Chinese Families in the Post-Mao Era

EDITED BY

Deborah Davis
and
Stevan Harrell

UNIVERSITY OF CALIFORNIA PRESS

Berkeley　Los Angeles　London

This book is a print-on-demand volume. It is manufactured
using toner in place of ink. Type and images may be less
sharp than the same material seen in traditionally printed
University of California Press editions.

University of California Press
Berkeley and Los Angeles, California

University of California Press, Ltd.
London, England

© 1993 by
The Regents of the University of California,
with the exception of chapter 6, "Family Strategies and Structures in Rural
North China," 1993 by Mark Selden

Library of Congress Cataloging-in-Publication Data

Chinese families in the post-Mao era / edited by Deborah Davis, Stevan
Harrell.
    p.   cm.—(Studies on China : 17)
    Papers from a conference sponsored by the Joint Committee on
Chinese Studies, held at Roche Harbor, Wash., June 12–17, 1990.
    Includes bibliographical references and index.
    ISBN 0-520-07797-0 (alk. paper).—ISBN 0-520-08222-2 (pbk. :
alk. paper)
    1. Family—China—History—20th century—Congresses.   2. Marriage—
China—History—20th century—Congresses.   3. China—Social
conditions—1949-   —Congresses.   I. Davis, Deborah, 1945-
II. Harrell, Stevan.   III. Joint Committee on Chinese Studies (U.S.)
IV. Series.
HQ684.A225   1993
306.85'0951—dc20   92-23163
                                                                          CIP

Printed in the United States of America

The paper used in this publication meets the minimum requirements of
American National Standard for Information Sciences—Permanence of Paper
for Printed Library Materials, ANSI Z39.48-1984 ∞

STUDIES ON CHINA

A series of conference volumes sponsored by the Joint Committee on Chinese Studies of the American Council of Learned Societies and the Social Science Research Council.

CONTENTS

TABLES

ACKNOWLEDGMENTS

The chapters in this volume were first presented at a conference on "Family Strategies in Post-Mao China," held at Roche Harbor, Washington, June 12–17, 1990. Financial support for the conference and subsequent editorial expenses were provided by a grant from the Joint Committee on Chinese Studies of the American Council of Learned Societies and the Social Science Research Council. In addition to our nine fellow participants who worked so speedily and intensely on paper revisions, the editors would like to acknowledge the intellectual contributions of four other conference discussants: Anthony Carter, Shumin Huang, William Lavely, and Susan Watkins, as well as conference assistant Fu Yunqi. During the several phases of revisions, we also greatly benefited from the careful reading and thoughtful criticisms of two anonymous readers and Dorothy Solinger. For help with photo reproduction, we thank Joey Liao.

ONE

Introduction:
The Impact of Post-Mao Reforms on Family Life

Deborah Davis and Stevan Harrell

In the decade after the Communist victory in 1949, state orthodoxy created a new institutional and moral environment for Chinese families. The collectivization of the economy and the elimination of most private property destroyed much of the economic motivation that had previously shaped family loyalties, and the frontal attack on ancestor worship and lineage organization struck directly at the cultural and religious core of the extended family. It was not simply the case, however, as many predicted, that communism destroyed the traditional Chinese family. On the contrary, many key policies actually stabilized and strengthened families. For example, large investments in public health and famine relief dramatically reduced mortality; fewer infants died, more children survived to marry, old age became the norm, and people from all social classes had larger and more complex kin networks than had been possible before 1949.[1] Similarly, the severe restrictions on internal migration not only served the interest of the government in controlling individual autonomy, but they also intensified the flow of intergenerational aid because they tied most adult men (and their sons) to the villages and towns of their birth.[2] Thus the Communist revolution created contradictions. On the one hand, it undercut the power and authority of patriarchs and destroyed the economic logic of family farms and businesses. On the other hand, it created demographic and material conditions conducive to large, multigenerational households with extensive economic and social ties to nearby kin. In short, Chinese families between 1950 and 1976

---

1. Edward Tu, Jersey Liang, and Shaomin Li, "Mortality Decline and Chinese Family Structure," *Journal of Gerontology* 44, no. 4 (July 1989): 157–68.

2. Deborah Davis-Friedmann, *Long Lives*, 2d ed. (Stanford: Stanford University Press, 1991), chaps. 3–4.

survived and reproduced themselves within a paradoxical environment: the often repressive egalitarianism of communism permitted more Chinese parents and children than ever before to realize core ideals of traditional Chinese familism, while at the same time the revolution eliminated many of the original incentives for wanting to realize those ideals.

With the shift away from collectivization and toward entrepreneurship and privatization after 1978, the Maoist compromise between state policies and family self-interest entered a drastically altered environment. This was especially the case in the countryside, where the Deng reforms dismantled the People's Communes as a core political and economic unit and abruptly subcontracted more than 80 percent of all farmland to individual families on the basis of fifteen-year leases. Commune and village assets were similarly redistributed, rented, or sold to the highest bidders, and by the mid-1980s most rural families were operating in a political economy of family tenancy where the agents of state authority had less control over the labor, land, and loyalty of rural residents than at any time since the Land Reform of the early 1950s.[3]

In the cities, the Deng reforms were far more modest and incremental. Private entrepreneurship was encouraged rhetorically, but the great majority of urban residents remained wage earners, and most households were units of consumption.[4] Moreover, the paradoxical relationship between the Maoist state and traditional familism had never been as pronounced in the cities as it had been in the villages. Urban families had very few welfare functions, income was highly individuated, and relations with kin could be very weak. Few households had continued as units of production following the collectivization of artisan workshops and services in the mid-1950s, and generous medical and pension plans for all state employees reduced the

3. For detailed discussion and varied interpretations of this process, see Philip C. C. Huang, *The Peasant Family and Rural Development in the Yangzi Delta* (Stanford: Stanford University Press, 1990), 286, 321–22; Victor Nee and Su Sijin, "Institutional Change and Economic Growth in China," *Journal of Asian Studies* 49, no. 1 (Feb. 1990): 3–25; Sulamith H. Potter and Jack M. Potter, *China's Peasants* (Cambridge: Cambridge University Press, 1990), 158–79; Louis Putterman, "Entering the Post-Collective Economy in North China," *Modern China* 15, no. 3 (July 1989): 275–320; Helen Siu, *Agents and Victims in South China* (New Haven: Yale University Press, 1989), 273–90; Vivienne Shue, *The Reach of the State* (Stanford: Stanford University Press, 1988), esp. 148–52; Terry Sicular, "Rural Marketing and Exchange," in *The Political Economy of Reform in Post-Mao China*, ed. Elizabeth Perry and Christine Wong (Cambridge: Harvard University Press, 1985), 83–110.

4. Deborah Davis, "Urban Job Mobility," in *Chinese Society on the Eve of Tiananmen*, ed. Deborah Davis and Ezra F. Vogel, 85–108 (Cambridge: Harvard University Press, 1990); Dorothy Solinger, "Capitalist Measures with Chinese Characteristics," *Problems of Communism* 38 (Jan.–Feb. 1989): 19–33. In December 1984 there were 86.3 million employees in state enterprises and 3.3 million working privately. By December 1989 these totals were 101 million and 6.5 million respectively. *Zhongguo Tongji Nianjian (ZGTJNJ) 1988*, 153, and *Renmin Ribao (RMRB)*, Feb. 21, 1990.

need for kin-based networks of mutual obligation. For these reasons, the main thrust of the Deng reforms in the cities had virtually no direct impact on the urban household economy. Nevertheless, urban families also entered into a new relationship with the state during the 1980s.

First, there was the challenge of prosperity, and if there were no great disparities of wealth, there was increasing economic differentiation and competition. Between 1978 and 1989 urban wages trebled, and consumer items such as color televisions, refrigerators, and electric fans, which in the 1970s had represented unimaginable luxury, became commonplace.[5] Equally important was the availability of the products of capitalist culture—Hong Kong and Taiwan soap operas, American movies and magazines, and the dance and video music of European and Japanese teenagers. Thus, while urban reforms did not commodify economic relationships within (and between) families as did decollectivization of agriculture, they did introduce a new range of cultural choices as well as the prosperity to permit individuals to act on preference, not merely respond to necessity.[6]

At the same time, however, the state continued to play a highly intrusive and coercive role vis-à-vis all Chinese families. Simultaneous with policies to decollectivize agriculture, encourage petty capitalism, and permit importation of the cultural products of the bourgeois West, the post-Mao leaders designed and implemented the most draconian birth control campaign in history. As first outlined in 1979, the birth control regulations prohibited any woman from having more than one child unless her first had died of a noninheritable disease or handicap. In one stroke of the bureaucratic pen, Chinese leaders decided that henceforth only half of all families would have a son to carry on the family name, that the sibling relationship would disappear, and that failure to use contraception would be a punishable offense. In terms of economic and political initiatives the reform leaders moved to disengage the state from control over land, labor, and markets; in terms of family reproduction they demanded that the state control the fertility of

---

5. In 1978 urban staff and workers had an average annual wage of 615 yuan; by 1989 it had risen to 1,950 yuan. *ZGTJNJ, 1989 (Chinese Statistical Yearbook)*, 125; *Guowuyuan Gongbao (GWYGB)* (Bulletin of the State Council), March 3, 1990, 85. For gains in consumer items, *ZGTJNJ 1989*, 728.

6. There are indications that the state-dependency of urban families may decline more rapidly in the near future. Nicholas Lardy reports that by 1990, 45 percent of China's *industrial* output was the product of the nonstate sector. While this includes many products of rural industries as well as urban collective enterprises, the growth rates of the private sector are about eight times those of the state sector, and continuation of current trends would mean that in a few years, a greater percentage of urban families in China will be unambiguously in the private sector and cast further adrift from the state-organized welfare net than is now the case. See Lardy, "Redefining U.S.–China Economic Relations," *NBR Analysis No. 5*, National Bureau of Asian and Soviet Research, Seattle, June 1991.

over one hundred million married couples. Rarely had the paradox of state power been more acute than between 1979 and 1983.

By the mid-1980s, however, the leadership had retreated from its original extreme position, and the ambitions of the state to dictate family size had moderated.[7] Rural families that could show that acceptance of the one-child limit would cause economic hardship or whose members were ethnic minorities were permitted to have a second or even a third child. And even in the cities, where pensions and social services eliminated the economic rationale for additional children, a variety of exceptions permitted some families a second birth.[8] Nevertheless, regardless of these modifications, the one-child policy continued to create tension and contradictions. For example, in designating the rural household as the basic unit of agricultural production, decollectivization increased the value of child labor. Yet the one-child quota demanded that families drastically curb fertility. If the one-child policy really succeeded, then approximately half the women born after 1955 would not have a son in their home to provide care for them in old age. There would have to be either a revolution in rural pension systems or massive construction of old-age homes. But with the collapse of the communes, rural pensions became even less extensive than they had been in the late 1970s, and village supports for the childless elderly precipitously declined in quality and coverage.[9]

In urban areas the clash between private and public interests created by the introduction of the one-child policy appeared in a different form. Thus even though young urban couples did not find the one-child campaign a threat to their immediate prosperity or to financial security in old age, they did perceive the campaign as an oppressive intervention of state power into an arena of family life that had remained private even during years of high political mobilization such as the Cultural Revolution.

The primary question, and the question that unites the chapters of this book, is this: What have been the initial consequences of these powerful and

7. Karen Hardee-Cleaveland and Judith Banister, "Fertility Policy and Implementation in China 1983–1986," *Population and Development Review* 14, no. 2 (June 1988): 276; Steven Mosher, "Birth Control: A View from a Chinese Village," *Asian Survey* 22, no. 4 (April 1982); Delia Davin, "The Single-Child Family Policy in the Countryside," in *China's One-Child Family Policy*, ed. Elisabeth Croll, Delia Davin, and Penny Kane (London: Macmillan, 1985) 74; Joan Kaufman, "Family Planning Policy and Practice in China," *Population and Development Review* 15, no. 4 (Dec. 1989): 707–30.

8. Birth control policies in minority areas were set locally and generally were looser than in Han areas. In urban areas, couples were permitted a second child when both spouses were only children, when the first child was seriously handicapped by a noninheritable defect, or when in remarriage the woman had had no children of her own. Nevertheless, second children are rare in the cities. Griffith Feeny, "Recent Fertility Dynamics in China," *Population and Development Review* 15, no. 2 (June 1989): 297–322.

9. Deborah Davis-Friedmann, *Long Lives*, 110–11.

contradictory initiatives for Chinese families in the 1980s? In particular, our authors have asked: What have been the consequences for household composition, for marriage arrangements, for fertility decisions, and for provision of care to kin unable to compete in the more individualized and commodified society of the 1980s? In terms of size and composition, has the percentage of joint and extended families declined? Has marriage age fallen and have parents lost control over a child's choice of spouse? Has veneration of ancestors become more elaborate, and have lineages returned as key brokers of local power? Where, overall, are the lines now drawn between public and private responsibilities, between the Deng party-state and Chinese society?

Drawing on William Goode's classic study of families in periods of economic change and growing prosperity, most observers would predict that the reforms of the 1980s would encourage nuclear households more focused on conjugal loyalties.[10] With greater affluence, higher rates of urban living, and increases in long-distance migration, the Goode model predicts that the influence of corporate kin groups should decline, brideprice and dowry become less prevalent, divorce rates rise, women's rights improve, age of marriage increase, and parents lose control over children's courtship and mate choices.[11]

But the Goode model, which drew heavily on the experience of Western Europe and North America and could not have used material on China after 1960, never dealt with a state as intrusive and coercive as the Chinese. In Goode's overview, state regulation of family life was a consequence of industrialization and urbanization. Clearly, in the People's Republic of China (PRC) state power and policies have been the creators, not the creations, of a transformed society. Thus, for example, formal, corporate kin groups such as lineage organizations were specifically replaced by Communist Party organizations and a people's militia as early as 1950, and in most parts of China family shrines and temples disappeared even as China remained an essentially rural and agrarian society.[12] The Marriage Law of 1950 prohibited concubinage and child betrothal and permitted women to sue for divorce. Within the first three years of the law nearly two million divorces were granted,[13] and concubinage and child marriage became almost unknown by the end of the decade. We could go on at length documenting how state policies in the areas of public health, education, and migration similarly pushed Chinese families toward a "modern family" form at a speed unknown in European or American experience. But here we empha-

10. William S. Goode, *The Family* (Englewood Cliffs, N.J.: Prentice-Hall), 183–85.

11. Ibid.

12. C. K. Yang, *The Chinese Family in the Communist Revolution* (Cambridge: MIT Press, 1965), chap. 11.

13. *Beijing Review*, Sept. 12, 1983.

size that because the state was so powerful in the past in shaping the resources and choices of family members and in defining the functional division of responsibility between private and public authorities, the retreat of the state during the 1980s may have permitted a revival of cultural preferences and economic forces that the Maoist state held in check but did not eliminate.

The interaction between these cultural preferences and economic forces is partially predicted by Jack Goody's models of the evolution of the family. These models stress the importance of property in shaping the functions a family holds in a particular society. For Goody the contrast is between periods when families derive their livelihood and social status from land or other productive resources they own or control, and periods when property belonged to the collective and status was based on political criteria. According to this model, extended-family ties and use of dowry and brideprice should weaken in the Maoist period but revive with the return of differences in social status within and among local communities after the Deng reform.[14]

In addition, it is possible that normative expectations rooted in sources independent of rational economic choices may prove decisive in an era when the party-state no longer intrudes as directly into cultural and religious life. Thus we may find by the late 1980s that in areas where government authority has dramatically retreated (most notably in rural areas) the dynamic of change for Chinese families may parallel that documented in John Caldwell's study of the demographic transition in western Africa, where family composition shifted in response to new ideologies rather than exclusively in response to new economic incentives and rationality.[15] Similarly, John Hajnal's study of marriage age and household type in Europe and Asia suggests that the key explanation of different household arrangements is likely to be culturally specific "rules for family formation" rather than the more global processes of urbanization, industrialization, or commodification.[16]

At the same time, in those areas where the state has strengthened its hand in the 1980s, we have a situation that is, as Susan Greenhalgh points out in chapter 9, unprecedented in world history and untouched by major theoreticians. The state, by implementing the planned-birth campaign, initially put itself at cross-purposes with just those cultural rules that shaped

14. See Jack Goody, *Production and Reproduction* (Cambridge University Press, 1976), and *The Oriental, the Ancient, and the Primitive* (Cambridge University Press, 1990).

15. John C. Caldwell, "Toward a Restatement of Demographic Transition," *Population and Development Review* 2, nos. 3 and 4 (Sept. and Dec. 1976): 321–66.

16. John Hajnal, "Two Kinds of Pre-industrial Household Formation Systems," *Population and Development Review* 8, no. 3 (Sept. 1982): 449–94.

the prerevolutionary Chinese family. That it later had to compromise and loosen the restrictions, at least in the rural areas, testifies to the resiliency of those cultural rules in the villages. That the compromise was much less evident in the cities suggests that urban couples held values fundamentally different from those of their rural peers or that the power of the party-state was still so dominant that urban men and women could not act on their personal preferences.

HOUSEHOLD COMPOSITION AND DIVISION

During most of the Maoist era, economic and political pressures fostered "family convergence." That is, in contrast to the two decades prior to 1949 when war, famines, and infectious disease prevented many from realizing the stable multigenerational households they desired, the overall legacy of the Maoist political economy was a remarkably uniform household structure, where differences in composition were increasingly due to the phase of the family life cycle, rather than to education or wealth, as had been true before 1949.

In the 1980s the new freedom to work outside of one's natal village and the introduction of the one-child campaign altered the external parameters shaping household size and composition, and in fact one can observe remarkable change within a short period. For example, in terms of average household size, families became noticeably smaller over the decade of the 1980s, and the number of households grew at a faster rate than the population.[17] In 1980 rural households averaged 5.5 members and urban households 4.4; by 1988 they had fallen to 4.9 and 3.6, respectively.[18] These declines, however, are explained almost entirely by declining fertility in response to the one-child campaign.[19] Thus macrodemographic indicators lend little support to an interpretation in line with Goode's initial predic-

17. Between 1982 and 1987 the number of people living in families rose by 8.2%, from 971 million to 1,051 million, while the number of family households rose by 12.7%, from 220 million to 248 million. *ZGTJNJ 1988*, 103, and *Zhongguo Shehui Tongji Ziliao 1987*, 31.

18. These figures should be treated as best estimates. For the 1980s figures there is no consistent national estimate, and for 1988 one must consider that after 1984 the definition of urban was relaxed to include many village residents in urban suburbs and also residents of small rural towns who had previously been excluded. The estimates used here are from Martin K. Whyte and William Parish, *Urban Life in Contemporary China* (Chicago: University of Chicago Press, 1984), 155 n.5, and *ZGTJNJ 1989*, 726, 742.

19. That is, because the percentage of women living with their husbands' parents upon marriage remained almost constant from the 1970s through the 1980s one presumes that it is the one-child campaign and not other factors that was most decisive. For estimates of these percentages, see Martin K. Whyte and William Parish, *Urban Life in Contemporary China*, 155 n.5, and *ZGTJNJ 1989*, 726, 742.

tion that economic development accelerates the nuclearization and individuation of family life. Rather, in China in the 1980s households became smaller, but not necessarily more nuclear.

A closer examination of field research on family composition in both urban and rural areas indicates that the trends in household size and composition have not been uniform; rather, they vary by the economic incentives of the local economy or the strictness of the planned-birth campaign. By the mid-1980s the most numerous incentives to preserve extended families were found in (1) villages where, as in industrializing Taiwan of the 1960s, reliance on labor-intensive cash crops or cottage industries rewarded unified budgets with one or more married sons or (2) cities where housing shortages forced newly married couples to remain in their parents' homes.[20] In short, while it is clear that average household size declined, it is still not clear to what extent the reforms have altered family composition or the meaning of joint budgets and shared property.

This is particularly true in urban areas where, as Unger (chapter 2), Davis (chapter 3), Phillips (chapter 11), and Ikels (chapter 12) indicate, residence in separate households does not necessarily mean functionally separate families. Cooking, childcare, care of the elderly or disabled, and monetary transfers all frequently take place among geographically divided branches of "networked" families. In addition, as is especially clear in Davis's longitudinal study of Shanghai families (chapter 3), the fluidity of household membership is highly sensitive to stages of the family developmental cycle, and if a survey captures families at that point when children are in prime years for marriage, or when parents pass into years with high risk of chronic illness and higher mortality, households may change membership rapidly over a short period. In Davis's Shanghai study, where households were observed once in 1987 and then again in 1990, 60 percent of the reinterviewed households had altered their membership, a rate of turnover that Davis attributes not only to the age of her newly retired respondents, but also to the new prosperity and freer social environment of the eighties. Jonathan Unger's review of the Chinese five-cities survey of 1983 (chapter 2) suggests, however, that the instability of urban households may be a short-term response to current housing shortages, and that in the long

---

20. Gu Jirui, *Jiating xiaofei jingjixue* (The economics of family consumption) (Beijing: zhongguo caizheng jingji chubanshe, 1985), 31; Isabelle Thireau and Mak Kong, "Travail en famille dans un village du Hebei," *Etudes chinoises* 8, no. 1 (Spring 1989), 7–40; Zhou Ying "Wo guo xiandaihua guocheng nongcun jiating" (Rural families in the transition to modernization), *Renkou yanjiu*, no. 2 (1988): 17–21. Zhang Yulin, "The Shift of Surplus Agricultural Labor," in *Small Towns in China*, ed. Fei Xiaotong (Beijing: New World Press), 186; William Lavely, "Industrialization and Household Complexity in Rural Taiwan," *Social Forces* 69, no. 1 (Sept. 1990): 235–51; Zhao Xishun, "Zhuanye jiating tedian qianxi" (An analysis of characteristics of specialized households), *Shehui kexue yanjiu*, 1985; Deborah Davis, chapter 3 of this volume.

term one would expect smaller, stable nuclear households, probably still linked in a variety of ways, to be the urban norm for both the newly married and the recently retired.[21]

In rural areas, housing shortages are not the problem they are in the cities, but there still exist factors that either retard formal family division or encourage links between families already divided. It is important to note, however, that these factors operate differentially in the varying economic circumstances of different rural areas. For example, in the western part of the Pearl River delta, where Graham Johnson has conducted fieldwork since the early 1970s (chapter 5), the new wealth and openness to the outside world have revived connections with overseas relatives and produced new forms of emigrant families, which favor female-headed households and delayed family division. In the central and eastern parts of the delta, by contrast, the main outside influences have come from Hong Kong capital investment, and families there tend to be male-headed and to divide more quickly. Harrell's comparison of three villages in the Sichuan-Yunnan border region (chapter 4) also illustrates the importance of increased economic opportunities. Here, despite the more stringent application of the one-child policy in the richest village, households in that village were still more complex than in villages practicing subsistence farming, because wealthier families postponed household division.

Given the short time that has elapsed since the implementation of the reforms and the still limited access to national-level data, none of the chapters in this volume will conclusively specify the degree to which initial shifts away from collectivist economy and ideology determine the shape of Chinese households. Yet by documenting a range of outcomes, the chapters challenge arguments that posit a uniform or direct process of household simplification. Future scholarship will thus need to scrutinize both the rules of family formation and the shifts in state power and policy that proved so decisive in the past, and to situate findings in specific local contexts of cultural difference, as well as in economic and political change.

MARRIAGE

In the first few years after 1949, the Chinese Communist Party (CCP) intervened directly to change many common elements of traditional marriage practices. The 1950 Marriage Law outlawed concubinage, child betrothal, multiple wives, and the sale of sons and daughters into marriage or prostitution. Village leaders and enterprise cadres exhorted the young people in their charge to delay marriage and in most cases enforced a policy of

---

21. See the critique of this aspect of Goode's formulation in Peter McDonald, "Adjustments of Rural Family Systems," unpublished paper, 1987.

late marriage by withholding choice job assignments, welfare benefits, or promotions.[22] They also condemned traditional rituals and elaborate feasts. Most of the ideals behind such policies were inspired by Engels's *The Origin of the Family, Private Property, and the State*, but the desired outcomes were also some of the very trends predicted by Goode for industrializing families. Success was mixed: the state succeeded in holding the line against such pre-communist practices as minor marriage and concubinage, but was much more successful in the cities (Whyte, chapter 8) than in the countryside in popularizing frugal weddings or eliminating brideprice and parental control of mate choice.

In September 1980 the National People's Congress passed a new Marriage Law, ostensibly motivated by a decision to strengthen the rule of law and bring the law more in line with practice. But in some areas the law actively encouraged "retrogression" to earlier practices of the precollectivist era. For example, the new law sanctioned minimal ages of marriage (20 for women and 22 for men [article 5]) that were significantly lower than the actual practices of the Cultural Revolution decade, and aside from a single sentence prohibiting "exaction of money or gifts" (article 3) there seemed to be no effort to control wedding expenses.[23] And in fact, in the decade following the passage of the new Marriage Law, marriages did indeed become decidedly "less modern" and more like those of the precommunist era. In 1978 the average age of marriage for women was 22.4 for rural brides and 25.1 for those in the city.[24] By 1987 the average age of marriage for all women had fallen to 21.0 years,[25] and teenage marriages and even child betrothal had begun to reappear in rural areas throughout the country.[26] The 1980s also saw an explosive increase in the overall expenses associated with marriage, as well as the return of lavish dowries and high brideprice.[27]

---

22. Whyte and Parish, *Urban Life in Contemporary China*, 113, found an average age of marriage for weddings between 1974 and 1978 to be 28.5 for males and 24.4 for females. William Parish and Martin Whyte, *Village and Family in Contemporary China* (Chicago: University of Chicago Press, 1978), 163, found average age at weddings between 1968 and 1974 to be 24.8 for males and 21.1 for females.

23. For an English translation, see *Beijing Review*, March 16, 1981, 24–27.

24. *Zhongguo Shehui Tongji Ziliao 1987* (Chinese Social Statistics for 1987) (Beijing: Zhongguo tongji chubanshe, 1987), 29.

25. *RMRB*, Feb. 19, 1989, 8.

26. The Hong Kong paper *Ming Bao*, on April 20, 1990, 8, reported 3.5 million underage marriages in 1988; *RMRB*, March 31,1989, 4, summarized a recent survey by the Women's Federation on betrothals of rural school girls.

27. Gu Jirui, *Jiating xiaofei jingjixue*, 344; Qian Jianghong et al., "Marriage Related Consumption," *Social Sciences in China*, no. 1 (1988): 208–28; *Beijing Review*, Dec. 25, 1989, 32; Sulamith H. and Jack M. Potter, *China's Peasants*, 209; Burton Pasternak, *Marriage and Fertility in Tianjin, China: Fifty Years of Transition*, papers of the East-West Population Institute, no. 99 (1986), 28–31; Martin K. Whyte, "Changes in Mate Choice in Chengdu," in *Chinese Society on the Eve of Tiananmen*, ed. Deborah Davis and Ezra F. Vogel, Contemporary China Series (Cambridge: Harvard University Press, 1990), 203.

Despite these clear trends away from Maoist preferences, however, not all of these shifts occur uniformly among rich and poor, or from region to region. Helen Siu (see chapter 7) suggests, in fact, that the trend follows Goody's general observation that dowry becomes more important in areas where competition for status is acute and parents need to endow their daughter richly in order to achieve a "good marriage." In her study of a Pearl River delta market town and its surrounding villages, she shows how connections to Hong Kong have greatly intensified the more general trend toward commodification and producing for the market. Overseas Chinese have invested heavily, and recent émigrés return frequently with gifts of consumer items and cash. As in the areas visited by Graham Johnson, families are eager for their daughters to marry an Overseas Chinese, and local men find themselves disadvantaged in the marriage market.

In the market town described by Siu, dowry had been a major investment among the precommunist merchant elite, but in the 1980s it became pervasive among many strata, as parents used a daughter's marriage to stabilize and advance family or individual interests in an era when the local political economy was in tumult and the Maoist bureaucratic hierarchies were in decline. In the outlying villages, at the same time, a shortage of female labor, caused partly by pressure on young women to marry into more prosperous town families, drove up brideprice. Thus in Siu's work we find an excellent example of where the immediate results of greater commodification and openness to the West were elaborate multigenerational investments that advanced corporate family interests as well as individual aspirations of the parents and the newly married couple. We also find traditional patterns seemingly revived but, as Siu herself points out, for purposes often quite different from those of precommunist years: village families pay high brideprices as much to keep their children from migrating away entirely as to assure the productive and reproductive contributions of future daughters-in-law.

Similar effects can be seen in the patterns of marriage ages and of village endogamy and exogamy, as is shown in Mark Selden's study of Wugong, a former model village in central Hebei, a region where brides were traditionally three to five years older than their husbands. During the collective era, age at marriage rose, and a long-standing prohibition against intravillage marriage fell into disregard. After only a short experience with economic decollectivization and political liberalization in Wugong, however, age at marriage fell, and village daughters were again marrying at a slightly older age (23.4 years) than village sons (22.7 years), although the traditional pattern of brides two to four years older than grooms did not appear and intravillage marriage continued. In other words, some but not all traditional preferences reappeared after the reforms. A similar pattern obtained in the relatively poor Shaanxi villages studied by Susan Greenhalgh in 1988 (chapter 9), where Maoist ideals of late marriage quickly crumbled, and the average age for a bride's first marriage fell precipitously from twenty-three to twenty between 1979 and 1987.[28]

Based on a survey of almost six hundred women in Chengdu, Martin Whyte shows somewhat similar patterns in urban areas. Some but not all precollective wedding practices have reemerged—for example, weddings, simple and cheap under Maoism, have once again become more elaborate in the reform era, but freedom of choice of spouse, introduced in the collective era, has remained under the reforms. In addition, the considerable social class variation in marriage practices in the precollective era was largely eliminated during the period of "high Maoism," but in the reform era, Whyte finds, even though weddings have once again become more elaborate, there has been no reemergence of class-stratified patterns in freedom to choose a mate, elaborateness of weddings, presence or absence of a dowry, the share of the wedding expenses paid by the couple, or the pattern of postmarital residence. Whyte provisionally attributes this to the continuation in the 1980s of a "rank/network/bureaucracy" social system that originally replaced the "status group/class/market" system with the imposition of state socialism in the 1950s. According to this logic, urban wedding behavior had not revived class-based differences in the 1980s, as had rural behavior, because the urban society of the 1980s was fundamentally still what Andrew Walder called "communist neo-Traditionalist,"[29] basically untransformed from the social structure of the Maoist period.

The diverse paths of change in marriage practices might cause us to reexamine a claim made in the important earlier study of urban marriages in the late Mao era carried out by Whyte and William Parish. In that study, the authors emphasized that after 1949 urban Chinese marriages resembled those of other developing societies. In line with Goode's predictions, there was a steady rise in marriage age, widespread disapproval of arranged marriages, and a convergence in the behavior of mate selection across different economic and educational strata. What was distinctive about China was the speed of the changes, the low cost of weddings, and the absence of a dating culture, characteristics Whyte and Parish attributed to CCP organizational and political resources not present among other rapidly modernizing or industrializing agrarian societies.[30] Nevertheless,

28. This pattern, however, was not uniform over the whole country either. In the three villages studied by Stevan Harrell in southernmost Sichuan, marriage age continued to be low from the 1950s through the late 1980s—there late marriage was never rigidly enforced in the collective era, and so there was no perceptible drop with the new law of 1980 or with the rise of the family farming economy. See Stevan Harrell, "Aspects of Marriage in Three Southwestern Villages," *China Quarterly* 130 (June 1992): 323–37.

29. See Andrew Walder, *Communist Neo-Traditionalism: Work and Authority in Chinese Industry* (Berkeley: University of California Press, 1986).

30. Whyte and Parish, *Urban Life*, 147–51.

they stressed that the causes of change lay primarily in the economic and social transformation and only secondarily in specific government policies aimed at reform of marriage practices.

Much of the "backsliding" that has gone on in the 1980s, however, makes the attribution of causality much more doubtful. Many of the changes in marriage during the Maoist era fulfilled Goode's predictions because the Chinese state was operating according to a political agenda, derived from Engels, that made behaviors that for Goode were predicted outcomes into explicit policy goals. The state planners probably thought they were just helping the inevitable along, but in fact they were creating a structure of inevitability much more narrowly restricted than the structure that would have been created by economic and cultural transformations. During the decade of the eighties, the state withdrew from close supervision of the local rural economies, and there was no single opportunity structure in the countryside. In the cities, the structure remained much more uniform, but several of its parameters evolved rapidly away from the Maoist period ideal, particularly the cost and lavishness of weddings. In retrospect, then, it seems that state policy had more effect in the Maoist period than Parish and Whyte originally gave it credit for, though the situation during the reforms is much more in tune with their model of primary causality residing in social and economic change. In any case, the situation is clearly more complex than any unilineal model of change would predict.[31]

CHILDBEARING

The relative importance of state power and economic imperatives is addressed with regard to a different area—fertility—by Susan Greenhalgh and Hill Gates in chapters 9 and 10. Although there is considerable disagreement about the fertility levels of the Chinese population before the early decades of the twentieth century,[32] it is clear that from the 1920s through the 1950s virtually all Chinese couples considered it essential that they have enough sons to ensure that at least one would grow to maturity and continue the patriline. Given the high mortality of infants and young adults during these war-ravaged decades, the goal of one surviving son encouraged most women to bear as many children as possible.

Throughout most of the 1950s the Chinese government took a decidedly

31. For example, see Arland Thornton and Thomas E. Fricke, "Social Change and the Family: Comparative Perspectives from the West, China, and South Asia," *Sociological Forum* 2, no. 4 (1987): 746–79.

32. See the debate between Arthur P. Wolf, in "Fertility in Prerevolutionary China," and Ansley J. Coale, in "Fertility in Rural China: A Reconfirmation of the Barclay Reassessment," both in *Family and Population in East Asian History*, ed. Susan B. Hanley and Arthur P. Wolf (Stanford: Stanford University Press, 1985).

TABLE 1.1. Changing Fertility Trends

	Crude Birth Rate	Total Fertility Rate (Urban Total Fertility Rate)
1950	37	5.8 (5.0)
1955	32	6.2 (5.6)
1960	20	4.0 (4.0)
1965	37	6.0 (3.7)
1970	33	5.8 (3.2)
1975	23	3.8 (2.1)
1980	18	2.5 (1.5)
1981	20	2.4 (1.3)
1982	21	2.8 (1.7)
1983	18	2.5 (1.6)
1984	17	2.3 (1.4)
1985	17	2.2 (1.2)
1986	20	2.3 (1.4)
1987	21	2.4 (1.3)

SOURCES: For crude birth rate, 1950–1987, *ZGTJNJ*, *1989*, 88; for total fertility rate, 1950–1970, Banister, *China's Changing Population*, 243; for total fertility rate, 1975–1987, Feeney et al., "Fertility Dynamics in China: Results from the 1987 One Percent Population Survey," 304.

pronatalist position and did little to alter traditional expectations of marital fertility.[33] After 1960 there was a shift, and the government began to promote birth control in cities, and urban fertility began to diverge from national trends (table 1.1). The real revolution, however, occurred during the decade of the 1970s when, as a result of both explicit government birth control campaigns and altered definitions of ideal family size, China's total fertility rate (TFR) fell from 5.8 in 1970 to 2.7 in 1978,[34] a drop without historical precedent in a society that had not suffered war, epidemic, or famine, and a rate that resembled that of Canada more closely than those of more comparable countries, such as Brazil, Iran, or Mexico.[35] In short, even in advance of the one-child campaign, Chinese women, in both rural and urban

33. There is a vast literature on Chinese fertility shifts. In this chapter we have relied primarily on work that has drawn on demographic work in the 1980s. Judith Banister, *China's Changing Population* (Stanford: Stanford University Press, 1987); William Lavely and Ronald Freedman, "The Origins of the Chinese Fertility Decline," *Demography* 27, no. 3 (August 1990), 357–67. Burton Pasternak, *Marriage and Fertility in Tianjin, China: Fifty Years of Transition*; Peng Xizhe, "Major Determinants of China's Fertility Transition," *China Quarterly*, no. 117 (March 1989), 1–37.

34. Judith Banister, "Population Policy and Trends in China 1978–1983," *China Quarterly*, no. 100 (Dec. 1984): 717–41.

35. *Statistical Abstract of the United States 1982–83*, 661.

TABLE 1.2.   Distribution of Births by Parity (percentages)

	First Births	Second Births	Third or Higher Births
1970	20.7	27.1	62.2
1977	30.8	24.7	44.5
1981	46.5	25.5	28.0
1984	51.8	28.3	19.9
1985	50.2	30.1	19.7
1986	51.2	31.5	17.3
1987	52.7	32.2	14.9
1988	52.2	32.4	15.3

SOURCES: For 1970, 1977, 1981, 1987, *RMRB*, Oct. 28, 1988, 3; for 1985 and 1986, Whyte and Gu, "Popular Response," 474; for 1988, interview with Peng Peiyun, *RMRB*, Sept. 20, 1989, 5.

areas, had reduced their fertility well below that of their peers in other developing nations.

In contrast, however, to the changes demanded by the one-child campaign, the shifts of the 1970s had been achieved without requiring half the population to forgo a son or all couples to risk a childless old age if their singleton died. Balanced against the substantial decreases in infant and child mortality rates, in fact, these early birth-limitation campaigns may not have produced much perceived difference from precommunist expectations of having a son survive adulthood. The one-child campaign unveiled in 1979 marked, therefore, a very radical departure from past efforts and, particularly in light of the new opportunities for considerable return on child labor, created the conditions for direct confrontation between family and state self-interest.[36]

Based on observations in the late 1980s, however, the impact of the policy is not clear-cut. That is, when one examines the overall trends in fertility and parity for the decade of the eighties, it appears that overall fertility has declined very little (see table 1.1). However, when one examines trends in terms of percentage of births that are third- or higher-order parities, the one-child policy has had a significant impact (table 1.2). The question, therefore, is what were the conditions that produced this record of mixed success. Was it the uneven efficacy of birth control cadres who had to rely primarily on intimidation and coercion, or the more universal pattern of variation by the economic and educational status of childbearing women?

Greenhalgh's and Gates's chapters, both based on 1988 fieldwork, confirm previous conclusions that the two-child norm has been widely

36. Steven Mosher, "Birth Control: A View from a Chinese Village"; Delia Davin, "The Single-Child Family Policy in the Countryside," 74.

accepted,[37] but they focus more extensively on the particular balances of socioeconomic incentives and state coercion that favor compliance and very low fertility. Working in Shaanxi periurban villages, Greenhalgh found that by 1987 local cadres had essentially given up enforcing a one-child policy: the fining system had collapsed, second children were spaced even more closely than they had been in 1980, marriage age had dropped to twenty, and more than 8 percent of women married in their teens. On the other hand, a two-child family appeared to be the mode, and if a family had two boys or a boy and a girl, parents were in most cases satisfied that they had achieved an ideal size. In short, Greenhalgh concludes that as a result of successful bargaining with local cadres, village families had "peasantized" population policy: it was not the state's enforcement power but the rational calculations of peasant families that brought rural fertility close to compliance with state goals.

In Gates's study of small-scale entrepreneurs in urban Chengdu and Taiwan, the focus is also on negotiations. But in this case the author stresses negotiations between a wife and other members of her (husband's) family. Interviewing several generations of women who bore children both before and after 1949, and across all decades since 1949, Gates finds that women entrepreneurs rationalized childbearing as a means to meet specific obligations, and that their willingness to have a child depended on their own individual relationship to the market. In the PRC during the one-child era, there is of course little official space in which to negotiate. There is a question, however, about delaying the first birth that can be (and is) subject to negotiation, and also there is a question about the degree to which a one-child norm would ever be acceptable to Chinese women and their families given pronatalist preferences and behavior in earlier decades and in Taiwan. Based on the Chengdu respondents, Gates finds a clear relationship between increased capital assets and what she terms "antiphiloprogenitivism." That is, urban petty capitalists do not desire more than the minimum number of children to meet their family obligations; therefore, in the 1980s when the state limited them to one child, these particular women found no difficulty in accepting that limit.

Certainly Gates's respondents represent only a small minority of urban women, since most urbanites are employed in state enterprises where they have no personal assets and no entrepreneurial ambitions. However, it is also true that the model of kinship that Gates has defined, whereby a woman's childbearing desires can be explained in terms of how her particular household relates to the larger economy, is in no way limited to urban

37. After completing four rural surveys in Fujian and Heilongjiang during 1987, Joan Kaufman found that enforcement at village level appeared weak and that while the household-responsibility system rewarded higher fertility, a two-child norm appeared to have been widely achieved; Joan Kaufman, "Family Planning Policy and Practice in China."

petty capitalists, but rather establishes a conceptual model that could be applied to all women, whether they live in cities, towns, or villages.

In fact, this conceptual model clearly fits with Harrell's data on the wealthiest of the three villages he investigated, where leading economic roles for women, readier acceptance of childbearing limits, and possibly even a tendency to pool capital, were most pronounced among entrepreneurial households. Given this parallel, it would be prudent to revise the ubiquitous urban-rural dichotomy and replace it, at least provisionally, with a three-way division between subsistence farmers, urban state/collective employees, and a third, entrepreneurial category that spans both cities and villages. And given the direction of China's economy toward an ever-larger private sector, we can expect that entrepreneurial households, a tiny minority at present, will come to constitute a much greater percentage of all Chinese families in the near future.

It is this third category of households that calls most sharply into question the unilineal theories of family change. While these petty capitalist households, as Gates and Harrell both suggest, do exhibit the predicted trends of lower fertility, at the same time they may well tend to greater household complexity because of capital and labor-pooling needs. In addition, as property owners they are more likely to be concerned with dowries, wedding banquets, and other forms of conspicuously displayed wealth. Whether or not the entrepreneurial category gains further prominence, the very fact that their family behavior differs from that of agriculturalists or state-sector employees once again points out that the process of family change, relatively homogeneous in the Maoist period, has become complex and heterogeneous.

DEPENDENTS AND FAMILY OBLIGATIONS

One of the explicit rationales for several aspects of the ideal model of traditional Chinese family organization, with its early and universal marriage and strong intergenerational interdependencies, was that such a system not only facilitated the continuation of the patriline but also provided for the frail and the vulnerable. If the family were to modernize in accord with a Marxist blueprint, families would relinquish these responsibilities, and the weak and the needy would turn first to public institutions. To quite an extraordinary degree, the Chinese Communist leadership in the collectivist period realized a large portion of these Marxist ideals. As might be expected in a state where the proletariat is by definition the vanguard, the greatest investments were made in cities, and within ten years of 1949 urban families enjoyed free primary education, free basic health care, and very inexpensive housing. In the countryside, where programs were funded by local communities and per capita fees, services were far more meager and families continued to be the primary source of aid for the young, old, and disabled. Nevertheless, money from central coffers subsidized construction of schools in small villages throughout the country, colleges sent thousands of new graduates to county and commune schools and clinics, and village cadres created welfare funds that supported cooperative clinics and guaranteed subsistence to all village households.

With the collapse of the commune as a political and economic unit, and the rapid commodification of rural labor, the structural supports for public welfare collapsed in the countryside and fees for services rapidly multiplied.[38] Tuitions became onerous, village welfare funds served only the most destitute, and most small clinics became privately run.[39] Even in the cities, where welfare provisions remained structurally intact and fully funded, there were also steps to monetize. Urban parents paid more extraneous school fees, and firms began to exclude some services from the health benefit. Bribes to medical personnel became more ubiquitous, and the cost of medicines not covered by health plans rose very fast as pharmacies and clinics tried to increase profits.[40] In short, the reforms noticeably reduced collective responsibility for care of the young, the sick, and the needy, and increased the financial burden of illness and disability on individuals and families.

The question here is how these cutbacks in public services have affected family behavior, and in particular whether the retreat of the state has affected family solidarity. Because of the more complete decollectivization of rural services, one would assume that village families have been most immediately and decisively affected, and that individuals who come from the poorest households or have the weakest network of extended kin will find themselves less secure than they had been under the collective. Conversely, given new incentives for individuals to develop family- and kin-based strategies of cooperation, one would also expect a resurgence of such risk-sharing institutions as burial societies, crop-watching associations, or lineage schools and scholarship funds. Reports from Guangdong, where lineage activities were traditionally strong, suggest that kinship associations have begun to assume welfare functions that were previously the responsibility of the village or commune.[41] But as Michael Phillips, working in

38. Deborah Davis, "Chinese Social Welfare," *China Quarterly*, no. 119 (Sept. 1989): 577–97.

39. Gail Henderson, "Increased Inequality in Health Care," in *Chinese Society on the Eve of Tiananmen*, ed. Deborah Davis and Ezra F. Vogel, 263–82 (Cambridge: Harvard University Press, 1990).

40. Ibid.

41. See chapter 5 in this volume, by Graham Johnson; also Sulamith H. and Jack M. Potter, *China's Peasants*, 266 and 337; and Helen Siu, "Recycling Tradition," *Comparative Studies in Society and History* 32, no. 4 (Oct. 1990): 765–94.

Hubei province, noted during discussion at our conference, lineage resources appear to be available for only a tiny percentage of rural families. Thus, at his hospital he has observed that the increased cost of hospital care and the collapse of collective medical insurance programs in the countryside have reduced the number of rural patients and shortened the stay of those whose family members are able and willing to pay the fees. Similarly, studies of rural enrollment rates show marked declines in entry to school and decreased completion rates from primary and secondary school.[42]

In this volume there are no studies of the impact of Deng reforms on rural families in distress. But in chapters 11 and 12, which analyze caregiving dynamics in urban families, we do find evidence of negative impact. In the families of schizophrenic patients he treated, Phillips observed how the more individuated reward structures and higher medical fees of the late 1980s increased tension between two core values of urban Chinese families: the desire to sacrifice for dependents, and the commitment to "judicious investment of family resources . . . [for the advancement] of the social status of the family." In the Mao years, when many employers were rather lax in their demands of the least skilled workers, families could find a place for their schizophrenic child or spouse. Treatment costs were covered by employers, and although families were often deeply ashamed by their relative's behavior, they still could maintain a veneer of normalcy. Moreover, the loss of this individual's full economic potential did not pose heavy financial costs in the absence of many alternative demands for surplus income. In the more competitive society of the 1980s employers can refuse to employ mentally ill people even for menial jobs, health insurance has reduced payments for medication, and the family, because of its heavier medical expenses and lost income potential, can become impoverished. In general, the cost to families of having a profoundly ill member increased during the reform years, and families with the fewest social and economic resources were hardest hit. Families continued to assume the main obligations, but financial burdens made the disability more immediately costly, and greater competition at the workplace and more approval of individualistic striving undermined the willingness of some family members to sacrifice for another.

In the final chapter of this volume, Charlotte Ikels discusses what the reforms have meant for elderly residents of Guangzhou. Overall, there have been no efforts to undermine financial security; in fact, over the decade of the 1980s pensions grew at about the same rate as wages, and the percentage of urban residents over age sixty who received a pension steadily rose.[43] However, for the same reasons that Phillips found schizophrenics more of a burden on their kin, so Ikels found Guangzhou elderly and their

42. *RMRB*, Feb. 15, 1989, 1; Aug. 7, 1989, 1.
43. Davis-Friedmann, *Long Lives*, 107–16.

children increasingly aware of the costs of providing services to the weakest and least socially active. Among her respondents the reforms did not directly reduce security or increase family conflict, but they did intensify anxieties about the future, and Ikels found elderly parents reaching out to make themselves useful or less needy, in anticipation of a day when they would need to draw heavily on the goodwill and filial loyalty of one or more of their children.

CHINESE FAMILIES IN THE POST-MAO ERA

Through the presentation of these research findings, we hope to establish a baseline, and perhaps even set an agenda, for future research on families in China. We believe that the approach taken here, looking at family behavior as the adaptation of cultural rules to changing and diverse political and economic circumstances, helps us do several things. It takes us beyond either/or debates about culture and political economy, or about state policy versus economic change, to examine the interaction of these factors. It moves us away from sweeping generalizations about *the* Chinese family, or even the urban or rural Chinese family, to consider different outcomes of adaptation to different circumstances. And it allows us, on the basis of empirical case studies, to begin to make certain generalizations, not so much about outcomes as about processes.

The first generalization is that many key characteristics of family life during the Maoist period—high age of marriage, elimination of polygamy and concubinage, reduced (or absent) dowry, and weak corporate kin groups—which earlier students of family life such as William Goode had expected to find as consequences of industrialization, may in the case of China be best explained by family laws, which Goode had presented as a consequence, not a cause, of change.[44] Thus we suggest that the Maoist period witnessed a rapid shift away from corporate kin groups, elaborate weddings, concubinage, and early marriage, not because the economic and social transformations of the 1950s and 1960s made such changes irresistible to individual men and women, but because the state drafted laws or regulations that required immediate compliance.[45] Therefore, it is in the interaction of preexisting "family culture" with both convergent processes of industrialization and particular state policies that we should look for explanations of the complex patterns of family changes in revolutionary China.

The second generalization responds to the resurgence of traditional

44. Goode, *The Family*, 186.

45. This point has also been made by William Lavely and Burton Pasternak in their studies of fertility decline. Lavely and Freeman, "The Origins of the Chinese Fertility Decline," and Pasternak, *Marriage and Fertility in Tianjin*.

rituals, ceremonies, and family behavior such as child betrothal, bride-wealth, lavish dowry, and joint family households, that initially appear to document a "step backward." None of these traditional practices should be interpreted as a simple return to the status quo ante. Rather, the return of precommunist festivals and traditions is first and foremost a response to the post-Mao political economy, and by examining these rituals in their con-temporary context one may identify the emergence of new boundaries be-tween kin and nonkin and the emerging character of intergenerational obligations in an era of political uncertainty. Thus, from such material we can perhaps more clearly see the family ideals and the rules guiding house-hold formation that Caldwell and Hajnal found decisive but that currently are still not well articulated in scholarly discussion of China.

The third generalization is that, when explicit state policies do not force homogeneity, the general tendency is for Chinese families to adapt their marital, parental, and welfare strategies to local economic conditions. Re-cent family behavior does not converge on a uniform pattern of extended patrilocal households with strong corporate links and equal inheritance among all sons, much less on an evolutionarily determined isolated nuclear family. Nor is there an urban form and a rural form. Instead, today's Chinese mainland, like twentieth-century Hong Kong and Taiwan, displays a variegated mosaic of family forms and behaviors, each demonstrating the adaptation of basic principles to differing conditions.

In his introductory comments to Louise Tilly and Joan Scott's study of English and French families in the early years of the industrial revolution, historian Michael Katz remarked:

> A close relationship exists between the organization of the family and the mode of production at any given time. Yet [Scott and Tilly] also show that the relationship is very complex. Domestic organization does not change quickly or easily. Families adopt complex strategies which enable them to preserve elements of customary practices in altered circumstances, and the family patterns that emerge represent adaptations, complex compromises between tradition and new organizational and social structures.[46]

Observations of Chinese families during the economic and political up-heavals of the 1980s confirm much of what Katz found to be the case for European families in another era of rapid change. But as we and most of the authors in this volume stress, in China neither the family nor the in-dividual is as autonomous as were Europeans in the eighteenth and nine-teenth centuries. Because during the second half of the twentieth century a powerful, intrusive Chinese state frequently rewrote the basic "laws" of eco-nomic exchange and terms of trade, the "complex compromises" that Katz

46. Louise A. Tilly and Joan W. Scott, *Women, Work, and Family* (New York: Holt, Rinehart and Winston, 1978), xi.

found in Tilly and Scott's discussion of gradual shifts from the household as a mode of production to a family wage economy may be quite different for the PRC.

As is obvious in our description of the several ways in which the Communist revolution served traditional family goals, and in the ways in which families have prospered under the Deng reforms, members of Chinese families, like those of Europe and North America, seek to maximize their resources under different modes of production. Economic constraints are critical in family form and family behaviors, but economics alone cannot capture all the external constraints. Politics also matter, and no study of Chinese families can be complete unless it is as concerned with the state as it is with the economy. And as everywhere, the changes that stem from politics and economics all play themselves out against the background of a Chinese family culture that does change, but only slowly.

PART ONE

Household Structure

TWO

Urban Families in the Eighties: An Analysis of Chinese Surveys

Jonathan Unger

During the 1980s our knowledge of the shape of urban family life in the People's Republic of China increased several fold. Some quite excellent research, to be sure, had been conducted by Western scholars in the 1970s through interviews with emigrants in Hong Kong.[1] But it was only in the eighties that Western sociologists, anthropologists, and demographers at long last were able to conduct research inside China. And perhaps more important, it was only in the 1980s that China's own social scientists were able to begin serious research of their own.

Under Mao, scholarship in the social sciences had been sacrificed to the whims and dictates of politics. The government had deemed sociology potentially dangerous, in that it intruded on the Party's desire to hold a monopoly over analyses of society. All sociology departments were abolished in 1952,[2] and it was not until 1979–80 that three departments—in Beijing, Tianjin, and Shanghai—were reestablished by the government as a first step in rebuilding a capacity to monitor and analyze social problems. Sociology departments soon opened at universities in other cities, with staff hurriedly recruited from other disciplines.

Though the field was still new, a substantial number of Chinese surveys on urban family composition were conducted between the years 1982 and 1985. The most significant of these projects was a coordinated effort in 1982–83 to study family patterns of eight residential districts in five of

1. See, for example, Martin King Whyte and William L. Parish, *Urban Life in Contemporary China* (Chicago: University of Chicago Press, 1984), and Deborah Davis-Friedmann, *Long Lives: Chinese Elderly and the Communist Revolution* (Cambridge: Harvard University Press, 1983).

2. Martin K. Whyte and Burton Pasternak, "Sociology and Anthropology," in *Humanistic and Social Science Research in China*, ed. Anne F. Thurston and Jason H. Parker (New York: Social Science Research Council, 1980).

China's major cities: Beijing, Shanghai, Tianjin, Nanjing, and Chengdu. The more than a dozen scholars who cooperated in this endeavor published a 566-page book that not only included essays on their separate findings but also provided appendices with hundreds of tables of local and cumulative data.[3] A rush of other surveys followed: of young marrieds, of middle-aged women, of the elderly, and so forth. By 1986, however, this boomlet in survey research was on the wane, and the number of new survey findings that were openly published declined precipitously thereafter.

Not all of this research was methodologically sound in sampling techniques, nor did commonsense always prevail in the composition of questionnaire questions. Some of the researchers, without training and new to this mode of social science research, were obviously learning on the job. Perhaps a third of the survey reports from those years are of little use on account of such problems. But the other two-thirds, those that appear to have been reasonably sound methodologically, are invaluable in promoting our understanding of social change in urban China. Cumulatively, they enable us to see the broader outlines of urban family structures and the changes these were undergoing.

Unfortunately, this is not at all true with respect to rural surveys—which is why this book does not contain a parallel chapter on Chinese findings about peasant families. Rural surveys by Chinese sociologists are hard to come by,[4] and the comparatively few that do exist generally seem to have been conducted hurriedly, using abnormally small samples. Overwhelmingly, Chinese scholars have concentrated instead on the residents of big-city neighborhoods.

This chapter will draw upon some thirty-five of these urban surveys. Since almost all of them date from 1982 to 1986, much of my analysis will concentrate on the shape of urban Chinese families in the first half of the eighties. In a number of places my analysis will differ from those of the Chinese authors, and my citation of their statistical findings does not imply that they are responsible for the interpretations I have placed upon this data. The first sections of the chapter will draw heavily upon the statistics of the five-city survey, to set out the circumstances of families at the opening of the eighties. The latter sections will refer almost exclusively to other, later surveys.

3. Wu chengshi jiating yanjiu xiangmu zu (Research Project Group on the Families of Five Cities), *Zhongguo chengshi jiating* (Chinese urban families) (Jinan: Shandong renmin chubanshe, 1985). The scholars involved in this project subsequently published two edited conference volumes of papers that discussed the findings: Pan Yunkang, ed., *Zhongguo chengshi hunyin yu jiating* (Chinese urban marriages and families) (Jinan: Shandong renmin chubanshe, 1987); and Liu Ying and Bi Suzhen, eds., *Zhongguo hunyin jiating yanjiu* (Research on Chinese marriages and families) (Beijing: Shehui kexue wenxian chubanshe, 1987).

4. The major exception is the native village of the grand old man of Chinese sociology, Fei Xiaotong. Fei has sent assistants into the field to survey this one village repeatedly.

TABLE 2.1.   Structure of Households in Five Major Cities, 1982

	Single-Member Households	Nuclear Household	Stem Family	Joint Family	Other	Total
Percentage	2.4	66.4	24.3	2.3	4.6	100
No. of households surveyed	107	2,912	1,065	101	200	4,385

SOURCE: Wu chengshi jiating yanjiu xiangmu zu (Research Project Group on the Families of Five Cities), *Zhongguo chengshi jiating* (Chinese urban families), Jinan: Shandong renmin chubanshe, 1985, 450.

MAKING A CHOICE: NUCLEAR AND STEM FAMILIES

First the simple facts. As of the early 1980s, according to the five-cities survey, some two-thirds of all the households in China's major cities were nuclear in composition: that is, they consisted only of parents and their children. We often think of Chinese families as including not just a married couple and their children but also one or more grandparents—that is, stem families[5]—and the data showed that, while urban China was largely composed of nuclear families, stem families, too, were indeed commonplace, constituting a quarter of all households. The 1982–83 survey of eight neighborhoods in five of China's major cities revealed that nuclear and stem families combined accounted for more than 90 percent of all households (table 2.1).

What was the prevalent trend, though? Were increasing numbers of newlyweds setting up their own independent households rather than living with parents-in-law in stem families? Not if we go by the figures gathered by the five-cities survey. These show that prior to the establishment of the People's Republic of China in 1949, the numbers of urban newlyweds who formed independent households were already on the rise, and that this trend had continued into the 1950s, but leveled off and subsequently dipped sharply. As can be observed in table 2.2, approximately 57 percent of the urban newlyweds who married during the dozen years between 1954 and 1965 had established their own households, but the incidence of this practice had been cut almost in half, to 32 percent, within the next dozen years.

One plausible explanation for the earlier shift into independent households is that the first decade of Communist Party rule had witnessed a large wave of immigration of single young adults into China's cities from the

5. In the early 1980s, Chinese scholars devised various translations for the term "stem family." The two most common translations were *zhugan jiating* and *zhixi jiating*. By the latter part of the 1980s the usage of *zhugan jiating* had prevailed.

TABLE 2.2.   Where Couples Who Wed in Different Time Periods Lived Directly after Marriage
(percentages)

Year of Wedding	–1937 (N = 563)	1938–45 (N = 611)	1946–49 (N = 463)	1950–53 (N = 471)	1954–57 (N = 494)	1958–65 (N = 627)	1966–76 (N = 870)	1977–82 (N = 883)
Independent household	31	40	42	53	58	56	48	32
With husband's parents	60	50	48	37	32	28	35	47
With wife's parents	9	9	8	8	8.5	12	14	18
Other	1	1	2	2	1.5	3	3	3
Totals	100	100	100	100	100	99	100	100

SOURCE: Wu chengshi . . . , 318; the same table is also discussed in Liu Ying, "Wo guo chengshi jiating jiegoude guimo he leixing" ("The size and types of family structure in China's cities), *Shehui* (Society), no. 5 (1984): 6.

countryside. They had had no families in the cities to fall back on, and when they married had necessarily set up independent families. This inflow of migrants was cut off in 1958, and strict controls against new migrants were introduced thereafter. We may presume that for at least the half decade immediately after the inflow from the countryside was halted, large numbers of the young adults who had arrived before 1959 were continuing to marry, which would explain the persistence during 1958–65 of a relatively high level of independent households of newlyweds (see table 2.2). But from the mid-sixties onward, the vast bulk of the marriage-age young people were from established urban families and, accordingly, could move in with parents after marriage.

Notably, it is also evident in table 2.2 that among the couples who married in the half-decade following Mao's death (the years 1977–82), the proportion establishing independent families was substantially lower than in the prior decade of 1966–76 and scarcely higher than for newlyweds in the years before 1937.[6] What accounts for the overwhelming preponderance of stem families among this younger generation of newlyweds? It should be remembered that a large portion of China's urban young people had been shipped off to the countryside to settle as peasants in 1968, when the Red Guards were crushed and the Cultural Revolution violence ended. They were joined in the countryside during the 1970s by a large proportion of the new urban secondary-school graduates, under a government policy of having the villages absorb the great bulk of the urban young people who were surplus to the needs of the urban labor force.[7] By the late 1970s, fully eighteen million urban youths had been forced into the countryside. Very few of them married during this decade of enforced rustication, in the belief that married couples would be less likely to receive permission to return to the cities. The wait was rewarded, for between 1975 and 1979 one province after another abandoned the hated to-the-countryside movement and ordered

6. Most of the other neighborhood surveys of the early 1980s support the evidence of the five-cities survey. One provides contrary evidence, though. A 1982 survey of an urban neighborhood of Chengdu, Sichuan, claims that in the parents' generation (396 households), 59% of young couples had lived in households separate from their parents; 33% lived with the husband's parents; and 8% lived with the wife's parents. In comparison, among the 333 young Chengdu couples of 1982, a considerably higher percentage, fully 74%, reportedly lived independently; 14% lived with the husband's family; and 11% lived with the wife's parents. See Li Dongshan, "Lun ju zhi" (On systems of accommodation), *Shehui diaocha yu yanjiu* (Social Investigations and Research), no. 5 (1985): 58. In short, the data for the parents' generation are very much in line with that of the five-cities survey; and the Chengdu data for the present generation are very much at odds with the five-cities data. It seems quite possible that the Chengdu investigators' data for the present generation records as "nuclear" those young couples who initially had resided with parents but who had already moved out of the parents' home.

7. Jonathan Unger, "China's Troubled Down-to-the-Countryside Campaign," *Contemporary China* 3, no. 2 (Summer 1979): 79–92.

most of the youths back to the cities. During the succeeding years, covering the period 1977–82, a large number of this horde of returned young people were not able to secure any regular urban employment nor the wherewithal to obtain separate accommodations when, after so many years of delay, they finally married. Such couples crowded into parents' apartments (the bride's if adequate space was not available at the groom's)[8] until separate housing became available.

That a temporary lack of alternative accommodations was a fundamental reason for the high proportion of stem families among newlyweds is suggested by the fact that most young couples moved out of the parents' home after only several years. A 1985 survey of 419 such multigenerational households in the city of Tianjin nicely illustrates this: 65 percent of the younger couples who had initially participated in stem families had moved out within the first five years of their marriage; and a further 17 percent moved out in the sixth to the tenth year of marriage: that is, in all, more than 80 percent of such stem-family participants moved out to form independent households within the first ten years of marriage.[9] This phenomenon was true not only for the most recent generation of young couples; the same shift out of parental homes had been true, too, of older cohorts of couples.

The consequence was that a clear majority of middle-aged couples, as of the early 1980s, were living in independent nuclear families, not with parents-in-law. Table 2.3, based on a survey of a Beijing neighborhood in late 1982, shows this very much to be the case for wives aged thirty-three to forty-five.

Demographics alone would dictate that many of these middle-aged couples would by necessity live as nuclear households. In past decades, from the 1940s through the end of the 1950s, urban families very often were giving birth to three to five children; and with the near-abandonment of the joint-family tradition (see below), when these children grew up all but one of them necessarily had to leave the household, either immediately at the time of their wedding or when their next younger brother married. This goes far in explaining the phenomenon, seen above, whereby a high propor-

8. The proportion of young couples moving into the groom's home as compared to the bride's home remained relatively stable from 1958 through 1982, though with a slightly rising bias in favor of living with the groom's parents, according to the data contained in table 2.2. In the period 1958–65 the ratio stood at 2.26:1; for the period 1966–76, 2.47:1; and for the period 1977–82, 2.58:1.

9. Pan Yunkang and Lin Nan, "Zhongguo chengshi xiandai jiating moshi" (A model of contemporary Chinese urban families), *Shehuixue yanjiu* (Sociological Research), no. 3 (1987): 61. (The number of individual respondents was not given; the survey covered 989 households.) This Tianjin neighborhood survey found that when first married, 52% of the newlyweds in the sample lived with the husband's parents; only 4% lived with the wife's parents; 42% lived in an independent household; and 2% other (p. 60).

TABLE 2.3. Structure of Households, as of 1982, of Women of Different
Age Groups: A Beijing Neighborhood Survey
(percentages)

Women's Age	70+ (N = 53)	60+ (N = 76)	46+ (N = 264)	33+ (N = 151)	24+ (N = 157)	Total (N = 701)
Single-member household	13	8	3	1	0	3
Nuclear	17	28	58	77	46	53
Stem	58	62	35	19	49	40
Joint	6	3	2	2	4	3
Other	6	0	2	1	1	2
Totals	100	101	100	100	100	101

SOURCE: Wu chengshi . . . , 9; also in Liu Ying, 7. (See sources for tables 2.1 and 2.2.)

tion of young couples shifted out of the parental home within the first five
years of marriage. The longer-term stem families usually have comprised
the elder couple, the youngest son, and his wife and children.

The shift of young married couples into nuclear households may have
gone beyond this, however. Chinese statistics suggest that in many cases
even the last remaining child moved out, leaving the older couple on their
own. Table 2.3, for example, shows that fully 77 percent of the surveyed
Beijing women who in 1982 were in the age group thirty-three to forty-five
lived in their own nuclear family—and that only 21 percent of the women
in that age group lived in a stem or joint family. This latter statistic must
have included a substantial number of women in their forties who were
living in a stem family with their *own* newly married children, rather than
living with their old parents-in-law. In short, the great bulk of the younger
middle-aged women were living entirely apart from their elders.

Are we viewing here new trends in intrafamily patterns, or instead long-
time mores? This question can be answered by examining the situation of
the households of interviewees' parents, on the eve of interviewees' weddings, as observed in table 2.4. On average, the parents of a groom would
have been in their late forties or early fifties (and since brides generally
have wed at a younger age than have grooms, the brides' parents would
have been a few years younger than the grooms' parents: say, in their early
to late forties). By examining the data vis-à-vis people who wed in different
time periods, we can derive a picture of the changing status of the households of these two age-sets of middle-aged couples. Table 2.4 is again based
on data from the five-cities survey of 1982–83.

TABLE 2.4. Household Structures of Grooms' and Brides' Natal Families,
for Different Time Periods
(percentages)

Year of Marriage	−1937	1938–45	1946–49	1950–53	1954–57	1958–65	1966–76	1977–82
Groom's Natal Family on Eve of Wedding								
Single-parent household[a]	15	19	16	21	19	20	16	6
Nuclear family	51	50	51	51	49	53	60	68
Stem family	18	18	19	18	18	18	17	19
Joint family	9	7	9	4	6	3	4	2
Other	7	6	6	7	7	6	3	5
Totals (*N* = 557)	100	100	101	101	99	100	100	100
Bride's Natal Family on Eve of Wedding								
Single-parent household[a]	6	7	8	9	8	7	4	2
Nuclear family	56	56	54	49	52	58	67	69
Stem family	26	21	24	28	23	23	20	21
Joint family	9	7	9	7	10	7	4	4
Other	4	8	6	8	8	5	4	4
Totals (*N* = 561)	101	99	101	101	101	100	99	100

SOURCE: Wu chengshi . . . , 484, 508.
[a] This line of the table literally reads "Single-person family," but p. 112 of the five-cities-project book defines that category as including widowed and divorced family heads.

It is evident from table 2.4 that as of the early 1980s, the nuclear-family form was more frequent among the middle-aged than in any previous decade, but this had *not* led to declines in the incidence of stem-family organization. Rather, it can be seen from the table that over these decades both forms of family organization had been the beneficiaries of sharp declines in single-member households and of a sharp decline, too, in the incidence of joint families (that is, families in which two or more married children and their spouses live together, normally with an elderly parent or parents). Similar trends have been evident in Taiwan.[10]

In urban China, this decline in single-member households is presum-

10. The data available to me from Taiwan are not entirely comparable, in that the Taiwan statistics are for urban and rural households combined. These Taiwan-wide statistics do, however, exhibit trends similar to urban China:

ably the dual consequence both of lower levels of bachelorhood and spinstership[11] and, among all the elderly who had married, of a rising survival rate among offspring. That is to say, a considerably higher proportion of elderly widows today presumably can count on having one or more grown children who can take them in if the need arises.

The decline in the numbers of joint families can largely be attributed to the changed class structure of post-1949 China; many of the joint families of earlier times had been built upon and held together by the wealth and property of the paterfamilias. The scarcity of joint families can also be attributed in part to the cramped living conditions that are almost universal in modern Chinese cities, and which preclude the sharing of the parents' meager accommodations by a large number of people. Whatever the exact factors that have been at work here, the incidence of joint families in a 1935–37 survey in Shanghai ranged from 7 percent among working-class families to 19 percent among the upper classes,[12] whereas quite different figures apply for more recent decades. In a survey by Whyte and Parish of Guangdong urban families as of the mid-1970s, joint families constituted only some 2 percent of households.[13] That same figure held true for China's large cities as of the early 1980s. As is seen in table 2.1, joint families constituted only 2.3 percent of households in the five-cities survey of 1982–83. (In many cases, I would surmise, these are households containing more

Household Composition, Taiwan 1965–85
(percentages, based on surveys of 2,700–4,500 for each period)

	1965	1967	1973	1980	1985
Nuclear	35	36	43	50	56
Stem	36	35	37	35	35
Joint	30	29	20	15	8

SOURCE: Maxine Weinstein, T. H. Sun, M. C. Chang, and R. Freedman, "Household Composition, Extended Kinship, and Reproduction in Taiwan, 1965–1985," *Population Studies* 44, no. 2 (July 1990): 217–39.

These Taiwan data show a far sharper rise in the nuclear-family form than was true for urban China. One possible explanation is that there was a far more rapid rural-to-urban migration in Taiwan than was allowed in the People's Republic. This rapid urban expansion resulted in the creation of a great many smaller households in Taiwan, with the younger couples in the cities and the older couple on the land.

11. According to the figures of the 1982 census, only 6.8% of all Beijing men and a mere 3.3% of all Beijing women in the 30–34 age group had not already married, and in the 35–39 age group only 3.9% of the men and 0.8% of the women. Chen Wanzhen, "Wo guo hunyin zhuangkuang de tongji fenxi" (A statistical analysis of the state of affairs of marriage in China), *Renkouxue kan* (Journal of Demography), no. 1 (1987): 19.

12. Martin King Whyte and William L. Parish, *Urban Life in Contemporary China* (Chicago: University of Chicago Press, 1984), 154.

13. Ibid.

than one set of newlyweds who have not yet been able to find suitable accommodations elsewhere.

THE DETERMINING FACTORS

Among what types of families do we find the highest proportion of nuclear as against stem families? Are there any "class" differences?

The answer to this latter question is yes. The most obvious "class" influence here may relate to geographic mobility. People who have moved into a city from the countryside or have moved from one city to another generally have not been able to bring kin with them because of residency-card restrictions. These same government restrictions have also more generally limited geographic mobility among ordinary people—the net result being low rates of geographic mobility but high rates of separation of relatives when mobility does occur. The net effect, according to a survey in the mid-eighties of an industrial district in Wuhan, was that, overall, 39 percent of the interviewees in the district lived in a different city or region than their parents, and 12 percent of the interviewees lived in a different city than all of their own children. University graduates and government officials most frequently have been assigned to jobs away from their place of origin, and this Wuhan survey revealed, not surprisingly, that residence at a distance from one's parents or children or both was highest among intellectuals, then cadres, and was least true of workers. One consequence, the survey indicated, is that a "class" distinction can be found in family composition. The incidence of stem/joint households in the district stood at 40.2 percent of working-class families, at only 33.1 percent of cadre families, and a mere 15.6 percent of intellectuals' families.[14]

A low level of stem-family organization may not just reflect enforced separation, however. Surveys show that even when relatives reside in the same city, most interviewees report that they *want* to live in separate nuclear households. The "class" differences in the above Wuhan survey may therefore also partly reflect the varying abilities of people of different professions to obtain the separate housing needed to set up new households. Certainly, surveys of stem-family participants variously show that somewhere between 21–27 percent of such families (based on interviewing parents) and 36 percent (based on interviewing married children) would want to divide the stem household if additional housing became available.[15]

14. Cai He, "Chengshi jiating jiegoude bianhua ji qushi" (Alterations and trends in the structure of the urban family), *Juece yu xinxi* (Policy and News) (Wuhan), no. 9, 1987, republished in *Shehuixue* (Sociology), People's University Reprint Series C4, no. 6 (1987): 96.

15. Hu Ruquan, "Cong Tianjin, Wuhan deng chengshide diaocha kan woguo chengshi laonianren jiating shenghuo" (The family life of elderly urban Chinese, as witnessed through surveys of Tianjin, Wuhan, and other cities), *Shehuixue yanjiu* (Sociological Research), no. 4

Overall, attitude surveys of young *unmarried* adults in the major cities have shown that a very large proportion would prefer to live separate from parents after marriage. A survey of a Beijing district in the first half of the eighties claimed that 88 percent of the surveyed youths felt this way, and that only 12 percent preferred to continue to live with their elders after they married.[16] Other surveys show the same general preferences, albeit not so dramatically. A 1985 survey of a Tianjin urban district, for instance, showed that 63 percent of the youths would prefer to live separately once married.[17]

The Chinese surveys do not directly offer data on any possible class differences in such attitudes, but indirect circumstantial evidence would suggest only a modest difference between working-class youths and other young people in this respect. One illustrative example is a survey among young unmarried female textile workers in the city of Harbin, in which 43 percent of the respondents ($N = 127$) expressed a preference to live in future with in-laws, and 57 percent a preference to live independently.[18] This finding among young working-class women differs only moderately from the Tianjin survey results for the populace as a whole. (To be sure, the question of gender differences may also have entered strongly into the Harbin survey findings; it is highly possible that young working-class *men*, had they been included in the survey, might have been more amenable to living with their own parents.)

City size may be as much a factor as social class in the statistics showing

---

(1986): 104, provides tables of surveys of Tianjin in 1984 (21%) and Wuhan in 1985 (27%) of *parents* in stem families, who stated that lack of housing was the principal reason for the stem family. Similarly, in an eighteen-city survey of married *young* people in stem families (1986), 36% of them reported that the main reason for the stem-family arrangement was that alternative housing was unavailable. Qian Jianghong et al., "Wo guo da zhong chengshi qingnian jiehun xiaofei yanjiu" (Research into the marriage expenditures of young people in China's large and medium-size cities), *Zhongguo shehui kexue* (Chinese Social Science), no. 3 (1987): 121. Parallel to this finding, in a 1985 survey of 431 stem households that had already divided up, 35% of respondents cited their obtaining additional accommodations as the principal reason for the family division. (Pan Yunkang and Lin Nan, 62–63.)

16. Pan Yunkang, "Shilun Zhongguo hexin jiating he xifang hexin jiatingde yi tong" (An attempt to discuss the differences and similarities between Chinese and Western nuclear families), *Tianjin shehui kexue* (Tianjin Social Science), no. 2 (1985): republished in *Shehuixue*, no. 3 (1985): 111.

17. Pan Yunkang and Lin Nan, 57.

18. Zou Naixian, "Qingnian fangzhi nugong shenghuo fangshi xuqiu bianhuade diaocha" (Survey of changes in young female textile workers' demands on life), *Qingnian yanjiu* (Youth Studies), no. 10 (1985); republished in English in *Chinese Sociology and Anthropology* 20, no. 2 (Winter, 1987–88): 15. The published data included a high proportion of women who declined to respond one way or the other, and I have excluded them in the figures here.

distinctions in family structure. The available data are not particularly reliable regarding the actual differences in family composition between China's largest, medium-size, and smaller cities, but scattered sources do suggest a higher incidence of nuclear families in China's large cities than in smaller ones.[19] Attitude surveys show a similar, albeit small, distinction in preferences. For example, a 1985 sample of fifty urban households in a small city in Fujian province, all of the households containing unmarried young adults, came up with a greater balance in the youths' postmarital preferences than was true of either Beijing or Tianjin: that is, only 51 percent of the Fujian youths wished to live apart from parents after marriage, while 41 percent thought it preferable to live with their elders. (In turn, the parents in these fifty households were generally much more favorable toward stem households than were their offspring: 69 percent of the parents thought it best that a married child live with them, and only 28 percent felt it best that married children live separately.)[20]

PARENTS AND CHILDREN: GENERATIONS AND ATTITUDES

Should we even expect the preferences of young people to count heavily in determining whether they remain in the home or leave upon marrying? Would a young man and woman or would his parents generally have the greater say in such a matter?

19. One source that makes this claim is Xu Jingze, "Wo guo jiating jiegoude tedian jiqi fazhan qushi chutan" (Initial investigation into the characteristics and developmental trends in the structure of Chinese families), *Wenshizhe* (Literature, History and Philosophy) (Jinan City), no. 1 (1985), reprinted in *Shehuixue* (Sociology), People's University Reprint Series C4, no. 2 (1985): 109–10. As circumstantial evidence, this article provides tables showing, e.g., a higher proportion of nuclear families in a 1982 Tianjin neighborhood survey than in a survey of a semi-industrialized suburban district of a Shandong city.

Such a conjecture is reinforced by the available data on family size. The 1982 census, for example, revealed that the households in China's 239 largest cities averaged, overall, 4.09 members. Households in the 38 cities that had populations of at least one million averaged 4.01 members, while those in the three largest cities were smaller yet: Tianjin, 3.90 persons; Beijing, 3.69 persons; and Shanghai, the largest city, 3.60 persons. Yuan Fang, "Zhongguo Laonianren zai jiating, shehui zhongde diwei he zuoyong" (The status and functions of the Chinese elderly in the family and society), *Beijing daxue xuebao, zhe she ban* (Beijing University Studies, Philosophy and Social Science edition) 3, no. 1 (1987), reprinted in *Shehuixue*, no. 4 (1987): 115.

20. Zhuang Jia, *Ren yu ren* (The Human Relationship), Guangdong renmin chubanshe (Canton: Guangdong People's Publisher), 1988, 147. A parallel sample of 50 households from villages in nearby counties found, as expected, that the surveyed young unmarried peasants were more amenable to living in stem families than their urban cousins: 54% of them thought it best that children live with elders after marriage (and 84% of their parents thought so). A rather high 41% of the unmarried village youths thought it best to live apart (compared to only 14% of the surveyed rural parents).

TABLE 2.5. Ways in Which Married Couples Initially Met, for Different Generations
(percentages, based on responses of 4,858 already married women)

Year of Marriage	−1937	1938–45	1946–49	1950–53	1954–57	1958–65	1966–76	1977–82
Parents arranged marriage	55	37	32	21	12	3	1	1
Relatives introduced	24	28	27	27	25	22	18	16
Friends introduced	15	24	25.5	31	36	45	46	50
Got to know each other ourselves	5	10	15	19	27	28	35	33
Other	1	1	0.5	2	1	1	1	0
Totals	100	100	100	100	101	99	101	100

SOURCE: Wu chengshi..., 307.

Certainly, young adults have gained a somewhat larger say over their own lives than in generations past. Whereas parents once very frequently arranged their children's marriages, that custom and the power it represented have all but disappeared in urban areas. More than that, parents play a markedly diminished role even in introducing their children to potential mates. As is seen in table 2.5, more than 80 percent of young marrieds during 1977–82 either had been introduced to each other by friends or had met on their own. Yet other surveys show, nevertheless, that young people still very seriously take their parents' advice into account in deciding whether to marry a particular person. As one example, a survey of 970 young workers in a district of Wuhan in the early eighties found that only 21 percent had made that decision entirely on their own. Another 63 percent sought out and respected their parents' counsel, and another 10 percent let their parents play the predominant role, asking only that they themselves consent to the parents' choice; 2.5 percent left the decision entirely in their parents' hands.[21] Other surveys came up with somewhat similar findings.[22]

21. Li Minghua et al., "Wuchang qu qinggong lian'ai hunyin xianzhuang diaocha" (Investigation into the current circumstances of falling in love and marriage among young workers in a Wuchang [Wuhan] district), *Shehui* (Society), no. 6 (1983): 31.

22. See, e.g., Liu Ying, "Tianjin Huningrong wu chengshi jiating diaocha chuxi" (Initial analysis of Tianjin's Huningrong neighborhood in the five-cities family survey), *Shehuixue yanjiu* (Sociological Research), no. 4 (1986), table, 80. Also see Zhuang Jia, table 2, 147; and Hu Ruquan, "Family Life," table, 98. Also see Martin K. Whyte's similar survey findings in Whyte's "Changes in Mate Choice in Chengdu," in *Chinese Society on the Eve of Tiananmen*, ed. Deborah Davis and Ezra F. Vogel, 185 (Cambridge: Harvard University Press, 1990).

One reason why the young still turn to their parents for advice and approval in such matters is that they remain largely dependent on their parents to get on in life, especially financially. The elder couple's earnings normally are considerably higher than the young person's,[23] and young people usually cannot afford the expenses of getting married and setting up a new family without parental help. A 1983 survey in Tianjin of 121 households found that 84 percent of young couples had obtained financial support from their parents in order to get married; only 16 percent of the marriages had occurred without the parents' financial help.[24]

Perhaps more important, young people normally are unable to obtain separate accommodations on their own; after marriage they need either to live with parents or to obtain the parents' aid in securing housing. In 1986 an eighteen-city survey of married young people between the ages of 18 and 35 ($N = 726$) found that only 27 percent had themselves been responsible for acquiring publicly owned housing (this was mostly provided by the husband's work unit, not the wife's).[25] The great majority either lived with the husband's parents (35 percent), or with the wife's parents (7 percent), or in publicly owned housing obtained for them by the parents (14 percent), or lived apart in private housing (7 percent), which in most cases presumably was owned by the parents.[26]

The parents, in short, have the wherewithal to play a very major role in determining their children's postmarriage arrangements. Yet, as was observed earlier, a very high proportion of young people in the major cities prefer to live apart from their parents. Is there a high degree of dissension and conflict, therefore, between the generations?

The answer appears to be, not usually: for during the first half of the eighties a shift was occurring in the attitudes of parents. Their views came largely to mirror those of their children. By 1984–85 surveys were revealing that the percentage of parents in the major cities who expressed a wish to live apart from all their children once the children got married was almost exactly as high as the percentage of young people expressing a wish to live apart from their parents (table 2.6).

According to the 1985 survey data from Tianjin, the desire to live apart from all of one's children once they got married depended partly on whether the parents had one child or more than one (table 2.7). Almost half of those with only one child were looking ahead to living together as a stem family, whereas some three-quarters of the parents with more than one growing child looked forward to the peace and quiet of the departure of all of them! (Note, too, that parents with more than two children who desired

23. Li Dongshan, table, 64.
24. Hu Ruquan, 109.
25. Qian Jianghong et al. (n.15 above), 120.
26. Ibid.

TABLE 2.6.   Preferences of Parents of Unmarried Adult Children:
After Children's Marriage, Do They Wish to Live with Them or to Live Separately?
(percentages)

	Wish More Than One Child to Live with Them	Wish to Live with a Son	Wish to Live with a Daughter	Wish to Live Separately from All Children	Other	Total
Tianjin, 1983 (N = 375)	22	31	8	39	—	100
Tianjin, 1984 (N = 1040)	14	20	6	58[a]	2	100
Wuhan, 1985 (N = 474)	19	20	9	46	6	100
Shanghai, 1985 or 1986 (N = 85)	27	9	8	55	—	99

Compare these figures with a 1985 survey of parents of a yet younger generation: parents whose children were not yet adults.

Tianjin, 1985[b]	5	19	9	67		100

SOURCES: For Tianjin, 1983; Tianjin, 1984; Wuhan, 1985, see Hu Ruquan, "Cong Tianjin, Wuhan deng chengshide diaocha kan woguo chengshi laonianren jiating shenghuo" (The family life of elderly urban Chinese, as witnessed through surveys of Tianjin, Wuhan, and other cities), *Shehuixue yanjiu* (Sociological Research), no. 4 (1986): 104.

For Shanghai, see Chen Gusong and Zhao Dehua, "Zhongguo jiating ningju li pouxi" (Analysis of the cohesive power of the Chinese family), in Liu Ying and Xue Suzhen, eds., *Zhongguo hunyin jiating yanjiu* (Research on Chinese marriages and families), Beijing: Shehui kexue wenxian chubanshe, 1987, 292.

For Tianjin, 1985, see Pan Yunkang and Lin Nan, "Zhongguo chengshi xiandai jiating moshi" (A model of contemporary Chinese urban families), *Shehuixue yanjiu*, no. 3 (1987): 57.

[a] Similarly, 63 percent of grown unmarried *children* in the 1985 Tianjin survey wanted to live separately from parents (57).

[b] Numbers of interviewees not given, but drawn from a survey of 989 households.

to be part of a stem family—that is, those parents who could be expected to have a choice as to whether to live with a married son or daughter—were unanimous in their preference for the traditional form of stem family: that is, for living with a son instead of a daughter.)

Not only did a majority of both parents and adult children in urban China prefer, by the mid-eighties, to live in separate households; increasingly during the eighties they were able to see those desires fulfilled. Lack of alternative accommodations had held something like a quarter to a third of all stem families together, as has been noted. By the latter half of the 1980s, the severe scarcity in urban housing had been considerably alleviated through a massive program of public-housing construction. (On this, see the beginning of chapter 3, by Deborah Davis.) Whereas urban resi-

TABLE 2.7. Attitudes of Parents of Differing Numbers of
Ungrown Children: Would They Want to Live Separately from, or
Together with, Married Children?

	No. of Children					
	1	2	3	4	5	6+
Best to live apart from all children	55%	77%	70%	75%	71%	93%
Want to live with a son	24	12	21	19	27	7
Want to live with a daughter	17	5	0	0	0	0
Want to live with all the children	4	6	7	6	2	0
Totals	100%	100%	98%	100%	100%	100%
No. of families in sample	255	256	123	88	41	30

SOURCE: Pan Yunkang and Lin Nan, 58, Table 7.

dents had had, per capita, only 5 square meters of living space in 1980, by the end of 1987 they enjoyed 8.5 square meters. That increase in living space had been brought about largely through the construction of large numbers of small new apartments rather than through any substantial enlargement in the size of new apartments. The opportunities for the establishment of new nuclear families had been substantially enhanced; the living conditions for stem families had not. As of the close of 1987, urban accommodations, on average, consisted of only 2.44 rooms.[27]

NETWORKED FAMILIES

In urban China today, even those parents who live apart from their married children still tend to maintain very close mutual contact, more so than would be the norm in most Western societies. A multifaceted interdependency between the households of parents and married children very frequently is deliberately sustained even when they live apart. This can be seen particularly clearly in relation to the interchange of gifts of money.

27. "Changes in the Life-Style of Urban Residents," *Beijing Review*, November 14, 1988, 27.

Although Burton Pasternak's 1981 study of a Tianjin neighborhood and the 1982–83 five-cities study both found that only some 36–38 percent of all households sent regular remittances of money to close relatives outside their own household, and that only 11 percent of urban households regularly received such remittances,[28] a later and more detailed study draws a rather different picture. This 1984 survey, conducted in Tianjin, focused on 181 households of younger married couples and the 312 households of the couples' parents. Thus, unlike the earlier studies, the statistics in this 1984 survey referred only to families where married children lived apart from parents, providing a more accurate picture of such families' interrelationships. It found that 84 percent of the married children gave money to both sets of parents and, notably, that 91 percent of the households of married children *received* financial help from one or more sets of parents. Examining this group of 91 percent, it found that fully 61 percent of them regularly received parental gifts of money to cover their daily expenses.[29] The survey revealed, moreover, that among these 181 households of married children, 44 percent received noticeably more money from their parents than they gave the parents, while only 27 percent of the children gave more money to their parents than they received in return.[30] In short, while children often provided small monthly remittances to parents as an accustomed way of showing filial respect, these same married children quite frequently were actually net financial dependents on their parents.

This should not surprise us, inasmuch as the Chinese government for decades has promoted a steeply inclined seniority system in state-sector wages. A 1982 survey of a Chengdu district accordingly found that each of the parents taken separately—74 percent of fathers and 65 percent of mothers—earned more than their surveyed married child.[31] At the same

28. On this, see Burton Pasternak, *Marriage and Fertility in Tianjin, China: Fifty Years of Transition*, Papers of the East-West Population Center, no. 99 (July 1986): 37–38; also Wu chengshi . . . , 428, 432. Pasternak's survey discovered, interestingly, that of the parents who did receive remittances from children, 71% were receiving regular monthly gifts of money from daughters, and only 55% from sons. Similarly, among the households of married children that sent money to parents, 66% of such households were sending money to the wife's parents, more than the 55% who were sending money to the husband's parents (27). Undoubtedly, one factor contributing to these statistics is that a considerably higher number of parents would already be living with the family of a married son than with the family of a married daughter, and such parents would not, by definition, be receiving inflowing remittances from their live-in son, but only from their daughter. But several survey reports have noted that parents frequently cite their married daughters as more filial and more emotionally caring than their married sons.

29. The survey found, moreover, that 74% of them received financial support from parents at the time of festivals; 8% to buy major consumer items; 11% just when in straitened circumstances (*jieju*); and 7% only in emergencies.

30. Pan Yunkang (n.16 above), 110–11; also Pan Yunkang and Lin Nan, 65.

31. Li Dongshan, table, 64.

time, their married children's financial needs, with young children to raise, were now frequently greater than their own. Middle-aged urban parents consequently quite often, as a matter of course, subsidize their married children.

Yet it should be remembered that the gifts of money regularly crossed both ways. It was and is a practice that tangibly symbolizes the mutual affection and sustaining support that bind the families to each other, cutting across the fact that normally the help that is actually needed lies largely on one side.

It is not just in financial terms that the younger couples are often dependent on one or both of their two sets of parents. They also frequently rely on one or more of their parents for daily childcare. Almost invariably, a young husband and wife in urban China both work full-time, and if one of their parents is retired—women in state-sector employment tend to retire at age fifty or fifty-five—they will want to rely on her to take care of their young children. In the 1984 Tianjin survey, 12 percent of the younger couples sent children to the grandparents on the father's side to be minded; and a further 8 percent sent children to the maternal grandparents. Some busy parents even sent the little ones to live full-time with the grandparents.[32]

More than that, this Tianjin survey found that in fully 86 percent of the younger couples' households, one or more family members regularly went to eat meals at one or both of the elder couples' houses. In examining this group of 86 percent, it was found that only 34 percent of them shared fewer than twenty meals a month at the homes of parents who lived apart from them (these figures, incidentally, include grandchildren minded by grandparents). Another 21 percent shared twenty-one to forty meals a month at the parents' homes, a further 11 percent shared forty-one to sixty meals, and a final 20 percent shared sixty or more meals a month.[33]

In other words, while living apart, they tended to interact almost like stem or extended families. Chinese social scientists have come up with the term "enwebbed" or "networked families" (*wangluo jiating*) to describe this situation, which some researchers claim has become increasingly common during the eighties. One scholar, based on yet another Tianjin study, reports that although young couples and their elders increasingly prefer to live apart, they want to live *near* each other, in order to be able to carry on such a "networked" arrangement.[34] Thus, families maneuver to acquire housing that will enable one or more of the married children's homes to be

32. Pan Yunkang, 111.
33. Ibid.
34. Hu Ruquan, "Shitan 'Wangluo jiating'" (A discussion of 'Networked families'), *Zhong-guo funu bao* (China Woman's Paper), March 7, 1986, 3.

clustered near the original home. A different strategy in "networked" living arrangements is for the younger couple to "network" almost equally with *both* sets of grandparents.

With one-child families enforced by government *diktat* and now the norm in China's cities, we might expect the incidence of *stem* families to begin increasing in the future at the expense of a "networking" of separate young and middle-aged nuclear families. After all, no longer will most grown children, as in the past, be obliged to leave the household after their marriage so as to leave room for yet younger siblings. In fact, in future a young couple would have a *choice* of parents' homes to live in. But the predictions that have been made in China of a sharp future rise in the proportion of urban stem households could be premature.

The percentage may well rise, but perhaps not by as much as one might expect by purely demographic reasoning. For one thing, as we have seen, a clear majority of parents as well as of children today prefer to live in separate housing. This was even true in 1985 with a majority of the parents who had only one ungrown child, as is seen in table 2.7.

In future, such feelings may well be strengthened, moreover, by the very fact that each of the two sets of parents will normally have only one child. Such a circumstance could well promote fears of "losing" their only child to another family after the child's marriage. A "networked" family/household structure would resolve such fears. Given that fact, at the turn of the next century it might well be a strongly favored form of family organization for the majority of the present generation of single-child urban families.

FAMILY ARRANGEMENTS OF THE ELDERLY

Nuclear households, as we saw above, already predominate among the urban middle-aged, often in a "networked" relationship with their married children. As we saw also, such nuclear-household arrangements are also preferred by a large majority of young marrieds. But what of the elderly— all those who are in their sixties and seventies and eighties? As people enter the tail-end of their lives do they prefer to live separately from their children? Did many of them indeed live apart from their children's families during the eighties, or did most of them live in stem-family households? And finally, what type of living arrangement seems most probable for the urban elderly of the decades to come?

First, the facts about living arrangements among the elderly during the eighties: at the same time that a very large proportion of middle-aged couples maintained their own nuclear family, a high portion of the elderly lived with one or more of their married children. Among the very elderly, as we shall see, more than 80 percent were members of stem or joint households.

In short, most urban Chinese, as they have passed from one stage of life

nuclear	stem	stem
As a child	As a teenager (elderly grand-parent joining household)	Early in own marriage (in parents' house)

nuclear	stem	nuclear
As middle-aged couple with children	As middle-aged couple (with married child briefly in household)	As middle-aged couple "networking" with children's households

stem	nuclear	stem
As late middle-aged couple supporting elderly parent	As couple in their sixties	In late old age, as widow or widower (with a married child's family)

NOTE: No given person is likely to pass through all of these phases in family arrangements, but a great many people will pass through a majority of them during their lives.

Fig. 2.1. A Life Cycle in Family Arrangements

to another, have swung between the stem and the nuclear form of household, often more than once. Instead of living continuously with the family of a married child, many members of the elder generation have preferred to live apart and then have joined the home of a married child only after their own spouse dies or when they become increasingly frail in advanced age. This was observed in table 2.3, which showed 64 percent of all women over age sixty living in stem or joint families. Other neighborhood surveys have suggested a lower proportion, but still high. In Shanghai (where more than 7.5 percent of the total population as of 1986 was over the age of sixty, a percentage that has been climbing yearly)[35] a 1983 neighborhood survey of 613 people aged sixty and older revealed that 52 percent lived in stem or joint families.[36]

35. Yuan Jihui, Chou Liping, and Dong Jiahua, "Shanghai shiqu gaoling laoren shenghuo zhuangkuang diaocha baogao" (An investigative report into the living conditions of the truly aged of a Shanghai urban district), *Shehuixue yanjiu* (Sociological Research), no. 3 (1987): 75.

36. Zheng Guizhen, "Shanghai shi jiating jiegou yu yang lao shiye" (Shanghai's urban family structure and facilities for the care of the elderly), *Zhongguo renkou kexue* (Chinese Demography), no. 5 (1988): 136. A similar Shanghai survey from 1982 showed that among 681 elderly aged sixty or over, only 7% lived alone; 35% lived in a nuclear family (e.g., with their spouse); and 53%, again a majority, lived in a stem or joint family. (Liu Ying, "Tianjin . . . ," 79.)

These figures do not reveal the complete picture, however. A *higher* number of elderly lived with one or more grown children than the above statistics would suggest—for a substantial proportion of them lived with an unmarried child (which would have placed them in the column of "nuclear households"). A 1984 Tianjin survey of 1,032 elderly shows this clearly. The pool of interviewees included only those elderly people who had one or more already married children. Of these elderly, 44 percent lived with a married child, but another 31 percent of them lived with one or more unmarried children. Only 24.5 percent of them lived just with their spouse or by themselves.[37]

Other surveys suggest, moreover, that as the elderly became increasingly aged, they were ever more likely to enter the family of a married child. A 1986 survey of 835 truly aged Shanghai residents—over eighty years of age—revealed that fully 80 percent of these octogenarians and nonagenarians lived with married children,[38] far greater than the 52–53 percent of Shanghai elderly sixty years old and over who were living with married children.[39]

Opinion polls reveal that the preferences of the elderly run parallel to their actual living arrangements. The more aged they are, the more apt they are to desire to live together with married children. A 1985 survey in Shanghai ($N = 2,556$) found that whereas 52 percent of the elderly aged sixty to sixty-four preferred to live in the vicinity of, but not with, their children (i.e., preferred a "networked" situation), that number had dropped to 25 percent among respondents aged seventy-five and older.[40]

37. Hu Ruquan, "Cong Tianjin . . . ," 103. If the elderly people who did not have any married children are added to this pool of interviewees, and if we ask simply what proportion of all the elderly lived in the same household as a grown child, the 1984 data from Tianjin show that fully 71% of the elderly were residing with children. Only 6% were living alone, another 17% were living with a spouse, and 6% were living with a grandchild. (Some in this last category, with or without spouse, were living with small grandchildren sent to them by working parents to be tended full-time.) Hu Ruquan, 97.

38. Yuan Jihui et al., 76. According to this survey, a further 10% of those eighty and over lived in a nuclear household, in most cases presumably consisting of themselves and their spouse. Only 8% lived alone.

39. To be sure, the two sets of surveys are not entirely comparable, inasmuch as a sizeable number of the Shanghai elderly over sixty presumably would still have been living with unmarried children; and these children almost invariably would have married by the time their parents were in their eighties. This can be observed in yet another Shanghai survey ($N = 3,614$), this one from 1985, in which it was found that 30% of the elderly between the ages of sixty and sixty-four lived with unmarried children, compared with 10% for the surveyed elderly over the age of eighty. In this 1985 survey, 47% of the elderly aged sixty to sixty-four were living with married children, compared with 62% of the octogenarians (Gu Quanzhong, Chen Yangming, and Qian Fang, "Status and Needs of the Elderly in Urban Shanghai: Analysis of Some Preliminary Statistics," *Journal of Cross-Cultural Gerontology* 2 [1987]: 180).

40. Ibid., 182.

TABLE 2.8. Shanghai Elderly Who Would Prefer to Live with a Married Child

Age	60–64	65–69	70–79	80+	Total	Men	Women
Prefer to live with married child	52%	60.5%	63.5%	71.5%	59%	56.5%	61%
N	326	271	260	56	913	405	508

SOURCE: Ling Bi, "Shanghai shide laoren jiating" (Families of the elderly in urban Shanghai), *Shehuixue yanjiu* (Sociological Research), no. 4 (1986): 89.

NOTE: This table is reproduced and analyzed in Qiu Liping, "Wo guo chengshi jiating jiegou biandong jiqi fazhan moxing yanjiu" (Research into changes and developmental models relating to China's urban family structures), *Renkou yanjiu* (Demographic Research), no. 5 (1987): 2.

A different 1985 opinion survey, conducted in a Shanghai neighborhood, shows this change in preferences clearly (table 2.8).

Among these interviewees, as one would expect, a rather higher proportion of widows and widowers desired to live in a married child's family than was the case where spouses were still alive. Perhaps more surprising, according to this 1985 Shanghai survey, 87 percent of widowers ($N = 37$), but only 64 percent of widows ($N = 214$), preferred to live with a married child.[41] If this finding from a small sample is true more generally, we can surmise that widowed men may feel more at a loss to cope for themselves, and considerably less self-reliant in terms of their own domestic life, than do widowed women.

In addition to the two factors of very advanced age and widowhood, survey data reveal a third salient factor that strongly predisposes some of the elderly to seek to live with a married child's family—if they do not receive a pension after retirement, or, if they do, if that pension does not amount to enough to make them financially self-sufficient.

Pensions in urban China normally range from 60 to 80 percent of preretirement pay,[42] and given the steeply inclined nature of state-sector salaries, even a couple in retirement often earns more than a married child's household with two wage earners. But not all elderly people are so fortunate. A great many urban retirees are not entitled to pensions, particularly those who had been employed in "collective" neighborhood enterprises rather than the state sector; and the great majority of these are retired women.[43]

41. As is obvious from the above statistics—37 widowers and 214 widows—Chinese urban women, to an overwhelming extent, tend to outlive their husbands. The five-cities survey of 1982–83 (518) found that 13% of *all* ever-married women are widows—and this in a survey that included women of all ages.

42. Yuan Fang, 117.

43. The consequence is that among Shanghai octogenarians, the great majority of whom are women, only 42% receive pension incomes, while 58% do not. (Yuan Jihui et al., 76). An

To be sure, a fair proportion of the elderly obtain new employment after retirement: as of the mid-eighties, 27 percent of retirees in Tianjin and 22 percent in Beijing had taken up paying jobs.[44] But that still leaves a large number of elderly without independent incomes. Since most retired men hold pensions, in most cases nonpensioned women can become dependents of their husbands. A 1984 survey in Tianjin found that fully 55 percent of the elderly without incomes ($N = 371$) could depend on a spouse's income; but, lacking that, 44 percent depended on children or grandchildren.[45]

Moreover, not even all pensioners are self-supporting. As of 1984, a survey in Shanghai found that retirees with pension incomes of fifty or more yuan a month (supposedly more than sufficient to support themselves) constituted 48 percent of the survey, and that those with pensions just sufficient for their own needs, between forty and fifty yuan a month, were a further 18 percent—leaving 31 percent of all pensioners with monthly pension payments below forty yuan, which, the author concluded, left them dependent on their spouse or children.[46] Since the level of pension payouts is determined by length of service and size of final salary, and since women generally are provided with considerably lower salaries than men,[47] and since they tend to work for fewer years (regulations normally require them to retire earlier), it is not surprising that women constitute the great bulk of these pensioners who obtain totally inadequate payouts.[48] And from the available data we can deduce that those who were in this situation and who did not have spouses to fall back on tended to move in with the family of a child as a dependent.

Data are more generally available showing a very sharp distinction between households with pensions and those without. In a survey in Wuhan in the mid-eighties, it was found that parents with pensions were four times more likely to live apart from all their children than were the elderly without pensions.[49] More than that, when attitudinal questions were posed of

---

excellent general study of the pension system is Deborah Davis-Friedmann, "Chinese Retirement: Policy and Practice," *Current Perspectives on Aging and the Life Cycle* 1 (1985): 295–313.

44. Yuan Fang, 120.

45. Hu Ruquan, "Cong Tianjin . . . ," table, 99.

46. Zheng Guizhen, 50. A second Shanghai survey, conducted among 6, 715 elderly people in late 1985, found that of those on pensions, 6% received 100 yuan or more; 20% received 71–100 yuan; 27% received 51–70 yuan; 32% received 31–50 yuan; and fully 15%, mostly old women, received 30 yuan or less: in other words, one out of seven pensioners obtained extremely meager monthly incomes (Gu, Chen, and Qian, 173).

47. A 1982 survey of a Tianjin neighborhood found, for example, that whereas 29% of all employed wives earned less than 40 yuan a month, only 6% of all employed husbands earned that little (Wu chengshi . . . , 69).

48. On this, see Gu, Chen, and Qian, 173.

49. Cai He, 96.

married children in stem and joint families, fully 93 percent of the children in such households where the elderly were without pensions expressed a willingness to retain the expanded family over the long term, compared with only 54 percent of those in stem or joint families where the parents were eligible for pensions and other benefits.[50]

There is a fascinating exception to this general tendency: retired cadres. Surveys during the eighties showed that the married children of retired officials lived at their parents' home at a far higher rate than was the case with other strata. A 1984 survey of 251 households of retired cadres in Tianjin found that fully 84 percent of them lived with their children.[51] A survey in 1983–84 of 570 households of retired cadres in the northern city of Harbin similarly found that, extraordinarily, fully 93 percent were living together with children.[52] Moreover, these retired cadres reportedly continued to be described by themselves and by their families as the "family head," to a far greater extent than was true in the stem families of other social strata.[53] The reason is probably as follows: it is a commonplace that officials can continue to exert a measure of bureaucratic power and influence even after retirement, enabling them to continue to be the pivotal movers within their families, much like the paterfamilias of old.

This is not to aver that the elderly in other families tend to lack much say in family affairs. In a 1985 Shanghai survey of 961 people aged sixty and over who resided in stem families, fully 87 percent felt that their views were listened to in the home, whereas only 10 percent felt that they had no say. Moreover, the great majority responded that they felt their children were appropriately filial.[54] Only 16 percent reported that their household was disharmonious.[55]

50. Ibid.

51. Hu Ruquan, "Cong Tianjin . . . ," 98. Among the 16% of retired cadre households whose children all lived apart, 14% had children living in the same city; in another 2% of the cases the children all lived in a different city or region; and in 0.4% of the sample the retired cadre had no children (ibid.).

52. Ibid. (a separate table on the same page); 0.5% of the retired cadres in Harbin were living alone; 5% were living with their spouse; another 6% with a child or children but without a spouse; fully 54% were living together with spouse *and* one or more children; and 33% were living with spouse, one or more married children, and grandchildren.

53. Yuan Fang, 117.

54. Ling Bi, "Shanghai shide laoren jiating" (Families of the elderly in urban Shanghai), *Shehuixue yanjiu* (Sociological Research), no. 4 (1986): 92. Also Zheng Guizhen, 136–37. Also see Liu Bingfu, "Wo guo jiating zai 'hexinhua' ma?" (Are Chinese families 'nuclearizing'?), *Xuexi yu shijian* (Study and Practice), no. 5 (1986), reprinted in *Shihuixue*, no. 3 (1986): 64. Also Hu Ruquan, "Cong Tianjin . . . ," table, 101—a Tianjin survey of 1,064 elderly in stem or joint families, in which 72% reported that their children/grandchildren were very respectful, and 26% that they were comparatively respectful, while a mere 2% related that the younger generation were not respectful (*bu da zunjing*). A 1988 survey of several smaller cities in Jiangsu province came up with quite similar findings: 65% of the elderly reported that their children were quite filial; 30% said the children were average in this respect, and only 5% reported

To the extent that their physical abilities allow, in almost all such stem households the elderly pull their own weight by taking care of the housework, minding the grandchildren, doing the marketing, and so forth, while the younger couple is off at full-time jobs. Inasmuch as the elderly handle most of the household's daily purchases during these daylight hours, they also normally end up controlling most of the household's money for daily living expenses; in fact, the 1985 Shanghai survey found that they did so in fully 88 percent of the households.[56] In other words, the younger couple hands over a good portion of their income, and in many cases a majority of it, to the elderly. The elderly not only feel they get respect; they even hold responsibility for most of the household budget.

In short, while a heavy preponderance of middle-aged couples and even a majority of the elderly prefer to live apart from all their married children, they do not do so because the alternative is in some respect onerous. Most of the elderly who *do* live in stem families seem to find it a relatively satisfactory and harmonious arrangement. And for those who are truly aged or infirm, it is a needed lifeline.

Here perhaps lies the rub in the government's enforced one-child family policy. It was observed earlier that the "networked" family of separate but linked households provides an increasingly popular living arrangement for the middle-aged parents of married children, and that it perhaps will become increasingly popular in future when two middle-aged couples will have to "share" one couple of married children. But what will be the situation several decades further into the future, when two pairs of quite elderly couples, or two widows, feel a need to move in with their married child's family, in circumstances where the elderly of both sides of the family share only one set of married children? A great many elderly, *against* their will, may be obliged to retain a "networked" form of family organization into advanced old age. It promises to pose one of the great social dilemmas in urban China's future.

---

that the children were not filial. Among these interviewees, 89% claimed harmonious relations with their children and only 11% reported conflict (*maodun*). Ye Nanke and Tang Zhongxun, "Laonianren shenghuo zhiliang chutan" (A preliminary investigation into elderly people's quality of life), *Renkou yanjiu* (Population Research), no. 6 (1989), republished in *Shehuixue* (Sociology), no. 1 (1990): 124.

55. Ling Bi, 92. Of this 16% of the elderly who reported a disharmonious stem or joint household, 43% felt the problem stemmed from tense mother-in-law/daughter-in-law relations, and a further 21% from conflicts between the elderly parent(s) and their married child. All told, these statistics suggest, though, that only some 7% of the elderly in stem households faced acute mother-in-law/daughter-in-law conflicts, a lower proportion than the scholarly literature on Chinese culture would have led us to predict.

56. Ling Bi, 91. A breakdown of this 88% shows that 70% were women and 18% men. (On the elderly's management of household funds, also see Hu Ruquan, "Cong Tianjin . . . ," 99).

THREE

Urban Households:
Supplicants to a Socialist State

Deborah Davis

Household size and composition are shaped by demographic, economic, and cultural factors. Mortality and fertility rates determine the number of potential members as well as the relative size and completeness of each generation. Availability of housing and the ease with which individuals move between homes or between cities affect the composition and stability, while culturally specific "rules of family formation" decide which kin are most likely to be coresident.[1] To the extent that state policies create or alter any of these constraints on living arrangements, government actions and priorities decisively shape family life. In much of the scholarly work on the family, however, the state has been assumed to be a secondary actor, and primary emphasis has been given to how increased urbanization and industrialization alter the economic utility of family relations or how new ideals emerge from long-term secularization or altered market incentives.[2] In China, and especially in urban China under the governance of the Communist Party, such assumptions do not hold because the state has assumed a central role in establishing the economic, cultural, and even demographic parameters that decide the size and composition of urban households.

In 1955 the government established a national system of household (*hukou*) registration as part of a plan to control rural to urban migration and to administer food rationing. As a result, all changes of address or any alterations in household membership were registered at the local police sta-

---

1. John Hajnal, "Two Kinds of Pre-industrial Household Formation Systems," *Population and Development Review* 8, no. 3 (Sept. 1982): 449–94.

2. Classic statements of these two positions are found in William Goode, *World Revolution and Family Patterns* (New York: Free Press, 1970), and Gary Becker, *A Treatise on the Family* (Cambridge: Harvard University Press, 1981).

tion, and any residential move required police approval.[3] A new Marriage Law required children to support (and house) elderly parents, and only elderly without responsible kin could turn to social welfare agencies to support independent living or institutional shelter.[4] During the massive push to collectivize the urban economy in 1958 virtually all women under the age of forty-five were required to work full-time outside the home, and as a consequence the career of full-time housewife disappeared among women under the age of fifty, and the typical urban household became one with two working parents.[5]

Equally decisive was the bureaucratic system of allocation that replaced the markets of the precommunist era and transformed urban residents from consumers and employees into clients of a socialist state.[6] In the case of housing, the shift from market to plan had immediate and far-ranging consequences for urban households. The building of new housing became the responsibility of municipal housing bureaus and individual enterprises.[7] Allocation of new apartments and redistribution of old flats depended on bureaucratic decisions rather than on a family's ability to pay. Households that felt they were inadequately housed or preferred a new location applied to the housing office of their neighborhood or their place of employment; then they waited until they were informed of a favorable decision. In rural

3. In the first years after the CCP victory, citizens could change residence quite freely. But with the strict enforcement of the 1955 household registration (*hukou*) system after 1958, residential mobility between and within cities greatly declined. In a study of three residential districts of Shanghai, it was reported that 35 percent of the urban population moved in 1954 and 43 percent in 1955, but by 1958 the rate fell below 10 percent. Christopher Howe, *Employment and Economic Growth in Urban China 1949–1957* (Cambridge: Cambridge University Press, 1971), 65–66, 72. In their study of Guangdong in the 1970s Martin Whyte and William Parish found that only 10 percent had changed residence in the past five years. *Urban Life in Contemporary China* (Chicago: University of Chicago Press, 1984), 21. Comparison of overall rates of urban growth in Beijing, Shanghai, and Tianjin also document a sharp decline after 1957 and before 1982. See Judith Banister, *China's Changing Population* (Stanford: Stanford University Press, 1987), 302–3. For a description of how the system operated, see Lynn T. White, *Careers in Shanghai* (Berkeley: University of California Press, 1978), 148–54.

4. Deborah Davis-Friedmann, *Long Lives* (Stanford: Stanford University Press, 1991), 34–60.

5. Whyte and Parish, *Urban Life in Contemporary China*, 201.

6. For the fullest exploration of the evolution and consequences of this process, see Andrew Walder, *Communist Neo-Traditionalism* (Berkeley: University of California Press, 1986). Also see chapter 8 by Whyte in this volume for the consequences for choice of mate.

7. In the early eighties 15 to 20% of urban families still owned homes purchased in the years immediately before or after 1949; however, the majority of urban residents lived in public housing allocated either through their place of employment or a municipal housing bureau. In December 1981, 54% of urban housing was owned by units, 28.5% by municipal real estate bureaus, and 17.5% by private individuals. *Beijing Review*, Oct. 11,1982, 27–28. In Wuhan in 1985, 21% of housing was owned by real estate bureaus and 62.7% by enterprises. *Wuhan Nianjian 1986*, 566.

China, where families were responsible for building their own shelter, people wanting more space raised their savings rate as a primary strategy for better housing.[8] By contrast, urban residents faced with a noncommodified, welfare system of housing developed strategies to present themselves as deserving supplicants.

After 1980 Chinese Communist Party (CCP) leadership under Deng Xiaoping inaugurated a development policy that initially promised urban residents significant departures from the Maoist political economy. Consumer industries were given a new priority, vast sums were invested in residential construction, and there was a revolution in the comfort and convenience of urban life. Average living space rose from 4.96 square meters per urban resident in 1980 to 8.7 square meters in 1988, and the percentage of households that had less than 4 square meters per capita fell from 33 percent to 15 percent.[9]

Increased availability of consumer goods and more plentiful housing, however, did not signal a renunciation by the CCP leadership of their role as social engineers. On the contrary, with the inauguration of the campaign to universalize a one-child family in 1979, the state assumed the right to dictate the fertility of every urban woman and thereby control family size more completely than any previous regime. In the long term, this decision would produce urban families with no siblings and very high ratios of elderly as a percentage of family dependents. But in the short term, the impact of the one-child campaign, especially as it affected household composition and the processes of household formation, is more difficult to predict. Knowing that a first child is a last child, will young couples remain in multigenerational homes longer than did earlier generations, or will they experience a heightened desire to set up an independent household? How will the absence of a son affect the solidarity of marriages, or the absence of a grandson alter obligations between parents and adult children? Will sustained rates of low fertility foster the rapid proliferation of small households of two and three members, or stabilize multigenerational arrangements?

Drawing on a range of recent Chinese publications and a longitudinal study of one hundred families in urban Shanghai interviewed first in 1987 and then again in 1990, this chapter addresses several of these questions about the impact of the post-Mao reforms on household size and composition in Chinese cities. The first section introduces the neighborhood

8. Thus between 1957 and 1978 rural families on average spent less than 4% of their incomes on housing, but as their incomes rose not only did the absolute amounts invested in housing increase but so did the percentages. Thus, for example, in 1978 they spent on average 12.4%, in 1986 14.4%, in 1988 14.9%, but only 8.2% in 1989, a year of economic downturn. *Zhongguo Tongji Nianjian* (henceforth *ZGTJNJ*) *1989*, 743, and *Beijing Review*, March 19–25, 1990, 39–40.

9. *ZGTJNJ 1988*, 806, and *ZGTJNJ 1989*, 756.

where I conducted the interviews and describes the general changes in household size and composition that occurred between 1987 and 1990. The second section focuses on one particular characteristic of these households—a strong "tilt" toward joint living with sons—and analyzes the cultural and practical supports for the predominance of this apparently traditional arrangement in an era of rapid economic and social upheaval. In the third and last section, I briefly review the housing policies of the 1980s and then look closely at which families in my sample initially drew the greatest benefits. In this way the chapter explores not only the impact of the reforms on urban household composition but also raises questions about the emergence of new inequalities and class divisions. The underlying theme unifying the chapter is the degree to which the reforms have altered the dependency of all urban families on the state. More narrowly, the chapter focuses on the question, To what extent and in what ways did the process of household formation in large metropolitan cities diverge from that of the late Mao era?[10]

HOUSEHOLD FORMATION IN URBAN SHANGHAI

In 1987 as part of a multiyear study of occupational mobility in urban China, I interviewed one hundred Shanghai women born between 1925 and 1935. In addition to material on work histories of the respondents, their husbands, and their children, I also gathered information on household arrangements at the time of the interview and at the time of each respondent's first marriage. In July 1990 I returned to the original interview site to update the information on the household arrangements of the seventy-three women who could be reinterviewed and to inquire systematically about the housing arrangements of all their married children ($N = 188$).[11]

As a group, the household heads in my survey represented the upper reaches of the working class and the lower rungs of middle management.[12] Only 5 percent of the fathers and 15 percent of the mothers worked outside

10. In 1984 the official definition of urban life was relaxed to include suburban and small-town populations, which had been excluded from urban statistics since 1963. However, in this chapter when I cite changes in urban household figures I am drawing consistently from tables that identify the city core of urban areas, and with my Shanghai survey I am generalizing to family situations typical in the 31 large metropolitan cities with one million or more inhabitants, a population that as of 1986 equaled approximately 46 percent of all nonagricultural population living in the largest 354 cities and towns. *Zhongguo Chengshi Tongji Nianjian 1987*, 1.

11. Funds to support field research came from the Committee on Scholarly Communication with the PRC and Yale University. For professional support and essential introductions, I wish to thank the Retirement Committee of the Shanghai General Union and the Putuo District Government.

12. The percentage breakdown among respondents and their husbands by type of current or last job was as follows:

the state sector, and 38.5 percent and 18 percent, respectively, were Party members. All families lived in a new residential neighborhood built in 1979, where each apartment had two rooms, a balcony, and a private toilet.[13] The estate represented good housing, and my respondents should be seen as successful supplicants in the bureaucratic allocation of scarce resources.[14] When I first interviewed them in June 1987, almost all expressed high levels of satisfaction with their current arrangements, and in only three cases was I able to identify families who were actively looking to move to better apartments.[15] However, when I returned in 1990 to reinterview the original one hundred respondents, I found that fourteen had moved to a new neighborhood, two had died, and most astounding to me, 60 percent of those who agreed to be reinterviewed had altered household membership.[16] In 23 percent of these families households became larger, in 34 percent they had become smaller, and in 3 percent they were the same size but included

	husbands	*wives*
semiskilled manual	12.5	59.2
skilled manual	11.5	7.1
low-level political cadre	6.3	6.1
routine white-collar	8.3	7.1
nonroutine white-collar	21.9	14.3
middle manager	29.2	2.0
professional	10.4	4.1

13. In 1987 there were 3,016 residents living in 814 households.

14. Although all apartments in the estate had only two rooms, there were two different configurations of the rooms, so that one gave 27 square meters and the other only 24. At the time of the 1987 interviews families in the larger apartments averaged 5.8 square meters per person, those in the smaller apartments 4.8 square meters. By way of comparison, one can note that in 1985 Shanghai households averaged 5.5 square meters per person, while nationwide the average was 7.46 square meters or 6.1 square meters depending on how you defined city residents. Hu Renxi, "Shiqu gaoling laoren zhuzhu qingkuang chouyang diaocha" (Sample survey of the housing situation of the very old in the urban districts), in *Gaoling laoren wenti yanjiu*, ed. the Research Group of Shanghai Municipal Committee on Problems of the Elderly (Shanghai: Shanghai shi laonianxue xuehui mishuzhu, 1987), 71–80; *ZGTJNJ 1988*, 806; *China Reconstructs* 38, no. 8 (Aug. 1989).

15. All three households were headed by professionals (a head engineer, a surgeon, and an import-export executive), and each had only two children. By June 1990 the first two had moved out of the estate and the third had both children working in Hong Kong and appeared to be making plans to emigrate themselves.

16. Besides those who had moved or died and were therefore not available for the reinterview, three were in the hospital, four were traveling outside Shanghai, and four were at work on the scheduled interview days. A comparison of the household profiles of the Shanghai reinterviewees with the original sample of one hundred respondents, however, indicates no serious problem of selectivity. Those who were reinterviewed had lived in only marginally larger households (4.65 as opposed to 4.57 persons) and in both groups a majority had lived in three- or four-generation homes: 57% among those reinterviewed, 54% in the entire 1987 sample.

TABLE 3.1.   Generational Stability of Shanghai Households
1987–1990

No. of Generations in Household, 1987	% Unchanged, 1990	% Simpler, 1990	% More Complex, 1990	Total (%)
1 (N = 5)	80	0	20	100
2 (N = 26)	62	8	31	101[a]
3 (N = 38)	89	11	0	100
4 (N = 4)	0	100	0	100

[a] Exceeds 100% due to rounding.

different people. Equally noteworthy was that whereas only 11 percent of the three-generation households became generationally "simpler" by contracting to either one- or two-generation households, 31 percent of the two-generation families had become generationally "more complex," expanding to three-generation arrangements through the addition of a new grandchild, an elderly in-law, or a coresident niece or nephew (table 3.1).

Because of their rather uniform age, favorable occupational status, and high rates of Communist Party membership, these Shanghai families cannot represent the urban population, and readers should not conclude that annual turnover rates of 20 percent in household membership were the norm between 1987 and 1990. However, I do think that the experience of these families is typical of urban families at an especially transformative stage of the life cycle. All households in this study were selected because they included a woman born between 1925 and 1935, thereby guaranteeing that most respondents would be able to give information on both a parent and a child who had worked for a full decade after 1949. This focus on households with a mother in her late fifties or early sixties also meant that respondents and their husbands were at that stage of life where they were assuming new roles of in-law and grandparent but were also still fulfilling the role of child to an elderly parent and of parent to an unmarried child. Therefore, while my sample cannot represent the total urban population, it does speak to a universal stage of the life cycle where the processes of family formation and household division are typically most dynamic.

In Unger's table summarizing household composition among Beijing women of five different cohorts, those between ages forty-six and fifty-nine had markedly different households than those between the ages of sixty and sixty-nine (see chapter 2, table 2.3, of this volume). Specifically, while the modal household for the younger women was nuclear, that for the older women was stem. In addition, Unger's finding of greatest levels of coresidence among both the neediest pensioners and the wealthiest high-ranking cadres coincides with what I observed in Shanghai. That is, when parents were either especially impoverished or particularly privileged, Unger's surveys revealed large and complex households because there were strong expectations that the wealthier or more fortunate would shelter the needy and poorer. This expectation, which Ikels has so aptly called an unwritten contract of entitlement (see chapter 12 of this volume), encourages multigenerational homes when, as a result of real or relative poverty, one generation is perceived as unable to provide adequately for itself. Because my sample targeted families where adult children were in the prime marriage years and elderly parents likely to be frail, the study caught individuals at a point in life when demands for intergenerational reciprocity and entitlement were especially numerous. No national survey will produce the same frequencies of coresidence, but a national survey targeted at this same age group in major metropolitan cities would look quite similar.[17]

LIFE CYCLE DYNAMISM AND INTERGENERATIONAL OBLIGATIONS: THREE CASES

Among my respondents, as among those interviewed in Chinese surveys described by Jonathan Unger, the ideal housing arrangement was an independent household for each nuclear family. The housing goal of most of my respondents and their children, therefore, was a separate home for each married couple and shared homes only when elderly parents needed care or companionship. But, as was clear in the pattern of household arrangements among my respondents in 1987 and in 1990 (tables 3.1 and 3.2), few families realized the ideal. Instead, as the following three case histories illustrate, persistent housing shortages and intergenerational obligations

17. A second consideration about this sample is the uniformity of the neighborhood. Nationwide, depending on the specific city, between 50 and 60% of urban residents live in apartments built by their employers, and only 20 to 30% live in municipal housing. Without parallel samples drawn from enterprise estates or company towns I cannot know the consequences of this difference for patterns of household composition. But given the more anonymous environment of city housing estates and the "entrepreneurial talent" that allowed these families to trade previous housing into what was perceived in 1979 to be excellent housing, we might hypothesize that my respondents were somewhat more aggressive than the average urban resident in mobilizing resources to improve their housing situation. A third concern is the uniqueness of Shanghai. However, in terms of crowding, one of the best indicators of intercity differences, Shanghai by the late 1980s was not very different from other large metropolitan areas. In 1986 the average per capita space in all urban homes was 5.9 square meters, in Shanghai it was 6.0, in Beijing 6.3, in Tianjin 5.9, and in Wuhan 5.7. Average household size in Shanghai also did not vary from the national norm, suggesting that while Shanghai was much more densely populated than average (2,118 persons per square km as opposed to 118 in all of urban China in 1990), in terms of availability and crowding of residential space it was not very different from the other major cities. *Zhongguo Chengshi Tongji Nianjian 1987*, 19, 27, 29, 31, 32, 35, 37, 39, 40, 291, 323, 331, and *Beijing Review*, Nov. 19, 1990, 11.

TABLE 3.2. Household Size and Composition among Shanghai
Respondents

	1987 (N = 73)	1990 (N = 73)
Average size	4.65 persons	4.42 persons
Composition (percentages)		
Alone	1	0
Spouse only	5	11
Unmarried children	26	16
Married child		
Sons	41	40
Daughters	17	18
Other		
In-law	4	4
Grandchild[a]	6	10

[a] These are grandchildren who lived with respondents while their parents lived
elsewhere. Grandchildren living with respondents whose parents were also
coresident are not counted here, but are included in households whose composition was identified as "married child."

to less fortunate members repeatedly overrode the desire to establish nuclear
households, and the norm was multigenerational homes and persistent
complexity.

The Lis (a pseudonym)

When I first interviewed Mrs. Li in 1987, she was fifty-eight years old and
just recently retired from her job as a daycare worker in a textile mill. Originally she had come from Ningbo, where her father had been a shop clerk.
But after her marriage in 1948, she and her husband had moved to Shanghai. When they were first married, they rented a fourteen-square-meter
flat near the Huangpu River. Later three children and her husband's
mother joined them, and by 1979 they were designated a "hardship case"
qualified for quick resettlement.

When they moved to their new apartment the household was officially a
three-generation family of six members: Mr. and Mrs. Li, his widowed
mother, and three unmarried children between the ages of twenty-five and
thirty-one. In fact, Mr. Li slept in his office, and the daughter had a bed-
space at her factory, so the actual household consisted of the two sons in
one room, and the mother-in-law and Mrs. Li in the second room. Then,
within six months of their move to this apartment, the eldest son married,

and he and his bride took over the room that he had previously shared with his brother, while the younger son set up a cot in the hallway.

Two years later, the older brother, his wife, and their small daughter qualified for their own apartment on the grounds of hardship. But as soon as this couple moved out, Mrs. Li's second son married and immediately moved his bride into the room just vacated by his brother's family.

Mrs. Li's daughter had even greater difficulty in establishing her own household. Married in 1982, she and her husband were unable either to move in with in-laws or find a room of their own. As a result, for more than seven years they each lived in their factory dormitory, while their daughter was raised by the husband's mother. Finally in 1989, at age thirty-five and with seventeen years work experience, the daughter was assigned a two-room apartment with a private bath and kitchen in a housing block built by her husband's employer.

When interviewed in July 1990, Mrs. Li maintained a household of four: herself, her second son, his wife, and their son. Her mother-in-law had died, and her husband continued to spend most nights at his office. However, during the summer the household was even more crowded than the official registration booklet indicated because Mrs. Li was keeping the children of both her elder son and her daughter for the school holidays. Usually six people were sleeping in the apartment, and most evenings Mrs. Li cooked for eight or nine people, depending on which of the adult members of her family were off from work that day.

Ideally, Mrs. Li and her son would like to have their own homes. But at the moment this family has stopped even trying to find an alternate arrangement. By the criteria of hardship, they are comfortably housed. The building is in good order, and although they live on the sixth floor, they have piped gas, a private toilet, and most important, the married couple has a separate bedroom accessible from a central hallway. Seniority is also unlikely to help either the parents or the son. Although a Communist Party member and a manager, Mr. Li is officially retired, and like his wife he has lost the leverage at the old unit that would enable him to advance a claim for new housing. The son, a manager of thirty-seven and also a Party member, would ordinarily be a prime candidate for a new apartment. But in 1988 he moved to a new job in a joint venture, and although the salary is higher than average and in 1989 he received a major promotion, the Hong Kong management has made it clear that it will never build staff housing.

In the case of the Lis a statistical profile would document gradual "nuclearization" of urban family life. Two of the three children maintain small neolocal homes, and only one son is coresident with his parents. The reality of the several intermediate steps, the long periods of intense crowding and dormitory living, however, quickly contradict any such simple interpretation of nuclear predominance. Rather, the Lis' experience graphically illustrates how in the midst of China's longest and biggest housing boom multigenerational living persisted even as the neolocal ideal animated much of the ongoing maneuvering.

When the Lis moved from their fourteen-square-meter apartment in 1979 they gave up all claims on the room they had rented from the city, and there seemed to have been no opportunity for them to keep title to both the old and the new rooms. However, for many of my respondents, even among those who did not own their own flats, relocation had not required them to relinquish their previous apartment, and the family maintained claims to two places. Thus one strategy that became obvious amidst the greater prosperity and openly entrepreneurial culture of the Deng era was that families shifted members between old and new apartments to maximize their leverage, or simply to minimize the crowding that occurred as children married, grandchildren were born, or elderly parents needed nursing care. This was the experience of the Zhaos, a family that in terms of the formal household-registration system had become less extended between 1987 and 1990, but in reality was still actively involved in a complicated process of reconfiguration.

The Zhaos (a pseudonym)

When I first met Mrs. Zhao in 1987, she was a fifty-seven-year-old mother of two grown sons and temporarily employed as a service worker in a small hotel. Her household was a four-generation home, which included her husband, her husband's mother, her second son, his wife, and their toddler. By 1990 her life had been simplified. She had retired from her hotel job to care for her newly retired husband, and her household consisted only of herself, her husband, and his ailing father aged eighty-five. At first glance, it appeared that the household had become markedly less complex. Further conversation revealed a different interpretation.

Mrs. Zhao was born in a Jiangsu village and came to Shanghai before 1949 as a textile worker. She married in 1953 and immediately moved into the two-room home of her husband's parents. Her husband was an only child, and for the next twenty-five years she, her husband, and their two sons lived with her in-laws. In the late 1970s the city tore down their front room, and as compensation assigned the Zhaos two rooms in a new municipal housing estate. However, when Mrs. Zhao moved, her elder son stayed behind with his grandfather (Mrs. Zhao's father-in-law) in the back room, which had not been torn down, while Mrs. Zhao, her husband, her mother-in-law, and the younger son moved to the new home. In 1987 when I first interviewed Mrs. Zhao, the older son, who had married in 1985, was living with his wife and baby in a three-generation household headed by her father-in-law. Mrs. Zhao maintained the six-person, four-generation home described above.

How had the household reconfigured by 1990 as a two-generation home of an elderly couple and an even older father-in-law? The process reflects both the new opportunities of the late 1980s and the traditional obligations imposed by the norms of intergenerational reciprocity and interdependence that had also been decisive in the family life of the Lis.

In 1988 Mrs. Zhao's mother-in-law died, and soon after, her eldest son left China to study in Japan. At that point, her father-in-law moved to live with her, and her younger son, his wife, and their child moved back to their old house to live with the older daughter-in-law and her son.

For the Lis and the Zhaos family relations appeared harmonious, and the strategies that shaped their household shifts away from the nuclear ideal were animated by the morality of intergenerational entitlement. In other families, relations were tense, and in an era of greater choice, conflicts split some households apart. However, as we will see with the Wangs, even in situations of conflict, obligations to provide for the needy continued to be a major force sustaining and even elaborating already complex households.

The Wangs (a pseudonym)

Mrs. Wang was born in 1932 on a riverboat in northern Jiangsu province. As a small girl she had come to Shanghai with her mother, and before she was ten she was working full-time in the textile mills. She was married in 1950 to a street scavenger, and the couple set up their new home with both his mother and her mother in a timber and stucco hut that he had rented sometime around 1949. In 1979 the building was condemned, and as compensation they received not only a new two-room apartment but also two single rooms in other locations, one for each marriage-age son. At first Mrs. Wang, her mother-in-law, and her younger, unmarried son lived in one place; the elder son, his wife, and two children lived in another, and the two daughters shared the new two-room apartment. At this time, Mrs. Wang's husband was serving a five-year prison term for crimes committed during the Cultural Revolution and was not a member of the household.

In 1987 when I first interviewed Mrs. Wang the family no longer was living as they had in 1979. Mrs. Wang's mother-in-law had died, and her husband, who had returned from prison, had moved with her to the new apartment, which they then shared with their younger daughter, a son-in-law, and an infant granddaughter. The elder son and his family remained in the room he had received in 1979, the elder daughter had married and was living with her husband's parents, and the younger son was living alone in the room he previously had shared with his parents and grandmother.

Three years later the family had redistributed itself once again. Mrs.

Wang remained in the same apartment she had occupied in 1987, but her husband had moved out and now slept in a loft they had built in the home of the second son. This son had married in fall of 1987, and now he, his wife, and their child occupied the main room, although during the day the child was sent to Mrs. Wang while her daughter-in-law was at work. The younger daughter, the daughter's husband, and their four-year-old child continued to live in the same room they had used in 1987, but now they also shared the kitchen, toilet, and hallway with the older sister, who had moved back with her young daughter after her divorce in 1988. The explicit strategy that Mrs. Wang articulated without any prompting was that by registering as many people as possible in this modest two-room flat, she hoped that within two or three years the younger daughter and her family would be allocated a third room in this estate on the grounds of hardship, leaving Mr. and Mrs. Wang, the divorced elder daughter, and her child in this apartment. With six persons in two rooms, the family averaged only a bit more than four square meters per head. However, none of the four adults in the apartment had a work unit with good housing supplies. Mrs. Wang and her elder daughter were from the worker ranks at a textile mill with no staff housing, and the younger daughter and her husband both worked for a suburban collective that neither built staff housing nor gave cash subsidies for home purchase or rental. Because not one of the four had any chance of gaining their own place by moving up the seniority queue at their workplace and Mr. Wang had no responsible unit as a result of his prison sentence, the only realistic strategy was to accentuate their position as especially needy supplicants and hope that the district housing office would view them as a hardship case worthy of solicitude.

THE REFORMS AND PREFERENCE FOR SONS

In the experience of the Lis, the Wangs, and the Zhaos, the primary concern behind their search for new housing was to reduce crowding and improve the location and amenities of their homes. However, families also pursued strategies to achieve socially optimal membership, which among those forced to accept multigenerational arrangements encouraged coresidence with sons, not daughters, or dependency on the parents of the groom, not of the bride. For the Lis this ideal meant providing for needy sons before a needy daughter, and for the Wangs it meant establishing each married son in an independent home while using their own apartment as a refuge for a divorced daughter and as a temporary solution for a daughter who had married a man with poor housing resources.

This tilt toward sons was also explicitly articulated by Shanghai residents with whom I spoke about housing goals, and here I quote from a conversation I had in June 1987 with a middle-aged cadre from my research site.[18] She had just moved from a fairly spacious home within walking distance of her office to a new apartment that required a long commute, and I was curious about what had motivated a move that had created such inconvenience.

> *Q:* But, from what you have said, your new apartment doesn't really sound like an improvement.
>
> *A:* Well, my husband and I will retire in the next few years, and our son will probably get married soon.
>
> *Q:* But you have at least five more years in this job, and your husband won't retire until 1997. Is this new apartment especially close to the workplace of your future daughter-in-law?
>
> *A:* Oh, no, my son doesn't even have a [girl] friend.
>
> *Q:* Then I really don't understand; why did you take this apartment?
>
> *A:* It is the layout. In our old place we had two bigger rooms, but you had to walk through one to get to the other. When our son *does* marry, it will be much better for each couple to have separate doorways. If we didn't take this place while we could, he would have a harder time finding a wife.

Additional evidence of the expectation of joint living with sons was found in the household arrangements of the 188 married children of my Shanghai respondents. Among those living with parents at the time of the interview, sons were more than twice as likely as daughters to be coresident (see table 3.2, lines 6 and 7), and among all married children unable to establish an independent home at the time of marriage, 84 percent lived with the groom's parents (table 3.3). Moreover, in only one year between 1979 and 1989 did more than 25 percent of coresident children deviate from this virilocal pattern.

Yet, as we saw in the Li family, some young couples who lived jointly immediately after marriage later established their own independent homes, and therefore it is possible that the tilt toward sons captured in table 3.3 misrepresents long-term trends. However, a comparison of housing arrangements among firstborn sons at the time of their marriages and again as of July 1990 suggests that the male bias persisted even after couples left a parent's home. For example, if the couple moved into an apartment arranged by their parents either at the time of marriage or in subsequent years, the apartment was far more likely to have been set up by the hus-

18. This sentiment was also clearly articulated at a seminar in November 1990 at Yale when two former residents of China drew on their own early years of marriage in 1980. In both cases they recalled direct pressure not to move to the home of their wives' parents, saying that their colleagues would consider such a move, even when it meant having more space, a "disgrace." One also said that the patrilateral tilt even extended to avoiding taking an apartment in his wife's unit. In that case, he said, the problem was that he did not want to be a subordinate in her unit, and his unit should not be subordinate to her unit.

TABLE 3.3. Postmarital Housing Arrangements of Shanghai Newlyweds

Year of Marriage	% Coresident with In-laws in Month after Wedding (N = 188)	% of Coresident Newlyweds in Home of Groom's Parents (N = 117)
1971–78	50	66
1979	60	100
1980	63	100
1981	69	100
1982	61	76
1983	79	82
1984	56	89
1985	74	57
1986	69	91
1987	42	80
1988	58	100
1989 + 1990 (May)	71	80
Mean percentage	62 coresident	84 with groom's parents

SOURCE: 1990 Shanghai interviews.

band's parents than by the wife's. Or, if their own employer supplied housing, it was the man's unit more often than the woman's that served as the landlord (table 3.4).

While to some observers of Chinese society a concern about the degree of a male preference might seem uninteresting given China's traditional patriarchal culture and patrilineal ancestor worship, to me the predominance of coresidence with sons and the greater reliance on parents or employers of the groom raised central questions about the effect of the Deng reforms on family life. But before addressing these larger questions, let me explain briefly why this "tilt" toward sons in housing arrangements struck me as worthy of further scrutiny. First, from my respondents' reports of their early married life, I discovered that the postmarital households of my respondents who had married in the 1940s and early 1950s differed very little from the arrangements of their sons who had married in the 1970s and 1980s. In fact, to the extent that there was any shift, it was toward greater not less virilocality. At the time of their own marriages 42 percent of my respondents had lived with the groom's parents and only 9 percent with the bride's. Among their firstborn sons, however, the percentages were 52 percent and 2 percent, respectively. In short, based on a comparison of hous-

TABLE 3.4. Housing Arrangements among Firstborn Shanghai Sons ($N = 52$)
(percentages)

	At marriage[a]	In July 1990
With husband's parents	52	35
With wife's parents	2	2
In home set up by husband's parents	21	25
In home set up by wife's parents	4	2
In home from husband's unit[b]	9	17
In home from wife's unit	5	6
Rented room	6	2
Other	2	10

[a] Average year of first marriage was 1982.
[b] Where husband and wife were in the same unit, each got half credit.

ing arrangements immediately after marriage, it appeared that after many decades of CCP hegemony in which one might have presumed that ideological supports for traditional preferences would disappear, the onus of providing shelter continued to be a male or patriline responsibility.[19]

Second, although an examination of household arrangements among these different cohorts of newly married couples revealed continuity with traditional expectations, other material suggested that a preference for sons was not simply a continuity with the precommunist past, but possibly represented a more pronounced "tilt" toward sons after 1980. During a 1979 trip to China, where I interviewed urban elderly in Beijing, Shijiazhuang, and Changzhou, I found strong evidence of departures from past preferences for coresidence with married sons.[20] In addition, among children of the Shanghai respondents who had married between 1971 and 1978, only half had moved in with in-laws, and of these 34 percent of the coresident couples had departed from virilocal practice and lived with the wife's parents (see table 3.3). Therefore, I was quite struck both by the higher rate of coresidence and by the lower rates of uxorilocal living among the most recently married.

By examining how urban residents have benefited from the Deng economic and political reforms, the possibility that the late 1980s may have seen an increased emphasis on traditional preferences becomes more understandable. Between 1978 and 1988 city residents experienced a dramatic

19. This was also the bias that Whyte and Parish found in their study of Guangdong families in the 1970s (*Urban Life in Contemporary China*, 144–45).
20. Davis-Friedmann, *Long Lives*, 47–59.

improvement in their standard of living. Urban wages tripled,[21] rationing of most foodstuffs disappeared, and items that had been scarce luxuries became almost commonplace. But what did this new affluence mean for family life? Most immediately it incited a consumer revolution that dramatically redefined the external markings of social status. After 1980 status came increasingly to be defined in terms of material possessions. In most of the families I visited, older members were less obviously affected by the new materialism, but in decisions about wedding expenditures, middle-aged and newly retired parents were as vulnerable as the young. A big banquet, a large trousseau, and a complete bedroom set were the minimum purchases necessary for a socially acceptable wedding. Anything less not only made the family lose face, it also could cause the children to claim parental selfishness or neglect, and thus justify children's distancing themselves from parents and filial obligations.

During the 1970s the official media had praised young couples who celebrated their marriages with a simple tea party and began married life with nothing more than two new winter jackets, two quilts, and a thermos bottle. In practice, urban weddings of the seventies typically had involved far more elaborate celebrations. Most parents hosted a family feast, and brides expected several sets of new clothes, basic home furnishings, and when possible, a new bicycle or wristwatch. Expenses were variable, but on average the groom and his family spent three to five months' income, and the bride and her parents only somewhat less.[22] Yet in most cities a family's reputation did not absolutely demand an expensive wedding, and it was possible (and of course politically correct) to marry with not much more than a new set of bedding, a table, and two chairs. Therefore, a young couple could, if they wished, marry without any financial obligations or debts to their parents.

The relative affluence of the 1980s and the influx of new consumer goods effectively eliminated the option of a simple wedding and thereby increased the dependency of young couples on their parents. By the mid-1980s an urban wedding averaged between 5,000 and 6,000 yuan,[23] but most young adults needed at least 80 percent of their monthly salary of 100–120 yuan

21. In 1978 average wages in state enterprises were 615 yuan; by 1988 they had risen to 1,853 yuan. *Zhongguo Tongji Zhaiyao 1987*, 101; *ZGTJNJ 1989*,125, 130.

22. Whyte and Parish, *Urban Life in Contemporary China*, 137.

23. In a twenty-city survey of urban marriages, average costs in 1985–86 were 5,069 yuan, which included 1,000 yuan for the wedding and 4,000 yuan for presents. Gu Jirui, *Jiating xiaofei jingjixue*, 343. Based on a 1986 survey in 18 large and medium cities, Chinese researchers estimated that for marriages concluded between 1981 and 1985, a groom's family on average needed to save between 39 and 50 months, and the brides' families needed between 24 and 31 months. Qian Jianghong, "Marriage Related Consumption," *Social Sciences in China*, no. 1 (1988): 221.

just to cover necessities. Unable to accumulate savings of any size on their own, they leaned heavily on their parents to purchase the color television, refrigerator, and washing machine that had become the essentials for any respectable new home of the late 1980s. In light of the exponential growth in the cost of an acceptable wedding and the high levels of dependency on parents among this generation of young urbanites, it is not surprising that parents frequently expanded their home to include the spouse of a newly married child. The question remains, however, why did they welcome a daughter-in-law more frequently than a son-in-law?

If I were to take my respondents' replies to this question, the answer would be quite simply this: "If a man moves into his wife's house, he will have no status or power." In short, what these urban residents emphasized was that Chinese culture is patriarchal and discriminates against females. But this answer, while true and relevant, does not explain why the affluence and greater ideological freedom of the eighties maintained—perhaps even strengthened—these traditional patrilineal preferences, or why these biases were so pronounced among young urban couples establishing new families during the 1980s. However, if we place the explosion of consumerism and the prolonged dependency of urban youth into the larger framework of the post-Mao political and economic reforms, causal links do emerge.

The Deng reforms championed commodification, decollectivization, and privatization, and in rural areas, as Harrell, Johnson, and Selden have documented in chapters 4, 5, and 6 of this volume, the result was a dramatic departure from the household economy of the Mao era. In the cities, by contrast, the reforms had only a minimal effect on the core economic institutions. Households did not become units of production, and housing supplies continued to be a privilege distributed to deserving clients through the municipal governments or places of work. After 1980, however, there were changes in labor policies that affected the relative earning power of men and women, which in turn shaped a parent's choice of coresident child.

In the 1970s the job assignment procedures for young urbanites often ignored educational or gender differences.[24] In some years all secondary school graduates regardless of training or preferences would be sent to the countryside; in other years, only those with an older sibling already in a village or a state farm could be assigned a city job. Sometimes families could keep a child at home on the grounds that an elderly parent needed care. Where the parent was relatively young or in good health, the family would argue that the new graduate was too physically frail to withstand the

---

24. Susan L. Shirk, *Competitive Comrades* (Berkeley: University of California Press, 1982), 52–84; Jonathan Unger, *Education Under Mao* (New York: Columbia University Press, 1982), 164–70.

rigors of rural life. Parents worked energetically to protect the interests of whichever child—son or daughter—was scheduled for a job assignment that year.

In this environment, parents with several teenagers could not predict which one would ultimately be the best source of support in the future, or even which child would be allowed to live in the same city as the parents. Therefore, many parents were as intensely involved with their daughters' futures as with their sons', and strategies that favored sons might be discarded. During the 1970s the massive outmigration of secondary and university graduates to manual jobs in the countryside depressed career prospects of sons and daughters. But because males had historically been the primary candidates for leadership positions and high salaries, the labor policies of the Cultural Revolution years created greater relative losses for males. Therefore, in the Deng era, when job assignments more predictably rewarded credentials and discrimination against females was no longer a focus of policy,[25] parents could logically expect more material gains by living jointly with a son than with a daughter. In the more relaxed ideological climate of the eighties, urban residents were freer to act on traditional preferences for sons, and given the increased discrimination against women it was also quite rational to value a son's financial contribution more highly than a daughter's.

The depoliticization of work rationalized preferences for sons in another way. During the years when political stigma had created especially severe discrimination, daughters often offered more reliable support because the regime did not police female kin ties as closely as those of males.[26] Under these circumstances, it made sense for some families deliberately to develop a household with the bride's family rather than the groom's. In the more depoliticized atmosphere of the eighties political blemishes no longer so directly determined family wealth and status. Daughters therefore lost their previous comparative advantage, and elderly parents and young adults would spontaneously, and without embarrassment, tell a curious foreigner, "It is shameful for a man to move to his wife's home."

In the 1980s, as in the 1970s, housing shortages denied many newlyweds the independent home they desired. But daughters faced the same housing crisis as sons; in fact, because many units provided housing for male workers before female workers, the needs of daughters could actually be greater.[27] Daughters were also as reliable a source of care as a son and daughter-in-law. Thus while necessity and external constraints explain why

25. Emily Honig and Gail Hershatter, *Personal Voices* (Stanford: Stanford University Press, 1988), 244–63; Stanley Rosen, "Women, Education and Modernization," in *Education and Modernization: The Chinese Experience*, ed. Ruth Hayhoe (Elmsford, N.Y.: Pergamon Press, 1992).

26. Davis-Friedmann, *Long Lives*, 78–79.

27. Honig and Hershatter, *Personal Voices*, 140.

high percentages of urban households included two married couples, cultural preferences and discrimination against women explain the bias in favor of sons.

THE UNEQUAL AND UNEVEN OUTCOMES OF HOUSING REFORMS

In China between 1950 and 1975, urban housing policy went through several phases. In years when municipal and enterprise leaders decided to make housing a priority there was a steady increase in the supply of cheap housing. But in years when "more productive" investments were given priority (as was the case between 1961 and 1972), little was spent on new urban housing.[28] Young couples or single adults could only find new quarters as members of larger, multigenerational households, and even couples with several young children were often required to share a suite with another young family in an apartment designed for one household.[29] As a result, by the late 1970s crowding was almost as acute as it had been at the end of the civil war, and average per capita living space was actually 20 percent lower than it had been in the early 1950s.[30]

The post-Mao leaders responded to this crisis with alacrity. In 1980 as much new urban housing was built as had been constructed during the entire Great Leap Forward, and one government source estimated that between 1979 and 1981, enterprises and city governments had rehoused the equivalent to the entire populations of Beijing, Shanghai, Tianjin, Guangzhou, Wuhan, and Shenyang.[31] Surprisingly, however, given the rhetoric

28. Reeitsu Kojima, *Urbanization and Urban Problems in China* (Tokyo: Institute of Developing Economies, 1987), 36–37.

29. Liu Yirong, "Yinggai zhongshi yanjiu yishihu de sheji wenti" (We must research the problem of one-room apartments), *Jianzhu xuebao*, no. 5 (1981): 61–63; Shen Kuixu, "Zhengque quli zhujai sheji yu fen pei di guanxi" (Resolve the relationship between housing supply and allocation), *Jianzhu xuebao*, no. 12 (1981): 59–64.

30. In August 1955 rents that previously had been set to provide maintenance and replacement were lowered in absolute terms. They were again reduced during the Cultural Revolution, thereby further widening the gap between expenditures and rents. Nicholas Lardy, "Consumption and Living Standards in China, 1978–83," *China Quarterly*, no. 100 (Dec. 1984): 856. One official Chinese source estimated that in 1979 average rents were 0.10 yuan per square meter, while cost to state was 0.38 yuan. "Urban Housing Rental," *Beijing Review*, Oct. 11, 1982, 27–28. In 1978 in 182 large cities households averaged 3.6 square meters per person; in 1952 the average had been 4.2 square meters. *People's Daily*, Aug. 5, 1980, 5, translated in *FBIS*, Aug. 20, 1980, 15–22. On rate of investment 1951–81, see Reeitsu Kojima, *Urbanization and Urban Problems in China*, 36–37.

31. For 1953–1984, see Kojima, *Urbanization and Urban Problems*, 37, and *Beijing Review*, May 3, 1982, 9. In 1991 the second source estimated that between 1979 and 1989 three times as much housing was built nationwide than had been built in the preceding three decades, and 500 million people moved into new or rebuilt homes. *Beijing Review*, Jan. 14, 1991, 38.

TABLE 3.5.   Rent as a Percentage of Urban Household Budgets

	1984	1985	1986	1987	1988	1990 (March)
National average	1.3	0.9	0.9	0.8	0.7	0.8
Beijing	1.5	1.1	1.1	0.9	0.8	0.9
Guangzhou	—	—	—	1.0	0.7	0.7
Shanghai	1.5	1.3	1.2	1.1	0.9	1.1
Tianjin	1.2	1.3	1.2	1.1	—	1.0
Urban Hubei	1.2	0.8	0.7	0.8	—	—
Wuhan	—	—	—	—	—	1.0

SOURCES: *Beijing Shehui Jingji Tongji Nianjian 1987*, 609; *1988*, 609; *1989*, 563; *China Statistics Monthly*, May 1990, 45–47; *Guangzhou Tongji Nianjian 1988*, 370; *1989*, 422; *Hubei Tongji Nianjian 1988*, 262; *Shanghai Tongji Nianjian 1989*, 477–78; *Tianjin Tongji Nianjian 1985*, 192; *1988*, 257; *ZGTJNJ 1988*, 807; *ZGTJNJ 1989*, 727.

of commodification and privatization of the Deng reforms, there was no sustained effort to pass on the costs in the form of higher rents. Instead, housing reform, to the extent that it was a reform, consisted of a decision to treble the share of housing in the capital-construction budget.[32] The low-rent policy and the bureaucratic system of allocation remained in place (table 3.5).

By the mid-1980s, however, new ideas began to circulate, and for a brief period there was a flurry of publicity announcing a fundamental shift away from public housing.[33] One of the most widely publicized models of change, sometimes called the Yantai plan, was a system whereby each employee was given a voucher to cover the real cost of building and maintaining what was defined as an adequate number of square meters of space (no price appears to have been placed on the land). Those who had more space than was considered necessary for their current household size were then to pay higher rents that approximated market value, and those who had less than adequate space would be given priority for renting or purchasing new housing.[34] In addition, there were experiments in Yantai, and elsewhere, with outright sales both of newly built homes and of existing enterprise

32. In 1978 housing took 7.8 percent of the construction budget; in 1981 and 1982 it went above 25 percent. Barry Naughton, "The Decline of Central Control over Investment in Post-Mao China," in *Policy Implementation in Post-Mao China*, ed. D. Michael Lampton (Berkeley: University of California Press, 1987), 66–67.

33. *Guowuyuan Gongbao (Bulletin of the State Council)*, April 20, 1985, 270, and *Beijing Review*, Nov.14, 1988, 18–20. A good summary of the several reforms is found in a commercially available *neibu* publication, Zhou Ying (ed.), *Chengshi zhuzhai gaige cankao ziliao* (Xinhuashe "Jingji cankao" bienjibu, n.d.; est. date of publication early 1988).

34. *RMRB*, July 1, 1988, 5.

facilities.[35] But by 1989, and particularly after the massacre in Tiananmen, central and municipal-level planners realized that at current wage levels, commercialization in the largest cities would be financially infeasible and politically destabilizing. Reforms were reduced to mild statements in support of gradual rent increases or lower housing subsidies, and plans for massive privatization were shelved.[36] Housing continued to take a trivial fraction of a family's income, and in most instances one pack of high-quality cigarettes cost more than a month's rent.[37] In fact, because wages rose steadily over the decade, the actual fraction of monthly income paid to rent fell to under 1 percent (see table 3.5).

In distributing apartments housing officials continued to establish a priority list according to the degree of crowding. However, even with the cutoff points as low as two or three square meters per resident,[38] more families qualified for relocation than there were new flats available. As a result, housing cadres considered the composition as well as the size of the household in defining the degree of need. If a one-room household contained three generations, or if a two-room home had more than two married couples, the family was given priority. Even with these stringent guidelines, supplies were insufficient, and officials created priorities among the "needy" on the basis of the the family head's rank in the enterprise. Senior workers and staff jumped ahead of the more junior, and families of model workers or those who had suffered particular injury during the antirightist campaigns of the 1950s or the Cultural Revolution were given priority. Although the policy was not designed to encourage multigenerational homes, in practice it did. The most crowded homes were those like the Lis, the Zhaos, or the

35. *RMRB*, March 11, 1988, 1; Oct. 11, 1988, 2.

36. See *Guofa*, no. 11 and no. 13 (1988) in *Guowuyuan Gongbao*, 1988, 179–88; *RMRB*, Aug. 21, 1989, 1; Lu Shiming and Hu Anqi, "Shanghai zhufang zhidu"; Lu Xing, "Shanghai zhumin dui shangpinfang de xianchuan he qianjing de kanfa"; and Jan Middelhoek, "Urban Housing Reform in the PRC," *China Information* 4, no. 3 (Winter 1989–90), 56–72; *Ming Bao* (Hong Kong), July 4, 1990, 49, reports that in Guangzhou private building and buying continues, but at a cost of over 2,000 yuan per square meter it is simply beyond the average consumer. Similar sentiments were expressed by most Shanghai and Wuhan residents I met during my 1988 and 1990 fieldwork, although not in smaller Sha City where new blocks had entered the market at 200 yuan per square meter in December 1986, and rose to only 500 yuan by July 1988.

37. In Shanghai in 1987 out of an average per capita income of 1,147 yuan, only 16 yuan (1.3%) went to rent and 30 yuan (2.6%) to utilities. *Shanghai Tongji Nianjian 1988*, 410.

38. In 1987 in Shanghai city, families with under 2 square meters per person were ranked as families in special need, but in practice, because after 1980 individual units supplied approximately 85 percent of new housing, the criteria varied from one enterprise to another and from one year to the next. In one collective enterprise described to me the cutoff in 1987 was 2.5 square meters, whereas in Watch Factory no. 4 it was 3 square meters in 1986 and 3.8 square meters by 1987, and in Textile Mill no. 6 it rose from 2.3 square meters in 1987 to 3 square meters in 1988.

Wangs, where a middle-aged couple had responsibility for sheltering an elderly in-law and several adult children. Newly married couples could apply to their workplace for a new apartment, but as a two-person household with little seniority they generally were deemed a low priority. Therefore, throughout the 1980s many newly married couples moved into the home of one of their parents, increasing the crowding of an existing household, but also moving the entire extended family further up the waiting list. Under this system, one should note that the household in line for the new apartment was that of the older generation, and thus when new flats did become available, the parents were assigned the new flat, and only through the intervention of the parents did the young couple receive an apartment of their "own." Moreover, if the parents had only one son or if a parent was already widowed, the housing authorities would allocate space with an eye to the parents' housing needs in old age and give priority to a joint or stem household rather than to the young couple. After new apartments were distributed to the most "deserving," the enterprise would then offer the recently vacated old flats to the more junior staff. Certainly some young couples did move into the newest estates immediately after their marriages, but among my respondents most of these lucky families obtained their new apartments through the intervention of their parents (see table 3.4). In a typical situation a parent (usually the father) had been assigned a new apartment as a reward for his seniority, but instead of moving to the new home himself he allowed a newly married child (usually a son) to live in the new apartment while the parents remained in the original place with other unmarried children or an elderly parent.

Urban China is hardly unique in its reliance on bureaucratic procedures rather than markets to distribute housing. Throughout the socialist world, and in segments of the capitalist economies, public housing allocated on the basis of need is commonplace. Moreover, in all these settings some families are more successful than others. Studies of urban housing in Eastern Europe in the 1960s and 1970s suggested that higher socioeconomic status often translated into more space and better amenities,[39] and that the characteristics that predicted success in the workplace—Party membership, advanced education, urban birthplace—also determined housing outcomes. However, in Whyte and Parish's study of urban China in the 1970s, China appeared a somewhat deviant case. Professionals and Communist Party functionaries reaped few advantages from their social status, and overall urban housing was distributed more in proportion to need than to political position or wealth.[40] The question is, to what extent did this egalitarian outcome persist during the housing boom of the 1980s?

39. William Parish, "Destratification in China," in *Class and Social Stratification in Post-Revolution China*, ed. James L. Watson (London: Cambridge University Press, 1984), 93–96.
40. Parish, "Destratification," 93–95.

Data from the official Chinese press suggest that the Deng reforms did not noticeably erode the basically egalitarian distribution of rents. For example, in Guangzhou in 1988, per capita monthly income was three times higher for families in the highest decile than in the lowest decile, yet rental burdens were virtually identical: 1.0 percent for families who averaged 84 yuan and 0.7 percent for those who averaged 245 yuan.[41] Similar egalitarian outcomes were documented in official statistics and independent fieldwork.[42] However, in the only report I have found that specifically compares distribution of residential space by the occupation of household head before and after the reforms, there is clear evidence of increasing inequality.[43] In 1978 average per capita housing space for respondents in this study ranged from 4.8m² for families headed by a service worker to 6.3m² for those headed by a factory leader. By 1988 average household space had increased for all categories of staff, but the gains for those previously at the top were greater than for those at the bottom, and the absolute disparity between the lowest and highest had doubled.[44]

Closer examination of the distribution of living space among the Shanghai families interviewed in 1987 documents similar discrimination against families headed by blue-collar fathers and also suggests how these inequalities in housing were created by the continuing role of enterprises as the brokers for most urban housing. All the families in my original 1987 sample lived in one new housing estate built in the first years of the post-Mao construction boom. Each apartment had the same number of rooms, but the layout and size varied in relation to the placement toward the staircases. Flats that ran parallel to the stairs had two rooms of equal size and contained twenty-four square meters of living space; those that were at the head of the staircase had one large room and one small room and contained twenty-seven square meters. Using the number of residents and the address of each family, I calculated the number of square feet each household occupied at the time of the first interview. And it is on the basis of these calculations that I was able to link the quality of housing and individual characteristics such as occupation and Party membership.

We can see from table 3.6 that despite the many shared characteristics of my respondents in terms of their age and their generally privileged

41. *Guangzhou Tongji Nianjian 1989*, 422.

42. *Guangxi Tongji Nianjian 1989*, 342; *Beijing Shehui Jingji Tongji Nianjian 1989*, 564; Andrew Walder, "Collective Benefits and Social Stratification in Urban China," paper presented at the 42nd Annual Meeting of the Association for Asian Studies, Chicago, April 5–8, 1990.

43. A study in five urban industrial units is summarized in *Zhongguo Laodong Gongzi Tongji Nianjian 1989*, 350.

44. Thus while service worker families gained on average 1.4m², production workers 1.6m², engineers gained 2.5m² and factory leaders 3.3m². *Zhongguo Laodong Gongzi Tongji Nianjian 1989*, 350.

TABLE 3.6.   Background Characteristics among Five Different Housing Levels

	Excellent (N = 10)	Very Good (N = 13)	Good (N = 26)	Fair (N = 29)	Poor (N = 21)	Sample Average
Square meters/person	12–13	8–8.6	6–6.5	4.8–5.2	3–4.3	5.5
Average no. births to women in parent generation	3.10	3.46	3.07	3.03	3.76	3.27
With CCP mother or father (%)	40	23	50	45	52	44
With father as manual worker (%)	0	31	31	31	48	30

SOURCE: 1987 interviews with 99 Shanghai families.

NOTE: Categorization was not done according to a continuous measure of space because families fell into these discrete clusters. Particularly among the 23 living in the most spacious apartments, it seemed best to break them into two groups, excellent and very good, so as not to lose the information on the clearly most privileged.

socioeconomic position, families in this sample did not have equal, or even roughly uniform, shares of housing space. A small elite (N = 10) enjoyed more than twice the average space, while nearly a quarter of the families (N = 21) lived at the hardship level of three to four square meters per capita. In terms of family or individual characteristics that might explain this pattern of inequality, three items immediately seem salient. Those in poor housing had more children, fathers were more likely to be manual workers, and as a group they had the highest percentage of Party members.[45] At first glance these observations seem contradictory. Upon further scrutiny, the outcome is consonant with what we know about the provision of urban housing in the semireformed political economy of Chinese cities of the 1980s.

The inequalities identified in table 3.6 document a bias against manual workers; they also reflect the impact of unequal institutional resources and the importance of unit-level patronage networks that reinforced class differences. The apartments in the neighborhood where I interviewed were built by the city government. However, the city had not taken sole responsibility for distributing the apartments. Instead, approximately half of the units

45. I also examined age of mother, history of past political problems, and work status of mother. There was absolutely no difference by age of mother (57 years old in 1987) and thus it appears stage in the life cycle was irrelevant. Similarly the percentage with past political problems ranged between 9% and 10%, indicating no variation on this dimension. Only with percentage of mothers with blue-collar jobs did I find a difference, parallel with that found for fathers; the worst housed had average percentage (71%) while the best housed were far below average (20%).

had been sold to more than thirty different enterprises, which then in turn allocated flats among employees waiting for better housing. Therefore, while all families in my sample moved to these apartments as the result of successful supplication, the focus of entreaty and the criteria to establish a family's priority in the housing queue varied among employers. As a result, some of the inequalities documented in table 3.6 may be as attributable to the different resources of the units that had purchased the flats as to the different needs or prestige of the individual families. That is, it is possible that for the city slaughterhouse or district bottling plant, which had previously had no staff housing, this estate represented the first and best housing option, while for the import-export bureau, which was a long commute from this estate and which had long had its own hostels for its largely white-collar staff, the estate was not highly desirable. As a result, families who received their apartments from the import-export bureau were viewed by their unit as receiving only moderately good housing and did not have to document the same level of hardship to their enterprise housing office to qualify for relocation as those coming from the nearby slaughterhouse or bottling plant.

This is not to say that I found no individual characteristics that patterned the inequalities beyond the disadvantaged position of families headed by manual workers. On the contrary, both number of children and membership in the Party appeared to have an influence. In the case of family size the effect was in the expected direction. Parents with the most children had the greatest burden and therefore were most likely to live in the most crowded apartments. In the case of the disadvantage of Party membership, the result was quite unexpected. Placing this negative return on Party membership in the context of the bureaucratic allocation of housing, however, this anomalous finding becomes reasonable.

In urban China after 1955 most job changes were initiated by supervisors redeploying scarce talent.[46] Blue-collar workers, therefore, had lower geographic mobility than white-collar, and Communist Party members, who were overrepresented in the professional and managerial roles, were more mobile than non-Party members.[47] But because in urban China employees needed to cultivate personal connections in order to gain favorable treatment in the distribution of such benefits as new housing, mobility could be costly to the individual and his or her dependents. As a result,

46. For a fuller description of this situation, see Deborah Davis, "Urban Job Mobility," in *Chinese Society on the Eve of Tiananmen*, ed. Deborah Davis and Ezra F. Vogel (Cambridge: Harvard University Press, 1990), 85–108.

47. In the Shanghai sample, for example, 84% of blue-collar parents and 84% of nonparty members had worked in no more than two enterprises between 1949 and 1987; by contrast among the professionals only 40% were as immobile, and among Party members, it was only 39%. By the chi-square statistic both distributions were significant at the .001 level.

Party membership with its attendant higher rates of mobility could have negative rather than positive outcomes. Certainly at this point in our study of Chinese families, this conclusion is offered only as a hypothesis. However, it should be noted that in the case of these Shanghai families there is a clearly negative return to high mobility. Overall, 18 percent of fathers worked in four or more units between 1950 and 1987. Yet among the twenty-one families with the worst housing, 24 percent of fathers were this mobile, while among the ten who lived in the most spacious quarters there was not a single case of the highly mobile.

CONCLUSION: THE DENG REFORMS AND URBAN FAMILIES

The economic and political reforms of the 1980s altered the larger environment in which urban residents created and maintained their homes. They gave urban residents an unprecedented opportunity to indulge their desires for a comfortable and, by Maoist criteria, luxurious private life. Freed from political pressure to denigrate individual preferences, urban residents made choices that the Maoist party-state had censored for three decades. Supplied with more plentiful and better-quality housing, they also had unprecedented opportunity to upgrade their accommodations and enjoy more space and privacy. In terms of material conditions the results were more homes with running water, indoor plumbing, separate kitchens, as well as a massive upgrading in terms of the outward trappings of modern households: color televisions, velour bedspreads, refrigerators, and even VCRs. But as we saw in the high rates of multigenerational living at the time of marriage and the tendency to share a home with a son rather than a daughter, the reform decade appeared to have had little effect on traditional rules of family formation. In fact, the comparisons between the experience of parents and firstborn sons, and between older and younger siblings in this Shanghai sample, suggest that the new consumerism and the freedom to fulfill personal dreams may actually have strengthened precommunist preferences for virilocal living.

Close study of these one hundred families also reminds us that despite the new affluence and the freedom to satisfy more materialistic and individual pleasures, the Chinese party-state had by no means renounced its ability to impose binding limitations on urban family structure and behavior. The most extreme example of this persistent power was found in the one-child policy, from which virtually no young urban family could deviate.[48] But equally important for understanding the general context in which households were created and maintained were the continuities with

48. In 1988 urban Total Fertility Rate (TFR) was 1.09, and in the city of Shanghai 96.3% of all births in that year were first births. *RMRB*, Jan. 14, 1989, 3, and Sept. 20, 1989, 5.

the Maoist political economy and the police controls over internal migration. Throughout the 1980s housing continued to be a welfare benefit allocated by employers primarily on the basis of seniority. Domestic space legally still fell under the purview of the police, and it seems telling that the 1982 constitution, which introduced several new safeguards against state intervention into private life, did not restore "freedom to change...residence," a right that *had* been protected by the earlier constitution of 1954.[49]

Urban families of the 1980s enjoyed new consumer freedoms, but they still were highly constrained in deciding when and where they could establish their homes. As a result of the reforms, there was some realignment in the relative strength of the defining parameters, but overall the prototypical urban household under Deng, as under Mao, could best be described as a supplicant to a socialist state.

49. *Beijing Review*, Dec. 27, 1982, 10–29.

FOUR

Geography, Demography, and Family Composition in Three Southwestern Villages

Stevan Harrell

Since 1979 the political economy of rural China has undergone two fundamental changes, one in the sphere of production and one in the sphere of reproduction. In the productive sphere, economic reforms have both decollectivized farming and allowed for family entrepreneurship; in the reproductive sphere the planned-birth campaign has severely limited the number of children a family may have. These two changes have been so fundamental as to transform both the physical and the social landscape of rural China, with unprecedented material prosperity, the disappearance of large, collective fields, the virtual disappearance of the once all-important production team, and the rise of family enterprise in commercial agriculture and cottage industry. Given these fundamental changes in society at large, we might expect the structure and organization of families and households to also experience widespread changes. At the same time, the societal changes brought about by economic reform and the birth-planning campaign have not had the same effect everywhere in the Chinese countryside, and we might expect changes in family patterns to also show local variation. For example, the economic reforms have *permitted* entrepreneurship everywhere, but they have actually *facilitated* it only in those places where geographic and market conditions are otherwise favorable. The planned-birth campaign has been implemented more strictly in some places than in others, so both the plan and compliance with the plan have varied. The result is that there is still, even after the implementation of the reforms and the planned-birth program, considerable local variation in the way Chinese rural households organize for production and reproduce themselves. There is also a difference in the way the birth-planning campaign and the economic reforms have affected family organization. The effects of the birth-planning campaign on the family are direct and easily observable: as fertility declines so do household size and the ratio of children to adults. In areas where the fertility-control campaign has been implemented more strictly, these changes are more noticeable. The effects of the economic reforms, however, are more indirect. While the reforms have had a visible effect on the ways families organize their labor for production, especially in areas where entrepreneurship has begun to flourish, the effects on the family developmental cycle are less easily proven, though some trends can certainly be detected. This chapter examines household organization in three villages whose economy in the 1980s varied from almost pure subsistence to freewheeling entrepreneurial, and examines the differential effects of the planned-birth program and the economic reforms in each village.

VARIATION IN CHINESE FAMILY SIZE AND COMPOSITION

In premodern society, Chinese families everywhere strove toward an ideal model developmental cycle in which a couple's daughters would marry out and their sons' wives would marry in, forming a patrilocal joint family. While this joint family could not be expected to last forever in reality, it was an ideal that ought to be achieved in every generation for at least a few years before the sons divided their household economies and took their individual equal shares of the family property, thus beginning the cycle over again. But in fact even this temporary joint form did not occur in every family in every generation: sometimes a couple had only one son who grew to maturity (or perhaps none at all), or sometimes a family's resources were too meager to support all its sons, in which case one or more might have to leave the family to make a living elsewhere.

And even where demography permitted, the joint phase of the family cycle was not always of equal length. As in so many societies with this and other forms of family organization, there was a series of centripetal and centrifugal factors that united brothers in pursuit of common economic goals or divided them in suspicion of each other's and each other's wives' motives.[1] When the centrifugal factors were stronger—when there was little economic motivation to hold the joint family together in the face of the psychological tensions among its branches—the joint phase in the cycle was short or nonexistent. When, however, as in the case of pooled labor, pooled capital,

---

1. For examples showing the effect of economic change on the series of decisions determining household form, see the several articles in Robert McC. Netting, Richard R. Wilk, and Eric J. Arnould, eds., *Households* (Berkeley and Los Angeles: University of California Press, 1984); the general introduction by Netting and Wilk, as well as contributions by Wilk, "Households in Process: Agricultural Change and Domestic Transformation among the Kekchi Maya of Belize," and Andrejs Plakans, "Serf Emancipation and the Changing Structure of Rural Domestic Groups in the Russian Baltic Provinces: Linden Estate, 1797–1858," are particularly useful as models.

or a diversified economy,[2] the potential for common gain outweighed the frustration of common domesticity, the joint phase was likely to last longer.

In looking at variation in Chinese family size and composition, then, we can see two kinds of causal factors that may explain variation over time or between one sample of families and another. Demographic factors will determine the personnel available for the formation of stem and joint families,[3] while various other social factors will influence the perceived balance between the advantages and disadvantages of staying together or splitting apart.[4]

In addition, any convincing look at variation from demographic or social factors must consider interaction between these factors. Demographic behavior is constrained by social norms, and particularly by the complex of choices within which members of a family frame and plan their strategies. In explaining the differences among communities, we must look for the effects that recent social changes have had on demographic behavior (fertility in particular, but also age at marriage), as well as their effects on decisions to divide the family or keep it together under certain circumstances.

RECENT SOCIAL CHANGES AND THEIR POSITED EFFECTS ON FAMILY ORGANIZATION

The importance of the planned-birth program and the rural economic reforms for household organization can be illustrated rather easily. The planned-birth policy has reduced the total fertility of Chinese women from

2. See Myron L. Cohen, "A Case Study of Chinese Family Economy and Development," *Journal of Asian and African Studies*, 1968; "The Developmental Cycle in Chinese Family Groups," in *Kinship and Marriage in Chinese Society*, ed. Maurice Freedman (Stanford University Press, 1970), and *House United, House Divided: The Chinese Family in Taiwan* (Columbia University Press, 1976). See also Burton Pasternak, *Guests in the Dragon: The Social Demography of a Chinese District* (Columbia University Press, 1983), and Stevan Harrell, *Ploughshare Village: Culture and Context in Taiwan* (University of Washington Press, 1982).

3. For studies pertaining to China, see Arthur P. Wolf, "Chinese Family Size: A Myth Revitalized," in *The Chinese Family and Its Ritual Behavior*, ed. Chuang Ying-chang and Hsieh Jih-chang (Taipei: Academia Sinica, 1985), and Stevan Harrell, "Marriage, Mortality, and the Developmental Cycle in Three Zhejiang Lineages," as well as Ts'ui-jung Liu, "Demographic Constraint and Family Structure in Chinese Lineages," both in *Chinese Historical Microdemography*, ed. Stevan Harrell (Berkeley: University of California Press, forthcoming).

More theoretical treatments of the interaction of demographic and cultural factors in determining household membership can be found in K. W. Wachter, E. A. Hammel, and Peter Laslett, *Statistical Studies of Historical Social Structure* (New York: Academic Press, 1978); an interesting discussion of the interaction of these factors in specific cases is Anthony Carter, "Household Histories," in *Households*, ed. Netting, Wilk, and Arnould.

4. Like previous authors, I propose to hold culture constant in the initial analysis, assuming that Chinese norms and ideals of family size and composition are the same everywhere. This becomes more problematic the further industrialization proceeds, but it is probably no great worry in the rural areas of Panzhihua city in 1988.

6.5 in 1965 and 6.3 in 1970 to 2.6 in 1980 and 2.3 in 1986.[5] Because of the discrepancies in both the policy and the practice of its implementation,[6] however, its effect has not been uniform. The number of children born has an obvious and immediate effect on the size of the family; though it does not affect the family's composition (its structure as nuclear, stem, or joint) immediately, it will have important structural effects in the future, so that communities where the planned-birth policy weighs more heavily will present different statistical pictures of the household size and composition that are reflections of the underlying developmental cycle.

The effects of the rural economic reforms are considerably more indirect and complex, but potentially no less important for understanding changes in family organization. Returning land to individual families for farming, and permitting or even encouraging various kinds of entrepreneurship, have meant that many families who under the collective system did little but contribute to the collective economy and thus try to survive, with very little leeway for entrepreneurship or planned growth, now enjoy a wide range of choices in where and how to invest their resources. An earlier calculus involving little but the contribution of various work-point earners to the family's grain share-out, and perhaps some marginal decisions about what to do with the small private plot, has been replaced by a complex of possible costs and benefits involving subsistence versus cash crops, possibilities of local or migratory employment, and for some families real opportunities for various kinds of investments of labor and capital.

Like the planned-birth program, however, the rural economic reforms have had differential effects in different places. Villages with convenient transport, or those that are close to urban centers, have seen the growth of wide ranges of wage-labor and entrepreneurial opportunities. This has meant the growth of inequalities in income within these villages, in addition to general growth. Remoter villages, however, have often seen a collective subsistence economy simply turn into an individual subsistence economy, and have also experienced considerably less internal inequality.

These differential effects of the economic reforms can be expected to have differential effects on family strategies, at least if we are correct in assuming that family strategies of fertility, marriage, and division are all affected by the perceived costs and gains to be incurred in having a child, in taking in a daughter-in-law or marrying out a daughter, or in dividing the family or keeping it together.

The three villages treated in this chapter lie within about sixty kilo-

5. Norman Y. Luther, Griffith Feeny, and Weiman Zhang, "One Child Family or Baby Boom? Evidence from China's 1987 One-per-hundred Survey," *Population Studies* 44 (1990): 341–57.

6. See Jeffrey Wasserstrom, "Resistance to the One-Child Family," *Modern China* 10 (1984): 345–474.

TABLE 4.1.   Average Family Size, 1973–1988

	1973	1978	1983	1988
Renhe village	5.82	6.10	6.36	4.80
Yishala village	5.77	5.96	5.63	5.29
Zhuangshang village	5.95	6.32	5.69	4.92

TABLE 4.2.   Family Composition, 1973–1988

	1973 (%)	1978 (%)	1983 (%)	1988 (%)
Renhe village				
Nuclear	44 (57)	45 (58)	44 (56)	41 (51)
Stem	33 (43)	32 (41)	31 (39)	37 (46)
Joint	0 (00)	1 (01)	4 (05)	2 (03)
Yishala village				
Nuclear	56 (57)	52 (53)	53 (54)	48 (49)
Stem	42 (43)	41 (42)	41 (42)	48 (49)
Joint	0 (00)	5 (05)	4 (04)	2 (02)
Zhuangshang village				
Nuclear	39 (68)	35 (61)	37 (64)	42 (70)
Stem	15 (26)	21 (37)	21 (36)	18 (30)
Joint	3 (05)	1 (02)	0 (00)	0 (00)

NOTE: For 1988 figures, if stem and joint are combined for purposes of statistical analysis, $\chi^2 = 8.30$, $p < .02$.

meters of each other in Panzhihua city, Sichuan, but they have been affected quite differently by the reforms and the planned-birth campaign. As a result, there are considerable differences visible in their patterns of fertility and household economy, and these, in turn, have affected household size and composition over the last two decades, differences that reflect underlying differences in the demographic and economic processes that constitute the developmental cycle. The relevant figures are presented in tables 4.1 and 4.2.

Although there are no consistent differences in household size among the three villages, notice that household size has contracted considerably more rapidly in Renhe with the effective implementation of a one-child policy there. More important, Renhe and Yishala consistently show higher percentages of stem families, and correspondingly lower percentages of nuclear families, than are found in Zhuangshang. This reflects differences in the processes of family growth and division in the three villages, differences that

are at least partially explicable in terms of the effects of the twin changes of
the planned-birth campaign and the economic reforms.

THREE VILLAGES IN PANZHIHUA CITY

Panzhihua city stands at the intersection of the Chengdu-Kunming railroad
and the Jinsha (upper Yangtze) River; as an administrative area, it includes the city of 400,000 people, built from scratch after 1965 to process
one of China's richest ferrous metal deposits, and three rural, county-sized
areas, whose combined population is about the same as that of the city (see
map 4.1). The most accessible and developed of these is Renhe *qu*, or district, a mostly rural area the size of a county. The three villages discussed
in this chapter are all in Renhe *qu*; our research team spent from eight
to fourteen days in each. Questionnaires covering the history of family
composition since 1949,[7] as well as details of the family economy from 1985
to 1987, were administered to 290 families randomly sampled in four
communities,[8] including 80 families in Renhe, 60 in Zhuangshang, and 98
in Yishala. What has become clear from the analyses of the data collected
in this survey is that geographic position has made a big difference in the
effect of recent policy changes on family process.[9]

Renhe Cun, a Prosperous, Commercialized Village
The capital of Renhe *qu* is Renhe *zhen*, a town of about 20,000 residents
about twenty minutes' drive on a smoothly paved highway from the southern edge of Panzhihua city proper. We interviewed in Renhe *cun*, an area of
about 1,200 households stretching eastward from the outer streets of the

---

7. All retrospective questions designed to elicit information on family composition reached
back to 1949, but my impression is that the data are less reliable before about 1970. For that
reason and because the conference dealt with changes since the beginning of the reforms, I
have chosen to concentrate here on the period from about 1970, which covers several years
under collectivization as well as the period since.

8. To be precise, in Renhe we selected five of the ten production cooperatives (formerly
teams), according to local cadres' descriptions of their economic activities. Thus one of the two
grain-growing cooperatives was sampled, one of the two where fish raising was important, and
so forth. In each selected team, we took a random sample of all households. Where a household could not be interviewed because there was no competent adult, we selected the household immediately below it in the household registers. In Yishala, we took a random sample of
the main village (80 households) and a random sample of the satellite village of Xiachang (10
households). In Zhuangshang, we took a random sample of each of the village's three cooperatives.

9. Geographic differentials in economic development in rural Panzhihua have also been
treated by Li Shaoming in a paper entitled "Panzhihua shi gongyequ de jianshe dui zhoubian
nongcun de yingxiang" (The effect of the construction of the industrial district in Panzhihua
city on surrounding villages), presented at the Conference on Urban Anthropology held in
Beijing in December 1989.

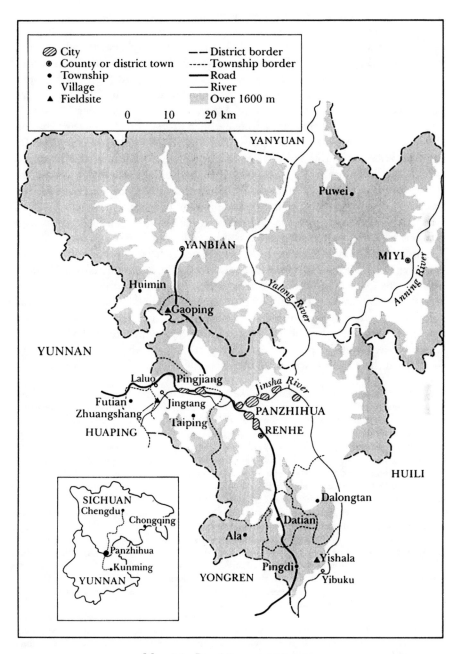

Map 4.1. Panzhihua and Vicinity

town itself into the foothills surrounding the rich valley where the town is located.[10] Renhe and the other *cun* that make up Renhe *zhen*, along with the neighboring *xiang*, or townships, of Qianjin and Zongfa, are probably the wealthiest villages in all of Panzhihua city; we chose Renhe partly as a contrast to the poorer, more remote villages that were our other interview sites. The mean per capita income in our sample households in 1987 was 1,024 yuan (with a household median of 4,800, or about 1,000 per person),[11] which puts Renhe comfortably above the national rural average, though still short of really wealthy villages in the Pearl River delta, as described by Johnson and Siu in this volume, or on the Chengdu plain or the Jiangnan area outside Shanghai.[12] About four-fifths of Renhe villagers' reported income was in cash. Most houses in Renhe are still built of mud (people say brick housing is too hot in the summer), but modern appliances such as televisions and tape players are ubiquitous, and several families own refrigerators, color televisions, or washing machines.

There has been a market at Renhe since at least the early nineteenth century, but the area remained a sleepy backwater of north central Yunnan until it was given to Sichuan in 1965, when the construction of the Panzhihua steel complex was begun. At that time, the flat land in the valley surrounding the town was converted to vegetable cultivation to serve the markets of the new city. To this day, eight of the ten cooperatives that make up Renhe village are engaged in vegetable cultivation; the ninth and tenth, in the hills to the east of town, cultivate grains.[13]

10. The village and the urban area of Renhe district town overlap spatially, with farmhouses interspersed between the apartment buildings occupied by government and construction company employees. The difference between village and town residents lies technically, not in the type of housing, but in the *hukou* registration: if you have *nongcun hukou*, or village household registration, you belong to Renhe *cun*; if you have *danwei hukou*, or unit household registration, you belong to the urban population of Panzhihua city. Some families have both; a man, for example, who has a state-sector job in the city will not have his household registration with his family, even though he lives with them. When some of the former agricultural areas of Renhe were taken over by Shijiu Ye (19th Metallurgy, which is actually a giant state construction company) and some residents took Shijiu Ye jobs, the affected production teams lost population, even though nobody actually moved.

11. The absolute level of these income figures should not be taken too seriously when comparing these villages with communities in other parts of China. We did not have access to the official methods of calculating income in kind (agricultural goods both produced and consumed by the household), and so we devised our own formulas. My impression is that our method yields a figure about 25 percent higher than the methods used in official reports.

12. I visited a village in Jiangyin county, Jiangsu, where the announced per capita income was over 1,200 yuan in 1985. It did not look much different from the surrounding villages. But officially reported average household incomes for Chinese province-level units showed only rural Shanghai to be slightly above Renhe at 1,059 yuan; the richest *provinces* were Guangdong at 644 and Jiangsu at 626. See *Zhongguo Tongji Nianjian 1989*, 746–47.

13. Called production "teams" during the collective period, these groups of up to a hundred or more households changed their name to production "groups" in the early 1980s; in

Vegetable growing, in its own right, can be very lucrative. The figures for the vegetables sown by one family on their tiny plot of .63 *mu*, or about a tenth of an acre, illustrate why.[14] Multiple cropping gives them a sown area of about 2.4 *mu*, on which, in 1987, they grew tomatoes, peppers, eggplant, cucumbers, green beans, cabbage, "Chinese" cabbage, and a kind of greens known as *wosun*. The family has minimal production costs for seed, fertilizer, and paying someone to plow their land; subtracting these from the total market price they gained for their vegetables, about 2,400 yuan, shows a probable profit of over 2,000 yuan. And they have much less land than certain other families that specialize in vegetables and sometimes make as much as 4,000 per year. There is skill in growing vegetables and in knowing when to sell to get the best prices, and some families do not do nearly as well. But vegetables are far more profitable than grain farming, even with the tiny plots available to Renhe villagers.

Only nineteen of the eighty households we interviewed in Renhe obtained all their income from farming, however. This is a great change from the 1970s and is attributable to two kinds of changing economic opportunities that are a direct result of the rural reforms.

First, there is salaried labor. While only four of our sample families earned all their income from wages, another twenty-six combined wage labor and farming, four wage labor and capital investment, and eight wage labor, capital investment, and farming. Wage labor has become increasingly available as industrial development spreads outward from Panzhihua city proper into the near suburbs such as Renhe. When industrial enterprises take over farmland, they are required to offer jobs to the farmers they displace. In the 1980s this has meant that most of the families in the seventh cooperative, which houses a large plant of the city construction company, have given up farming altogether: only three of the twelve families interviewed in that cooperative still received any income from farming, while eleven had some wage income and six lived partly by entrepreneurship. Wages vary, of course, and the wages of one worker are usually insufficient to support a family of more than two or three. For example, the family income of a man whose 110 yuan per month as a tractor driver is supplemented only by sale of an occasional pig is on the low side at 2,100 per year for four people. Another family, with three wage earners supporting six mouths, manages to make about 4,500 per year, still below average for Renhe, but enough to allow the family to save nearly 1,000 a year after expenses.

1988 the name was changed again to "cooperatives," though this does not indicate a recollectivization of agriculture.

14. It might be useful for nonfarmers to visualize the size of this plot: a square of about 20.5 meters on a side.

It is in entrepreneurial investment of capital, however, that the real opportunities lie. Sometimes this can be something that one person can do alone, as in the chicken-raising business run by the wife in the vegetable-farming family described above. Her husband orders fertilized eggs from Chengdu, or even from Beijing or Shanghai, several times a year; his wife raises them until they are at about the transition from furry to feathery, at which point she sells them for .20 yuan profit each. At 30,000 chickens per year, that is a net income of 6,000 yuan for one person's labor. Added to the aforementioned vegetable gardening and a fledgling fish-raising business, this pushes the family very close to the fabled category of *wanyuan hu* (ten thousand) household.

A few families in Renhe have made it to *wanyuan hu* status and beyond; there were five in our sample. As an example, take the leader of the ninth cooperative, a grain-growing community in the area called Longtangou, in the hills to the east of town. His family has three trucks used to haul sand and gravel. His two grown sons drive two of the trucks; he hires a driver for the other vehicle, as well as about three laborers to load and unload the construction materials. After paying wages and operating costs, this business netted the family about 18,000 yuan in 1987; added to about 1,000 from pig raising and another 1,000 from fish farming, plus in-kind income from grain farming, this brought the family's income to about 22,300, the second highest of any family we interviewed. The family head thought he was probably about the eighth wealthiest in Renhe *cun.* He had just enlarged his family mansion to twenty-nine rooms (six of them currently empty) built in two stories around a spacious courtyard, for a total of about eight hundred square meters of floor space.

From these few examples, it is easy to see how much the possibilities for family economy have changed since the basic reliance on collective agriculture came apart at the end of the 1970s. I should emphasize, however, that not all families have benefited equally, or even benefited much at all from the reforms. The closest neighbors to the family with the twenty-nine-room house live in a one-room mud cottage, and the poorest families in our sample had incomes of 300 yuan or less per person. In addition, families with several televisions and a truck live side by side with people who do not even own a watch or a radio.[15]

A visitor to Renhe thus goes away with a general impression of a dynamic economy. Families have a variety of economic alternatives, many of them involving investment of capital, and those who are successful in this have not only increased their wealth dramatically since the reforms, they

15. The topic of reemergence of social classes in prosperous parts of the Chinese countryside ought to be addressed systematically. The official position, cited to us by Panzhihua vice-mayor Tan Huizhang, is that differences in income, because they do not involve exploitation, represent divisions among strata within a class rather than differences between classes.

have also positioned themselves for further growth in perhaps new and as yet unknown directions. There are almost no Renhe families whose major income still derives from subsistence farming; except for some of the families in the ninth and tenth production cooperatives up in the hills, even the farmers are in business for profit through the growth and sale of vegetables.

Yishala, a Model Minority Village with a Mostly Subsistence Economy

When visitors from outside Panzhihua, Chinese or foreign, come to the area and ask to be taken to a minority village, Yishala is often the one chosen. It lies in Pingdi *xiang* at the southernmost tip of Renhe *qu*, high above the Jinsha River at an altitude of about 1,680 meters. From Panzhihua city it is an hour-and-a-half drive on the paved highway to Pingdi town, which has a periodic market, and another twenty minutes or so on a good gravel road to Yishala.

Yishala is in many ways typical of Pingdi,[16] in that its population is composed entirely of farmers, most of whom belong to the officially designated Yi *minzu*. They call themselves *Lipuo* and their language *Libie*; they use this language in all everyday interactions, but almost all of them are fully bilingual and use the Han language with outsiders, as well as within the community for formal occasions such as weddings and funerals. Their customs, with a few minor exceptions that serve as ethnic markers, are the customs of the local Han; their family, lineage, and inheritance systems are likewise those of northern Yunnan peasants generally.

At the same time, however, Yishala is somewhat atypical, even of Pingdi, in that it is a model minority village for Panzhihua. This means that the city government, along with the provincial Office of Minority Affairs (*minwei*), has provided funds for investment in village improvements. The most important of these are the cement factory, whose dormitories housed us for our stay in Yishala, and the cultural center, a brick building that stands locked and unused next to one of the village irrigation ponds. For village families, however, model status makes only a minor difference: a few younger members are employed at the cement factory, which may raise the family cash income by the amount of wages (about 50 yuan a month for an average worker), but not all families take advantage of this opportunity, and the idle cultural center does not seem to do anybody any good.

16. There has been at least one previous survey of families in Yishala, conducted by the Panzhihua Office of Artifact Management in cooperation with the Anthropology Department of Zhongshan University in Guangzhou. See Chen Qinghua, "Pingdi Yizu de jiating bianqian" (Changes in the Yi family of Pingdi), unpublished paper, and Li Xiaorong, "Panzhihua shi Yishala Yi cun shehui jingji diaocha" (An investigation of the society and economy of Yishala Yi village in Panzhihua city). Aside from their greater emphasis on the Yi ethnicity of Yishala villagers, the findings of both Chen and Li are in general and specific agreement with mine.

TABLE 4.3. Sources of Income in Renhe, Yishala, and Zhuangshang

	No. of Households (%)		
	Renhe	Yishala	Zhuangshang
Farming only	18 (23)	21 (21)	39 (65)
Wage labor only	5 (06)	0	0
Nonfarm production only	3 (04)	0	0
Farming and wage labor	25 (31)	42 (43)	19 (32)
Farming and nonfarm production	17 (21)	17 (17)	1 (02)
Wage labor and nonfarm production	4 (05)	0	0
Farming, wage labor, and nonfarm production	8 (10)	18 (18)	1 (02)

The major crops in Yishala are winter wheat and barley, summer rice and corn, supplemented by draft cattle, as well as goats, pigs, and chickens raised both for consumption and for sale. Vegetables are grown for family consumption only. A comparison of family income sources in the three villages is found in table 4.3.

Superficially, the occupational structure of Yishala bears some resemblance to that of Renhe, in that only twenty-one families of the ninety-eight we interviewed in Yishala and its small satellite hamlet of Xiachang made their living entirely by farming; this is an even smaller percentage than in Renhe. The largest category (forty-two households) combined farming and wage labor of some sort, while another seventeen combined farming and small-scale sideline production (construction lime in Yishala; incense in Xiachang), and eighteen derived income from all three—farming, sidelines, and wage labor. But in another sense, Yishala is like the subsistence-oriented village of Zhuangshang: in neither village was there a single family that did *not* farm, while in Renhe 15 percent of the families had given up farming altogether.

When we look at the economic nature of nonfarm production in Yishala and Renhe, however, we find a fundamental difference. Many people in Renhe are true entrepreneurs—they invest capital in the hopes of a return, which in turn will bring greater capital. They also innovate; there is a wide range of activities from hauling sand to raising chickens, and families are tied, not to one enterprise or another, but rather to the principle of investing in anticipation of profits. For vegetable farmers such as those described above, even farming is an entrepreneurial activity.

Nonfarm production in Yishala, in contrast, is not really entrepreneurial in most cases. Though thirty-four families in our Yishala sample engaged in selling a product for a profit, only eight of these realized a profit of more than 500 yuan in 1987, and none earned more than 2,500 from such activity. In addition, most of the petty industry of Yishala families consists of quarrying limestone and making lime for sale, an activity that requires only a small capital outlay (one has to own or have access to a small tractor to haul the heavy rock) and realizes only a small profit, too inconsequential to provide much capital for reinvestment. In other words, this is not the building of a financial base independent of farming, as is the case with Renhe entrepreneurs; it is merely the supplementing of income.

Zhuangshang, a Poor Village of Subsistence Farmers

It is possible to drive to Zhuangshang, but it is faster if you park your car at the neighbor village of Jingtang and walk: by trail from Jingtang to Zhuangshang is about thirty minutes for a fast hiker.

Zhuangshang lies just above the banks of the Jinsha River, in the township of Pingjiang (see map 4.1). Parts of Pingjiang are prosperous (it overlaps with the urban district of Geliping in the same way that Renhe *cun* overlaps with the urban population of Renhe town), but the southwestern corner of the township, where Jingtang, Kuqiao, Laluo, and Zhuangshang lie, is dry, undeveloped, and poorly served by transport. Zhuangshang itself is the poorest village in this corner of the township, with a per capita income in our survey of only about 424 yuan, not low enough to qualify it for state aid as an officially impoverished (*pinkun*) area, but so low that it has no electricity, no bicycles (some families could afford them, but they could get nowhere on them, so people use donkeys as their main means of carrying things), many people dress in patches, and all houses are built of unplastered mud walls.

Zhuangshang is officially a minority village; the people consider themselves to be members of the Shuitian *minzu*, a group not officially recognized by the state, which places them in the larger category of Yi.[17] But the Shuitian people in Zhuangshang and in neighboring Futian township and Huaping county practice very little that would enable an outsider to distinguish them from local Han Chinese without specifically asking. Their customs, language, and social organization seemed from our investigations to be identical to those of the neighboring Han villages. The only practical difference that may be connected to their official Yi identity is state permission to have two children,[18] a factor that, as we will see below, has had noticeable effects on family size and composition in the 1980s.

17. For a detailed description of ethnicity in several villages in the Panzhihua area, including Zhuangshang, see Stevan Harrell, "Ethnicity, Local Interests, and the State: Yi Villages in Southwest China," *Comparative Studies in Society and History*, July 1990.

18. It is not even clear how big a factor ethnicity is in the Zhuangshang villagers' permis-

In contrast to the variety of family economies found in Renhe, and the typical Yishala pattern of farming supplemented by wage labor, Zhuang-shang villagers are all primarily farmers. In our sample of sixty households, we found only two families with any members engaged in any sort of entrepreneurial activity—both made small amounts of cash by buying miscellaneous goods cheap in one local market and selling them slightly dearer in another. One of these households also contained a wage laborer, as did nineteen other households in the sample, leaving thirty-nine households dependent entirely on farming (or in a few cases also fishing in the Jinsha River or gathering medicinal roots for sale).

Even here, not all agricultural activity is purely subsistence-oriented. One family, whose income of 7,304 yuan (over 3,000 in cash) in 1987 was the highest in our sample, may nonetheless provide an example of a slightly more successful version of the typical Zhuangshang family economy. On their allotted 4 *mu* of irrigated land and 2 *mu* of dry land, they produced 6,530 *jin* of rice, 400 of wheat, 2,000 of corn, and 6,000 of sweet potatoes. In addition, their banana groves netted them about 100 yuan profit (much less than some families with more trees), and three months of fishing in the Jinsha River by the household head and two of his sons brought in another 1,500 in income. In addition, they sold two pigs for a total of 800 yuan, and about twenty chickens for a total of 160. With this income, this family was extraordinarily prosperous by Zhuangshang standards. They owned a black-and-white television (useless since electricity to the village was terminated a few years before), a radio, a sewing machine, and five watches. Their house had floors of lime plaster and contained four bedrooms, two common rooms, two kitchens, and three storerooms, in addition to numerous stables.

More typical, though in fact somewhat below average, was another family consisting of the household head, his wife, and two teenaged sons. On their two *mu* of irrigable land, they grew 2,000 *jin* of rice in the summer seasons, and 200 of wheat in the winter;[19] dry land produced 800 *jin* of corn

---

sion to have two children. Birth quotas in Pingjiang *xiang* are determined by relative wealth and prosperity, rather than exclusively by ethnicity, so that villagers in Geliping and Dashuijing, two urban-overlap villages, may have only one child; people in Jingtang and other moderately prosperous places may have two if the first is a girl; people in Zhuangshang may have two, and Miao people in a couple of remote mountain areas may have three if the first two are girls.

19. The low wheat-yields are due to the lack of irrigation water in the winter season. Ever since a state-owned coal mine diverted water in 1980 from an irrigation channel used by Zhuangshang and Jingtang to a coal-washing facility, it has been difficult to grow a winter-wheat crop in this area. Villagers are still angry about this: they have attacked the coal mine physically and submitted several formal complaints to city authorities and asked us to bring the matter to the authorities' attention (which we did), but so far they have not gotten their

and 400 of sweet potatoes. Except for the compulsory quotas sold to the state at low prices, they ate these food crops. Banana and papaya trees brought most of their cash income; together with the sale of a few chickens, these fruits netted them about 160 yuan cash. Since they had no income from wages, fishing, or entrepreneurial activity, the rest of their 1,200 yuan for the year was income in kind—the aforementioned subsistence crops plus one pig slaughtered at New Year's. This left them with a shortfall of about 400 yuan to meet their basic expenses; they borrowed this in small amounts from a variety of people.

This latter family, obviously, was poor. Their house, built in 1968 and not renovated since, had dirt floors; they had none of the appliances or amenities asked about on our questionnaire—not even a watch or a battery-operated radio. They were not starving—nobody we saw in Zhuang-shang had any signs of malnutrition or lack of food—but theirs was truly a subsistence economy.

These two families represent something of the extremes of Zhuangshang villagers, but they are in fact not very different from each other—the only real distinction is the first family's rather profitable fishing activity. But even this activity is not really entrepreneurial, in the sense that it involves little capital investment (fishnets are about all), and seems unlikely to grow except by the marginal addition of another laborer or two. And most of the families in Zhuangshang, although they fall quantitatively somewhere between the incomes of our two examples, are qualitatively more like the second—only about a third of Zhuangshang families' total income is in cash, and even most of their cash income comes from primary production (bananas, papayas, wild grasses, and fish from the river). And aside from the marginal gains in agricultural productivity that might come from a more secure supply of irrigation water, there is little visible chance that they will be able to increase their income in the near future. They seem bound to remain subsistence farmers, with perhaps a slight increase in income from migratory wage labor, for the next few years at least.

If the general agricultural regime and the low level of income make Zhuangshang family economies seem not very different from those of Yi-shala, there is still a difference between them. Per capita income in our Yi-shala families was 430 yuan, essentially the same as we found in Zhuang-shang, but it was distributed differently, with about one-half of the typical family's income in cash, mostly from wages or the manufacture of lime or both. This was reflected in the different standards of living in the two

---

water back. As a result, disputes over irrigation are extremely common, especially during the nighttime, when people accuse others of stealing or diverting their water. Cadres in both villages told us they spend most of their time in the late winter and early spring mediating irrigation disputes.

TABLE 4.4.   Recent Birth Cohorts in Renhe, Yishala, and Zhuangshang, with Crude Birth Rates and General Marital Fertility

| | Year of Birth | | | |
No. of Births	1968–72	1973–78	1978–82	1983–87
Renhe				
Males	30	30	11	11
Females	38	18	1[c]	3[c]
CBR[a]	30	21	5[c]	6[c]
GMFR[b]	—	.200	.045–.083[d]	.045–.070[d]
Yishala				
Males	60	31	11	15
Females	37	31	15	16
CBR[a]	34	21	9	12
GMFR[b]	—	.180	.079	.084
Zhuangshang				
Males	30	18	13	10
Females	19	22	15	16
CBR[a]	29	23	16	16
GMFR[b]	—	.234	.165	.126

[a] Crude birth rate per thousand population per year.

[b] General marital fertility rate = number of children per year per married woman of childbearing age (15–45 years). This gives a better measure of the success of planned-birth campaigns than does crude birth rate, which does not control for the age structure of the population.

[c] These figures are so low as to be suspect, especially since they show the number of girls as only a fraction of the number of boys. It seems unlikely that the imbalance is entirely due to chance, but it is impossible to tell how much of it is due to chance and how much to infanticide or, more likely, underreporting. Even if we assume the statistically worst case, that people are concealing a large number of daughters, and the number of daughters are actually equal to the number of sons, this only brings the crude birth rates for these intervals up to about nine per thousand, still very low.

[d] The high and low fertility rates for Renhe are based on the uncorrected number of births (low figure) and on the number of births assuming a sex ratio of 100 (high figure).

places—people in Yishala had considerably more consumer goods on the level of bicycles, sewing machines, and black-and-white televisions, though none of them had a car, a refrigerator, or a color television.

DEMOGRAPHIC CHANGES: THE FERTILITY DECLINE

These differential economic patterns have had considerable effects on family size and structure. In order to understand the changes in family in general, however, we also need to look at the other kind of factors influencing family process: the differential decline in the birth rate during the same period.

TABLE 4.5.   Parity of Wives in Recent Marriage Cohorts

| | *Year Married* | | |
Parity	1970–74	1975–79	1980–84
Renhe			
0	0	0	2
1	0	4	15
2	4	2	0
3	4	0	0
4	0	0	0
Yishala			
0	0	0	3
1	0	1	5
2	11	5	7
3	7	1	0
4	0	0	0
Zhuangshang			
0	0	0	0
1	0	0	1
2	2	3	12
3	8	2	0
4	1	0	0

The basic facts are indicated in tables 4.4 and 4.5, which present various
kinds of evidence pertinent to changes in fertility over the last fifteen years
in the two villages.

All three villages can be seen to have undergone a sharp decline in fertility in recent years, but the decline in Renhe is sharpest, followed by Yishala
and then Zhuangshang. These differences in fertility among the three villages, indicated both in the declining size of recent birth-cohorts and in the
declining parity of recent marriage-cohorts, hint at an explanation of the
more precipitous decline in the size of Renhe families, even though those
families are more complex than those of Zhuangshang. In Yishala, family
size has not declined so rapidly, in spite of fertility decline, because families
have remained even slightly more complex than those in Renhe. But what
accounts for the more abrupt fertility decline in Renhe and Yishala?

One factor is simply the difference in birth quotas, under what appears
from our data to be a very effective regime of implementation. The birth
quota for Renhe, as a Han village and a periurban one, is a single child,
whereas Zhuangshang and Yishala families are allowed to have two, because of either their poverty or their ethnicity, or perhaps both (the township governments in Panzhihua set their own quotas; the standards vary

considerably from one township to another). In the first years of the planned-birth campaign, corresponding roughly to the 1978 to 1982 birth cohort, Yishala seems to have implemented a policy stricter even than was allowed by its two-child quota, causing its birth rates to drop temporarily to levels resembling those in Renhe, but since then implementation has loosened considerably. The question thus becomes one of how Renhe has managed to keep the lid on births even in the more relaxed atmosphere of the late 1980s.

The low birth quota may not be the whole story. The number of children born in Renhe dropped more suddenly in 1978 than even during the famine years of the late fifties and early sixties,[20] and has remained low until the present. This has not been the case everywhere, even in our own study—note the slight rise in the Yishala birthrate between 1978–82 and 1983–88[21]—and it has also been reported from many parts of China that enforcing the single-child policy is particularly difficult in the rural areas, where children are seen both as potential labor-power and as necessary old-age insurance.[22] In fact, Greenhalgh's chapter (9) in this volume argues that the state and the local community have in essence negotiated a two-child policy in the Han villages she studied in Shaanxi, which like Renhe were vegetable-growing communities. Enforcement has worked, though, in Renhe, and I think the reason has partly to do with three interconnected factors that distinguish Renhe's experience in the reforms. These are physical and economic proximity to the city, entrepreneurship, and the status of women. Renhe, of all the rural areas in Panzhihua at least, is most like an urban area and thus most susceptible to effective population control. The many families that live partly from state wages will have pensions, as have urban workers; this lessens the value of children as old-age insurance. Also, the relatively high standard of living expected in Renhe these days (considerably higher than in the villages surveyed by Greenhalgh, which seem comparable to Yishala, though lower than in the Pearl River delta villages surveyed by Johnson), along with the cash basis of the economy, in which children's labor contribution declines relative to their consumption needs, also makes children seem less profitable, and the pressure to have

20. A Renhe resident whom I interviewed about the famine of 1960–62 told me it was not particularly serious in this area. People were hungry, he said, for six to eight months in 1960, but a good winter harvest in 1961 saved the area from starvation, and harvests after that time were reasonably good. Our figures support this interpretation, but I did not pursue this point systematically with other people.

21. There is little increase in the General Marital Fertility Rate in Yishala between these two cohorts, indicating that the rise in the birth rate is due to a change in the age structure of the female population. However, if we consider that village birth quotas are based on total population, rather than on the population of married women, to the cadres of the planned-birth campaign this would look like a slackening of enforcement.

22. Wasserstrom, "Resistance."

fewer of them thus less onerous. And even entrepreneurial families, which are often larger than their farming or wage-earning counterparts in other places, are usually larger because they tend to retard family division, not because they are particularly fertile.

Zhuangshang and Yishala share none of these characteristics that Renhe has in common with the nearby city. The standard of living itself is lower, and with the continuing battles over irrigation water, Zhuangshang villagers are ever mindful of the possibility of food shortages. What food they do manage to produce will come from hard labor, and hard labor belongs to the young and middle-aged; this along with the impossibility of any savings and the unlikelihood of the implementation of any sort of pension plan (nobody interviewed in Zhuangshang earns wages in the state sector; in Yishala we know of only one state-sector wage earner, a cadre in the *xiang* government at Pingdi), means that old-age insurance in the form of children is still a crucial consideration. All but one of the thirteen women who married into Zhuangshang families from 1980 to 1984 already had their legal maximum of two children by the beginning of 1988; although Yishala brides seemed somewhat slower to reproduce, about half of the comparable cohort there had already borne a second child by 1988.

The other two factors contributing to the relative ease of enforcement of the one-child quota are entrepreneurship and the status of women, and the two are closely interconnected. Entrepreneurship in its own right undoubtedly releases the pressure to have more children; those who replace a subsistence economy with an entrepreneurial one trade a strategy of survival for a strategy of advancement, and advancement relies on the accumulation of capital rather than of labor, especially since successful entrepreneurs such as the sand-hauling family described above can actually afford to hire laborers.

It is important to distinguish nonentrepreneurial productive sidelines, such as the ubiquitous lime production in Yishala, from true entrepreneurship as found in Renhe. Making lime is a welcome source of income for Yishala villagers; five hundred yuan in cash is a considerable supplement to a family's average of two or three thousand total, and enables not only saving but the purchase of bicycles, tape players, and in some cases televisions or small tractors. Zhuangshang villagers, of course, do not even have these meager opportunities, and indeed they are poorer than their counterparts in Yishala. But the presence in Yishala of a cash income source of this kind does not alleviate the pressure to build old-age security through children; it is a supplement rather than an alternative strategy.

In a similar manner, the status of women is a factor in the calculus of fertility strategies. Hill Gates suggests in her chapter (10) in this volume that for entrepreneurial women in Chengdu, "anti-philoprogenitivism," or restricting the numbers of one's offspring, is a strategy pursued by women

TABLE 4.6. Average Years of School by Birth Cohort,
Renhe, Yishala, and Zhuangshang

	Renhe		Yishala		Zhuangshang	
Birth Cohort	Males	Females	Males	Females	Males	Females
1953–57	6.43	4.92	5.64	2.72	5.50	2.91
1958–62	6.71	6.94	7.75	3.31	7.50	5.00
1963–67	6.93	6.21	6.11	3.72	5.79	4.00
1968–72	5.43	6.33	5.11	4.14	6.26	5.13
1973–78	5.21	5.42	4.74	4.07	5.28	4.25
1978–82	2.00	3.00	1.45	1.00	1.69	1.20
Total	5.15	5.64	4.77	3.02	5.09	3.17

who want to shepherd available capital for reinvestment and also wish to reduce the burdens of childcare so they can devote more time and energy to business. But if fertility restriction is a women's strategy, women must have enough control or leverage in family decision making to be allowed to pursue this strategy.

There is considerable evidence that the status of women is higher in Renhe than in Zhuangshang or Yishala. One of our more surprising findings concerns the amount of schooling given to boys and girls in the three villages, as shown in table 4.6. As the table indicates, despite the considerable differences in income and urban cultural influences in the three villages, the average years of schooling for males differ very little. The Communist Party's program to bring basic education to villagers seems to have succeeded rather spectacularly in the case of Zhuangshang, which is otherwise a poor and remote village.[23] What does differ, however, is the imbalance of education between girls and boys. In Renhe, girls born since 1950 have received slightly more education on the average than have boys, though the difference is not significant.[24] In both Zhuangshang and Yishala, boys have been to school for almost two years more, and the difference is fairly consistent across all cohorts. Only one female in eight from Zhuangshang, and one in nine from Yishala, has gone beyond elementary school, while at least a quarter of Zhuangshang and Yishala males, and Renhe residents of both sexes, have had more than a primary education.

23. Zhuangshang is particularly noteworthy here, since it got such a late start. In Yishala, the first school was established in 1906, and most males received some primary education in the decades before 1949. In Zhuangshang, however, there was only a short-lived attempt at a school in the 1930s, and most men born before 1940 are still illiterate.

24. There is, of course, some right-censoring in the data for the later cohorts, since many of the people in those cohorts are still in school.

This male-female difference in education seems to reflect the difference between the subsistence pursued by the Zhuangshang villagers and the partly entrepreneurial economy now flourishing in Renhe. The subsistence economy usually entails the retention of the patrilineal, androcentric social system, in which livelihood comes from the property-and-labor-managing patriline, in which men and women play the traditional roles—even the few people we did find in Zhuangshang who engaged in production for profit were men, as were all the participants in the grueling labor of lime manufacture in Yishala. In Renhe entrepreneurship is a departure from the traditional system and centers around individual initiative. This initiative can be taken by either men or women, and women are thus seen to be just as productive and to have just as much potential as men; perhaps this is why people send their girls to school for at least as many years as they send their boys.

But it is not merely the potential for entrepreneurial activity that is shared by men and women in Renhe; many of the actual prime movers in Renhe's entrepreneurial families are women. I have already mentioned the vegetable farmer's wife with her chickens; there is also the entrepreneuse who took out a contract on a formerly collective fishpond in 1987; though she barely recovered her investment that year, she expected to net over 7,500 in 1988. Ren Hai and I interviewed her because we were interested in talking to someone who had recently contracted for one of the fishponds; we spent a couple of hours discussing her balance sheet and her plans for expansion. When we had taken enough notes she insisted on leading us out to the pond and giving us a tour; in particular she wanted to show us the brick shed she had recently had built, which not only housed her gear but was planned as a little office for the rent-a-rod business she was planning to open for Sunday visitors from the city.

In addition, many of the vegetable-growing enterprises in Renhe are run and managed by women. This is particularly true in a large number of families whose male members hold salaried jobs; the women plant, grow, and sell the vegetables. This was brought out strongly to me in an interview with a man who was a professional cook (a state employee); he was hard-pressed to come up with any figures on acreage, fertilizer, yields, or profits from agriculture. His twelve-year-old son, who helped his mother out in the fields after school, knew much more than the father, but I had to wait until his mother got home to get the figures straight.

This is not to suggest that the women of either Zhuangshang or Yishala act retiring or submissive. In Yishala, which we knew better because we lived there, women were publicly very visible on all sorts of formal and informal occasions, and they often took the initiative in helping us with our interviewing and other tasks; our limited time in Zhuangshang showed the same sorts of patterns. But in neither place do women control capital; as

Gates points out in chapter 10, this seems to be the crucial difference, not just in granting them some independence, but also in permitting a strategy that would allow low fertility. Even if a woman were fully in control of the family economy in a place like Zhuangshang or Yishala, her rational strategy, despite the possible hardships involved, would still be to have enough children to ensure a comfortable old age.[25]

This still leaves open the reasons for the relative success of the planned-birth campaign in Yishala, where a two-child policy was negotiated only later, and where it was very effectively implemented. I would suggest provisionally that this has something to do with Yishala's model-village status; it may have been possible to acquire and preserve such status because the villagers were behaving in model ways, including controlling their fertility. This supposition was strengthened on my visit to Pingdi in September 1991, where township cadres told me Yishala has become a provincial-level Civilized Village, preserving its model-community status.

FAMILY DIVISION AND FAMILY COMPLEXITY

All these factors, I propose, combine with the single-child birth quota to contribute to the dramatic diminution in the size of Renhe families between 1983 and 1988. As urban proximity, entrepreneurship, and the status of women have made this decline in family size more dramatic than the corresponding declines in Zhuangshang and Yishala, we must remember a rather contrary fact expressed in the opening tables of this chapter—Renhe families, although the same size as those of Zhuangshang, are nevertheless consistently more complex, while Yishala families are as complex as those of Renhe and larger than those in either Renhe or Zhuangshang. Stem families have accounted for from 39 to 46 percent of the families in Renhe over the last fifteen years, and from 41 to 48 percent in Yishala, while in Zhuangshang they have been as little as 26 percent and have never exceeded 37; the current percentage figures at the time of our survey were 46 in Renhe, 48 in Yishala, and 30 in Zhuangshang. In addition, though the figures are probably too small to carry much weight, Zhuangshang has had *no* joint families since the late seventies, whereas Renhe and Yishala have always had a few. What is the reason for this?

It might be possible to explain different proportions of stem and nuclear families by demographic variables. For example, if the eldest generation is living longer, there will be a higher proportion of stem families, with everything else held constant, since there will be a higher probability of three generations being alive at once. For the villages discussed here, however,

---

25. Sons are preferred, here as elsewhere. But a daughter will do; uxorilocal marriage is a continuing option in all three villages and has always accounted for about 10 percent of marriages in each place.

there seems to be no difference—the average age at death for members of our Renhe families who lived to age 20 was 55.3 for women and 57.7 for men, in Zhuangshang it was 56.5 for women and 55.2 for men, and in Yishala it was 56.8 for women and 57.1 for men.

Age at marriage would also affect the proportion of joint families in a population, since earlier marriage would also mean earlier childbearing and a consequently greater chance that three generations would be alive at once. But again, we find no significant differences in the two villages—for male age at marriage, the crucial variable in a patrilocal family system, the average for Renhe is 23.2, for Zhuangshang 22.2, and for Yishala 22.1; certainly no significant difference.

Finally, the size of the brother-set might affect the proportions of stem and nuclear families. If there are more brothers, and if most families divide before the death of the parents, then there will be more nuclear families (including brothers who do not stay with the parents) for each stem family (the brother who does stay with the parents). I have calculated numbers of surviving children for mothers in the three villages who married from 1951 to 1960 (whose sons grew to manhood and faced family division in the 1970s and 1980s), and indeed the numbers were slightly larger in Zhuangshang than in Yishala or Renhe, but only slightly so—4.7 children in Zhuangshang and 4.4 in both Renhe and Yishala. This is not enough to account for the differential proportions of nuclear and stem families.[26]

To explain this difference, then, we must turn away from demographic factors and look at the causes of variation in the pattern of family division. We might at first suspect that Renhe and Yishala families are dividing later than those in Zhuangshang. The late division of Renhe families would go along with previous findings that entrepreneurial families tend to stay together longer in order to pool labor, capital, or both. But if this were the case, we would expect to see a high proportion of joint families in Renhe, and we would also expect that a higher proportion of entrepreneurial families would be of the more complex, stem or joint type. Figures do not bear

26. If we figure that in every brother-set, one will stay with the parents upon marriage, while the others move away to form nuclear families, then if the brother-set averages 2.35, as in Zhuangshang, 42% of the families formed upon marriages of the sons will be of the stem type, while an average brother-set size of 2.2, as in Yishala and Renhe, will produce 46% stem families. The actual percentages, as indicated above, diverge much more widely than that.

If parity makes little difference for family complexity now, it is bound to matter more in the future. If Renhe people continue to have only one child, every person with living parents at the time of marriage will form some sort of three- or four-generation family; perhaps many of these will be of the double-grandparent type, in which both the husband's and the wife's parents live with the couple. The alternative is a large proportion of old people living alone with none of their children, and the kind of "networked family" described by Ikels and Unger in this volume. In Yishala and Zhuangshang, however, there ought to be just enough children for everybody to form a stem family.

TABLE 4.7. Types of Family Division, 1973–1987

	Type A	Type B
Renhe		
1973–77	2	7
1978–82	2	7
1983–87	9	12
Yishala		
1973–77	2	3
1978–82	6	12
1983–87	5	4
Zhuangshang		
1973–77	2	2
1978–82	1	14
1983–87	0	13

this out. There have been a few joint families in Renhe in the last ten years, but always less than 5 percent of the population. And the relationship between family economy and family composition is not much more convincing: in a cross tabulation of family complexity and family economy, we find essentially no relationship.[27]

But in fact there is an important difference between Renhe and Yishala, on the one hand, and Zhuangshang, on the other, with regard to the process of family division. We can see this if we classify family divisions into two types. One, which I call type A, is family division after the brothers have already formed a joint family. This is the classical *fen jia* of Chinese ethnology (as described by Cohen in *House United, House Divided*). The other, type B, consists of brothers either hiving off one by one soon after their own marriages, or in some cases, even before marriage. Table 4.7 shows the prevalence of type A and type B family divisions in the last three five-year intervals.

It is apparent that type A divisions, those in which brothers wait until they have formed a joint family for at least a few months or years before they divide, have increased as a proportion of all family divisions in Renhe in the years since the economic reforms; whereas they were less than a fourth of family divisions from 1973 to 1982, they constituted almost half the divisions in the more recent interval. In Yishala, this type of family division has always constituted a significant proportion of all divisions. If there is no visible difference between the timing of divisions *within* Renhe or

27. Since no significant results were found, this tabulation has been omitted from this chapter.

Yishala, from one category of family economy to another, there is still a very real difference between these villages and Zhuangshang, where essentially all family divisions come piecemeal at the time of each brother's marriage; this explains the complete absence of joint families in that poor village in the 1983 and 1988 cross sections.

Moreover, this pattern has emerged in Renhe with the economic reforms, with the transition from a subsistence economy to an entrepreneurial economy, while the families of Zhuangshang continued to be constrained to an almost purely subsistence-farming economy. In this kind of economy, it matters little whether brothers stay together after their marriages. There are no economies of scale in subsistence grain farming, and there are few if any opportunities to save and invest in an economy as poor as Zhuangshang's. So the stresses of joint family life are avoided, and each brother and his family go their own way when they marry.

But why the lack of differences between entrepreneurial and other families in Renhe? Perhaps this is because almost all families in Renhe are entrepreneurial to an extent; even those not currently engaged in entrepreneurial activity face the possibility not only of entrepreneurship but of diversification in general, which in today's economy is a strategy of advancement. It may be best not to make too much of the current differences in each individual family's economy when all families are caught up in an expanding, petty-capitalist race for income and status. And as such they are not automatically dividing their households as soon as brothers marry.

The problem for this kind of argument, of course, is Yishala. The families there are in no sense entrepreneurial; though they supplement their farm income with lime manufacture and have enough cash to invest in a few modern conveniences, they are not plunging headlong into the pursuit of profit, as are so many families in Renhe. Nevertheless, for the last twenty years at least, nearly half their families have grown to the joint phase before dividing. It is possible that the additional labor requirements of lime production may retard family division somewhat, but it seems doubtful that this is a major consideration. In addition, the typical family cycle does not seem to have changed from the pre-1978 period to the period of the reforms. Perhaps it is simply local tradition; certainly there need not be a rational economic calculus behind every change in family composition.

Nevertheless, no family in Renhe has remained in a joint state for more than two years, at least since before 1968. In Yishala, the longest recorded period of joint-family organization is six years, with another family having stayed together four years before dividing. It appears that even in Renhe's entrepreneurial environment and in the face of Yishala's long-held customary practices, the centrifugal pressures still outweigh the perceived advantages of staying together. Or perhaps really significant entrepreneurship, the kind where capital-pooling confers a perceptible advantage in expansion, is just now under way in Renhe, and we will see more families remaining into the joint phase in the next few years. Of the two joint families in our survey in 1988, one was the transport, fish-farming, and stockraising enterprise of the family with the twenty-nine-room house; perhaps they will remain together longer. However, at least three entrepreneurial joint families divided between 1983 and 1988.

CONCLUSION

It is clear that family process in the rural areas around Panzhihua city is changing and that the changes have something to do with the twin policy initiatives of the post-Mao government: strict population control and liberalizing economic reforms. Population control has been important everywhere, but has had a differential effect on the three villages studied, with Renhe effectively reduced to one-child families and a consequent drop in household size, Yishala showing a more moderate drop, and Zhuangshang, where people are allowed to have two children, seeing family size decline more slowly.

The other factor, the economic reforms, seem to have had a less universal effect on family process and composition. The cycle of growth and division in Yishala and Zhuangshang has changed little because of the reforms; in Yishala before the reforms, people often allowed their families to grow to the joint form; this tendency has remained. In Zhuangshang, the prereform tendency not to form joint families has also continued. That neither of these villages has seen much change in this aspect of family process is not surprising, since the transformation from collective to individual farming in these villages has not resulted in a massive shift away from subsistence farming. The villagers of Yishala have experienced some prosperity with the reforms, but no great transformation in the physical rhythm of their lives or in the expenditure of their labor. In Zhuangshang, even the increase in prosperity has been quite modest.

Renhe is another kind of place altogether; there the entrepreneurial, petty-capitalist economy is in full swing, and there is some suggestion that it has prompted some families to pool their resources by remaining undivided longer than they would previously have done. It will take another decade of such entrepreneurial expansion, however, before we can determine with any certainty whether there has been a fundamental change in family process as a result of the economic reforms. As it now stands, the most important factor influencing changes in family process is the birth-limitation campaign.

FIVE

Family Strategies and Economic Transformation in Rural China: Some Evidence from the Pearl River Delta

Graham E. Johnson

The arrangement of familial economic roles such as redistributor, manager or worker and the pooling and redistribution of resources are characteristics of [Chinese] family life adaptable to a great variety of economic activities.
MYRON L. COHEN, HOUSE UNITED, HOUSE DIVIDED

The great majority of the Chinese population lives in rural settlements, and their economic activities are largely agricultural. Rural policies in China were shaped by distinct ideological directions after 1949 and had profound implications for the operation of rural households and rural kinship organization. Chinese rural cultivators were first caught up in land reform and then in the process of the collectivization of production. The fundamental attributes of a peasant economy relate to land, the allocation of household labor to work the land or to meet cultivation responsibilities, and the link with nonpeasants through an elaborate network of marketing. Land reform affected cultivation rights. Collectivization compromised the household allocation of labor. From the mid-1950s, planned purchase and supply of major agricultural commodities transformed marketing behavior. The consequences for the economic organization of rural households were far-reaching. In 1979 China embarked on a new developmental course, which was first charted in the countryside. There quickly emerged different possibilities for rural Chinese households and their members to pursue economic and other goals different from those that had prevailed during the first three decades of the People's Republic of China.

There is a consensus that the Chinese peasant household is a corporate entity in which its members cooperate to meet (economic) goals.[1] That co-

---

1. Thoroughly described in Cohen, *House United, House Divided* (New York: Columbia University Press), 57–85.

operation is reinforced by religious and ritual solidarities. The intimate linkages between economic requirements and domestic social organization give rise to the pooling of labor and the allocation of labor by household units. In south China, especially Guangdong and Fujian, localized lineages elaborated principles of Chinese kinship and were central features of rural social structure. Administrative change and political leadership after the formation of the People's Republic of China compromised well-understood methods of family and kinship organization. The active administrative interventions from the cooperative movement in the early 1950s up to the formal demise of the commune system in 1983 disrupted traditional methods of household economic organization. Control over decision making by households for the three decades after land reform was lost, not to world economic forces, but to a bureaucratic state and its intervention.[2] Lineage organization in south China was compromised by land reform and was thereafter ideologically suspect.

This chapter will examine aspects of the characteristics of Chinese households and kin groups in rural areas of the Pearl River delta in Guangdong province in the mid-1980s. The Pearl River delta is a distinctive and well-described cultural setting for Chinese households and kin groups. The economic transformations as a consequence of policy initiatives since 1979 have been substantial in all the coastal provinces of China. They have been especially marked in Guangdong and the Pearl River delta.[3] The Pearl River delta, more than any other region of China, has become firmly incorporated into the global economy and has assumed a particular role in the new international division of labor.[4] Major rural economic change has occurred as a consequence of incorporation into the world system. There has been a shift from a relatively insulated, state-dominated economic system to one that is open to outside influence, one in which rural households and the communities of which they form part have assumed, or reassumed, control over production activities. Peasant households in the Pearl River delta have responded with alacrity to opportunities in the wake of reform. In certain regions of the Pearl River delta, and especially those where the Overseas Chinese presence is marked, lineages have been revived and elaborated.

2. The broad dimensions of the process are most provocatively explored by Vivienne Shue in *The Reach of the State: Sketches of the Chinese Body Politic* (Stanford: Stanford University Press, 1988). Some of Shue's arguments are also explored in Helen Siu, *Agents and Victims in South China: Accomplices in Rural Revolution* (New Haven: Yale University Press, 1989), which are placed in the historical context of developments in Xinhui in the Pearl River delta. See especially 189–211.

3. E. Vogel, *One Step Ahead in China: Guangdong under Reform* (Cambridge: Harvard University Press, 1989).

4. David Thorns, "The New International Division of Labor and Urban Change: A New Zealand Case Study," in *Pacific Rim Cities in the World Economy*, ed. M. P. Smith, 68–101 (New Brunswick: Transaction Books, 1989).

Within Third World rural development, the critical social stratum is the peasantry. The sociology of the peasantry is not part of an extensive literature and has assumed major significance only in the modern period.[5] The analysis of the role of Chinese peasants in development is compounded by three decades of policies that were formulated to create "purposive change."[6] The best-documented accounts of the transformation of traditional peasantries, and yet ones that have become subject to considerable controversy, are European examples.[7] The transformation of the peasants of European Russia constitute one example directly comparable to the Chinese case, in which their "awkward" character has been clearly demonstrated.[8]

The issues in the transformation of Asian peasantries have been explored in the debate between Scott and Popkin.[9] How peasants react to their incorporation into the world-system is a critical question raised by those discussions. Scott has most recently provided a finely worked case study,[10] which has gone some way in meeting Keyes's comment that "theories . . . can shape significant questions but answers to those questions if they are to be good answers must take into account not only objective conditions that constrain social action but also the historically situated 'social space' within which action actually occurs."[11]

Households and the communities of which they are a part are key elements in the "social space" of a peasant social stratum. It is a generally held view that peasant households are adept at meeting threats to the integrity of their basic cultural structures. Peasant households can be

5. Eric Wolf, *Peasants* (Englewood Cliffs, N.J.: Prentice-Hall, 1965), remains one of the best general statements. See also his "The Vicissitudes of the Closed Corporate Peasant Community," *American Ethnologist* 13 (1986): 325–29.

6. W. L. Parish and M. K. Whyte, *Village and Family in Contemporary China* (Chicago: Chicago University Press, 1978), 8–15.

7. See T. H. Aston and C. H. E. Philpin, *The Brenner Debate: Agrarian Class Structure and Economic Development in Pre-Industrial Europe* (Cambridge: Cambridge University Press, 1985).

8. See T. Shanin, *The Awkward Class: Political Sociology of a Peasantry in a Developing Society: Russia 1910–1925* (Oxford: Oxford University Press, 1972), and Robert Edelman, *Proletarian Peasants: The Revolution of 1905 in Russia's Southwest* (Ithaca: Cornell University Press, 1987).

9. James C. Scott, *The Moral Economy of the Peasant: Rebellion and Subsistence in Southeast Asia* (New Haven: Yale University Press, 1976); Samuel I. Popkin, *The Rational Peasant: The Political Economy of Rural Society in Vietnam* (Berkeley: University of California Press, 1979). See also the provocative arguments in Daniel Little, *Understanding Peasant China: Case Studies in the Philosophy of Social Science* (New Haven: Yale University Press, 1989), and the study by Wan Hashim, *Peasants Under Peripheral Capitalism* (Bangi: Penerbit Universiti Kebangsaan Malaysia, 1988).

10. James C. Scott, *Weapons of the Weak: Everyday Forms of Peasant Existence* (New Haven: Yale University Press, 1985). See also the examples in Forest D. Colburn (ed.), *Everyday Forms of Peasant Resistance* (Armonk, N.Y.: M.E. Sharpe, 1989).

11. Charles F. Keyes, "Peasant Strategies in Asian Societies: Moral and Rational Economic Approaches—A Symposium: Introduction," *Journal of Asian Studies* 42, no. 4 (August 1983): 754.

highly flexible in their responses to new economic and social opportunities. Equally, the communities that groups of peasant households form may become part of a collective strategy in the response to new opportunities implicit in incorporation into the world-system.

It is often assumed in the contemporary period that rural peoples are overwhelmed by the forces unleashed as a consequence of incorporation into the global economy.[12] Instead of their becoming passive victims of world forces, a community-led response by these peoples to new economic opportunities may create protection against global forces that threaten to disrupt the delicate social fabric of rural areas. Such responses may reveal the resilience of long-established social units, not least family and kin groups, that major theoretical paradigms have argued are readily compromised by major economic transformation.[13] Peasant kinship structures may not be weakened by new economic forms. On the contrary, they may become spatially more ramified to take advantage of new economic opportunities. Further, the arguments proposed by Skinner that markets and marketing create a major focus for Chinese peasant social existence are sustained as market areas themselves undergo a domestic renewal and form the major link with the global economy.[14]

THE CHINESE CASE, GUANGDONG AND THE PEARL RIVER DELTA

The rural sector has been a key element in China's development strategy. The record up to 1979, however, was an uneven one.[15] In the thirty years after 1949 a collective approach to rural production was created in which the traditional link between peasant households and the cultivation of privately owned land was compromised, and a large state-organized planning apparatus intervened in the Chinese peasant economy.

In 1979 major changes in China's policies began in the countryside. Theories and practices of a thirty-year period were significantly modified. There was significant decentralization of responsibility for agricultural pro-

12. Peter Worsley has described this as "the undoing of the peasantry." See his *The Three Worlds: Culture and World Development* (London: Weidenfeld and Nicholson, 1984), 61–167; see also William E. James, Seiji Naya, and Gerald M. Meier, *Asian Development: Economic Success and Policy Lessons* (San Francisco: International Center for Economic Growth, 1987), 157–90.

13. See the arguments, for example, in Neil J. Smelser, "Mechanisms of Change and Adjustments to Change," in *Industrialization and Society*, ed. Bert F. Hoselitz and Wilbert E. Moore, 32–54 (Paris: UNESCO and Mouton, 1963).

14. G. William Skinner, "Rural Marketing in China: Repression and Revival," *China Quarterly*, no. 103 (September 1985): 393–413.

15. Nicholas Lardy, *Agriculture in China's Modern Economic Development* (London: Cambridge University Press, 1983).

duction, and peasant households once again became the focal point of the agricultural sector of the rural economy. After 1979 Chinese peasant households assumed major management responsibility over agricultural production, including both subsistence grain production and economic crops, which became increasingly subject to market forces. At the same time, rural development policy encouraged diversification of the rural economy and promoted a shift away from a central reliance on agricultural production.[16]

While Chinese peasant households could contemplate new forms of (private sector) economic participation, the major transformation of local economies in some of China's regions was led by a dramatic growth in collectively managed enterprises, the lineal descendants of the commune and brigade industries, whose growth had been severely limited in the period before 1979. The formal demise of the system of the People's Communes is linked to "decollectivization" and the increased ability of peasant households to determine the allocation of household labor.[17] It is nonetheless paralleled by an intense reorganization of local administration in which the entrepreneurial and business skills of local cadres have become more critical in their judgment of performance than political and ideological accomplishments, which had prevailed for much of the previous thirty years.

Community control of nonagricultural (and especially industrial) activities was vigorously pursued, which augmented household control over strictly agricultural production. Economic opportunity in nonagricultural production expanded throughout rural China and had major consequences for peasant households, which could deploy their members into an array of decidedly new economic activities. Major changes in China's rural development policies and their impact in a variety of regional contexts since 1979 have been extensively documented.[18] The Pearl River delta in Guangdong has been favorably located to take advantage of new directions in policy.

Guangdong, located strategically along China's south coast, is a large province of substantial geographic, economic, and cultural diversity. Its economic core is the Pearl River delta, with Guangzhou as its regional center. The delta also contains Hong Kong and Macao and two of the three

16. Jeffrey R. Taylor, "Rural Employment Trends and the Legacy of Surplus Labour, 1978–1986," *China Quarterly*, no. 116 (December 1988): 736–66.

17. A point made by Vivienne Shue, "The Fate of the Commune," *Modern China* 10, no. 3 (July 1984): 259–83.

18. See the essays in W. L. Parish, *Chinese Rural Development: The Great Transformation* (Armonk, N.Y.: Sharpe, 1985); K. Griffin (ed.), *Institutional Reform and Economic Development in the Chinese Countryside* (London: Macmillan, 1984); E. Perry and C. Wong, *The Political Economy of Reform in Post-Mao China* (Cambridge: Harvard University Press, 1985), 1–194; Robert F. Ash, "The Evolution of Agricultural Policy," *China Quarterly*, no. 116 (December 1988): 529–55; Jorgen Delman, Clemens S. Ostergaard, and Flemming Christiansen (eds.), *Remaking Peasant China: Problems of Rural Development and Institutions at the Start of the 1990s* (Aarhus: Aarhus University Press, 1990).

Special Economic Zones (SEZ) that were located in Guangdong after the promulgation of the new "open door" policies in 1979. Outside the delta, the province is mountainous and therefore relatively poor, with inadequate communications and a pronounced ethnic diversity. Guangdong is one of China's great rural regions, ranking third in terms of the total value of rural production in 1988. Although deficient in grain production, it produces over 40 percent of China's sugarcane and is the largest producer of fruit, fish, and forest products. The province's heavy industrial base is relatively small, although it is an important center of light industry. Only Shanghai produces more sewing machines, and the province leads the nation in the production of electric fans. It is a major producer of bicycles, refined aluminum products, hand tractors, and certain food products, of which refined sugar is most significant. Since 1979 there have been sharp increases in the production of domestic appliances, electronic goods, and cameras. Overall economic growth rates have been especially marked since the middle of the 1980s. Guangdong has consistently attracted the bulk of China's foreign investment,[19] which has had consequences for the province as a whole but which has been especially marked in the Pearl River delta.

Aggregate statistics for Guangdong province, although impressive, tend to mask the performance of the delta region which, since early 1985, has been designated an "open economic region" (*jingji kaifang qu*).[20] The delta region occupies a commanding position in the Guangdong provincial economy. With less than a fifth of the provincial population, it has built on its advantageous location, closely proximate to Hong Kong and, through it, to the world economy. Guangdong was unable to take full advantage of its long tradition of commercialized production before 1978 but, nonetheless, was the major provincial producer of cash crops such as fish, silk cocoons,

19. Yang Dali, "Patterns of China's Regional Development Strategy," *China Quarterly*, no. 122 (June 1990): 248.

20. The core of the delta is composed of the two "municipalities" (*shi*) of Foshan and Jiangmen, which were created out of the former Foshan prefecture, in the early period of reform. The western part of the delta is composed of the four *xian* (Enping, Taishan, Kaiping, Xinhui), from which the bulk of the North American Chinese population traces its ancestry, Doumen and Heshan; the central delta extends from Guangzhou south and includes Nanhai, Punyu, Shunde, and Zhongshan and also mountainous Gaoming and Sanshui. The eastern delta consists of Dongguan and Bao'an, adjacent to the Shenzhen Special Economic Zone and Hong Kong. In 1987 the administrative definition of the "Open Economic Area" was expanded up the West River to include Zhaoqing *shi*, north of Guangzhou to include Huaxian and Conghua *xian*, and eastward to include much of what had formerly been Huiyang prefecture. Most of these new additions are not strictly delta, are mountainous and Hakka-speaking. They had begun to share in the prosperity of what is known as "the small delta," the original, essentially Cantonese-speaking, core. For a discussion of the "small" and "large" delta, see *Guangdongsheng Nianjian 1989* (1989 Guangdong Yearbook), 252–53; 492; 496.

fruit, and vegetables. In the wake of rural reform its agricultural sector flourished under the newly liberalized policies. While sericulture in the central delta declined, the production of fish, fruit, and vegetables expanded dramatically, destined for the domestic market as well as Hong Kong and Macao. The major transformation in the rural sector, however, was not in agriculture. Rapid economic growth occurred as the rural sector shifted to nonagricultural production. Entrepreneurial energies were released in a flurry of industrial growth, concentrated, initially, in certain regions of the delta. The central delta from Guangzhou south to Macao and the Zhuhai Special Economic Zone and the eastern corridor to Hong Kong and the rapidly expanding Shenzhen area comprised the major areas of new economic activity. These developments were possible partly because national policy allowed the province considerable autonomy to pursue innovative measures to seek capital and to retain foreign exchange earnings. The delta was able to mobilize the extensive links it possessed with its expatriate kinsmen who live in Hong Kong, Macao, and overseas.

The entire delta has long been an area of out-migration. From the mid-nineteenth century large numbers of émigrés from south and southeast China met some of the developmental needs of the burgeoning global economy and worked as unskilled laborers in the Americas and in Southeast Asia. The western reaches of the delta have provided the great majority of Americans and Canadians of Chinese origin. Under different circumstances, a large number of delta residents left for Hong Kong in the late 1940s and 1950s, and many contributed to Hong Kong's economic transformation after 1950.

In the 1980s the entrepreneurial skills and capital of these émigrés were actively sought. Kinship connections and local loyalties have become a central part of local development initiatives. In the process the delta has become firmly linked to the global economy through its Hong Kong connections. It has thus begun to share with other parts of East and Southeast Asia some of the developmental characteristics that McGee has described as the "desakota process," in which an intense mixture of agricultural and nonagricultural activities stretch along linear corridors between large city cores. The process typically occurs in regions characterized by high population densities and which were formerly dominated by wet rice agriculture.[21] The Pearl River delta constitutes one of those regions.

21. T. G. McGee, "Urbanasasi or Kotadesasi? Evolving Patterns of Urbanization in Asia," in *Urbanization in Asia*, ed. L. Ma, A. Noble, and A. Dutt, 93–108 (Honolulu: University of Hawaii Press, 1989); G. E. Johnson, "The Political Economy of Chinese Urbanization: Guangdong and the Pearl River Delta," in *Urbanizing China*, ed. Gregory Guldin, 185–220 (Westport, Conn.: Greenwood Press, 1992).

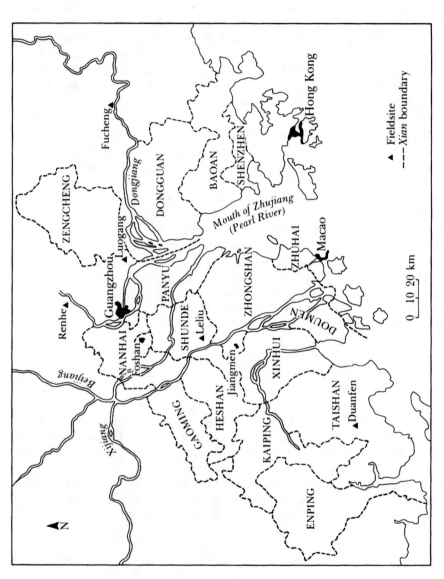

Map 5.1. The Pearl River Delta

RESEARCH SITES

I have been examining the process of rural development within the Pearl River delta since the reforms began. Building on work begun in the 1970s,[22] I have worked in five sites across the delta. I chose the sites in the 1970s, when each was administratively a commune, because each had some distinguishing characteristics. Duanfen, located in Taishan *xian* in the western delta, was a center of out-migration to North America. Leliu in Shunde *xian*, in the central delta, had a distinctive cash-cropping economy and possessed some unique cultural characteristics.[23] Luogang and Renhe are close to Guangzhou, located in Baiyun *qu* (formerly the "suburban district"). Although Luogang is mountainous, it is notable for fruit production. Renhe, to the north, was a grain specialist area, known for its radical political character in the Cultural Revolution and coincidentally a major source of migration to Canada. Fucheng, in Dongguan *shi* (formerly, *xian*) is a major source of migrants to Hong Kong, where I had worked in the 1960s.[24]

The economies of the five units and the villages that compose them have changed substantially since reform got under way in 1979.[25] One index of the change and the broadly successful response to the reform initiatives that they have enjoyed is substantial growth in per capita income (table 5.1). The opportunities for economic transformation are a consequence of internal factors, of which the indigenous economy and leadership are key, and location. Since initiation of the reforms linkages with expatriates in Hong Kong or Macao or in Overseas Chinese communities have become of increasing importance.

22. Elizabeth and Graham Johnson, *Walking on Two Legs: Rural Development in South China* (Ottawa: International Development Research Centre, 1976).

23. The distinctive ecological features of Shunde (and of Leliu in particular) are described in Kenneth Ruddle and Zhong Gongfu, *Integrated Agriculture-Aquaculture in South China: The Dyke-Pond System of the Zhujiang Delta* (Cambridge: Cambridge University Press, 1988).

24. For much of the 1980s I interviewed cadres at a variety of administrative levels associated with the units. In the summer of 1986 I selected five villages from among the units, based on my general knowledge of them. Using the household records I drew random samples of village households and administered a standard questionnaire. Much of the information that follows comes from this survey. The survey was funded by a research grant from the Social Sciences and Humanities Research Council of Canada. The Chinese Academy of Social Sciences gave me every assistance. In Guangdong I was greatly helped by the Guangdong Academy of Social Science and by the Department of Sociology at Zhongshan (Sun Yat-sen) University. I express my thanks to Li Ruichang and Chen Daojin and to Professor He Zhaofa. Mr. Tan Xiaobing assisted me in collecting the survey data and doing a great deal of coding, data cleaning, and analysis in Canada. His efforts are greatly appreciated.

25. Some general findings are indicated in the following: G. E. Johnson, "The Production Responsibility System in Chinese Agriculture: Some Examples from Guangdong," *Pacific Affairs* 55, no. 3 (Fall 1982): 430–52; "1997 and After: Will Hong Kong Survive? A Personal View," *Pacific Affairs* 59, no. 2 (Summer 1986): 237–54; "Rural Transformation in South China? Views from the Locality," *Revue Européene des Sciences Sociales* 27, no. 84 (1989): 191–226.

TABLE 5.1.   Per Capita Income, Selected Production Units, 1979–1987
(yuan)

Unit	1979	1984	1987	Annual Growth (%)
Duanfen	90	494	756	49.9
Leliu	180	701	1,400	75.3
Luogang	119	961	1,500	129.0
Renhe	157	448	1,200	73.7
Fucheng	352	865	1,659	41.2

SOURCE: Interviews, 1979–87.

Duanfen, located in southern Taishan, has benefited the least of the five units from the opportunities of the reform period. It is distant from Guangzhou and Hong Kong and its prospects for growth and development were, until recently, hampered by inadequate communications. As an Overseas Chinese area it suffered disabilities from almost the moment of its incorporation into the People's Republic of China. The overseas connections and linkages were political liabilities for much of the three decades from 1949 to 1979, which were especially marked during the period of the Cultural Revolution. It remained a subsistence economy with a substantial dependence on remittances from abroad. Per capita income in the middle 1970s was below a hundred yuan.

After 1979 the overseas linkages were viewed in a positive light, and many of the harsh political judgments that had colored local policy options were reversed. Although the economy has remained agricultural and firmly based on grain production, its base has diversified. Cash crops, such as fruit and sugarcane and the raising of poultry, have become widespread. Duanfen has prospered since reform, but its incorporation into the world-system has not occurred on the same scale as other units in central and eastern portions of the Pearl River delta. The question is partly one of location but also one of the particular nature of Duanfen's linkages to the global economy.

Leliu lies in Shunde in the central region of the delta. It enjoyed a distinctive economy based on fish farming and silkworm cultivation. There are no rice paddies in Leliu, and its commercialized (and export-oriented) agricultural production allowed its peasant cultivators to enjoy relative prosperity even before the reform period. It was an area of extensive out-migration to Hong Kong before 1949, and the linkages with its expatriates were vitalized in the wake of reform. A young and dynamic leadership sought to involve the entrepreneurial energies of Hong Kong in its economic transformation. Its agricultural economy, especially fish farming, has remained buoyant, although sericulture has been eliminated as a consequence of pollution and low prices for cocoons. Dramatic growth in nonagricultural production has overwhelmed its agriculture. The market towns of Shunde have become the centers of light industrial production, which has allowed its households to enjoy the highest per capita incomes in rural China.

Luogang is located off the main highway that links Guangzhou to eastern Guangdong at the eastern edge of Baiyun *qu* of Guangzhou municipality.[26] Formerly part of Panyu *xian*, it has a long history of specialization in fruit production. Changes in pricing policies and release from the highly bureaucratized purchase and supply of fruit has allowed peasant cultivators to increase household income. The region did not have a history of extensive out-migration, and the local economy has seen no growth in its small-enterprise sector since the reform period began. Its villages remain firmly agricultural, although their proximity to major markets (and especially Guangzhou) has allowed them to take full advantage of its new commercial opportunities and profit from high prices paid to fruit growers. Grain production remains important. Proximity to centers of labor demand (especially in construction) has allowed members of peasant households to seek employment opportunities outside agriculture.

Renhe is located at the northern edge of Baiyun *qu*. The large and dense population is largely engaged in grain production. Renhe lies beyond the zone of intense vegetable cultivation that has developed to meet the needs of the Guangzhou market, and has relatively little involvement in cash-cropping, although it has had some success in raising poultry. Outmigration was substantial in the past, and there are significant numbers of its natives overseas and in Hong Kong. Its industrial capacity at the *zhen*, village, and individual levels has grown since the reform period, often in cooperation with Hong Kong entrepreneurial interests. Yet, the degree of Renhe's incorporation into the broader economy of the delta is less extensive than that of other units in the central delta or of those closer to Guangzhou or Hong Kong. The capacity of the local economy to absorb surplus labor is limited. Large numbers of men, especially those under forty years of age, have left the area to seek work in Guangzhou and elsewhere in the delta, leaving the management of the agricultural economy in the hands of women and older men.

Fucheng extends in a wedge to the south and east from Dongguan city. The economic growth of Dongguan since the reform period got under way has been remarkable. Fucheng has fully shared in the transformation of the

26. For a broad account of Baiyun *qu* (formerly the "suburban district"), see *Guangzhou Nianjian 1989* (Guangzhou Yearbook) (Guangzhou: Wenhua chubanshe, 1989), 487–89.

entire *shi*.[27] Dongguan has benefited from its close proximity to the Shenzhen Special Economic Zone (SEZ) and Hong Kong. It has fully utilized investment resources and skills of its expatriates in Hong Kong who have provided much of the capital for an extensive array of enterprises, both industrial and agricultural, which have transformed the rural economy of Dongguan. Fucheng has over four hundred enterprises, whose foreign exchange earnings in 1987 were over $HK50 million. They include plastics, garment manufacture, electronics, and toys, virtually all destined for the world market as subsidiaries of Hong Kong–based manufacturers; they also include large shipments of vegetables for the Hong Kong markets and fruit for both Hong Kong and domestic markets throughout China.

The five units are broadly representative of the Pearl River delta. They extend across the delta, representing differing production regimes, which are historically determined but also a consequence of different leadership strategies and different developmental possibilities in the wake of rural reform after 1979. The villages within the five units and their constituent households have responded with alacrity to the new possibilities. I will first outline the consequences for peasant households in general and then discuss peasant household strategies in the central and eastern delta (what Vogel calls "the inner delta").[28] I will finally give an account of household strategies in the distinctive western reaches of the delta, in which overseas-Chinese connections are a dominant characteristic.

PEARL RIVER DELTA HOUSEHOLDS: A DESCRIPTIVE PROFILE

Households in the sample population had a mean size of 5.1, not dramatically different from household size in other national rural samples in the 1980s,[29] from the 1970s estimate of 5.0 for Guangdong by Parish and Whyte,[30] or from the 1930s figure for Guangdong of 5.2.[31] Household size ranged from single individuals to an enormous household of 26. There were

27. The performance of Dongguan is detailed in Zhonggong Zhongyang Bangongting, *Dongguan Shi'nian: 1979–1988* (Dongguan Ten Years: 1979–1988) (Shanghai: Shanghai renmin chubanshe, 1989). Fucheng's performance is detailed at pp. 219–20.

28. Ezra Vogel, "Guangdong's Dynamic Inner Delta," *China Business Review*, September–October 1989, 56–62.

29. Household size from a national sample of rural households in 1986 was 5.07, cited in *Zhongguo Tongji Nianjian 1988* (Statistical Yearbook of China 1988) (Beijing: Zhongguo tongji chubanshe, 1989), 822; Guangdong samples indicate a decline from 5.74 in 1978 to 5.12 in 1985, cited in *Guangdong Tongji Nianjian 1988* (Statistical Yearbook of Guangdong 1988) (Beijing: Zhongguo tongji chubanshe, 1989), 415.

30. Parish and Whyte, *Family and Village*, 134.

31. Irene B. Taeuber, "The Families of Chinese Farmers," in *Family and Kinship in Chinese Society*, ed. M. Freedman, 71 (Stanford: Stanford University Press, 1970).

TABLE 5.2. Peasant Family Types, Selected Villages

Type	Villages					
	Kongluen (Duanfen)	Naamshui (Leliu)	Tsimkong (Luogang)	Ngawu (Renhe)	Wantong (Fucheng)	Total
Isolate	17.0%	11.0%	13.0%	7.0%	11.6%	11.9%
Nuclear	31.0	49.0	56.0	51.0	55.4	48.8
Stem	46.0	35.0	27.0	33.0	28.1	35.6
Joint	6.0%	5.0%	4.0%	9.0%	5.0%	5.8%
Households (N)	100	100	100	100	121	521

SOURCE: Household Survey, 1986.
$\chi^2 = 22.76$ $p = 0.03$

TABLE 5.3. Family Relationships, 1930–86

Relation	1930	1973	1986
Head	1.00	1.00	1.00
Spouse	.78	.69	.74
Child	1.91	2.54	2.59
Parents[a]	.23	.32	.20
Child's spouse	.31	.12	.24
Grandchild	.36	.12	.12
Siblings	.23	.14	.12
Others	.14	.02	.02
Mean size	5.03	4.95	5.09
Households (N)	20,066	249	521

SOURCE: The 1930 figure is derived from Frank W. Notestein and Ch'iao Ch'i-ming, "Population," cited in Parish and Whyte, *Village and Family*, 134. The 1973 data are in Parish and Whyte, 134. The 1986 data are from the household survey.
[a] Includes in-laws (but very few).

26 single-person households (5.0 per cent), 18 (older) women and 8 men. The modal household as in the 1970s was nuclear in structure. There were relatively few joint households, though a large number of stem or broken stem households (table 5.2). Family relationships in the sample of households are similar to the patterns detailed by Parish and Whyte in their study of Lingnan villages in the 1970s (table 5.3).

Certain kinds of household relationships that existed in the past—and were familiar in the studies of household and family in the peripheries of Hong Kong and Taiwan in the 1960s[32]—either are nonexistent in the contemporary period or are extremely rare. Polygyny became illegal in 1950 as a result of the Marriage Law, and its economic possibility was compromised by land reform and later collectivization. Plural wives are a characteristic of the past. "Minor" forms of marriage, such as "small daughters-in-law," once common throughout the delta, become impossible in the context of a legally enforceable age of marriage,[33] and certainly the logic for most forms of minor marriage is less compelling than in the pre-Liberation context.[34] Households are no smaller than they were in the past, although they were likely to be somewhat larger in the late 1970s, but they are less complex. There are fewer members of senior generations than there were in the past, and there is an almost total absence of father's brothers and father's brothers' wives. Similarly, there are only few siblings (and their wives) and a virtual absence of kin outside direct lines of descent.[35]

One of the more obvious elements of continuity is patrilocal marriage.[36] The dominant form of postmarital residence is firmly patrilocal. A close adherence to well-defined areas from which to draw brides is clearly appar-

32. Summarized most effectively in Maurice Freedman, *Chinese Lineage and Society: Fukien and Kwangtung* (London: Athlone Press, 1966), which inspired the first generation of anthropological fieldwork in Chinese settings after the formation of the People's Republic of China.

33. This is not to suggest that all unions occur only upon the assumption of legal age. There are ways that socially recognized marriages can occur regardless of formal legality. See Parish and Whyte, *Village and Family*, 164–66.

34. See, for example, the arguments in James P. McGough, "The Domestic Mode of Production and Peasant Social Organization: The Chinese Case," in *Chayanov, Peasants and Economic Anthropology*, ed. E. Paul Durrenberger, 183–201 (Orlando, Fla.: Academic Press, 1984).

35. There is a virtual absence of unrelated kin. There was one (legal) household of unrelated men (in the Shunde village). The villages did contain substantial numbers of individuals who were unrelated by either kinship or marriage to the indigenous people of the villages. They were not living in legal households with formal registrations. I could not discover any way to interview such individuals, who generally appeared to be non-Cantonese-speaking males working as day laborers. The situation had changed by the end of the decade when non-Cantonese-speaking households began to contract land for two- and three-year periods and build houses and small hamlets in styles distinct from those of the indigenous delta villages.

36. It is not easy in survey situations to distinguish minor marriage or distinctive local customs. Divorce appears to be very low. The three cases of divorce in Naamshui (Leliu, Shunde) were sought by men from women who had refused to consummate their marriages and move from their natal households. See Janice Stockard, *Daughters of the Canton Delta* (Stanford: Stanford University Press, 1989), for a discussion of marriage patterns in Shunde, which were anything but "major." In the Leliu village of Naamshui I also came across a household headed by an unmarried sister well past marriage age, who was keeping house for her younger brothers, had engaged special tutors for them, encouraged them to study hard, and was delighted to find two of them at university. The commitment of Shunde women to their natal homes is a very strong one.

TABLE 5.4.   Marriage Provenance: Mothers, Spouses, and
Daughters-in-law

Provenance	Mother	Spouse	1st Daughter-in-law	2d Daughter-in-law
Same *xiang*	11.4%	22.6%	18.6%	21.3%
Same *zhen*	46.4	43.8	44.3	44.3
Adjacent *zhen*	26.7	22.9	23.6	21.3
Other	15.3%	10.7%	13.5%	13.1%
Households (*N*)	75	354	140	61

SOURCE: Household Survey, 1986. Parish and Whyte, 1978, 134.
NOTE: The categories used by Parish and Whyte to collect data on marriage provenance are not strictly comparable to mine. They report 35.0% of marriages were with brides whose natal homes were outside the commune in the 1968–74 period. My figure for brides who come from outside the *zhen* (the former commune) is 34.4 percent.

ent. Village endogamy is uncommon in all but the large multiple-surname village of Wantong in Dongguan. The marriage area may be somewhat more tightly drawn than in a previous generation. More spouses and daughters-in-law tend to be from the same *xiang* than are mothers. The most common provenance for wives is within the bounds of the production unit (the former commune, now typically called *zhen*) and rarely extends beyond the adjacent administrative entity (table 5.4).

The coincidence between former commune boundaries and standard markets was very close.[37] Marriage relations were most intense within the bounds of the market area. It was a pattern reinforced by administrative practice during the commune period and has not been compromised by new administrative arrangements, which in the Pearl River delta have seen few shifts in administrative boundaries, although much confusion in changes of name.[38] Administrative and other changes in the 1980s have only reinforced traditional boundaries that have salience for rural households.

37. This was first detailed in G. W. Skinner, "Marketing and Social Structure in Rural China: Part III," *Journal of Asian Studies* 24, no. 3 (May 1965): 363–99.

38. Rural Guangdong has a distinctive administrative structure, which is a consequence of its particular characteristics and historical developments. The basic unit of local government is called the *zhen* (market town) and is equivalent to the former commune. The former brigade, which was based on the pre-Liberation *xiang* (village alliance) became a unit of government for only a brief period in the mid-1980s and paralleled the creation of "township governments" (*xiang zhengfu*) in most other Chinese provinces. It is now officially referred to as the "village" (*cun*). The former production team, which may have formed a natural village or a village neighborhood during the commune period, is called the "village small group" (*cun xiaozu*).

Marriage is central to family continuity. The patrilocal system of marriage has been little affected by the dramatic changes of forty years. Brides are sought from other villages, which have tended over a long period of time to be linked in a system of bridal exchange. Administrative practice during the commune period likely contained and intensified the long-established system of marriage exchange. The renewal of the system of periodic markets has only reinforced the long-established contexts within which marriage occurs. To be sure, marriage is no longer "blind," and individuals have choice in the matter of whom they will marry. The decision to marry, nonetheless, occurs as part of clearly understood family consequences and is arranged in consultation with members of the kin group. Go-betweens make connections between families with eligible children. Their provenance is the area served by the periodic market, and their sphere of operation is the market town on market day.[39]

Demographic changes over the past forty years have had some major significance for rural household structure. Infant mortality rates have fallen progressively since the 1950s and especially after the Great Leap Forward.[40] Hence, rural households have more surviving children than was the case for rural households in the republican period. This likely has had effects for adoptions and other forms of incorporation into the household of individuals outside the direct line of patrilineal descent.[41]

There are more female heads of household (16.9 percent) than at earlier periods. If single-person households are excluded (the majority of these are elderly widows) the proportion of households headed by women is 14.1 percent. There is some regional variation. In the Overseas Chinese areas, households are much more likely to be headed by women. Women are least likely to head households in the two wealthy areas of Shunde and Dongguan.

The incidence of (recent) household division is substantial. While 30.0 percent of households remain undivided, 41.2 percent have divided since the beginning of reform. Households are most likely to have remained undivided in the Overseas-Chinese–dominated village of Kongluen in Duan-

---

39. Margery Wolf makes similar arguments. See her *Revolution Postponed: Women in Contemporary China* (Stanford: Stanford University Press, 1985), 167–68.

40. Judith Bannister, *China's Changing Population* (Stanford: Stanford University Press, 1987), 103–20.

41. Parish and Whyte, *Family and Village*, 136, reported a virtual absence of adopted sons (except among households headed by women) and an absence of adopted daughters and "small daughters-in-law." This is also the observation of Sulamith H. Potter and Jack M. Potter, *China's Peasants: The Anthropology of a Revolution* (Cambridge: Cambridge University Press, 1990). They note in the Dongguan village where they worked, which is adjacent to the one I surveyed, but in a different administrative unit, that "adoptions are rare" (220).

fen (Taishan). Division has been most marked in the fruit-growing village of Tsimkong in Luogang, Guangzhou. It was also high in Wantong in Fucheng (Dongguan) as the reform period got under way. I will offer an explanation below.

The past four decades have been characterized by dramatic shifts in economic and political organization in rural China. Rural households in the Pearl River delta are caught up in late-twentieth-century change. Although the context has changed, household structure at first appears to be characterized by continuities. Households are not immune to what occurs beyond their bounds. Change is, however, kept at arms length, and peasant families have devised strategies to deal with the economic and political threats to their integrity. The patrilineally structured rural household has not merely maintained its corporate character but has also used its intrinsic flexibility to meet new possibilities in the 1980s.

CHANGING ECONOMIC CHARACTERISTICS OF HOUSEHOLDS

The elaboration of the global economy and the creation of a new international division of labor has had sometimes catastrophic consequences for economic management by peasant households. There is a general assumption that in the twentieth century rural cultivators (peasants) have become less able to meet their own (or local) needs as their production activities become overwhelmed by the need to meet the demands of markets they do not control and participate in only indirectly.[42] As rural production becomes increasingly capitalized and incorporated into the world-system, nonsubsistence production and wage labor become increasingly important. Maclachlan has commented on the consequences of global economic change for rural households in the Third World. He has noted:

> In most cases of the capitalization of the countryside, the grounds for divorcing the needs of all or part of the peasantry from production decisions depend upon the character of intruding market forces, while the settlement, the division of costs and benefits, depends heavily on property institutions which prevail at the time of divorce. The role of judge in the whole process is played by government policy. . . . It makes a great deal of difference whether the agricultural sector is commercialized to produce export crops, or whether it is used to provide food and a source of labor for an urban industrial sector. It also makes a great deal of difference whether land tenure features powerful landlords or freeholding peasants. And it likewise makes a difference to know

---

42. This is an explicit part of the argument in Eric Wolf, *Peasant Wars of the Twentieth Century* (New York: Harper and Row, 1969), esp. 276–302.

TABLE 5.5. Peasant Household Economic Types, Selected Villages

| | Villages | | | | | |
Type	Kongluen (Duanfen)	Naamshui (Leliu)	Ngawu (Renhe)	Tsimkong (Luogang)	Wantong (Fucheng)	Tot:
Subsistence	70.3%	—	44.4%	—	—	21.9(
Cash-cropping	—	65.9%	—	95.9%	37.7%	40.6(
Multisector	29.7%	34.1%	55.6%	4.1%	62.3%	37.5(
Households (N)	91	91	90	97	97	475

SOURCE: Household Survey, 1986.

if a government's chief aim is the acquisition of foreign exchange, or import substitution, or the feeding of its people.[43]

The economic responses of peasant households in the Pearl River delta to the domestic and international pressures to which they have become subject in the 1980s are varied. There would seem to be three broad responses for those households that are economically active: (1) to remain in essentially subsistence production; (2) to become predominantly cash-cropping households; (3) to endeavor to place one or more members of the household in nonagricultural production. Peasant households will therefore fall into the following categories: subsistence, cash-cropping, multisector. The three types of economic households are to be found in all the villages I surveyed. Given the characteristics of the Pearl River delta, it would be expected that households engaged in other than subsistence production will be most numerous. The region has a highly commercialized agricultural sector, and the growth of the rural-enterprise sector has been marked in the 1980s. Table 5.5 indicates the distribution of household types, classified by their production orientations, in the five villages I surveyed.

Characteristics such as traditions of local production and location are important elements in determining why a village and its constituent households will likely shift from a subsistence to a nonsubsistence orientation. Given policy shifts, the cash-cropping tendencies of villages with well-established traditions of commercial production are intensified, and the proportions of cash-cropping households will therefore likely increase. Similarly, villages close to urban settlements will be subject to more extensive flows of information and capital, and both cash-cropping and multisectoral

43. Morgan D. Maclachlan, "From Intensification to Proletarianization," in *Household Economies and Their Transformation*, ed. M. D. Maclachlan, 15 (Lanham, Md.: University Press of America, 1987).

households will be greater. Finally, political leadership, the ability of leaders to establish connections and create entrepreneurial opportunities (for village- and community-based enterprise), will have consequences for economic diversification, a feature of rural development throughout rural China during the reform period.[44]

Both the size of household and its internal structure, in particular the number of adults, have consequences for labor-force attributes and the ability of households to meet productive goals. The resources a household has, such as the amount of land or available capital, determine the ability to expand productive horizons. Social (class) status and the assumption of administrative or political roles, as cadre or Party member, by household members can augment the ability of households to respond to the changing economic and social options.

Chayanov argued that peasants were adept at devising coping strategies and could utilize control over the deployment of household labor to meet new opportunities. Opportunity for Chinese peasant households was substantially restricted under conditions where collective structures took the major decisions for labor allocation. In the reform period, the devolution of responsibility for production decisions generated greater flexibility and greater possibilities to deploy household resources. If land parcels become small and the number of adults is large, households may pursue a strategy of moving some of their members into other sectors and, if it seems essential and possible, away from the local economy and into economic niches elsewhere.[45]

The capacities of peasant households to create strategies to meet (changing) economic and political challenges will be determined by internal and external factors of the kind outlined above. In the wake of reform policies, opportunities for delta peasant households have varied from locality to locality. The reform process has turned on "openness," and the external connections that villages possess have had a critical kinship dimension. The presence or absence of kinsmen outside of the village and the broad communities that villages form have been decisive for the development process in general and the kinds of strategies that village households have adopted. Kinsmen have become sources of investment and entrepreneurial skill. Yet, it is important to distinguish between the effects of kinsmen who are resi-

44. Jean Oi, *State and Peasant in Contemporary China* (Berkeley, University of California Press, 1989).

45. The very largest household in my sample had seven marital units: parents, five married sons, and a married grandson. In addition to contracting fishponds and cane lands in the natal village, the family corporation had contracted fishponds in the adjacent *zhen*, had further contracted fishponds in Dongguan, 100 kilometres away, and had assumed management responsibility over a brick kiln in Shaoguan, in northern Guangdong. Family income was in excess of 40,000 yuan in 1985.

dent in Hong Kong or Macao and those who are Overseas Chinese. Unquestionably, the areas in the western delta have benefited from extensive Overseas Chinese linkages. The substantial (and growing) funds that have flowed into the region from North America and elsewhere have been channeled, however, into projects such as roads, bridges, and public buildings, of which schools and hospitals are most common. Investment funds and entrepreneurial energies that have derived from Hong Kong and Macao, by contrast, have been directed toward the creation of productive enterprises and have had a major and direct effect on local systems of production. The consequences for household strategies in the eastern and central delta, where the presence of kinsmen based in Hong Kong and Macao is proportionally large, can be readily contrasted with those in the western delta, where the proportion of Overseas Chinese kinsmen and Overseas Chinese households is larger. Fundamental economic change, as a consequence of the entrepreneurial activities of Hong Kong–based kinsmen, has been greater in the central and eastern delta. The greater the degree of incorporation into the global economy, the greater will be the effect on household strategies and the greater the implications for changes in household structure. The extent of change will vary from village to village, depending on the extent and nature of the expatriate involvement in the local economy. The corporate kinship structures of the delta are the buffers that allow a highly flexible response to the dramatic possibilities of the reform period.

THE CENTRAL AND EASTERN DELTA: HONG KONG CONNECTIONS

The central and eastern delta areas have been most advantageously located in the 1980s to take advantage of new policy options. The region was historically highly commercialized and open to a variety of external linkages. The assumptions of development policy for much of the thirty years after 1949 compromised the operation of local economies, which turned inward under intense pressure from the Chinese state.[46] Peasant resistance was substantial, but the degrees of maneuverability were highly constrained.[47] The possibilities for household economic behavior changed dramatically after 1979.

46. Helen Siu, *Agents and Victims*, decribes the consequence of state policies from the 1950s for citrus and fan-palm production in Xinhui. Xinhui is on the highly commercialized eastern edge of the western delta. Her field sites are in and around the *xian* city. The arguments that she makes for Huancheng can be appropriately made for much of the central and eastern delta. Even where cash-cropping was extensive, its development was compromised by the emasculation of peasant marketing after 1956, and especially after the Great Leap Forward.
47. See David Zweig, "Struggling Over Land in China: Peasant Resistance After Collectivization, 1966–1986," in *Everyday Forms of Peasant Resistance*, ed. Forrest D. Colburn, esp. 153–62 for an account of peasant resistance to collectivist policies in the Lower Yangzi region.

The large multisurname village of Wantong in Fucheng, Dongguan, which had been a brigade during the commune period, responded with alacrity to the changed circumstances after 1979. It had responded well to collectivization, and a dynamic and highly respected leadership had organized major land reclamation during the Great Leap Forward, which resulted in high grain yields and relatively high per capita incomes even before 1979. Its Party secretary was transferred to the commune level shortly before the reforms got under way. Working closely with a *xian* leadership committed to exploring new economic relationships, he argued for mobilization of the capital and entrepreneurial resources among the substantial number of expatriates in Hong Kong. The success has been dramatic. It was helped by its proximity to the growing Shenzhen SEZ and the dramatic improvement in road communications with Hong Kong.

The consequences of local economic transformation have been major. There has been little mobility of local labor away from Fucheng as the village economies have intensified.[48] Only 34 percent of the indigenous labor force is engaged strictly in household-managed agricultural production. The rest works in enterprises, the bulk of which are run by the village as collective entities. There is no single lineage base to the village (as in neighboring Zengbu),[49] but there is an intense local loyalty, a loyalty that was furthered during the period of intense agricultural collectivism in the 1960s and the 1970s. It has been heightened with the extensive involvement of Hong Kong–based expatriates in the village economy in the 1980s. The links to the global economy are direct. Much of the production of the village-run enterprises, such as garments and plastics, is destined for Hong Kong and for reexport to Europe and North America. Not all the village-run enterprises are industrial. Vegetables are cultivated year round for the Hong Kong market by an enterprise that works jointly with a Hong Kong–based expatriate; it employs wage workers, the bulk of whom are villagers. The local economy is thus closely integrated with the world-system through Hong Kong.

The consequences for village households are various. In terms of economic strategies, none of the economically active households are engaged in subsistence production, and most are multisector households. Rapid economic advance has given rise to increased demand for household division, hence the number of nuclear households is higher than in all other villages,

48. On the contrary, growth in the number of enterprises in the *zhen* as a whole (there were 346 enterprises in 1987, of which 118 were wholly engaged in the processing of materials for the international market [*wailai jiagong*]) has resulted in the recruitment of several thousand workers from outside the area, many of whom are not Cantonese speakers.

49. See Potter and Potter, *China's Peasants*, esp. 251–69. Zengbu is across the river from Wantong, the village I surveyed in Fucheng, and draws the bulk of its brides from the village.

except for the fruit-growing village of Tsimkong (in Luogang), where rapid economic growth has also been marked.[50]

Management of the household (*dangjia*) is least likely to be in the hands of the household head (40.3 percent) than in the other sample villages and is almost as frequently (38.7 percent) in the hands of the spouse of the head. There are proportionately fewer female household heads in Wantong than in the other villages. Women in south China have long been noted for a high degree of economic independence. It is tempting to conclude that increased economic participation of Wantong women in wage labor has enhanced their importance as family managers. There is a common argument that women are increasingly marginalized as incorporation into the global economy grows.[51] The impact of incorporation into the world-system has been very dramatic for Wantong. It has not been at the expense of marginalizing women indigenous to the area.[52]

The fruit-growing village of Tsimkong (in Luogang) has prospered in the reform period but not as a consequence of global incorporation. Its major comparative advantage is a long history of growing fruit (oranges, lichee, and pineapple). Reform of the price system and the resurgence of private marketing have caused rapid increases in household income. Household economic strategy is less elaborate than in Wantong; it involves maximum allocation of household labor in highly commercialized agricultural production. There are only a few multisector households and none involved in subsistence production. There is little out-migration and a virtual absence of kin abroad or in Hong Kong or Macao. Household division in the wake of heightened economic opportunities has been marked, and the number of nuclear households is proportionately large. Household management, however, is typically in the hands of (male) household heads who both allocate household labor and retain control over its financial resources. The intensification of agricultural-sector activities, driven as they are by domestic

50. Margery Wolf, *Revolution Postponed: Women in Contemporary China*, discusses the issues of household division based on observations she made throughout China in the early 1980s, which, given earlier work in rural Taiwan, are instructive. See esp. 224–26.

51. The "classic" study is Esther Boserup, *Women's Role in Economic Development* (London: Allen and Unwin, 1970); Lourdes Beneria and Gita Sen, "Class and Gender Inequalities and Women's Role in Economic Development: Theoretical and Practical Implications," *Feminist Studies* 8, no. 1: 157–74; Also, J. C. Robinson, "Of Women and Washing Machines: Employment, Housework and the Reproduction of Motherhood in Socialist China," *China Quarterly*, no. 101 (March 1985): 32–57.

52. The same cannot be said of wage-workers who are recruited from outside the area. Large numbers of young unmarried females have been recruited to work in the Fucheng enterprises. They are paid well by local Chinese standards, and their accommodation, though spartan, is adequate. They are provided with subsidized food and have access to modest medical services. They are simply wage-workers. They do not participate in management or decision making. It is expected that they will return to their native places when they reach marriageable age.

market demands, seems to have done little to enhance roles for women in the household.

The other two villages in the eastern and central delta are different. Naamshui is less involved in the economic transformation of Leliu than other villages in the *zhen*. There has been a persistent inability, however, to develop industrial enterprises and thereby diversify the village economy. As a consequence, a large portion of the labor force remains in agricultural production, but significant numbers (40 percent), and most of the men under forty, have left the village and often Leliu itself. They work as carpenters, decorators, and temporary workers in construction and in commerce and transportation. They regularly return to the village, but they have no continuing role in village-based production activities. The village agricultural economy is dominated by women, despite the demise of sericulture, and by older men who have contracted fishponds, either individually or (which is more common) in cooperation with men from other households.

Village households make a steady living, if not spectacular by local standards (per capita income is about 1,100 yuan, slightly below the level of the *zhen*). One reason for the failure to diversify the village economy is that it is in a remote corner of the *zhen*. Its Hong Kong expatriates are few in number, and the village lacks the "connections" (*guanxi*) that have been so critical for the success of other villages in Shunde. There is an intense village solidarity, and the organization of production does not differ dramatically from its practice in the 1960s and 1970s. Fish production is organized about cooperative principles, and income from the contracted fishponds is distributed (*fen hong*) on an annual basis. The collective health care system works well, there are pensions, and only two "five-guarantee" households.[53]

Household economic strategy is to maximize opportunities in the cash-cropping skills that Naamshui has long developed, while placing its younger male members outside the village economy. Household division has been less pronounced than in other villages, which have experienced more dramatic internal change in the 1980s. Leliu has the fewest nuclear households and rather more stem households (35 percent) than others in the sample villages in the central and eastern delta. Household management is disproportionately in the hands of household heads, and only 7.2 percent of spouses assume these duties. It has the largest proportion of households with unusual structures, including a "collective" household of men, two headed by older unmarried women who keep house for their (as yet unmarried) brothers, and the only case in the sample of a household in

---

53. Five-guarantee households are those (normally elderly) with insufficient family resources to provide food, clothing, shelter, medical care, and a burial, which are provided (guaranteed) by the collective.

which the wife of the head is working elsewhere. Shunde in the past was distinguished by unusual domestic arrangements, of which delayed-transfer marriage was the most notable. Such distinctive practices are still clearly discernible.[54]

Ngawu, in Renhe, has also changed less dramatically than some other villages in the delta. It, too, is firmly agricultural and has only a small enterprise sector. A significant proportion of its (male) labor force is working outside the village. Ngawu has large numbers of expatriates abroad. They are, however, Overseas Chinese, many resident in Canada. The impact of Overseas Chinese kinsmen on local economies is distinctive and does not translate into economic transformation of the kind experienced in those parts of the delta where Hong Kong expatriates are numerous. There is a further complication in Renhe: it is a grain area with little commercialized crop production; it is too far away from the Guangzhou market to develop fully a specialization in vegetables; its local leadership also had many reservations about the responsibility system and was very tardy with its implementation.

Ngawu has not been able to capitalize on the opportunities to transform its system of production. A large proportion of the households remain in subsistence production. Household strategy therefore relies heavily on meeting basic grain requirements and in placing household members in nonagricultural production outside the village to augment household income. Only a few village households have members working in the *zhen*-managed enterprises, and there are only a few enterprises at the village level to absorb local surplus labor. The out-migration of household labor is therefore substantial but predominantly male.

Household division is not marked, and household structure reflects patterns that may have been more typical of a previous generation.[55] Ngawu has the largest proportion of joint households (9.0 percent) and also the lowest proportion of isolates (7.0 percent). Perhaps because of the frequent absence of household heads, there are relatively more spouses (21.1 percent) or individuals other than the head or spouse of the head (15.8 percent) who assume the role of household manager. The village economy has not been affected by incorporation into the global economy. Out-migration was important in the past as substantial numbers went abroad. Its émigrés,

54. The distinctive marriage system, which many attribute to its underlying economic base, is outlined in Janice Stockard, *Daughters of the Canton Delta*, esp. 1–30 and 134–66. See chapter 7 in this volume, by Helen Siu, which deals with this form of marriage and its implications in adjacent Zhongshan.

55. A 1930s study in the delta indicates rather more complex households (63 percent) and fewer isolates (3 percent) than appears to be the case in the contemporary period. See Lewis S. C. Smythe, "The Composition of the Chinese Family," *Chin-ling Hsueh-pao* 5, no. 1 (1935), cited in Parish and Whyte, *Family and Village*, 134.

however, have had little effect on village economic change in the contemporary period. Out-migration, on a temporary basis, is still important as household members find work in the burgeoning economy of the delta. They remain involved in household economic tasks and return at periods of heavy seasonal labor demands in their household responsibility fields. Their contribution of labor and earnings from outside employment is important for the well-being of village households. New economic opportunities appear to have no major effects on household structure in Ngawu.

THE WESTERN DELTA:
THE OVERSEAS CHINESE CONNECTION

Finally, I want to discuss some of the features of the distinctive western delta, the homeland of North Americans of Chinese origin.[56] Overseas Chinese have always been deeply conscious of their membership in elaborate kin groups and have remained fiercely loyal to their ancestral points of origin. Chinese communities abroad were constructed, in the past at least, about a set of organizations that had at their core principles of fictive kinship (family or surname associations) or common origin. It is the loyalty to ancestral points of origin on the part of expatriates that calls forth a willingness, even after decades abroad, to donate to homeland projects. It is this understanding that has been so important for local leadership in production units in the Pearl River delta to encourage the involvement of its expatriates in local economic development in the 1980s.

The great majority of households in Duanfen have relatives overseas. They are described as "Overseas Chinese dependents" (*qiaojuan*). A small proportion of households do not have kinsmen abroad. Among the *qiaojuan* households there are those whose kinsmen abroad are distant and others who have close kinsmen with a direct relationship, either through marriage or descent, such as husbands, wives, parents, or children. The closeness of relationships will determine the amount of support that relatives abroad will provide and, in the modern period, the likelihood of obtaining an immigration visa and the possibility of joining kinsmen abroad. In the western delta in the 1980s, family and kinship loyalty has resulted in the creation of distinct household strategies among villagers with extensive overseas link-

56. I have benefited from numerous conversations with Dr. Woon Yuen-fong of the University of Victoria about the western delta region. She has generously shared her findings from Chikan in neighboring Kaiping *xian*. See her "Social Change and Continuity in South China: Overseas Chinese and the Guan Lineage of Kaiping County, 1949–1987," *China Quarterly*, no. 118 (June 1989): 324–44; and her "International Links and Socio-economic Development of Modern China: An Emigrant Community in Guangdong," *Modern China* 16, no. 2 (1990): 139–72; "From Mao to Deng: Life Satisfaction Among Rural Women in an Emigrant Community in South China," *Australian Journal of Chinese Affairs* 25 (January 1991): 139–69.

ages. It has also resulted in the extensive revival of lineages, which had seemed forever compromised by land reform, collective forms of economic management, and firmly held ideological positions.

In the western delta it is important to distinguish the proportion of households with relatives abroad and, among these, whether their relatives are directly or more distantly related. It is possible to suggest that there are different strategies employed by households in the region, which are determined in large measure by the extent of their links with kinsmen abroad.

The consequences of extensive out-migration provide a possible explanation for the large (17 percent) proportion of "isolate" family types in the Duanfen village complex of Kongluen. Many are older women who have not yet left to join family in North America or have decided to stay. There is also a disproportionately large number of household heads who are widows (38.5 percent).[57] The high proportion of widowed household heads is a possible consequence of the high rates of out-migration to overseas settlements. Some men left and never returned or broke contact with their homeland villages. Some may have remarried abroad and established separate families. Contacts between the homeland and the points of migration were frequently disrupted and were severed for almost a decade during the Japanese occupation. Mortality was also very high in Taishan during the Japanese occupation.

Delayed household division (and the out-migration of recently divided families) results in a very small proportion of nuclear households (31 percent). There is a correspondingly large number of stem families (46 percent). Data on responsibilities of household management reflect some of the distinctive features of the consequences of extensive out-migration. There are more heads of households responsible for economic management in Kongluen than in any other village (69.8 percent) and, correspondingly, the lowest incidence of spouses taking on these responsibilities (4.6 percent). This can be partly explained by the large number of isolates and widowed household heads. Equally, household management by other than the household head (or spouse) (26.9 percent) is matched only in Ngawu, where the incidence of complex household forms, as in Kongluen, is high. In both, the numbers of Overseas Chinese households are large.

Among Pearl River delta villages, remittances have a marked significance for household income only in the Overseas Chinese homeland. This is true among households in Kongluen, where remittances are still the major determinant of income disparities. Household income per capita is

---

57. For the total sample, household heads who were widowers or widows constituted 19.0 percent. The proportions in the other sample villages are as follows: Naamshui, 13.8 percent; Tsimgong, 18.2 percent; Ngawu, 9.1 percent and Wantong, 16.2 percent. The number of widowers was less than 10 percent of the total number of widowers and widows.

highest among those with relatives abroad and lowest among those who do not have relatives abroad.[58]

Non-*qiaojuan* households have the fewest resources and must rely therefore on their own abilities. As a result, these households are more deeply involved in wage labor than are *qiaojuan* households. Their male members, for example, are the backbone personnel of the construction teams that have become so important for Taishan (and neighboring Kaiping and Enping) in meeting the labor needs of the Pearl River delta construction boom. Such activities take workers away from the villages for long periods, and they may return only infrequently but, as in Ngawu, typically for the busy season of transplanting and harvesting in midsummer. Their wives tend to bear a disproportionate share of agricultural tasks. Those who do remain in the villages and concentrate on agricultural production tend to contract larger amounts of land and to expand into lucrative sidelines, either within the agriculture sector or into transportation or commercial activities. Such households often become "specialist households" of one kind or another.

Distant *qiaojuan* households have remittances but have little or no opportunity to contemplate out-migration. Such households are therefore also deeply involved in local economic activity. As *qiaojuan* households they have some advantages when compared with the non-*qiaojuan* households. They have remittances that can become working capital. They have connections with relatives abroad who can become the source of capital inputs by either bringing in (tax free) or sending items that are unobtainable or in short supply, such as machinery, electric motors or generators, building materials, trucks, or motorcycles.

Changes in policy toward direct *qiaojuan* families have resulted in the return of confiscated property. In addition, since 1979 direct *qiaojuan* families have been leaving in large numbers as part of family reunification policies in such countries as Canada and the United States. As a consequence, there is a considerable amount of property standing empty, which is often managed by the remaining (distant) *qiaojuan* kinsmen. Such properties can be used as an economic resource. Thus, while non-*qiaojuan* families are typically engaged as wage laborers or on their own account in farm production, distant *qiaojuan* households are typically engaged in enterprises in the private sector or are in partnership with *zhen*-run enterprises. The access to capital by distant *qiaojuan* households has allowed them to contract formerly collectively managed facilities (such as orchards, general stores, or repair facilities) at the village level and therefore augment their participation in agriculture with private production activities in the tertiary sector.

58. This was also the pattern of income distribution even before the reform in the rural economy got under way, despite the obstacles that sometimes appeared for those households receiving remittances. It appears, however, that income differences have narrowed in the 1980s.

Direct *qiaojuan* households were the most advantaged in the 1980s in terms of both remittances and their potential ability to leave. As direct *qiaojuan* they were most severely affected by ideological hostility and the lack of labor power before 1979. Often bitter memories of the past and lack of confidence about the future increase their desire to leave the homeland. This group of households expects to leave, and, despite enjoying all the advantages that their distant *qiaojuan* kinsmen have in the villages, they are less committed to long-term economic benefit in the homeland. Many, particularly the women, who were left behind at an earlier period, are older, and their only economic activities relate to food production for themselves and whatever dependents remain. Older men who may be waiting for immigration visas spend a great deal of time socializing with their friends in the teahouses. The major concern of younger members of such households is preparing for emigration, and they spend much of their time acquiring a foreign language, typically English, or some other useful and marketable skill. Their levels of education are often high.

The possibility of family reunification abroad and migration away from the homeland has some marked effects on the social structure of villages throughout those parts of the Pearl River delta where direct *qiaojuan* households are concentrated. In Taishan, as well as other parts of the *siyi* area of migration to North America,[59] while the architecture stands as a testimony to foreign remittances in the past, many houses stand empty, some smaller villages are virtually deserted, and there is the constant movement of population away from the area. Over ten thousand people have left Duanfen since 1979, including at least three Party secretaries. There is a curious contradiction. On the one hand, some of the more prosperous residents abroad have returned to the homeland and donated to schools, hospitals, libraries, and other public monuments, often renewing their association with their native places after an interval of decades. On the other hand, there are households who are leaving to join their kinsmen in North America permanently, leaving behind splendid houses, familiarity, comfort, even a modicum of prestige, for an uncertain future in an alien environment.

In the late twentieth century the desire to go abroad is as intense as it was in the earlier part of the century. There is far more contact with a wider range of relatives living abroad, and a detailed knowledge of life outside China is certainly present. There are also visitors, with their obvious affluence and their ability to dispense largesse. There is also television with its seductive images. The direct *qiaojuan* households are awaiting their

59. Cantonese: *sze-yap*, literally "four districts." The four contiguous and culturally distinct *xian* (Xinhui, Kaiping, Taishan, and Enping) that constitute the ancestral points of origin for the great majority of Chinese in the Americas.

chances to leave, knowing that there is a certain inevitability. The distant *qiaojuan* and non-*qiaojuan* households are anxious to marry their daughters to direct *qiaojuan* or, better, an actual Overseas Chinese. In this way, over time, the entire household can be sponsored and take up residence abroad.[60]

LINEAGE REVIVAL

A dominant and distinctive feature of villages throughout the Pearl River delta is that they are lineage villages. Chinese lineages are property-holding corporations that socially integrate groups of households whose male heads trace their descent to an apical ancestor. They may be simple, small, and of only shallow genealogical depth, occupying a hamlet or a village fragment. They can also be large and complex, have a history of many tens of generations, and have a multisettlement character. In Duanfen a third of the households are surnamed Mei. Their development before 1949 was not dramatically different from that of the Guan in Chikan in neighboring Kaiping, as is described by Woon.[61] In the 1930s they struggled with the Jiang (Cantonese: Kong) who occupy eight adjacent villages (Kongluen) over the control of a major market. In the center of the main Jiang village stand three enormous ancestral halls. There are lesser halls and "study halls" (*shushi*) in the satellite villages.

During land reform in Duanfen, as well as other parts of south China, lineage properties were redistributed. At certain points in the history of the People's Republic of China, lineage rituals were attacked as feudal remnants, genealogies were ideologically suspect and hidden away, and ancestral tablets were destroyed—if not in 1958, most certainly in 1966. Ancestral halls, the most imposing structures in many villages, became team headquarters, warehouses, or workshops, and in some instances they were pulled down. Their granite floors and lintels became raw materials to repair village pathways and sometimes to build piggeries. After land reform, the operation of the south China lineage was compromised and its property basis was dismembered. At the same time, collectivization and rural

60. Some data on American Chinese who take brides from Taishan can be found in Wu Xingci and Li Zhen, "*Gum San Haak* in the 1980s: A Study of Chinese Who Return to Taishan County for Marriage," *Amerasia* 14, no. 2 (1988): 32–34. The article emphasizes the desire to leave and the high educational achievement of brides. It also indicates that the SES of the grooms is not high.

61. In Chikan, the Guan lineages occupied forty natural villages and competed, before 1949, with the powerful Situ lineage to control Chikan *zhen*, the intermediate market town. See Woon Yuen-fong, *Social Organization in South China, 1911–1949: The Case of the Kuan Lineage of K'ai-ping County* (Ann Arbor: Center for Chinese Studies, 1984).

development policies kept intact groups of families who were socially integrated by common descent. Old relationships and old conflicts could readily operate even in a changed political environment.[62]

Village architecture is a constant reminder of the principles of lineage organization, despite the efforts to dismember the lineage as an economic and ritual entity. The carefully crafted policies to destroy lineages in the Overseas Chinese areas (and elsewhere) reflected a sophisticated understanding of the operation of a Chinese lineage. In the revival of many aspects of lineage organization in the 1980s, in Duanfen and elsewhere, the impact of the foreign links are key.

Since 1950 the issue of how to attract investment by ethnic Chinese abroad has been an important and troublesome issue in the formulation of Overseas Chinese policy,[63] and it readily fell victim to conflicting domestic political currents in the past. After 1979 investment was actively sought abroad, and the involvement of both Overseas Chinese and émigrés from Hong Kong and Macao in the new economic program were important. In the traditional areas of Overseas Chinese migration, the willingness of Overseas Chinese to commit substantial funds to public projects depended on the resolution of some outstanding grievances. The fate of their lineage organizations was one of these.

While the full elaboration of all aspects of the operation of lineages cannot be contemplated, many of them are once again practiced. Graves have been repaired, rituals are performed at the graves of apical ancestors, ancestral halls are being restored, ritual feasts occur in the halls once more, lineage libraries are being refurbished, and lineage officers have begun to act as agents for members of the lineage, similar to the way the administrators of lineage trusts intervened on behalf of members in the period before 1949.

The restoration work that occurs is made possible by donations from local and external contributors. The major donations are from abroad. Funds are remitted through a network that is worldwide but energized from Hong Kong. The network is maintained by a sophisticated and widespread communications system. From the western delta there flows a large stream of local publications that focus on the reliance of local areas on the contributions of kinsmen and fellow countrymen overseas in maintaining local

62. Anita Chan, Richard Madsen, and Jonathan Unger, *Chen Village* (Berkeley: University of California Press, 1984), esp. 16–40; the point is also argued by Potter and Potter, *China's Peasants*, who state, "A core group of close patrilineal kinsmen has now replaced the collective as the major group larger than the household in the organization of agricultural production" (266). There is no evidence from their account that lineage revival has been carried to quite the same degree in Dongguan as in the western delta regions.

63. Stephen Fitzgerald, *China and the Overseas Chinese* (Cambridge: Cambridge University Press, 1972), 121–26.

integrity. Local history and local tradition are emphasized, and while economic advances receive careful attention, they are seen to be in harmony with a local cultural base that is firmly rooted in kinship.

In the Overseas Chinese areas, schools and education funded by the Overseas Chinese speak of upward mobility and lineage integrity. Before 1949 in Taishan, class and kinship were linked to overseas connections. In the thirty years after land reform, those connections were often a liability, although they continued to be of importance. In the past ten years, the liabilities have become advantages and have contributed to a developmental process that reflects national policies but, as a consequence of intense and distinctive patterns of overseas linkages, has developed some differentiating features of its own.

CONCLUSION

I have outlined in this chapter some of the features of Pearl River delta households and kin groups in the contemporary period. The delta has become caught up in a major rural transformation in the wake of reform efforts that began in the late 1970s. This process of economic change has proceeded further and faster than in any other region in the People's Republic of China.

Part of the explanation for the dramatic economic developments in the delta is its proximity to Hong Kong, which experienced its own transformation beginning in the 1950s. Hong Kong shifted from an economy based on entrepôt trade to become a major manufacturing center and a crucial part of the world system of banking and trade. A population largely of Pearl River delta émigrés, in concert with others from the Lower Yangzi and eastern Guangdong, led in establishing the links with the global economy. When reform initiatives were attempted in China after 1979, the entrepreneurial energies of Hong Kong were actively sought. Guangdong province was given distinctive authority to establish linkages with the world-system. These were developed through Hong Kong. By the late 1980s, Guangdong, and the Pearl River delta in particular, had become firmly incorporated into the world-system.

The consequences of that incorporation for Pearl River delta households and kin groups has been the focus of this chapter. Long an area of intense commercialization, the rural economy of the Pearl River became constrained by the assumptions of development policy for much of the three decades after 1949. The cellular character of rural China was reinforced by a high degree of bureaucratic control. The strategies of rural households in the Pearl River delta until the reform period were compromised by administrative practices that linked them firmly to their villages and to agricultural pursuits. Certain forms of kinship organization, notably lineages, and their ritual expression, were targets of official hostility. There appeared to be a commonality of structural form for peasant households across the Pearl River delta after land reform, despite some variation in local economic possibilities.

I have examined the effects of recent economic change for rural households in five villages across the delta. I have suggested that the ability of local administrative units to adapt to policy changes has increased economic opportunities for households. The ability to establish linkages with kinsmen abroad has been especially critical in generating local-level economic change and moving a village economy away from a reliance on subsistence agriculture. In those villages where economic changes have been widespread, peasant households have taken full advantage of the local transformation and have allocated household labor among the variety of new opportunities that are contained within the reformed village economy. In the Dongguan village of Wantong, where extensive incorporation into the global economy through the entrepreneurial activities of Hong Kong–based expatriates has been particularly marked, household economic strategy has been characterized by an ability to allocate household labor in a wide array of economic activities. In the Luogang village of Tsimkong, where there are few overseas connections, the impact of global incorporation has been slight. Economic growth has been substantial as a consequence of reform policies. An intensification of the village's commercialized agriculture has seen households committing their energies and maximizing returns by expanding the cultivation and sale of fruit and vegetables. The sources of economic growth in the two villages differ. In Wantong, joint economic enterprise between the village and Hong Kong–based entrepreneurs has added to the economic inventory. In Tsimkong, existing economic capabilites have been intensified, and its increased production meets the needs of the domestic market. In both instances, however, the consequence of rapid local economic growth for household structure has been substantial and has contributed to increased household division, which explains the large number of nuclear households. The issue here is one of a flexible response to economic opportunity, which was articulated by Cohen and specifically addressed by Harrell in this volume. Structural change in a village economy may have important consequences, not merely for the productive role of women but also for their position as household managers. The firm incorporation of Wantong into the global economy has augmented the role of women in household structure. In Tsimkong, where growth has not been a consequence of structural change, the dominance of male household heads as household managers has been maintained.

Where local structural change and economic growth have been less marked, the options for peasant households and the adaptive strategies that they have adopted have been fewer and different. In such contexts, village economies have been unable to absorb the labor that newer production arrangements in agriculture have released. In the rapidly growing economy of the Pearl River delta in the 1980s, economic opportunities have generally increased. Peasant households in villages in which structural change and economic growth have been modest have deployed their younger male members outside the village to take advantage of economic opportunities that the home villages cannot supply. The degree of change in household structure in such contexts is lessened. Household characteristics such as the incidence of household division or the allocation of responsibility for family management are determined less by change within the village economy than by the inability of the village economy to generate change and sufficient growth to absorb the labor surplus.

In the areas where Overseas Chinese ties are widespread, there are distinctive external linkages. Extensive out-migration has had profound structural consequences for peasant households. Linkages overseas only rarely translate into local economic transformation. Overseas Chinese have close and intense relationships to their ancestral homeland. Gifts by Overseas Chinese to their native places in the 1980s have contributed significantly to the infrastructure but not to major structural changes in the local economy. In contrast to the past, entrepreneurial activities by Overseas Chinese in the homeland are not extensive. The economic impact of Overseas Chinese monetary transfers is indirect. The impact of remittances for households in an Overseas Chinese area is, however, very great. Household strategies among peasant households in Overseas Chinese areas appear to be determined by the presence or absence of overseas linkages and the closeness of kinship to overseas relatives, when they are present. The absence of men has major effects for household form, household division, and household management. The very considerable sentiment for the homeland that exists among Overseas Chinese has led to regeneration of lineages to a degree unparalleled in those parts of the delta where the Overseas Chinese presence is less marked.

Chinese rural households in the Pearl River delta have been caught up in a change of great proportions during the 1980s. The change has been uneven in its effects across the region as a consequence of varying local characteristics, one of the most important of which has been the nature and intensity of relations with their kinsmen abroad. There are many continuities with the past. There is also a striking capacity on the part of peasant households in the Pearl River delta to respond creatively to opportunities and formulate strategies to maximize their possibilities. Households in the villages I surveyed are aware of the implications of the reform period for their well-being and have taken steps to deal with them. Some have been bold and innovative in their response. The local contexts have determined what the nature of their response can be. For delta households the past ten years have seen their material standard of living improve significantly. They have benefited directly or indirectly from the incorporation of the broad region into the global economy. They do not appear at this time to have been overwhelmed by the negative consequences of globalization, which has led to the undoing of peasantries in some other contexts. Their corporate kinship structures with their instrinsic flexibility have buffered the impact of change. They have been able to hold the world-system at arms length to an important degree and to protect themselves from some of its most pernicious effects.

PART TWO

Marriage

SIX

Family Strategies and Structures in Rural North China

Mark Selden

This chapter explores familial strategies and structures in response to socioeconomic and political changes over two generations in a peripheral region of rural North China. The primary data are household surveys conducted in Wugong village, Hebei, in 1978, at the end of the era of mobilizational collectivism; in 1984, two years after the reform agenda began to transform the village collective structure; and in 1987, when the household contract system had taken root. The surveys, which shed light on familial, demographic, and marital patterns from the 1920s to the 1980s, are supplemented by interviews conducted in the course of more than a decade of fieldwork in this and other villages in Raoyang county and throughout central Hebei. The focus of the study is on familial responses to macro political and economic change over the last half century, notably to the antimarket collectivism and the *hukou* population control system implemented by a powerful party-state from the 1950s forward, and the contractual and market-oriented reforms and birth control measures of the 1980s.

This study advances and assesses three hypotheses concerning changing familial strategies and structures in rural China in the era of mobilizational

Many of the ideas explored here are the product of collaborative research with Edward Friedman, Paul Pickowicz, and Kay Johnson. For background on Wugong and rural Hebei, see Friedman, Pickowicz, and Selden (1991). I am indebted to Richard Ratcliff, who introduced me to computer design and helped conceptualize computer elements of the survey, as well as to Zhu Hong and especially Shih Miin-wen for research assistance in the design and implementation of computer manipulation of the data. Cheng Tiejun, a sociologist, and a native of Raoyang county, who lived and worked in Wugong for several years in the 1970s, has been a source of knowledge, sources, and insight into the issues explored here. Deborah Davis and Stevan Harrell provided insightful critique of successive drafts, as did Edward Friedman, Gail Arrigo, Joan Smith, and an anonymous reader of the penultimate draft.

collectivism (the 1950s through the 1970s) and contractual and market-oriented reforms (since the 1980s):[1]

1. Collectivization, by weakening the household as a productive unit, undermined the economic rationale for the extended family. The result was a sharp reduction in average household size and in the number of stem and joint families as smaller nuclear families became the norm in the years 1955–1980.

2. Collectivization, the suppression of private markets, and restrictions on population mobility from the early 1950s through the 1970s, reinforced village involution in two distinct but intertwined senses. First, the ensemble of policies associated with mobilizational collectivism reversed the historical tendency of progressive expansion of the economic and social world of the peasant from the village to the standard marketing community and beyond. Beginning in the 1950s, the world of rural residents contracted back toward the natural village (see Skinner 1964–65). Second, with extravillage income-earning opportunities reduced or eliminated, with rapid population growth continuing through the 1970s, with expansion in the number of labor days per capita, and with collectives absorbing virtually unlimited supplies of labor, labor input increased substantially while marginal productivity of labor declined (see Geertz 1963; Huang 1985, 7–14; Huang 1990, 11–18; Chayanov 1986). This chapter explores some of the manifestations of village involution at the level of the family, particularly the pronounced tendency toward intravillage marriage, shrinking familial size, and simplification of structure associated with mobilizational collectivism in the years 1955–1980.

3. The resurgence of the household economy and the market in the 1980s reversed a number of trends of the collective era, giving rise to a bimodal pattern in household structures. On the one hand, rural household division accelerated as contracts took effect and the central economic role of households was restored. On the other hand, we observe signs of a resurgence of extended families, notably among entrepreneurial households emphasizing nonagricultural activities, capital accumulation, and expanded access to labor power, in ways that invite comparison with pre-land-reform patterns including the relationship between social class and family size and structure. Both cases suggest the growing autonomy and economic role of the household. At the same time, however, the continued strength and penetration of the state is revealed in the enforcement of the one-child (later the tacit two-child) family planning policy.

These theses are examined in relation to Wugong village, with comparisons to patterns observed in other rural regions and communities.

---

1. My approach to mobilizational collectivism and the political economy of reform is spelled out in Selden 1992.

WUGONG VILLAGE

Wugong, a village founded more than thirteen hundred years ago during the Sui dynasty, is located in Raoyang county in south central Hebei, one of the poorest areas of the North China Plain. Although the village is just 120 miles south of Beijing and Tianjin, throughout the twentieth century Raoyang has remained a poor and peripheral region, whose saline and alkaline soil and dearth of above-ground water sources together with periodic eruptions of drought and flood have proved inhospitable to agriculture. Equally important, its primitive transportation and communications—no railroad, poor highways, and lack of waterways[2]—left the region beyond the pale of dynamic metropolitan centers of industry, commerce, and modern thought as they experienced capitalist development and incorporation in the global economy in the first half of the twentieth century.

In the 1940s the region was incorporated in the networks of power that eventually brought the Communist Party to power. Its very peripheral character proved advantageous in insulating the locality from Japanese control and forging bonds of nation and community that linked Wugong and Raoyang to the Party and the army. Raoyang was located in the Central Hebei base area, one of the few plains regions to sustain organized resistance throughout the anti-Japanese war. Beginning in 1943 with a four-household land-pooling group, Wugong villagers embarked on a path of cooperative transformation that would eventually transform a marginal and poor community into a thriving provincial and even a national model of cooperation, before receding into anonymity with the resurgence of the household economy and market forces in the 1980s (Friedman, Pickowicz, and Selden 1991).

In 1978, when research began, Wugong was a large and relatively prosperous wheat- and cotton-growing village with a registered population of 2,552. With per capita distributed collective income of 190 yuan, it was more than 50 percent richer than the second most prosperous of the ten villages that constituted the Wugong Commune, and three times richer than the poorest village. It was also approximately 50 percent higher than China's average 1978 rural per capita income of 133 yuan (*Changes and Development in China*, 242). Team Three, the largest and most prosperous of three teams and the focus of our household surveys, had a 1978 population

2. Until 1954 the Hutuo River was Raoyang's lifeline to Tianjin for several months each year. Damming the river eliminated this connection to the major commercial and industrial center in the region. The state's attack on the market and its controls on population movement reinforced the county's isolation. Raoyang was a major casualty of the general prioritizing of irrigation over transportation and of self-reliant production over market ties that characterized national development from the 1950s through the 1970s. A new Beijing-Guangzhou railroad, in the initial stages of construction, is scheduled to pass through Wugong.

of 232 households and 996 people: 514 females, 480 males, and 2 whose gender was not recorded. This was comparable in size to many brigades in rural China, the size being emblematic of the high levels of collectivization ("advanced socialist production relations") maintained since the 1950s. In 1984, as household- and market-oriented reforms were beginning to take root in a region and a village whose leaders long resisted reform, the registered population of the team was 244 households with 939 people: 480 females and 459 males.[3] In 1987 its population had dropped to 845 people in 250 households.

As the village that boasted the oldest continuous cooperative in Hebei, the home of national model peasant Geng Changsuo, and, beginning in 1953, the site of a provincial tractor station, Wugong attained national prominence as a large-scale mechanized cooperative. It sustained its status and special access to state resources through the twists and turns of national policy until the early 1980s. In the late 1970s and early 1980s, as national policies changed, Hebei province remained a bastion of opposition to contractual and market-oriented reforms. Wugong too stood in the forefront of defenders of the collective road that had brought fame and fortune to a once peripheral community. Thus it was not until 1982, following the ouster of its provincial patrons, that Wugong adopted the contract system, and even then the collective continued to play a prominent role in both agricultural and sideline production. Like many other model villages, such as Dazhai and Long Bow, just across the border in Shanxi, Wugong was the last village in its commune to ratify fundamental changes in the collective regimen (Hinton 1990, 31–47; 124–39). Our data capture familial dynamics spanning the decades prior to land reform, the collective era, and the early years of the contractual reforms of the 1980s.

CHANGING PATTERNS IN FAMILY SIZE AND STRUCTURE

Land reform, collectivization, and market closure led to village involution and to important changes in household size and structure. The most important of these changes were the reduction in average household size and

3. The 1978 officially registered Team Three population was 232 households with 1,053 people. This number included, however, 53 women who had left the team, in most cases by marriage, and in many instances 30–40 years earlier. Our data indicate that they neither contributed financially nor had husbands or children residing in Team Three. We have excluded such individuals from our sample, while retaining others who lived and worked or studied outside the village. These include spouses who work outside and provide financial support to family members in the village, and youth who were studying or serving in the military. All of these maintain important local ties and most are expected to return to the village. In 1978 there were 49 individuals working outside the village, 32 holding jobs in factories, as teachers or cadres, 11 in the army, and 6 studying in universities or technical schools. All of these are included in our Team Three sample.

TABLE 6.1.   Frequency of Household Size in North China Villages,
1929–1933

No. of household members	North China Villages, 1933 (Gamble)	North China Villages, 1929–31 (Buck)	North China Villages, 1929–31 (Chiao)
1	5.6%	2.8%	3.8%
2	8.2	8.4	8.6
3	16.1	14.4	13.4
4	20.1	17.4	16.3
5	16.1	17.0	15.5
6	10.6	13.0	13.7
7	8.7	9.1	8.9
8	5.2	5.8	6.1
9	3.5	3.9	3.6
10	2.6	1.6	3.0
11 and more	7.3%	5.8%	6.9%
Total persons	5,217	17,581	28,738
Total households	1,022	3,317	5,178
Average household size	5.1	5.3	5.5

SOURCES: Sidney Gamble, *North China Villages: Social, Political and Economic Activities Before 1933* (Berkeley: University of California Press, 1963), 319. Survey of 1,022 families in rural Beiping and Hebei. John Lossing Buck, *Land Utilization in China* (Nanking: University of Nanking, 1937), 368–69. Survey of 17,581 families in Anhui, Hebei, Henan, Shanxi, Shandong, Shaanxi, and Suiyuan. Chi-ming Chiao, "Rural Population and Vital Statistics for Selected Areas of China, 1929–1931" (Cornell University M.S. in Agriculture, 1933), 7, 17. A sample of 5,178 North China families in Hebei, Shandong, Shanxi, Henan, and Anhui.

number of generations, and the rise to dominance of smaller nuclear families. Data on other communities and regions suggest that many of the demographic changes described below for Wugong reflect broad tendencies found in villages across North China. Our discussion differentiates outcomes specific to a model village from more representative patterns.

Rural surveys of four Hebei villages in the vicinity of Beijing compiled by Sidney Gamble, a large North China sample of 17,581 households studied by John Buck, and Chi-ming Chiao's North China sample of 28,738 households, provide baseline data on household size and structure in rural North China (table 6.1). Gamble found average household size to be 5.1 members, Buck 5.3 members, and Chiao 5.5 members in the 1930s. In Gamble's 1933 sample, 26 percent of households had 7 or more members and 9 percent had 10 or more members (Gamble 1954, 26–27). Twenty-seven percent of Buck's North China households had 7 or more members, including 8 percent with more than 10 members (Buck 1937, 368). Chiao found that 29 percent of households had 7 or more members, including 10 percent with 10 or more members (Chiao 1933, 17).

In the 1930s, household size correlated closely with landownership and wealth. The large household was economically advantaged, and it was only the prosperous that could sustain large households. Greater size facilitated division of labor, diversification, and accumulation. In his 1927 survey of 400 Dingxian farm families, Sidney Gamble found that those with farms of less than 10 mu had an average of 3.8 members, those with 21–30 mu averaged 6.2, and families with over 100 mu averaged 13.5 members. Per capita landownership and wealth increased with size of farm. For example, there was 1.8 mu of land per person in farms of less than 10 mu, 4.1 mu per person in farms of 21–30 mu, and 9.1 mu per person in farms of over 100 mu (Gamble 1954, 84). In his 1929–33 national survey of 16,786 farms, Buck found that in the winter-wheat *gaoliang* areas that included Hebei province, the small farm had an average of 4.7 household members, whereas medium-sized farms had 6.0 members, large farms 8.5 members, and very large farms 10.7 members (Buck 1937, 278).

Comparing Wugong's Team Three in 1978 (table 6.2) with North China in the 1930s, we note the much smaller average household size, just 4.3 members, compared with approximately 5.3 members in the earlier period. By 1978 the number of large households with 7 or more members was small despite the fact that a prosperous village like Wugong could sustain relatively large households compared with poorer communities. In 1978, 11 percent of Team Three households had 7 or more members, the largest being 9 members. By contrast, 26–29 percent of North China households in the 1930s samples had 7 or more members, including nearly 10 percent with 10 or more members. By 1978 household size no longer correlated with wealth measured by per capita household income. Size was above all the product of life-cycle timing. Neither labor power, land, capital, nor special skills were any longer decisive factors in determining household opportunity and income. This meant that there was a close relationship between the ratio of labor power to dependency and per capita household income, but virtually no correlation between household size and per capita income. Households with large numbers of young children had low per capita incomes, but as these children moved into the labor force per capita incomes rose. With marriage and household division, the cycle repeated. We hypothesize that this pattern was widespread throughout rural China in the era of mobilizational collectivism.

In 1978, 25 of Team Three's 232 households boasted three generations, and 2 others had four generations. The 5 largest households had nine members, and just 6 others had eight. The four-generation households were

TABLE 6.2.   Frequency of Household Size in Wugong Village, Team Three, 1978–1987

	Wugong Team 3 1978		Wugong Team 3 1984		Wugong Team 3 1987	
	No.	(%)	No.	(%)	No.	(%)
No. of household members						
1	15	(6.5)	12	(4.9)	2	(0.8)
2	9	(3.9)	32	(13.1)	68	(27.2)
3	33	(14.2)	68	(27.9)	68	(27.2)
4	56	(24.1)	66	(27.0)	70	(28.0)
5	56	(24.1)	37	(15.2)	30	(12.0)
6	38	(16.4)	13	(5.3)	11	(4.4)
7	14	(6.0)	12	(4.9)	1	(0.4)
8	6	(2.6)	1	(0.4)	0	(0)
9	5	(2.2)	2	(0.8)	0	(0)
10	1	(0.4)	4	(1.6)	0	(0)
11 and more	0	(0)	0	(0)	0	(0)
Total persons	996		939		845	
Total households	232		244		250	
Average household size	4.3		3.8		3.4	

those of the deputy Party secretary of the commune and the leader of Team Three. These four-generation households reveal leading Party families living out a contemporary version of the big-family Confucian ideal.

The dominant trend from the 1950s forward, consistent with the logic of collectivization, was from larger to smaller and from complex to nuclear families. The social and economic logic favoring stem and joint families was weakened in a collective milieu. Collectivization reduced the power of the family head over sons once control over land and labor passed from the family to the collective. Stated differently, after 1955 the fortunes of adult males no longer rested as heavily on the goodwill of a father who could assure their incomes and their future. Moreover, the advantages of the large household for achieving prosperity, by facilitating both accumulation and a complex household division of labor, were irrelevant in the collective era. Young men working in the collective earned as much as their fathers through work-point allocations from their teenage years, and there were few outlets for household investment. In short, the economic logic of household accumulation and the extended family was irrelevant in the era of collective agriculture.

To be sure, the collective paid income earned by all members in a lump sum directly to the household head, not to individual earners, perpetuating certain forms of intrahousehold dependency on the family head.[4] The household also remained the primary consumption unit. But sons no longer depended on fathers to provide a share of household land and other property or to organize the household division of labor. Dependence on parents to assure a marriage and provide a home was also reduced if not eliminated in the collective era. In addition, a portion of welfare for the elderly and ill passed from household to collective responsibility, thereby further weakening intergenerational bonds. All these factors strengthened tendencies toward smaller and less complex households, toward reduced intergenerational dependence, and toward earlier household division. This was particularly true in a model village where household production for the market was tightly restricted and the range of collective economic and cultural activities was broad. The fact that model Wugong achieved notable success in birth control by the early 1970s, a decade before most rural communities, strengthened this tendency to reduce household size and complexity.[5]

How widespread was the tendency toward smaller and less complex household structures in rural China in the collective era? Fruitful comparisons in the changing patterns of household size and structure can be made between Wugong in the 1970s and Parish and Whyte's 1973 findings for Guangdong. First, no significant change in household size occurred in Guangdong as a result of collectivization or other factors. Average household size in South China in 1930 was 5.0 members compared with 4.8 members in Guangdong in 1973. By comparison, we have hypothesized that significant reduction in household size in Wugong by the 1970s was a product both of collectivization and of unusual rigor in implementing birth control guidelines in the model village. Why the difference? One important reason is that birth control was not widely propagated or practiced in Guangdong and in much of rural China at the time of Parish and Whyte's 1973 investigation. This situation would change dramatically across the countryside from the late 1970s, bringing north and south into close alignment with respect to fertility. What had changed in Guangdong by 1973 was the fact that both the nuclear family (50%) and the single-person family (12%) had increased sharply in number, improved health care and nutrition reduced mortality, and the number of stem and joint families

4. A fruitful area for future research is control of the family purse along both gender and generational lines, including savings to assure proper marriages and funerals.

5. The population of Wugong village increased from 1,700 in 1955 to 2,413 in 1969, a 42 percent increase, or 2.8 percent per year. Between 1970 and 1975 population increased at a rate slightly less than 1 percent per year, from 2,426 to a peak of 2,567, before declining slowly but steadily to 2,533 in 1979. Wugong's 1984 population of 2,552 remained below the 1975 peak level, and population has subsequently remained stable.

plummeted. Compared with 63 percent in the 1930 South China sample, in 1973 in Guangdong only 39 percent were stem and joint families (Parish and Whyte 1978, 132–36).[6] As in Wugong, we hypothesize that the shift to collective agriculture and the declining role of the family as an economic unit was the primary reason for the change in family structure leading to earlier division and reduction in the number of stem and joint families. At the same time, household size did not change significantly, because of continued high birth rates together with mortality rates substantially lower than those prevailing in the 1930s.

Between 1978 and 1987 significant changes occurred in Team Three household size and composition as household division accelerated following the implementation of household contracts. The 1984 survey gives years of household division for 83 of 244 Team Three households. Forty-four households divided in the five years 1979–83. By comparison, just 10 of the surveyed households indicated that they had divided in the decade 1966–75. The high rate of household division in the years 1979–83 constituted a response at the household level to the preparations for, and then the actual implementation of, contractual and market-oriented reforms.

Changes in household size and composition in the wake of partial decollectivization were particularly visible and significant among the elderly. Between 1978 and 1984, the average Team Three household size fell from 4.3 to 3.8 persons, and the number of two-person households increased from 9 to 32. Among two-person households, couples aged sixty-two and older increased from four to nineteen. By the mid-1980s, it was common for both spouses to remain alive, active, and self-sufficient long after their fifties, the time when most households customarily divided.

In 1978 fifteen people over age sixty-five lived alone, often in close proximity to sons or other family support networks. These included three women, ages seventy-nine, eighty, and eighty-three, two of whom continued to earn significant work-points permitting self-support with dignity. Their living alone was nevertheless a sensitive issue. Questionnaires repeatedly recorded the unsolicited information that sons performed household tasks and otherwise supported aged parents who lived alone. Responsibility for the aged remained a family affair. But whatever the assistance rendered, if we look at the utterly bare hovels in which some elderly people resided alone, and observe that such people frequently lacked even tea leaves to add to boiling water when serving a guest, it is difficult to escape the conclusion that in rural China as elsewhere the transition to the nuclear family imposes a heavy price on the rural elderly. By 1984 the number of single-

---

6. Sulamith Potter and Jack Potter, *China's Peasants: The Anthropology of a Revolution*, 217, found a smaller percentage of Zengbu brigade (Guangdong) households living in stem families in 1980, 25 percent. The joint family form did not exist in this community.

person households of those sixty-two or older had dropped to nine, including one seventy-nine-year-old woman and an eighty-four-year-old man.

Between 1978 and 1984 the number of three-person households virtually doubled while the number of five- and six-person households was halved and those with seven to ten members dropped from 26 to 19. The great majority of household divisions in these years took place within two years of marriage, most often at the time of birth of the first (and in these years only) child. Earlier and more frequent household division, together with effective birth control, gave rise in the 1980s to the new archetypal three-person household composed of parents and one child.[7]

These tendencies toward small, simpler, and more homogeneous households were carried further in the years 1984–87. By 1987 there were only two single-person households, and the largest household in the team had only seven members. Between 1984 and 1987 the number of households with seven to ten members dropped from seventeen to just one, and the size of the largest household fell from ten to seven. Household division occurred throughout the 1980s more frequently and earlier than in the 1930s or in the collective era. We see this clearly in a pattern that had no earlier twentieth-century precedent in Wugong or, to my knowledge, in most of rural China. Of the sixty-eight two-person households in 1987, twenty-three consisted of childless couples who married in the years 1980–86. This constitutes a break in two important ways. First, prior to the 1980s, it was extremely rare to establish one's own household before the birth of the first child, and frequently it was only after the birth of a second child, if at all, that the household divided. Our 1978 survey indicated no household composed of a recently married childless couple. Two such households existed by 1984. By 1987, twenty-three childless couples who had married within the previous five years had established independent households.

Prior to land reform, the economic logic of the household economy prevented early household division. At the heart of the family compact was the exchange between the care of aged parents by male offspring and the eventual transfer of land.[8] Collectivization eliminated both the element of land transfer and the household as the organizer of productive activity. The

7. A return visit in 1991 revealed that Wugong remained a leader in birth control, but with the new relaxed guidelines, more households took the opportunity to have a second child following the birth of a daughter. A second child was permitted four years after the birth of a daughter (or the death of a first child) on condition that one parent accept sterilization. In all but one known case, it was the wife who accepted sterilization.

8. This formulation of a compact excludes daughters. I tentatively suggest that a weaker and more ephemeral but not insignificant compact rested on parental obligations to nurture and to arrange a suitable marriage for a daughter in exchange for services rendered prior to marriage, after which the allegiance and obligation of a daughter was expected to be to her husband and his family.

household contract system of the 1980s offered young men and women equal and immediate access to their own land—if they established independent households. Moreover, with the village providing land for home construction, growing numbers of young people chose to free themselves from the constraints of parental and mother-in-law authority as quickly as possible following marriage.[9]

A second significant departure from earlier norms of both the republican era and the collective years is that by the late 1980s many young couples were not producing offspring in the first several years of marriage. By contrast, prior to the 1980s, virtually every couple produced a child within the first year or two of marriage. The changes noted here with respect to small nuclear families, autonomous households, and delayed reproduction bring the family in Wugong in the late 1980s closer to prevailing urban patterns in China, and indeed to norms prevailing in industrial societies elsewhere.

Important dimensions of the 1980s economic and social reforms impinge heavily on household size and structure: The household contract system weakened the former collective structure and strengthened the role of households as productive units both in agriculture and in sideline production and market activity. Between 1978 and 1984 the total number of those listed as working or studying outside the village or serving in the military dropped by nearly half to twenty-seven. Outside employees declined by one-fourth from thirty-two to twenty-four. The largest changes centered on outside study and the army. In 1984 no Team Three member was studying outside the village, and the number of those in the army had fallen from eleven to just three. The changes primarily reflect Wugong's loss of status as a model village coinciding with the opening of alternative channels of mobility associated with the private sector and the market, changes that Wugong people were relatively slow to act upon. The drop in the number of youth joining the army may also be a function of the declining prestige and shrinking size of the military in the 1980s.

The 1984 figures do not, however, suggest a trend toward village isolation, involution, and subsistence farming. Quite the opposite. In 1984, 107 households, nearly half of the households in Team Three, listed one or more members who were engaged in nonagricultural economic pursuits, including teachers, factory workers, and contractors in diverse industrial, craft, commercial, and handicraft activities. In 1978, when the collective

9. Did accompanying policy changes in, for example, access to land and housing for young newlyweds occur at the village level that facilitated the greater autonomy of young people in the 1980s? This is a subject for future research. Here I wish to observe the limits of the present research, which moves between national policy and household behavior but is unable to clarify the important intermediate range of local-level policies, particularly those at the village and county levels, affecting family decisions. Joan Smith drew my attention to these issues.

still held sway, 50 households, just over one-fifth, listed such activities exclusive of unpaid team and brigade political positions. Compared with 1978, many more people engaged in craft and industrial production, provided services, and produced for and sold in the market. While many of these were listed as living and working in the village, in 1984 their work regularly took them outside for commercial and other economic activities. As in the first half of the twentieth century, the Wugong economy was more fully embedded in a wider economic world extending from the standard marketing community to other parts of North China, including Beijing, Tianjin, and beyond to Inner Mongolia and the Northwest.

By 1984, two years after the implementation of household contracts, we observe a bimodal pattern in household strategies. On the one hand, there was continued reduction in household size from 4.3 people in 1978 to 3.8 in 1984. This was the product of large numbers of household divisions in the early 1980s and the continued effects of birth control. Most people lived in nuclear families, and by 1984 the number of four-generation households had further declined from two to none. In 1978, four- and five-person households predominated, accounting for 48 percent of the 232 households; approximately equal numbers of three- and six-person households made up an additional 31 percent. By 1984 three- and four-person households had become the norm, accounting for 134 (55 percent) of the 244 households. The number of households with six or more members plummeted from 64 (28 percent) in 1978 to 32 (13 percent) in 1984. Likewise, the percentage of households with zero or one registered child increased from 45 to 77 percent while the percentage of households with three or more children dropped from 43 to just 16 percent. The number of single-person households fell from 15 (7 percent) to 12 (5 percent) while the number of two-person households tripled from 9 (4 percent) to 32 (13 percent).

On the other hand, we observe apparently contradictory tendencies at work. Specifically, there was a resurgence of stem, joint, and multigenerational structures as a significant group of households reasserted themselves economically and socially and the reforms stimulated new and diverse individual and family strategies (table 6.3). The striking fact is that in a very brief time, and simultaneous with a sharp drop in numbers of births and in household size in response to the birth control program, the number of stem and joint families nearly doubled from 31 in 1978 to 53 in 1984. Among stem and joint families, the somewhat higher concentration of nonagricultural contracts and members in state-sector jobs as workers, cadres, or teachers underlines a degree of congruence between diversified cash-earning economic activity and extended family arrangements. Twenty-seven out of 53 stem and joint families (51 percent) recorded the existence of nonagricultural contracts, extravillage income, or members earning state

TABLE 6.3.   Wugong Team Three Family Structures in 1978, 1984, and 1987

	One-Person Families		Nuclear Families		Stem Families[a]		Joint Families[b]		Total Families
	No.	(%)	No.	(%)	No.	(%)	No.	(%)	No.
1978	15	(6.5)	186	(80.2)	29	(12.5)	2	(0.9)	232
1984	12	(4.9)	179	(73.4)	48	(19.7)	5	(2.0)	244
1987	2	(0.8)	202	(80.7)	41	(16.5)	5	(2.0)	250

SOURCES: 1978, 1984, and 1987 Team Three surveys.
[a] Stem families: A son and daughter-in-law and their unmarried child(ren), if any, living with son's parent(s).
[b] Joint families: Two or more sons and daughters-in-law with their unmarried child(ren), if any, living with sons' parent(s).

salaries. The comparable figure for nuclear and one-person households was 80 out of 191 (42 percent).

Our findings concerning the resurgence of extended families in the early 1980s, consistent with the Davis-Harrell hypothesis in the introduction to this volume, run directly counter to the modernization hypothesis that leads one to anticipate that the growth of the market, commodification, and growing cash income would all contribute to strengthening the nuclear family (Goode 1982).[10] Rather, with the opening of the household sector and the market, significant numbers of Wugong people, particularly those with an entrepreneurial bent, chose to reconstitute joint and stem families, reversing the pattern of their sharp decline following collectivization. In just six years, from 1978 to 1984, the number of stem and joint families increased from 31 to 53, even as the average size of family dropped from 4.3 to 3.8 persons. Team Three demographic experience in this respect lends weight to the suggestion by Davis and Harrell in this volume that for the 1980s and 1990s we replace the urban-rural dichotomy with a tripartite division between subsistence farmers, urban collective and state employees, and entrepreneurs in both city and countryside.

One interesting example of the trend toward extended families is provided by the sole Team Three family classified as "landlord." Li Maoxiu, the youngest son of a small landlord, was a resistance activist who rose to head the district children's organization in wartime while his brother joined

10. William Parish and Martin Whyte, in *Village and Family in Contemporary China*, 137, observe that, contrary to another modernization hypothesis, in Guangdong in the 1970s, no correlation existed between higher education and incidence of nuclear families.

the Party and the army en route to a government career in Shandong. With his father dead and his brother away, Li Maoxiu was branded a landlord in the 1947 land reform. Isolated, stigmatized, and barred from joining a cooperative, in 1952 Li Maoxiu committed the crime of flight, seeking, with the aid of a seal carved out of a turnip, to begin a new life as a teacher in the Northeast. He was caught and jailed for five years, and following his return to the village lived the life of a pariah. The Lis' only child, a son, married in 1964 at age nineteen. During the Cultural Revolution, to insulate the younger generation from the harassment heaped upon "class enemies," the family divided. Fifteen years later, in the early 1980s, the landlord cap having been officially removed, not only did Li Maoxiu initiate several family enterprises, including long distance trade and the opening of a bakery and a plastic workshop, but he also reconstituted a three-generation stem family. In 1984 the family included his wife, his son and daughter-in-law, and their teenage daughter and two sons. In 1990 the family redivided. Li Maoxiu and his wife lived alone in their original, dilapidated home, a grim reminder of their days of opprobrium. Their son and his wife and children moved into a new home at the other end of Team Three.

The 1987 data indicate that some trends already evident in 1984 have gone further. Average size of household continued to drop from 3.8 members in 1984 to 3.4 in 1987. The drop was particularly precipitous among households with 6 or more members. By 1984 such households had already declined to just 13 percent of the total. By 1987 they had dropped further to just 5 percent, and the number of households with 7 or more members fell from nineteen to one.

At the same time, the hypothesized bifurcating pattern in which the majority form small nuclear households while an entrepreneurial minority favors stem and joint households, appears less pronounced in 1987 than in 1984. While the number of stem and joint families increased significantly between 1978 and 1984, the trend reversed between 1984 and 1987 as the number of extended households dropped from 53 to 46 and their size was reduced. Unfortunately, our 1987 data do not permit clear differentiation between entrepreneurial and nonentrepreneurial households. In any event, the hypothesis concerning correlation between multigenerational extended families and entrepreneurship will require testing against the performance of other and larger samples.

INTRAVILLAGE MARRIAGE

In the decades following collectivization, the shrinking of the world of the villager from the standard marketing community and beyond to the natural village was manifested in the closing off of extravillage economic, social, cultural, and marital ties. Most rural people found their world restricted to the confines of the natural village. According to the 1978 survey, of the 985 Team Three residents whose birthplace is known, 771 were born in Wugong and 214 were born outside the village, nearly all of the latter being brides who married in. Famine, political turmoil, war, population pressures, and the hope for better opportunities had led millions of Chinese to flee ancestral villages in search of land, food, and work in the century prior to the founding of the People's Republic. Beginning in 1955, and with particular force after 1960, however, powerful institutional mechanisms associated with collectivization, market controls, and rigorous state enforcement of the *hukou* system of population control kept rural residents in place in the village of their birth or marriage. Village communities attained extraordinary levels of stability. Only a handful of households settled in Wugong after 1945, all of them prior to collectivization, and in every known case they had familial connections. Of 480 males registered in Team Three in 1978, only 11 were born outside the village, including 3 sons born in the Northeast where both parents were factory workers prior to their forced repatriation to Wugong. The repatriates were among the twenty million industrial workers and family members sent back to their villages of origin in 1962 following the failure of the Great Leap Forward. The combination of collectivization, market curbs, and household registration controls put a brake on the dynamic movement of the Chinese population both within China, where millions had migrated to the Northeast and other areas during the late Qing and the Republic, and abroad. This involutionary pattern too was a facet of the growing isolation of village communities associated with collectivization and population controls. In this respect Wugong's experience was representative of that of rural China.

One important change in marital practice in Wugong concerns intravillage marriage. There were deep structural reasons for the trend toward intravillage marriage following collectivization and market closure. Prior to the 1950s, the standard marketing community not only was the primary locus of trade and cultural activities but also defined the terrain within which most marriage contracts were negotiated. Team Three brides of the previous half century who are listed in the 1984 survey came from some forty villages in Raoyang county and sixteen villages in neighboring counties, nearly all within a ten-mile radius of the village. The combination of collectivization and market suppression substantially changed these patterns. With villagers prevented from buying and selling in the few remaining markets, with the closure of rural fairs and traditional cultural events after 1957, with the penetration of party-state networks deep into village life, and with attacks on old culture, customs, and ideas, including the purchase of brides, most people found their world restricted to the natural village. At the same time that extravillage social and economic ties were severed, with activities largely restricted within the team and brigade, the most valuable alliances for families struggling to survive shifted to within the village. From work assignments to income, from opportunity for higher education, to a place in the army or the right to build a house, villagers depended heavily on the goodwill of team and brigade cadres who ruled the village. This was the socioeconomic and political basis for the rise in intravillage marriage in rural communities during the collective era, a pattern that spread throughout much of rural China in the 1970s. Village involution was reflected in marital patterns as more and more brides were from Wugong.

There were, in addition, special reasons why Wugong, in this as in many other areas, led the way. As Wugong reaped the fruits of its status as a model village, per capita income soared above the levels of neighboring communities. In the process, marital strategies changed and taboos restricting intravillage or same-surname marriage began to erode.[11] Parents became reluctant to send daughters to live in much poorer villages that traditionally exchanged brides with Wugong. Moreover, with women sharing in the rapidly expanding educational opportunities that made primary school education the norm in Wugong in the 1950s, junior high education in the expanded village school the norm in the 1960s, and even enabled many to graduate from high school in the 1970s (in each instance Wugong was approximately a decade ahead of neighboring communities), young people in the model village had numerous opportunities to meet. Other villages shared in the expansion of education and accompanying social practices, but at a slower pace.

Participation in collective labor and group activities organized by the youth league, militia, and the county government provided important venues in which young people could meet and court. These opportunities were especially numerous in a model village whose youth enjoyed disproportionate opportunities to participate in state-sponsored cultural, social, and political activities. Growing numbers of young people took marital choice into their own hands, often enlisting the services of a matchmaker to legitimate and sanctify their choice after the fact.

There were limits to the related trends toward autonomous and intravillage marital arrangements throughout rural China, particularly constraints imposed by poverty. The poor were at times still forced to enter paired marriages. One young woman in a poor Raoyang village in the 1960s, for example, was forced to abandon her lover, an only child, to accept a blind-exchange marriage that simultaneously assured her brother a bride. Such exchange marriages were illegal, and the Women's Federation sporadically sought to eliminate them. Larger multiple marriages sometimes involved

11. In Wugong and other multilineage Hebei villages, certain kinds of intravillage marriage, including same-surname marriage, had long been acceptable.

TABLE 6.4.   Birthplace of Wugong Team Three Brides as of 1984

	Born in Wugong		Born Outside Wugong		No. of Brides
	No.	(%)	No.	(%)	
Married prior to 1970	31	(21)	120	(79)	151
Married 1970–84	40	(45)	48	(55)	89

SOURCE: 1984 Team Three survey.

package arrangements for six, eight, or more young people. The attractiveness of paired and multiple marriages lay in the fact that they often eliminated or greatly reduced costly brideprice and dowry, thus making it possible for the poor to wed. While frowned on by the state, this remained a recourse for poor rural households, for some their only hope to arrange a marriage.

Our 1984 survey reveals significant changes in intravillage marriage patterns related not only to collectivization and market closure, but also to Wugong's prosperity and prominence vis-à-vis neighboring communities. The year 1970 marked the divide with respect to intravillage marriage, and this tendency grew more pronounced with the passage of time (table 6.4). While examples of Team Three intravillage marriage are found as early as the 1930s, just 31 (21 percent) of the 151 brides marrying prior to 1970 were born in Wugong. By contrast, 48 (45 percent) of the 88 brides who married between 1970 and 1984 were born in the village, and 26 of 38 brides (68 percent) who married in the years 1984 to 1986 were born in Wugong. The pattern of intravillage marriage grew stronger throughout the 1980s, despite the fact that villagers again participated in a wider regional economy.

Many other Chinese rural communities followed Wugong in the shift toward intravillage marriage in the collective era. The literature abounds with examples from South China. Parish and Whyte (1978, 171) found that intravillage marriage in Guangdong increased from 3 percent prior to 1949 to more than 20 percent in the 1950s through the 1970s. Potter and Potter (1990, 217), in their Zengbu brigade research (Guangdong), noted an increase in intrabrigade marriage from 10 percent of the total in 1964–68 to 21 percent in 1979–81. In this single-lineage community, intrabrigade marriage had to overcome the taboo against same-surname marriage, which was considered incestuous prior to the 1950s.

Chan, Madsen, and Unger describe a "marriage revolution" in Chen village, Guangdong, during the Great Leap, when several youths dared to defy the taboo on intralineage (and intravillage) marriage and took local brides of the same surname. In the post-Leap famine, intravillage alliances became the marriage of choice, involving 70–80 percent of the total (Chan, Madsen, and Unger 1984, 188–91). Jan Myrdal provides an anecdotal example from the Northwest, noting that in the 1960s intravillage marriage was commonplace in Shaanxi's Liulin village (Myrdal 1965, 21).

In the 1980s, with the rise of the household contract system and the market, Wugong, slow to shift gears in step with the times, lost its model status. Within a few years neighboring communities rapidly overcame the income and productivity advantages that the model village had long enjoyed. The relative attractiveness of marriage into Wugong under these circumstances declined. Young people nevertheless continued their efforts to secure control over marriage and choose partners from their circle of local acquaintances.

New marital patterns in Wugong were not confined to intravillage marriage. Some Team Three marriages even began to take place within the narrow confines of the team. In 1978 a local schoolteacher and women's activist married the deputy battalion leader of the militia. Both were natives of Team Three. Some Wugong people privately worried over possible adverse genetic consequences of close inbreeding. Wugong had no historical taboo against intravillage marriage or same-surname marriage; indeed this multilineage village had a long history of such marriages. But the village was divided into four incest-taboo neighborhoods, and strict codes had long prohibited marriage within the neighborhood. Two of these areas eventually formed teams one and two, while the third and fourth, separated by a lane, combined to form Team Three.

Geneticists and demographers with whom I have consulted indicate that intermarriage within a community of 600 households (Wugong village), or even 300 households (Team Three), poses no serious threat of birth defects provided close relatives do not marry. Yet China has serious problems of birth defects, and a rash of articles in the Chinese media in the years 1988–90 warned darkly that rural inbreeding had reached serious proportions in the countryside. On December 6, 1988, and January 2, 1989, the *People's Daily* (overseas edition) cited surveys by sociologist Gao Caiqin to warn of the debilitating consequences of intravillage marriage. On the basis of a study of 1,441 peasant families in six provinces, Gao concluded that ever-closer consanguinity in single-lineage villages was "causing population degeneration and undermining social development." Gao found that 30 percent were marrying within their native villages and 51 percent in the township. On January 30, 1989, *People's Daily* (overseas edition) reported the existence of more than thirty million Chinese with congenital defects and warned that an important source of the problem in remote mountain areas lay in inbreeding. The *Impartial Daily*, a Party organ published in Hong Kong, presented even more alarming figures in its edition of April 12,

1990. It claimed that China had some fifty million people who were mentally or physically handicapped and again pointed to intravillage and intratownship marriage as a cause. What none of these sources mentioned was the fact that China's *hukou* system of population control, together with the antimarket collectivism that prevailed until the late 1970s, had strengthened the tendency toward intravillage reproduction.

By early 1989 the state began to act on findings like those mentioned above. Chen Muhua, chair of the Women's Association, told a symposium that the cost of raising children with congenital defects, which many attributed to close kin marriage, was seven to eight billion yuan per year. Chen announced the promulgation of a eugenics law, "Regulations to Prevent Mental Defectives (*chidai sharen*) from Bearing Children" in Gansu province (*People's Daily*, overseas edition, January 30,1989). The method: forced sterilization. The May 21, 1990, Taiwan newspaper *World* (Shijie) cited a *People's Daily* report that Gansu had already sterilized 5,500 of the province's 260,000 mental defectives. Officials stated that most of the rest would be sterilized within the year, and it seems likely that the Gansu sterilization program is a pilot project preparatory to national implementation. It is difficult to imagine a state program more susceptible to political manipulation and human tragedy. What criteria for "mental defectives" will be applied, and by whom?

Neither the broad marital policies of the state nor youth initiatives to take control of marriage challenged the patrilineal, patrilocal marital traditions that were particularly entrenched in North China. (Uxorilocal marriage had long been acceptable for families without sons in the southeast, east central, and southwest but not in the north; Wolf and Huang 1980, 11–15; 94–107; Goody 1990, 106–7.) Virtually the sole state initiative calling patrilineal, patrilocal practices into question in the People's Republic was the 1974–75 campaign pressed by Jiang Qing, with Xiaojinzhuang village in suburban Tianjin as its model. The campaign encouraged intravillage marriage and marriage into the family of a daughter who was an only child. One young man from neighboring Shen county did marry into Wugong at that time, enabling an only child to remain at home to care for her aged parents. The husband benefited by the move to a prosperous model village, doubtless a step up the economic ladder, but entailing some loss of face. With the end of the campaign, the issues disappeared from the political agenda.

The resurgence of the household economy and the market in the 1980s, and the weakening of restrictions on population movement, should reinforce trends toward extravillage marriage as the social and economic world again opens to marketing communities and beyond. Whether these effects will overcome other factors conducive to intravillage marriage, particularly changing patterns of youth courtship, remains to be seen.

MARRIAGE AGE

As the place of origin of Wugong brides changed, so too did age of first marriage. The earliest recorded age of marriage in our 1978 survey is that of an eighty-two-year-old poor peasant who married his sixteen-year-old bride when he was fourteen; one woman then in her fifties also married a middle peasant when she was fourteen.

Gamble's study of Dingxian in the 1930s produced numerous examples of much earlier marriages, particularly for boys, than those recorded in Wugong at that time.[12] In a sample of 5,255 rural families, 169 males and 33 females under age fifteen were married, including 21 boys age eleven and under. Girls married as young as age twelve. All but 5 women in Gamble's sample had married by age twenty-one, but as many as 10 percent of males had not married by age thirty-eight. In another study of 515 families, Gamble found the range of ages for first marriage for males to run from seven to fifty-one and for females twelve to thirty-eight (Gamble 1954, 37–41; 58–59). In Buck's 1929–31 North China rural sample of 1,600 married men and 1,760 married women, 58 percent of the men and 86 percent of the women married by age nineteen, including 12 percent of men and 13 percent of women who married prior to age fifteen (Buck 1937, 380). Comparable results were recorded in C. M. Chiao's 1929–31 survey of 12,456 farm families. He found that in North China 62 percent of men and 80 percent of women married before age nineteen (Chiao 1933, 28, 31).

Gamble's 1930 Dingxian sample of 515 families makes clear the high correlation between male marriage age and wealth, using landownership as a gauge for wealth. Among households with less than 50 mu of land, 33 percent of married males wed by age fourteen, and 11 percent first married between the ages of twenty-nine and thirty-five. By contrast, 81 percent of males in households with 100 mu or more of land married by age fourteen and all but five percent married by age seventeen (Gamble 1954, 59).

In another Dingxian sample of 5,225 families, Gamble found that more than 99 percent of females had married by age twenty-one. By contrast, just 60 percent of males married by age twenty-three, and it was not until age thirty-nine that 90 percent of males married (Gamble 1954, 39–40). The great majority of the unmarried 10 percent, virtually all of them males from poverty-stricken families, would never marry. They would face old age without familial support, and their family line would die out, thus violating the filial injunction to maintain the family line.

One measure of the degree of state penetration of village life during the collective era is the success of the campaign to postpone marriage for substantial numbers of rural youth, from the late teens to the early and even,

---

12. In the 1930s Wugong was the extreme southwest part of Dingxian prefecture.

TABLE 6.5. Average Age at First Marriage in Wugong Team Three,
Selected Years

	Males				Females			
	Avg.	Min.	Max.	No.	Avg.	Min.	Max.	No.
1965–69	21.6	19	26	26	21.8	18	26	26
1975–79	25.3	23	28	34	25.3	21	29	34
1982–84	22.7	20	24	22	23.4	22	26	23

SOURCE: 1984 Team Three survey.
NOTE: The sample includes brides who marry into Wugong as well as those born in the village. It excludes Team Three women who marry outside the team or village and for whom
no records are available.

for a period, to the late twenties. By the 1960s, early and child marriages
were largely eliminated and very late marriages (over age thirty) as well as
the number of men who were never able to wed, were sharply reduced in
most of rural China. From the 1950s through the mid-1970s, most Team
Three men and women married shortly after age twenty as both earlier and
later marriages declined in keeping with state directives and in response to
changes associated with land reform and collectivization (table 6.5). The
pattern shifted dramatically in the late 1970s. Marriage age for women and
men increased on average from twenty-one in the late 1960s to twenty-five
in the late 1970s. The explanation for the shifts in marriage age in the 1970s
lies in the intense campaign to postpone marriage beyond age twenty-five,
one of the pillars of China's birth control strategy at that time.

In the late 1970s campaign to delay marriage, as in so many others,
Wugong more scrupulously enforced state goals than did most communities. For model communities, their "capital" was political capital. The
advantages models enjoyed in higher income, access to state resources, and
prestige were mediated through ties to the state, not the market, although
the advantages of model status included higher incomes and privileged access to state resources. We hypothesize that the delay of marriage by five
years to the late twenties was unusually pronounced in Wugong and other
model villages, although the campaign had an impact far beyond such communities. After 1982 the state relaxed efforts to postpone marriage until the
late twenties while continuing to control fertility. With partial decollectivization and the resurgence of the household economy, the state's ability to
enforce marital postponement—and much else—generally weakened. The
result in Wugong was that the norm shifted back to the early twenties,
where it had been since the 1960s.

Older women and men in Team Three experienced a much broader
range of ages at first marriage than did younger generations. Of 56 Team

Three women who married between 1920 and 1949 and were alive at the time of our 1984 survey, 20 married between age fifteen and nineteen, 26 between twenty and twenty-four, 9 between twenty-five and twenty-nine, and 1 in her early thirties. Out of 60 Team Three married men whose marriage between 1910 and 1949 is recorded in our 1984 survey, 1 married at age thirteen, 13 between age fifteen and nineteen, and 4 in their thirties. By contrast, every one of the 100 women and 100 men who married between 1970 and 1984 married between age twenty and twenty-nine. The data for the years 1970 to 1984 reveal with particular clarity the effectiveness of state pressures to defer marriage in a model village. In the years 1970–74, 15 men and 14 women married between ages twenty and twenty-four, and just 3 men and 4 women married between twenty-five and twenty-nine. But between 1975 and 1979, as the state called for delayed marriage to age twenty-eight for men and twenty-five for women, the pattern shifted sharply. In the years 1975 to 1979 just 5 men and 8 women married between ages twenty and twenty-four, while 25 men and 22 women married between twenty-five and twenty-nine. In the years 1980–84, state pressures for delaying marriage to the late twenties eased, and the focus of birth control shifted from delayed marriage to contraception and abortion. The pendulum then shifted back toward somewhat earlier marriage. Of the 38 men and 38 women who married between 1984 and 1986, just 4 men and 4 women did so at ages twenty-five to twenty-six while the remaining 34 men and 34 women wed between age twenty and twenty-four.

Our surveys of Team Three contain no examples of destitute males who never married. In Wugong village, from the 1940s, apparently every male could afford to marry, and all, even the physically handicapped, did so. It is not of course the case that following land reform and collectivization all Chinese rural males were able to marry. In the early 1960s, males in poorer households and destitute communities faced continued difficulty in securing a spouse. A vivid example is provided by Duankou village, a poor community a few miles north of Wugong that was devastated during the Great Leap. In the early 1970s just 17 out of 80 men age twenty-five to forty-five had been able to marry. In frustration, unmarried males, led by a former war hero, organized a gang that set out to prevent other village males from achieving the marriages they had been denied. Their method was to launch a rumor war, warning of dire consequences for families of prospective brides who were contemplating marrying into Duankou.

Throughout rural China, land reform and collectivization not only eliminated extremes in inequality of landholding and economic opportunity, but also initiated processes that compressed wide variations in marriage age. This pattern of homogenization in which early and late marriages were virtually eliminated, illustrated with particular clarity in model Wugong, may be seen, if less sharply etched, throughout much of the countryside during the collective years.

The wide dispersion of marriage age, the inability of significant numbers of poorer men to marry at all, and substantial age differences between spouses, characteristic of rural China in the first half of the twentieth century, gave way in the decades following land reform and collectivization to the homogenization of marriage age in the early twenties. However, the hardcore poor, predominantly those living in chronic deficit areas, remained outside this process.

One other distinctive marital pattern in Hebei counties near Wugong bears mention. A popular local saying went: "A wife three years older is like a brick of gold; a wife five years older looks older than your mother." Sidney Gamble documented the predominant pattern of older wives for Dingxian in the 1930s. In a survey of 766 couples in 515 families, he found that wives were older in 70 percent of cases, husbands in 25 percent. In the case of older wives, the largest number were two to three years older, with a maximum difference of eleven years. Older husbands, however, averaged eight years older, up to a maximum of thirty-one years. Most of these cases involved poor males unable to marry until late in life (Gamble 1954, 45–46).

In Team Three, the greatest age disparity revealed in our 1978 survey was that of a male who took a bride eighteen years his junior in a 1932 union. Six other males, ranging in age from sixty-two to seventy-three, had wives ten to fifteen years younger. An additional thirty-one couples differed in age by five to nine years, with the male being older in twenty-six of these cases. In all but three of the forty-three instances in which the age difference of partners was five or more years, the male was above forty-five years of age, indicating that by the 1950s such marriages had become rare. Since the 1960s, all Team Three marriages have joined partners of roughly equal age; in no case did the difference exceed four years. The trend to marriages among people of comparable age coincided with homogenization in the age of first marriage.

Gamble (1954, 41–43) documented for Dingxian and rural Hebei in the 1930s a class-based pattern of differentiation in which the favored approach for the prosperous was to marry off a son at a very young age, averaging thirteen years for families owning more than 100 mu. Brides in such cases averaged 3.6 years older, to assure that they were ready both to bear children and to care for their in-laws and their child husbands. Wugong data likewise reveal class differentiation in marital patterns, although few men married as young as did Gamble's wealthy scions. The 1978 Team Three survey showed that among surviving couples, twenty-five men who married prior to 1955 had married women five to eighteen years younger. All but three of these men were classified as poor peasants in land reform (the others were middle peasants). Many of them first married when they were in their thirties or forties, and in one case the groom was sixty years of age. Eleven women married men four to seven years younger. In these marriages, favored by the more prosperous, eight of the husbands' households were middle peasants, and one a landlord. Just two were poor peasants.

Our 1984 survey of Team Three showed that the practice of taking a bride ten or more years younger, which persisted in Team Three into the 1950s, has long since disappeared. On the other hand, forty-three women were two to four years older than their husbands, and thirty-nine men two to four years older than their wives. The pattern of wives two to four years older continued in some relatively recent marriages, including twelve out of twenty-two cases in the years 1974–84. However, in none of the thirty-eight marriages consummated between 1984 and 1986 did the age differential exceed two years. The traditional preference for brides two to four years older appears to have declined. The emerging pattern in the mid- to late 1980s is one of close age parity and a preference for intravillage marriage, with husband and wife of similar age in their early twenties.

MARRIAGE AGE AND CLASS

The Team Three survey data provide striking confirmation of class-based differentiation in marital patterns prior to land reform. Wugong was part of the central Hebei base area during the anti-Japanese resistance. Landlord power in this region, with initially very low tenancy rates, was further reduced as a result of wartime reforms prior to the 1947 land reform. Consequently, when class labels (*chengfen*) in this village were fixed in 1947, the Party based them on politicized memories of landownership and social relations that purportedly existed in 1936, more than a decade earlier. Only in that way could the Party assure the existence of class enemies to target for struggle and expropriation. The labels nevertheless provide certain clues concerning differential marital patterns among the poorer and more prosperous in the years prior to land reform.

The sample is of twenty-seven males classified as poor peasants, twelve as middle peasants, and one as landlord who were either age sixty by the time of the 1978 survey or had married by 1947. The marital data for the middle peasants and landlords displays the preferred regional pattern of early marriage: eleven of thirteen men married between ages fifteen and twenty to women who were two to five years their senior. By contrast, only four of twenty-seven poor peasants were able to marry by age twenty. Thirteen others were unable to marry until age twenty-five or later, including eight who first married after age thirty. Only four of twenty-seven poor peasant men married an older woman. Sixteen out of twenty-seven of these poor peasant men married women five or more years younger, including four whose brides were ten to eighteen years younger.

The 1978 survey data reveal the expected correlation between class designation and marital patterns in Wugong in the years prior to land reform. By contrast, those who married in the 1970s and 1980s display no significant differences based on class designation, for all hewed to state guidelines for marriage in their twenties regardless of class origin or income.

MARRIAGE AGE AND PARTY MEMBERSHIP

Marital patterns for male Communist Party members differ significantly from those of non-Party members before and during the era of mobilizational collectivism. The 1978 survey reveals that all fifty-nine male Party members married between ages fifteen and twenty-nine. By contrast, the range of non-Party marriage ages spans the entire spectrum from age fourteen to sixty, with twenty-nine taking place after age thirty. The crux of the issue is the generation that included people who were in their sixties to their eighties at the time of our 1978 survey, since it was among them that later marriage, or no marriage, frequently occurred. Eight of the eleven male Party members age sixty and above had married by age twenty-four, and the remaining three married between twenty-five and twenty-seven. By contrast, the thirty-seven non-Party males for whom marital data is available included ten who married for the first time in their thirties, two in their forties, two in their fifties, and one at sixty. The fact that male Party members who reached marriage age prior to the 1947 land reform all married by age twenty-nine strongly suggests that in Team Three the Party did not recruit extensively from the very poorest strata, that is from marginal households whose sons could only marry very late if at all. Historical research documents the significant role played by prosperous peasants and landlords as well as independent cultivators in the anti-Japanese resistance in Wugong and throughout central Hebei. Such people had the resources to marry at relatively early ages. The Party also recruited among the poor, but rarely from the ranks of the utterly destitute and marginalized.

Party members responded only slightly more loyally than others to the campaign to delay marriage in the years 1975–84. Five of the six Party members who married in the years 1975–80, including two women, waited until ages twenty-five to twenty-eight. The remaining Party member, who was serving in the army, married at twenty-four. Of the eighty-nine non-Party members who married in those years, fifteen men and seventeen women, over one-third of the total, married prior to age twenty-five. Within the context of significant marriage delay for all, Party members tended to hew slightly more closely to state guidelines. But in a model village, nearly everyone conformed to state demands to delay marriage.

CONCLUSION

This chapter has highlighted changes in family size and structure, marriage age, location of marital partners, and the locus of marital decision in response to powerful state initiatives. Of particular importance are the following: collectivization and population control leading to village involution in the era of mobilizational collectivism, and market-oriented contractual reforms and rigorous birth control measures since the 1980s. The changes associated with the collective era in Wugong and in much of rural China led to homogenization in age of marriage in the range of twenty to twenty-four, a marked shift toward intravillage marriage, shrinking family size, and predominance of nuclear families long before the state succeeded in reducing fertility. Comparative data strongly suggest that these patterns, documented here with respect to Wugong, were widely shared throughout the Chinese countryside. Many trends, particularly delayed marriage and later reduced fertility (the one-child family), constitute direct responses to state policies and priorities. But others reveal the striving of rural inhabitants, and particularly rural youth, to expand opportunities to make autonomous decisions concerning marriage, family, and family division. Certain outcomes, such as the unusually early and high response rate to the state's delayed-marriage campaign, the early and rigorous implementation of birth control, and the trend to intravillage marriage, reflect Wugong's model status, a factor that peaked in the 1950s to 1970s before declining in the early 1980s.

The survey results suggest that the household contract system and expanded opportunity for market and mobility since the 1980s produced significant changes in family and individual marital strategies, including further shrinkage of family size, the existence for the first time of substantial numbers of new couples forming independent households prior to the birth of a child, and the decision to postpone conception for at least several years after marriage. Finally, we note signs of the emergence of a bimodal familial pattern that can best be understood in terms of new class divisions. At one pole we observe small nuclear farm families and at the other a significant number of joint and stem families, many of them engaged in significant entrepreneurial activity.

SEVEN

Reconstituting Dowry and Bbrideprice in South China

Helen F. Siu

The recent decade of reforms in the 1980s brought drastic changes to Nanxi Zhen, a market town with a rural hinterland.[1] Situated at the heart of the Pearl River delta, connected by easy road and water transport to Guangzhou, Macao, and Hong Kong, it has enjoyed an unprecedented boom.[2] Rows of new houses have mushroomed on the landscape. Some are funded by relatives living in Hong Kong and Macao. Many are built by local entrepreneurs themselves. There is also the ever-growing number of rural enterprises employing young migrant workers on the town's outskirts, accompanied by the bustling businesses on the roads and in shops and restaurants, by the common sight of color television sets, washing machines, hi-fi systems, and videos in private homes, and by the lavish rituals at funerals and weddings.[3]

Family dynamics have taken a sudden turn. Nearly everyone I encoun-

This chapter is based on fieldwork conducted periodically from 1986 to 1990, funded by the Committee on Scholarly Communication with the People's Republic of China and Wenner Gren Foundation for Anthropological Research. I am grateful for the comments from Deborah Davis, Jack Goody, Stevan Harrell, and participants in the conference on Family Strategies in Post-Mao China, June 12–17, 1990, Roche Harbor Resort, San Juan Island.

1. All the local place names in this chapter are pseudonyms. Nanxi Zhen went through a few administrative changes after the revolution. It was an administrative town after 1923, headquarters for the third district of Dagang county. It maintained a market-town status in the 1950s. In 1963 it was made into the Nanxi Zhen Commune. In 1987 it merged with the surrounding Nanxi Rural Commune to become a *zhen*.

2. This prosperity has been partly brought about by investments from natives who emigrated to Hong Kong, Macao, and Southeast Asia in the first half of the twentieth century and who have become successful businessmen and industrialists. The particularly successful counties in the delta are Nanhai, Panyu, Shunde, Dongguan, and Zhongshan.

3. See Helen Siu, "Socialist Peddlers and Princes in a Chinese Market Town," *American Ethnologist* 16, no. 2 (May 1989), for the economic changes.

tered in town with grown children complained that the young people of today are drunk with the new wealth. They are desperately energetic, but they are also said to be brash, uncaring for their parents, vulgar in their conspicuous life-styles, and lacking moral restraint. Surprisingly, the young people who show little knowledge of the Chinese cultural tradition eagerly participate in lavish funeral and wedding rituals and shoulder most of the expenses themselves.[4]

Town residents also complained that the escalating dowries, some reaching over 10,000 yuan, are ruining those who have daughters to marry off, and that sons and daughters keep most of their wages and bonuses for their own future homes instead of paying for their keep. With an average monthly income of 200–300 yuan, young workers give at the most 40 to 80 yuan per month to their parents. Although the payments from the groom's side averaged 1,000 yuan in cash, the demand on the groom's family to provide a new house for the young couple puts a considerable strain on relationships within the family and leads to intricate maneuvers with town cadres to obtain building sites and materials.[5]

In the villages surrounding the town, which represented an impoverished area in the prerevolutionary and the Maoist period, a similar lavishness is now displayed in the provision of new houses by the groom's side and large banquets.[6] Dowry from the bride's family remains small compared with that of the town, but contributions from the groom's side have increased several times, reaching an average of 2,000 yuan. Poor males are said to have resorted to taking in migrant women from Guangxi province because the amount demanded for marriage to local women has become unaffordable.[7]

Have the terms of marriage gotten out of reach and out of control during

4. See Helen Siu, "Recycling Rituals: Politics and Popular Culture in Contemporary Rural China," in *Unofficial China: Essays in Popular Culture and Thought*, ed. Richard Madson, Perry Link, Paul Pickowicz (Boulder: Westview Press, 1989), for the analysis of why young people are actively engaging in ritual activities.

5. In this area where properties belonging to emigrants had been confiscated in the Maoist era, one strategy today is for the emigrants to claim the properties back for their relatives. Cadres in Nanxi have expressed concern for such a trend because the town government has no resources either to compensate for these properties or to relocate those who are made to vacate.

6. See also the chapter on marriage practices in a rural community in the eastern part of the Pearl River delta, in Sulamith and Jack Potter, *China's Peasants: The Anthropology of a Revolution* (Cambridge: Cambridge University Press, 1990).

7. In the 1980s, Nanxi Zhen hired thousands of migrant laborers from other provinces, especially Jiangxi, Guangxi, and Hunan. They filled the lowest level of town factories and also became sharecroppers in the villages. Employment peaked in 1988 with over 15,000. For the pattern of migration, see Helen Siu, "The Politics of Migration in a Market Town," in *China on the Eve of Tiananmen*, ed. Deborah Davis and Ezra Vogel (Cambridge: Harvard University Press, 1990).

the recent decade of prosperity? Why do people feel compelled to pursue these ends? What do the marital transfers today tell us about family strategies four decades after the revolution? In addition, the different emphasis on contributions from the bride's and groom's sides in town and village is striking and requires our analytic attention. In pursuing these questions, I aim in this chapter to address theoretical debates in anthropology with regard to marital exchanges, and to use the debates to highlight the complexity of family dynamics and cultural exigencies as several generations of local residents experienced major transformations in the political economy during the last half-century.

Most scholars who work on dowry and brideprice would agree that marital transfers affect and reflect relationships between the generations and between families. Jack Goody starts out arguing that dowry, which establishes a conjugal fund, is a form of "diverging devolution" common to complex stratified societies in Europe and Asia. For purposes of maintaining economic standing, families find it important to advance the status of daughters as well as sons, and so to allocate them a share in the parental estate. He contrasts dowry with bridewealth, a circulating fund common in classless societies. Bridewealth is an exchange among senior men used to establish future marriages, especially for the sibling of the bride. Wealth goes one way, and rights over women another.[8] In Chinese studies (as elsewhere in Europe and Asia), the term "brideprice" applies to that portion of the marital transfers provided by the groom's kin; it is usually part of a wider set of transactions that includes the dowry, the contributions made by the family of the bride and normally destined for the daughter or for the married couple. Goody suggests an alternative phrase, "indirect dowry."[9] Here the term "brideprice" is retained for transfers from the groom's side, whatever their destination. What usually changes is the different weight given to one element as against the other, with higher status groups tending to stress direct dowry and lower ones brideprice, or indirect dowry.[10]

8. The term "brideprice" has been used to cover two different types of marital transfer. In Africa, it was earlier used for the transaction that passed from the family of the groom to that of the bride, where it was available for the marriage of her brothers or other male kinsfolk; the word was generally abandoned in favor of "bridewealth," since nothing like "price" in the usual sense of the word is involved.

9. Whether the former gifts are passed on to the daughter or used in the marriage festivities themselves, they constitute even less of a "price" than African bridewealth. However, among some lower-status groups, part or even all of these transfers may be retained by the bride's kin, possibly in compensation for the gift they have provided, possibly as a reserve on which the daughter can draw, possibly for their own use. See Jack Goody and S. J. Tambiah, *Bridewealth and Dowry* (Cambridge: Cambridge University Press, 1973).

10. Although I have sometimes indicated the element of endowment, it is essential to recognize the above complications and bear in mind that "brideprice" in the wider sense is rarely an alternative to direct dowry, but rather a counterpart.

Stressing prestige building rather than status maintenance, Harrell and Dickey refine Goody's original formulation by underscoring the social meaning of dowry.[11] They expect dowry to be a prominent feature of socially differentiated but openly competitive societies with urban commercial wealth. While recognizing that dowry also involves an economic transaction between families that reflects how woman's labor is calculated and valued, it is more important as part of a cultural, symbolic complex, a social statement for the upwardly mobile classes.

Before the revolution the marriage transfers of rural China usually consisted of indirect dowry; that is, the groom's family made a contribution, which was returned with the bride as part of the dowry. Only among the very poor would it be retained by her kin.[12] Maurice Freedman suggests that brideprice payments signify the superiority of the groom's family vis-à-vis the bride's, while Patricia Ebrey sees dowries in historical times as used by the upwardly mobile for purposes of status enhancement.[13]

Both claims are true in specific circumstances, but dowry is used in a much wider range of situations than social mobility alone, and brideprice is used for more purposes than affecting superiority, since they are elements in virtually all marriages. This point is made by Goody in his recent book where he refines his earlier analysis by arguing that in traditional China, the incorporation of women by their husbands' families was never abrupt or complete. She and her natal family maintained multiple ties through life. He sees only a limited role for marital transfers as a payment for the right to women's labor in the strict sense, but allows analytical room for the role of dowry as a means of prestige building. In the economics of status maintenance, he stresses the cultural and social importance of a woman to both her natal and her affinal kin in providing for "the continuation of the house," to which process the creation of conjugal funds was central. This was evident in China, where most scholars intuitively assume otherwise. Both families contributed to this fund. Direct dowry was the main instrument used by high-status families to endow the new conjugal units, and indirect dowry (or brideprice in the wider sense) by lower-status families for similar purposes.[14]

This theoretical material is useful for understanding the nature of mari-

11. See Stevan Harrell and Sara Dicky, "Dowry Systems in Complex Societies," *Ethnology* 24, no. 2 (1985): 105–20.

12. William Parish and Martin Whyte, *Village and Family in Contemporary China*, 180–92 (Chicago: University of Chicago Press, 1978).

13. Maurice Freedman, *Chinese Lineage and Society: Fukien and Kwangtung* (London: Athlone, 1966), 55; Patricia Ebrey, "Early Stages in the Development of Descent Group," in *Kinship Organization in Late Imperial China, 1000–1940*, ed. Patricia Ebrey and James Watson (Berkeley, University of California Press, 1986).

14. Jack Goody, *The Oriental, the Ancient and the Primitive: Systems of Marriage and the Family in the Pre-industrial Societies of Eurasia* (Cambridge: Cambridge University Press, 1990).

tal transfers in Nanxi Zhen and their recent developments. Local historians are eager to point out that the differences in terms of marriage between Nanxi town and the surrounding villages had existed over several centuries: The town elites used dowries to enhance their status, whereas the poor tenants in the villages "sell" their daughters to finance their sons' marriages by asking for a large brideprice. This view is of course debatable, but if it were true, it would confirm the analyses of Harrell and Dicky on a general level, and also the China-specific formulations of Freedman.

The issue is complicated, however, by the question of whether a similar set of factors can be used to explain the differences in the decade of the 1980s. Are the divergent terms of marriage observed today similar to those in the prerevolutionary period, revived after a hiatus of forty years? Or does the explosion of energies in the 1980s indicate how fundamentally family relationships had been changed by the Maoist state in the decades before, and how the post-Mao reforms have further restructured family life in both town and village?

Emphasizing again the social prestige–building element in marriage transfer, as Harrell and Dicky would, one may argue that the escalations of dowry in town today are due to a sudden prosperity combined with a largely untouched cultural tradition. Revived by liberalized policies in the 1980s, the ideal forms of transfer finally become a reality for the majority of people. In the town, the new wealth generates competitive display; parents want to provide for their children in their new households in order to confirm the family's social statuses. It is the same with the younger generation. Nanxi town consists of a large number of young workers, private entrepreneurs and cadres whose fortunes have exploded in the decade of reforms and who are eager to flaunt their newly acquired wealth for the purpose of social networking. Large dowries and at times equivalent contributions from the groom's side are ways to reinforce status. It is also shrewd business strategy, as with the financing of other rituals. This analytical position assumes that the socialist interlude in the past forty years has done little to change cultural expectations and strategies for the perpetuation of family wealth and status.

If one stresses the rights to women's labor in marriage transfer, analytical attention is drawn to the escalating brideprices in the villages and their relationship to labor needs among the farming families. Could the increased pace of economic activities in the 1980s have exacerbated these needs, which are reflected in the ways families strategize and negotiate marriage payments? Social statuses in the villages are changing with increased mobility and rapid out-migration. With an acute labor shortage, it seems logical to assume that families are paying a high brideprice in order to secure the rights of women to augment long-term field labor. That was a concern in the past, and it remains one today. This position regarding the role of marital transfers assumes that the traditional village-town divide, as well as the gender and generational division of labor, continues to structure the area's ongoing development in much the same way as before.

Observing the divergent terms of marriage in Nanxi town and the surrounding villages in the 1980s, I would caution against viewing these terms as representing two different political economies with their own cultural logic, which have sprung back to haunt the socialist government. On the surface, the town-dwellers' stress on dowry and the villagers' on brideprice seems to indicate that the strategies of prestige building and of the recruitment of women's labor have prevailed in the different sectors. But I suggest that these marital transfers arose in a single culturally constructed political economy, which had undergone drastic transformations in the Maoist period at one level and which had persisted at another. At the level of change, one can view the extravagant dowries in town today as public statements and shrewd networking in an era of entrepreneurial vigor; the peculiar form such vigor takes is based on the popular assumption that the party-state can exert its power against any formal civic organization. I would also show that in both town and village today the marital transfers negotiated involve not so much the exchange of material goods and prestige between the families of the bride and groom as the intense and rapid devolution of property to the conjugal couple at the time of marriage itself. This trend represents a very different intergenerational and interfamilial dynamics in the context of a much-changed political economy. On the issue of persistence, I shall argue that the involvement of women in "the continuation of the house" remains intact in both town and village after forty years of socialism. The peasants who face the rapid emigration of both sons and daughters can meet labor demands by making sharecropping arrangements with migrant laborers; they choose instead to pay a high brideprice in order to anchor much-valued family commitments in the village. Could it be that rather than the family's merely surviving the Maoist interlude, its importance may have been intensified in the last few decades by Maoist politics to the point that the older family members, confronted by a decreasing commitment from their children, are now pursuing family strategies with inexplicable fervor? Goody's analytical views on the importance of the conjugal fund may seem applicable in these circumstances.

Therefore, while appreciating the major roles of both cultural tradition and economic logic in shaping marriage transfers, I suggest that four decades of socialist politics have underlain the mutual impact of marriage and the economy, changing and at times preserving cultural expectations, restructuring economic needs, and at times reinforcing family strategies.[15]

15. This is close to the observations of Parish and Whyte for the postrevolutionary period up to the late 1970s. For north China, see Kay Johnson, *Women, the Family and Peasant Revolution in China* (Chicago: University of Chicago Press, 1983), 208–14.

That history highlights how much and in what ways family relationships have been transformed, and it is a crucial analytic element for understanding marital transfers in Nanxi Zhen today. Using a random sample survey of three hundred households collected in 1986 and on subsequent trips in 1987 and 1989, I explore these issues of the reconstitution of brideprice and dowry in Nanxi Zhen and the surrounding villages in relation to the process of decollectivization or privatization.[16]

PREREVOLUTIONARY MARITAL TRANSFERS IN NANXI

The Pearl River delta is a complex, ever-expanding social landscape. As the river continues to flow along a southeastern direction and forms marshes at its lower reaches, it attracts migrants who come to settle from different parts of south China. This process has given rise at various periods to communities with vastly different economic resources and cultural configurations. Nanxi town is one of a line of market towns situated between a well-populated part of the delta and these vast river marshes. Known locally as sands (*sha*), the marshes were reclaimed and converted to rice fields by lineage and merchant estates based in the town. In this way, Nanxi grew from an outpost in the sands during the Ming to a dominating center of wealth, power, and ritual by the late eighteenth century. At the turn of the present century, the residents consisted of a dynamic commercial class, together with its functionaries, who controlled the landed estates in the sands and the trading of grain, mulberry, silk cocoons, wine, fruit, and vegetables.[17]

Although the economies of Nanxi town and the villages have been interlocked, they are worlds apart in many ways. The inhabitants of the sands were mobile, boat-dwelling farmers and fishermen who were treated as an underclass by town dwellers. Generally referred to as the Dan, the sands people worked as hired hands and tenants when lineages reclaimed river marshes, and they engaged in the meaner trades, such as carrying coffins and digging graves. Prejudice against them was reinforced during the years of bad harvests when they fled the area in their boats with whatever they could glean from the fields. When they had gathered strength in numbers, they were portrayed as bandits and pirates.[18] Until the 1940s there were

16. The survey covers all fifteen of the town's residential neighborhoods and three villages at different distances from the town.

17. See Helen Siu, "Recycling Tradition: Culture, History and Political Economy in the Chrysanthemum Festivals of South China," *Comparative Studies in Society and History* 32, no. 4 (1990): 765–94.

18. See Dian Murray, *Pirates of the South China Coast, 1790–1810* (Stanford: Stanford University Press, 1987). See Helen Siu, *Agents and Victims in South China: Accomplices in Rural Revolution* (New Haven: Yale University Press, 1989), chaps. 2 and 3, on the historical development of the sands in the Pearl River delta.

seldom any real villages. The occasional straw huts on the dikes were in sharp contrast to the 393 ancestral halls and the 139 temples in the town before the 1949 revolution. Even today, the sands consists only of small villages between which lie extensive fields.

Nanxi was a place of residence for an unusual concentration of the wealthy and upwardly mobile until the land reform. An official document of 1971 records that the town then had 482 persons labeled as landlords and 57 as rich peasants. Most of them belonged to the town's four major lineages, whose members married each other. Before 1949 they and their families constituted a significant social group among the town's some 12,000 residents. For the women in these families, there was little extra-domestic employment and no need for it. In fact, a married daughter of the wealthy might not touch the food of her husband's household for at least a year, being supplied with foodstuffs from her natal home. The women were also provided with lavish dowries, which might include elaborate jewelry, double sets of *suanzhi* furniture, delicate porcelain dishes and vases, silverware, together with annual provisions of grain and large tracts of river marshes.[19] Brideprice was negligible. In 1986, older women whom I interviewed generally agreed that before the war the brideprice for a "respectable family" was about a hundred silver dollars, a few hundred wedding cakes, and banquet food. Whatever was received was largely consumed in the wedding feast. Both the bride's and the groom's family would hold a dinner for friends and relatives, each making up ten or more banquet tables. They insisted that except for the very poor, families accepted without argument whatever the bridegroom's family would offer. That custom remains unchanged today. Negotiating brideprice would have been a tremendous loss of face. "Only the sands people would act in such a manner," I was told.

To attribute this emphasis on dowry only to a strategy for status acquisition among rich families is to neglect the fact that a similar situation of low brideprice in relation to dowry existed in ordinary town families. It might be suggested that the terms of marriage had different meanings for households in various circumstances. But the life-styles of members of the wealthy lineages and what they provided for their daughters represented the cultural ideal in the area.[20] The smallness of brideprice might also be

19. I refer to those that controlled the development of the sands from the Ming dynasty on. See the genealogies of the Zhao of Sanjiang in Xinhui county, the Long and Luo of Shunde county, the Huo of Foshan. See Siu, "Where Were the Women? Rethinking Marriage Resistance and Regional Culture in South China," *Late Imperial China* 11, no. 2 (December 1990): 32–62, for details of marriage customs in the area.

20. The same was true for Shawan in Panyu county, another center of wealth and power at the edge of the sands. A large percentage of the town households in Shawan literally lived off

related to the practice of *buluojia*, the delayed removal of the bride to her husband's house.[21] The richer the families, the longer their daughters stayed at home. Ties with a married daughter continued to be important in various ways. As long as she remained at her home, the fruits of her labor were shared with her natal family. The significant break with her parents came when she was about to have a child, not when wedding gifts were negotiated and exchanged. When she joined her husband, provisions for continuing support were often made. If brideprice was used at all for acquiring the rights to a woman's labor, the custom of *buluojia* would have kept the payment low.

Town residents, whether from families that were formerly rich or poor, insisted that their terms of marriage and those of the sands were very different. The inhabitants of the sands did not practice *buluojia*; a woman settled with her husband's family immediately after the wedding. Among the fishermen, the mobility of their boat-dwellings made it difficult to do otherwise, since it was not a question of husband and wife being in adjacent villages. At the same time, their dowries were modest, consisting of several sets of clothes, a blanket, a mosquito net, washbasins, bowls, and plates; but the brideprice was large, usually twice that of the town. In my 1986 interviews I came across old men in Zhixi, a village in the sands, who had been married in the late 1920s and early 1930s. They quoted brideprice amounts of one hundred to two hundred silver dollars, which seemed extraordinarily high given the standard of living in the sands at the time. One part of the brideprice consisted of banquet food for the relatives and friends of the bride. In the town only selected members of households (other than those of close relatives) were invited to attend wedding banquets, but in the sands such occasions involved every aquaintance far and near, young and old. Feasting lasted for three whole days. Meals were served for those guests who had moored their boats the night before. They were feasted again on the wedding day, and on the third day meals were served before the guests left the area. As in Africa, the remainder of the brideprice was

---

the focal ancestral estate, Liugeng Tang, which owned 60,000 mu of the sands. As in Nanxi, women learned sewing and helped with family chores until they settled with their husbands. For the historical evolution of lineages in Shawan, see Liu Zhiwei, "Lineage on the Sands: The Case of Shawan," a paper presented at the panel "Lineage Power and Community Change in Republican South China," annual meetings of the Association for Asian Studies, April 1990.

21. Historical documents through the Qing recorded it as common in parts of the Pearl River delta both among the elites and commoners. It involved women marrying at an early age but continuing for a few years to reside at their natal home. They would briefly visit their husband's home for important ritual occasions and festivals, but not until they were about to give birth to their first child would they settle there permanently. See Siu, "Where Were the Women?" for a summary of the relevant literature.

often used as a marriage fund for brothers,[22] a use that was scorned by town residents, who asserted that the sands people were "shamelessly aggressive" in negotiating brideprice and that "they had to marry off a daughter in order to get a daughter-in-law."[23] It seems that their strategy for coping with life at the bottom of a social hierarchy was regarded as a stigma in the eyes of the townsfolk, who used it as a way of dissociating themselves from the people of the sands.

THE WAR INTERLUDE

The domination of the town over the sands in the late imperial period continued through the republican period until the decade of the 1940s, when war and endemic disorder finally broke the power of the town-based ancestral trusts. Many tenant farmers in the sands were able to acquire land from their landlords by manipulating cash rents, grain prices, and taxes. In addition, local bosses who rose to the height of their power during the Japanese occupation took over vast estates by force.[24] Although built with straw and river mud, small villages with more permanent dwellings mushroomed in those places where local bosses set up their territorial bases.[25] Interviews suggested that in this particular decade marriage strategies changed with the shift in power. The rich households in the villages started to arrange marriages with elite families in town whose fortunes had declined in the years of war. In doing so, they adopted the prestigious custom of *buluojia* and displayed lavish dowries. My interviews show that several local bosses succeeded in marrying their daughters to the families of merchants and rich peasants from the neighborhoods adjacent to the town.[26] As for the ordinary people of the sands, the situation did not appear to change, although the new situation provided the basis for them later on to redefine their circumstances. In 1986 I interviewed a dozen of the old residents in one of these villages settled by migrant laborers, Zhixi. Although

22. See Jack Goody and S. J. Tambiah, *Bridewealth*, on the functions of brideprice and dowry in African and Indian societies. A circulating fund increases interdependence among siblings and between generations within a family.

23. The demand of high brideprices in the sands was told to me by many old women in town and confirmed by a marriage ritual specialist who attended many weddings in the area.

24. For the rise and fall of local bosses, see Helen Siu, *Agents and Victims*, chap. 5. For Nanxi, see Helen Siu, "Subverting Lineage Power: Local Bosses in the 1940's," a paper presented in the panel "Lineage Power and Community Change in Republican South China," AAS meetings, April 1990.

25. A richer household might have a tile roof. These houses are known as *chan ding ya* (wooden beams and bark holding up tiles).

26. For example, the Liu family of Zhixi village married a daughter into a prosperous Mai family of Yongding in the late 1940s. A great deal of jewelry was given as dowry. The father of the bride was the most powerful local boss in the village.

it was difficult for them to name any ancestor beyond their grandfather's generation, they nevertheless claimed that their families had originated from the older part of the delta where the ancestral halls stood. They insisted that as long as they could remember, they had practiced *buluojia*. They also disassociated themselves from the boat-dwelling inhabitants of the more recent river marshes further southeast, an area they termed *xia sha* (the lower sands).[27] But data from my survey contradicted their claims. Their families at the time demanded extraordinarily high brideprices of between one hundred and three hundred silver dollars. Families of the bride and groom both provided banquets that lasted for several days. Dowries were far below what was given by elite families in town and consisted of kitchen utensils and bedding, although in some cases a set of table and chairs and a chest were added.

Contrast the rural areas with the circumstances of households in town for that period. During the eight years of war with Japan, Nanxi town was ruled by an uneasy alliance of local bosses with the Japanese army that was stationed nearby. Everything was scarce owing to the blockades imposed both by the Japanese military and by what remained of the Nationalist government. The fortunes of landowning families and merchant houses declined rapidly, their estates being divided and sold off to the military bosses. The ideal marital payments were hard to come by. As for ordinary households, the ideal was even harder to imagine. Old women I interviewed claimed that ordinary households provided little dowry to speak of. Brides settled immediately with their husbands because family members were scattered or had perished. The most the couple got was enough food for a dinner with close relatives, together with some basic items of furniture. Those who were refugees from other counties were grateful to have any shelter.[28] Brideprice, if given, was often in the form of baskets of rice, ranging from one to ten *dan*.

Except for the local bosses who had risen rapidly during the war, families in town found lavish dowries for daughters harder to reach, and the embarrassment of asking for a brideprice became a necessity. In other words, the dislocations of war and the reversals of fortune for the area's elite families had eroded the traditional terms of marriage before the Communists arrived on the scene. It is this period that provides a realistic baseline for an evaluation of the relationship between the terms of marriage and the transformed social hierarchy after 1949.

27. Some of the residents of Zhixi might have been poor urbanites who migrated to the villages. They attended the lineage ceremonies in the ancestral halls in town and continued to observe town customs.

28. In my household survey of 1986, I found many heads of households, men or women, who had come from other counties in Guangdong during the war and who settled in Nanxi afterward.

SOCIALIST TRANSFORMATIONS

Since family continuation, social prestige, the devolution of wealth, and the labor needs for households were important factors in marital transfers, family strategies were bound to change during the Maoist period from the 1950s to the late 1970s because the consolidating party-state had made a serious attempt to redefine the ideological principles and to restructure the political economy and the social hierarchy. In Nanxi the step-by-step transformation started immediately after the Communists took power. During the land reform of 1952, the former elites of the town—managers of lineage estates, merchants, administrators of the Nationalist government, and local bosses who came to power in the 1940s—were killed, imprisoned, or had their properties confiscated. Those who had set the standards of wealth and power were then reduced to a caste of untouchables. Not only were the means no longer available for continuing such a life-style, but the policy of overturning the hegemony of "tradition" was actively pursued during political campaigns when activists were brought in from outside the community. Those activists who had often been poor tenant farmers in the sands set about destroying ancestral halls and important public buildings, and carted the materials off to the villages. The political fervor extended to social life itself. Through the 1950s and 1960s, lavish dowries and wedding feasts were periodically stigmatized as "feudal extravagance." Brideprice was condemned as "buying and selling in marriage," and large payments were prohibited. But the uneven ebb and flow of politics meant that local cadres were sometimes compromising and permissive. The uneven pattern of policy implementation was quite similar to the one found by Parish and Whyte in rural Guangdong.

People interviewed in the late 1980s repeatedly expressed resignation about the stripping down of traditional practices in Nanxi town through the Maoist decades. The ideals of traditional marriage payments lingered on after the land reform. It was impossible for the town residents to afford the lavish transfers of the former elites, but dowries did consist of moderate provisions of household furniture, utensils, and jewelry. People recalled carrying brides on sedan chairs and attending wedding feasts. At the time, agriculture and commerce had recovered somewhat from the war. Family fortunes and private property were inheritable. But the subsequent collectivization of town enterprises followed by the famine years of 1958–61 left little for wedding festivities. My friends remembered how they sent their children around the neighborhood streets to gather leaves for fuel, and how fried dough wrapped in banana leaves became a delicacy. When the economy recovered in the early 1960s, local cadres had to brace themselves for the *siqing* campaigns.[29] For fear of corruption charges made by

29. "The four clean-ups" campaigns preceded the Cultural Revolution. The major targets of attack were village cadres who had risen with the Party bureaucracy.

work teams sent from outside, local cadres asked the inhabitants to behave with moderation. Guests could attend wedding dinners only in small groups because the town leadership explicitly limited the number of banquet tables to four per gathering.

The Cultural Revolution tried to kill off whatever remained of the old practices in town, giving rise to severe factional disputes among the town's leadership. Although actual fighting was rare, groups of Red Guards were formed, cadres were challenged by activists recruited from the sands, former landlords were paraded around the town, and ancestral tablets were burnt. The official model for wedding celebrations was to hold tea receptions instead of dinner banquets. Interviews show that because of the concentration of cadres, Party members, union workers, and teachers in town, the official line for simple wedding rituals was imposed more effectively than in the villages. Furthermore, the concentration of ancestral and merchant estates there in the prerevolutionary period meant that there were many families with bad class labels. Reduced to being a group of untouchables, members of these families had to marry among themselves or else "marry down" to whoever would take them. In the latter case the husbands were mostly poor petty traders who could not afford any marriage prestations.

By the mid 1970s those who remained unconvinced by socialist rhetoric were too afraid of the Party's organizational power to express their sentiments publicly. A new generation came of age under the shadow of the Maoist ideological purity who had been denied the appreciation of cultural depth and historical sensitivity. In the eyes of their parents, they had little sympathy for tradition.

Nevertheless, despite economic hardships and the government's explicit restrictions, dowry and brideprice remained an important concern for the local residents. The highest sum for brideprice quoted to me was about a hundred yuan, balanced by a few dowry items, such as bedding, household utensils, chairs, and a table. Such payments were not substantial enough to be viewed as means for prestige building or as shrewd calculations to obtain a woman's labor. But their persistence did reflect the continual importance of family commitments in everyday life under the changing socioeconomic conditions.[30]

The economy of Nanxi town had been drastically restructured and removed from the sphere of local agriculture. Instead of a place of residence for rentier landlords who lived off the grain from the sands, residents were

---

30. The reinforcement of family and patriarchy by socialist transformation has been dealt with by Judith Stacey, *Patriarchy and Socialist Revolution in China* (Berkeley: University of California Press, 1983); Margery Wolf, *Revolution Postponed: Women in Contemporary China* (Stanford: Stanford University Press, 1985); Emily Honig and Gail Hershatter, *Personal Voices* (Stanford: Stanford University Press, 1988). See also the works of Kay Johnson and Elizabeth Croll, and most recently, Deborah Davis's chapter in this volume.

employed in collective enterprises, which increasingly entered into subcontracts with state factories and commercial units at the county capital. While private resources were stripped away, wages in these collective factories were low, and the security or social services offered could not be compared with employment in the state sector. Nevertheless, town residents anxiously held on to their meager earnings and unflattering status, hoping that the government would not look for an excuse to send them to the sands and demote them to the status of peasants. Their fear of such arbitrary political reversals was not unjustified. Their status as town dwellers had been redefined when the adjacent rural commune was administratively merged with the town between 1958 and 1963. Ironically, it was their urban status that also led their children to be sent off to the sands in the wake of the Cultural Revolution.

Factory employment meant that the next generation worked with collective town enterprises rather than with their families. With wage employment, young workers might be expected to develop more individualized marriage strategies highlighting the concerns of the conjugal pair. But because of the relatively stagnant town economy and the post-1949 wage structure favoring seniority and the practice of *dingti*, young workers continued to be dependent on their parents and were expected to contribute to the family budget.[31] In the collective town enterprises workers received a great deal less of social services than those in the state sector, and the family continued to provide important support. My survey shows that one-generation families were rare. Many households consisted of the parents, a married son and his children, and unmarried children. Because of the continued practice of *buluojia*, it was not unusual for a married daughter to eat her meals at home. In other words, intergenerational and sibling ties remained strong despite wage employment outside the home and despite government efforts to replace loyalties to the family with those to the Party and the state.[32]

Indeed, families relied increasingly on an informal network of relatives because many traditional civic organizations had been eliminated.[33] This

31. *Dingti* is a system of job assignment in which a retiring person's job can be taken over by his or her children.

32. On age cohorts and structured life chances, see Deborah Davis, *Long Lives*, 1991 paperback ed., chap. 8; "Intergenerational Inequalities and the Chinese Revolution," *Modern China* 11, no. 2 (April 1985): 177–201; "Unequal Chances, Unequal Outcomes: Pension Reform and Urban Inequality," *China Quarterly*, 1989, 223–42; on dependent relationships in the urban industrial structure, see her review of Andrew Walder's book *Communist Neo-traditionalism: Work and Authority in Chinese Society* (Berkeley: University of California Press, 1986), in "Patrons and Clients in Chinese Industry," *Modern China* 14, no. 4 (October 1988): 487–97.

33. I refer to marketing networks, temple and credit associations, neighborhood shrines, and ritual specialists. For example, residents relied more on their relatives for funerals when ritual specialists and coffin-bearers were not readily available.

dependence was compounded by the general bureaucratization of life—for example, in the allocation of housing, for the establishment of quotas in various neighborhoods to send educated youths to the sands, or for the recruitment of soldiers and students based on class background.[34] Maneuvering the power of the state became a feature of everyday life. It showed even in household registration: married children delayed the registration of their new household until it was strategic to do so. A paradox existed for the town residents: while they relied heavily on the family for services not available through state channels, coping with the power of the state had become a cultural given in domestic decisions. The terms of marriage were negotiated within the framework of this politicized environment.

Maoist politics brought about drastic economic transformations in the sands as well as in the town. Nevertheless, marriage transfers continued to be significant for the local population. Instead of mooring their boats along a wide network of rivers, the inhabitants of the sands were forced to settle on land, where they were increasingly confined to their cellularized villages.[35] But under the policy of the Maoist period, settlement rights had strings attached. An exclusively grain-growing economy tightly controlled under the state pricing system kept their incomes low and their lives isolated from the towns and cities. Their daughters, whose children would automatically be assigned rural status, were no longer an available choice as marriage partners for those outside the sands. By the late 1950s the traditional strategy of achieving upward mobility by marrying into town mainly as second wives was closed off. Despite government claims to the contrary, the social gap between rural and urban residents widened.[36]

Brideprice negotiations continued in the Maoist era. Rural women described the marriage market and the transfer of payments at that time as unpredictable. Families with many daughters were fortunate to get them married off and had to choose from whoever was available in the village. At times, they took whatever brideprice was offered. In other villages men complained that there were not enough women around even when their families offered a good brideprice. A big change came about when people took wives from within the village. Daughters naturally remained nearby

---

34. For the bureaucratization of urban life, see Martin Whyte and William Parish, *Urban Life in Contemporary China* (Chicago: University of Chicago Press, 1984); Jonathan Unger, *Education Under Mao: Class and Competition in Canton Schools, 1960–1980* (New York: Columbia University Press, 1982); Gail Henderson, *The Chinese Hospital: A Socialist Work Unit* (New Haven: Yale University Press, 1984).

35. Cadres in the sands of Nanxi Zhen complained that it was difficult to make the sands people settle in houses clustered in a village, which was achieved only in the 1970s. See Helen Siu, *Agents and Victims*, on the step-by-step cellularization of rural communities in south China.

36. On the village-town divide, see Helen Siu, "The Politics of Migration in a Market Town."

even after marriage, and they continued to help out at home. When a family was short of labor, daughters stayed longer at home, like the town people. The collectivization of the economy of the sands and the corresponding cellularization of rural communities paradoxically intensified interdependence within local families as well as between them.

Villagers in Zhixi, Yongding, and Jiuji celebrated their weddings with banquets of a dozen or so tables throughout the 1950s until the late 1970s, except for the very lean years 1958 to 1962 and during the high tide of the Cultural Revolution, when officials explicitly demanded ritual simplicity.[37] Still, a brideprice of a hundred yuan plus wedding cakes was not uncommon. As for the dowry element, it was not until the 1970s when "the three treasures," a bicycle, a watch, and a sewing machine, were added to the ideal dowry list. They were largely "luxuries" reserved for the families of rural cadres.

THE RECONSTITUTION OF DOWRY AND BRIDEPRICE IN THE 1980s

Is the renaissance today a reinstatement of earlier practices spurred on by new prosperity? Not entirely. If both the terms of marriage and the political economy on which they were based were redefined by the state, their expansion today is further shaped by the entrepreneurial energies in town and in the sands. In two earlier papers, I interpreted the upsurge of seemingly "traditional" ritual practices not simply as a revival but also as having undergone great changes as a result of the socialist period. A similar argument can be applied to dowry and brideprice.

In Nanxi Zhen, the ten years of liberalization since 1980 have brought much prosperity for both town and village. Two categories of residents have made remarkable fortunes. First, party cadres have used official connections to make business deals; they have accepted "bribes" to facilitate those transactions, and they have anticipated the new policies of privatization, moving ahead of others to get the best resources for their families. The large modern villas that have sprung up in town are mostly theirs. Second, there are the entrepreneurs whose interests conflicted with the monopolizing powers of officials but who also colluded with them to gain a share of the profits. Many inhabitants of Nanxi town have been able to make contact with relatives in Hong Kong and Macao, who contributed to the building of houses, bought them imported consumer goods, or invested in joint ven-

37. Yongding, a village adjacent to Nanxi, is a rural settlement older than Nanxi town itself and containing established lineages. Jiuji, three kilometers southwest of Nanxi town, was a sizable village by the late Qing. Zhixi became a permanent settlement in the republican period. Traditional customs in the villages did not disappear until the late 1950s. A village cadre in Zhixi said that when his daughter married in 1953, she was carried in a sedan chair.

tures; these residents are known as having "a southern window" (*nanfeng chuang*). Those relatives who contribute to the enterprises are duly rewarded, but meanwhile the local entrepreneurs make profits and are asserting their independence. This assertion of independence is particularly prevalent among the younger entrepreneurs in town, where the life-styles and preferences of these two categories have become models for emulation and envy among the society as a whole.

The marriage transfers for these privileged families are elaborate. In town, brideprice demands are still not explicitly made, but new calls are made on the groom's family, and the expenses incurred by them are large. It has become essential for the groom to provide a new house for his bride.[38] Because of the shortage of building sites in town, the cost of a square meter of land is about 180 yuan. Together with building materials, decorating, and labor, a standard house can easily cost 70,000 yuan. Cadre families are particularly under pressure to make such contributions because, as one said, "people expect us to use administrative means to secure the prime sites, the imported tiles, and the color television. When we take the lead, others eagerly follow, claiming that present policies allow everyone to be prosperous."[39] According to another cadre, such transactions not only assure people that wealth is politically acceptable, but also enable them to convince themselves and others that they have not lost control of the situation in an era of ideological redefinition.

Similar pressure was felt by the nouveaux riches, because to spread the impression that "they have the means" is necessary for business. These families are now ignoring the official norms for the age of marriage. In one case, a marriage was contracted and a house built for a twenty-one-year-old, the only son in the family, because the parents, who were former landlords and who had migrated to Macao a few years earlier, were anxious to have male progeny to receive the family wealth.[40]

Besides the expenses of the house, the groom's family also pays a substantial brideprice, which has reached a norm of 800 to 1,000 yuan. The sum is mainly used to help pay for the wedding feast at the bride's natal

38. The provision of a house for the married couple illustrates what Jack Goody speaks of as "indirect dowry," which is generally stressed by poorer families, whereas direct dowry is stressed by richer social groups (such as the former landlord and merchant families).

39. The price for building land shot up in the town as well as in the villages adjacent to the town. In 1988, the price reached 200 yuan per square meter, compared with about 80 yuan for the villages farther away. The head of Nanxi was notorious for having secured some prime sites cheaply for his children and friends because he was in control of town planning and construction. A modern five-bedroom villa in town was 40,000 yuan in 1986 and rose to 150,000 yuan in 1989.

40. I attended the wedding of this young man, who had two older married sisters. He seemed not to know what he was doing throughout the entire affair. Earlier, I had interviewed him in my random sample survey as the head of a household.

home.[41] The standard in town is now at least thirty banquet tables at the local restaurant, at a cost of about 6,000 to 9,000 yuan.[42] Of course, the wealthy give more, as in the case of a successful private entrepreneur where the parents of the groom offered 1,200 yuan as brideprice, another 50 yuan as lucky money for the bride's brother, together with the cost of thirty-two banquet tables for the bride's family, who resided in a village on the outskirts of town.[43] They also provided thirty banquet tables on the wedding day for their own friends and relatives. Their banquet food included imported beer and soft drinks from Hong Kong, expensive dried mushrooms, squids, scallops, pork and chicken, and six hundred wedding cakes.[44]

It is difficult to insist that these prosperous families are attempting to "compensate" for the bride's labor. More appropriately, it has become a strategy for the upwardly mobile to win a bride of appropriate background, to acquire prestige in the local community, and to strengthen personal networks in a volatile system where formal organizational ties are still unreliable. For the common folk, the new standard is making it hard for their sons, because they have neither the wealth nor the political means to meet these expectations and would have to wait to get married until the richer households had chosen their brides. One might argue that this state of affairs is no different from the old days. But in the old days, no poor household would be competing with a rich one for a wife, in accordance with the saying "Bamboo door matches bamboo door, and wood door matches wood door." Now it is a tougher game when the woman one fancies in the workplace finally decides to marry a co-worker whose family has the "southern window" and can provide a house and thirty banquet tables for the marriage. A new hierarchy is in the course of defining itself through marriage and marital transfers.

In town, the expenses for the bride's family can be just as high if not higher. Among the wealthy, dowry items include modern furniture, a bicycle, electric fans, a sewing machine, imported color television, a washing machine, a hi-fi system, totaling over 15,000 yuan. It seems natural to argue that there are many upwardly mobile families created by the sudden opening up of economic opportunities in this area, who use the marriage of their sons and daughters to make an impression in town. However, there is

41. The sum is about four to five times the average wage of a young worker.

42. In 1986, a standard wedding gift from friends was 5 yuan. In 1989, I was told to give 25 yuan whenever I was invited to a wedding.

43. The family used to work on bamboo handicrafts. In the 1980s the head of the household worked as a manager for foreign trade in the largest factory in Nanxi Zhen. His annual salary and benefits easily reached 60,000 yuan, according to friends. One of the sons opened a small factory for metal parts and had his own prosperous business. In the previous three years, the family had built two three-story houses, costing over 100,000 yuan each.

44. In traditional marriages, wedding cakes and banquet food were listed together with the brideprice and other items and presented to the bride's family before the wedding.

an added dimension. Even for the very rich families, the bride and groom both contribute to the sum by saving up over the preceding few years. The self-accumulating dowry has arrived, and the couple are no longer entirely dependent upon their parents. The objects will be publicly transported and displayed during the course of the wedding day when they go to fill the new house assigned to the young married couple.[45] Dowry may still consist partly of the inheritance due a daughter, but it increasingly takes on the meaning of a conjugal fund created by and for the newlyweds themselves. Among the young workers, technicians and private entrepreneurs, who now earn a great deal more than their parents because of bonuses and shared dividends, the creation of their own independent conjugal fund is both possible and preferred.[46] Their eagerness to start the union in a new house symbolizes this concern. They take great care and pride in building and decorating their house according to the styles that are promoted in the television programs beamed from Hong Kong and in magazines for home living.[47]

Although the younger generation in Nanxi have taken the initiative in building their own conjugal funds, parents who have the means eagerly contribute, for both their sons and their daughters. Given their economic situation, it is not difficult to see the logic behind their efforts. Old age security becomes an important concern when the changing political winds and the subsequent competition from private entrepreneurs have shaken the town's collective economy in which they have participated. In fact, the town's enterprises experienced a great deal of uncertainty in the mid-1980s when faced with fierce competition from the mushrooming industries in the nearby villages. When businesses folded, workers were laid off with little prospect of a pension. Retirees have also found their pensions too meager to catch up with the severe inflation. If one argues that the function of the family as the basic provider persisted during the Maoist era, it is reasonable to expect that those with the means contribute to the consolidation of their

45. The *huiyou*, close companions of the groom, often collectively give large decorative mirrors for the new couple to hang in their own house. In the case of the successful entrepreneur mentioned earlier, the groom asked the bride's family to buy whatever dowry items it wanted and then have them billed to his family. When asked why they did that, the answer was the concern for "face."

46. I am not sure how far these attitudes are due to the impact of the television and media of Hong Kong, which promote the individualistic energies of young entrepreneurs. In fact, young people in Nanxi copy the Hong Kong life-style; for example, they buy imported clothes and electrical goods, smoke American cigarettes, drink Hong Kong beer, and use the vocabulary of Hong Kong television.

47. Two of my good friends, both young entrepreneurs with a good education and contacts in Hong Kong, live apart from their parents, although the latter come to care for their infant daughters. The interior design of their houses, each of which is equipped with a color television, a hi-fi system, and video, matches that of upper-middle-class families in Hong Kong.

children's marriages, with the hope that some measure of intergenerational dependence can be maintained under such conditions. In one case, two retired teachers saved up enough to buy a color television for their married son who had taken a job in a research unit in Hunan. When the young couple had a baby, the mother-in-law went to Hunan for several months to take care of the newborn, leaving her husband behind with an unmarried son. She eventually brought her grandson back to Nanxi. I asked why she did all that, well knowing that their resources and energies were strained. Her reply was straightforward: she would maintain a good relationship with her sons in the hope that they would reciprocate when needed. Whether her strategy works or not remains to be seen.

The sands have also been rapidly transformed in the last decade. Wedding banquets have grown even more elaborate, and it is common to have thirty or more tables. According to town residents, the sands people have adopted the custom of the town by sitting around tables, where courses were brought out one by one. This differs from their habit of serving food in large bowls all at once, with the guests squatting around to help themselves. New houses are provided by the groom's family for the newlyweds, but these belong mainly to cadre families.

If marriage practices were only mainly a means for families to work their way up the social hierarchy, one would expect the people in the sands to reduce their demand for brideprice, inasmuch as this has been such a stigma in the eyes of the town residents. Surprisingly enough, dowry remains moderate, but the monetary demands for brideprice have escalated sharply, reaching an average of 2,000 yuan, twice that of the town and more than the annual income of an adult worker in the villages.

To understand this phenomenon, it is necessary to trace the history of the socialist transformation in the sands. Today wedding festivities provide a sharp contrast to the normally quiet life in the villages. These rural areas are devoid of young workers, either men or women, with only old men and women doing light farmwork and carrying grandchildren on their backs. Most of the younger ones have migrated to the periurban neighborhoods, women to work in factories, men on construction sites. Farm labor is in such short supply that farmers increasingly make sharecropping arrangements with migrant farmers from the provinces of Guangxi, Jiangxi, and Hunan. Sometimes they hire workers outright by giving them room and board plus 80 to 100 yuan a month during the busy season. Not all of these migrant workers are good farmers. In 1986 the municipality in which Nanxi situates turned back 20,000 illegal migrants because, according to a municipal cadre, the region had suffered poor harvests for the last few years as a result of the poor quality of their labor.

One may wonder why many families continue to enter into contracts for large areas of land for growing grain despite such acute labor shortages.

The reason is simple: grain prices are high in the open markets, often over 100 yuan per *dan*, in contrast to the negotiated state price of about 25 to 30 yuan. The high price is due either to the fact that many families have switched to the growing of turfs, fruit, and sugarcane, or to the fact that their children have gone into the towns and cities to work.[48] This forces them to buy grain in the markets in order to fill the delivery quotas that are part of the process of contracting land from the village.

Attachment to the land is also promoted by concerns of a cultural and historical kind, which have been sharpened by the migration of the young. During interviews, older farmers repeatedly expressed a heightened anxiety about maintaining a base in the village because of the past history of settlement rights, especially as their children do not share such sentiment and would often like to emigrate from the rural areas. It took centuries for the people of the sands to be recognized as permanent inhabitants on the land. During the socialist period, attachment to land was seen as a burden that tied families to rural poverty; only with difficulty did the government convince them to build permanent brick houses in order to form "villages." When land again became a valuable household resource in the 1980s, they felt they must defend settlement rights, which entitled their sons to build houses in the village, and from which later arrivals are in their turn excluded. Waves of migrant workers from Yangjiang in southern Guangdong, from Guangxi and Hunan provinces, have become the new underclass of the sands. The verdicts of criminal cases that came before the people's courts in the last few years show that many of the victims of extortion, robbery, rape, and murder in the sands are these recent migrant workers. History repeats itself; the recent migrants take up the social space formerly occupied by the people of the sands.

The increased mobility of the rural population in general has created a dilemma for the earlier families who want to maintain their rights in the sands. They complain that it is increasingly difficult to find brides for their sons because local women, just like the men, prefer factory employment near Nanxi town, with the added intention of finding spouses there. Families are reluctant to let their grown daughters be married off too soon, and when they take in a daughter-in-law with an ever-increasing brideprice, they try to keep her at home.

It is true that where there is ample land and where agriculture continues to rely on manual labor, labor becomes a prized commodity. The crucial issue is why, given the availability of cheap migrant labor, families in the sands choose to pay high brideprices in an effort to keep their women at

48. In the villages closer to Nanxi town, turf is grown to supply the offices and hotels in the coastal cities and in Hong Kong. In the farther corners of the sands, banana plantations are common. They also produce for both the internal and the export markets.

home. Today settlement rights in the sands are highly valued, especially for the older generation, who were discriminated against before and who finally feel that they have gained a productive foothold in the 1980s. The "continuation of the house," as Goody describes it, made possible by commitments from the parent's generation toward the new conjugal units, is the culturally acknowledged basis for claiming these settlement rights. It also secures for the family the much-needed long-term farm labor. Furthermore, the demand for a high brideprice distinguishes these families from the new underclass of migrant workers, who cannot afford such payments and would not be able to make such a demand. As before, marital strategies serve a political function by excluding those at the lowest end of the social hierarchy.

CONCLUSION

The analysis of marital payments in this chapter takes into account the history of political transformation of the regional economy. The resources available to families and the way they choose to maneuver within the constraints imposed by the state are intertwined with this political history, which shapes the available options as well as the perceptions of them. In general, marital transfers in Nanxi Zhen have to do with strategies of family continuity and advancement. In the early twentieth century, these transfers took place in a highly stratified socioeconomic context. Apart from endowing daughters, the giving of a lavish dowry in town was a strategy for building prestige among the elites; for the commoners, it was more a way to distinguish themselves from the sands people. The inhabitants of the sands and the town had regarded themselves as worlds apart precisely because their lives were connected in multiple and unequal ways to an evolving regional economy. There were fierce contestations in material relationships and symbolic arenas. Ethnic labels or terms of marriage among families were political statements in this expanding part of the delta. As in dialogues on lineage, community, and settlement history, they were means of exclusion, differentiation, and acculturation among the local population as they sought their respective places in the emergent polity.

It would be naive to expect the "equalizing" measures of the socialist regime to have reduced the inequality between Nanxi town and the sands. There were less status competition and fewer prestige-building strategies among former elite families in town who were condemned to be a caste of untouchables. This process might explain the drastic drop in the dowries in town. But the life chances of the residents of town and sands continued to differ. Their respective positions within the socialist state reinforced and even enlarged the town dweller's traditional discriminations against the people of the sands. Unlike the urban families in the large cities as de-

scribed by Whyte in chapter 8 in this volume, whose livelihoods have been
based on an established state sector, these families lived in a small market
town dependent on a shaky collective economy near the margin of the rural
collective sector. Their cultural strategies to distinguish themselves from the
people of the sands remained significant, although the strategies were sub-
dued by a general lowering of living standards of the elites who defined
them, and although the motives behind the strategies were based on the
realities of a different rural-urban hierarchy.

It would be equally naive to assume that collectivization from the late
1950s to the late 1970s had dwarfed concerns for inheritance and for the
continuation of the family, especially in view of the fact that the family has
once again become a focal point of social life in the 1980s, which has in turn
led to a revival of marital transfers. Interdependence among family members remained strong if not intensified in the Maoist era for both the town
dwellers and the villagers; hence the continual negotiation of marital payments despite the attempts of the government to restrict and undercut
them. This "preservation" of family commitment was a way for people to
cope with the transformed relationship of state and society, another unin-
tended consequence of the policies in the Maoist era.

Family dynamics and the related terms of marriage today cannot be seen
as a restoration of what had been put on hold since the late 1950s. Instead,
as Whyte observes in Chengdu and Huang in rural Shangdong, they resulted from several contradictory trends that had changed the meaning of
the family at one level and reinforced it at another. At the level of the institution of the family vis-à-vis the larger society and the state, relationships
have changed because other mediating aspects of the civil society had been
stripped away. At the level of commitments among family members, the
concerns for continuity have remained strong precisely because other institutions were redefined by political ideologies and were no longer viewed
as reliable for the individual.

The economic opportunities of today, which have been created by a
decade of liberalization, pose a new social reality for the residents in Nanxi
town as well as for those in the sands. The opportunities allow young urbanites to create viable conjugal funds on their own initiative by means of
exaggerated dowries and brideprices, largely self-accumulated. Their efforts
dovetail those of their parents, who are eager to gain some old age security
in a time of uncertainty and who contribute with this end in view. Rural
youths, both men and women, are anxious to shed their peasant status and
eagerly fill the gaps at the lower end of the town's employment hierarchy,
an opportunity that was denied them for over three decades. For the older
generation, with the drastic loss of their young at a time when agriculture
becomes profitable, settlement rights reemerge as an important issue. Their
concern is often not shared by their children. Mustering the cultural re-

sources at their disposal, they try to control marriages for reproduction and for continued commitment to the family. By maneuvering marriage payments, they hope to tie women to the household economy. This new concern increases the demand for a large brideprice in the sands. The "success" of these strategies pursued by the older generation remains to be seen. With the productive links between the rural generations broken by migration and urban employment, and in town by increased entrepreneurial opportunities for the young, generational conflicts are numerous and explicit. Prospects of retaining the young are not high, although some may be persuaded to stay.

In sum, factors leading to different payments of brideprice and dowry are complex. They involve intergenerational dependencies within the family, as well as the fortunes of individual family members in relation to the larger society and state. From the early twentieth century to the post-Mao era, three crucial political turning points—the war interlude, the Maoist era, and the post-Mao liberalization—have continued to create different life chances for the residents of the town and the sands and have triggered divergent strategies. In analyzing these terms of marital transfer in Nanxi town and the sands through this time, I hope I have given a historically grounded and meaning-focused account of the ways the transformations of political economy intertwine with the cultural, symbolic resources people use to make sense of their lives.

EIGHT

Wedding Behavior and Family Strategies in Chengdu

Martin King Whyte

Marriage decisions are central to any discussion of family strategies. Normally, marriage is a central step in the age-old Chinese effort to continue the family line.[1] It should also be obvious that not just any marriage will do. Which individuals sons or daughters marry may have important consequences for the future prospects not only of those sons and daughters, but also of the larger families in which they grew up. Which partners are chosen and how the wedding is celebrated may affect the social status and links to useful patrons and allies of those involved. And whether particular marriages result in an expansion of an existing family (by the couple's moving in with what I call an "old family") or the setting up of an independent household (which I call, for the sake of simplicity, a "new family") may influence the opportunities Chinese have to succeed in the world that confronts them. For these and other reasons it is obvious that marriage is a central focus of family strategic thinking. In this chapter I analyze survey data from one Chinese city in an effort to gain insight into how family strategic behavior in regard to getting married may have changed over time, and particularly in the post-Mao or reform period (i.e., since 1978).

With colleagues at Sichuan University I collected survey data in Chengdu, the capital of Sichuan province, in 1987.[2] Our interviewees were a probability sample of 586 ever-married women between the ages of twenty

1. Concubinage, adoption, and other steps may be taken to this end, but for most Chinese, and particularly since 1949, marriage has been an essential prerequisite to family continuity.

2. My Chinese collaborators are Yuan Yayu and Xu Xiaohe, both affiliated with the Sociology Research Office of Sichuan University. Our research was supported by the U.S.–China Cooperative Science Program of the National Science Foundation and also by the United Board for Christian Higher Education in Asia, Sichuan University, and China's State Education Commission.

and seventy who lived in the two main urban districts of that city. Since we asked our respondents a variety of questions about how they first got married, and since the dates of those first marriages ranged over the fifty-five years from 1933 to 1987, we are able to say quite a bit about how the marriage experiences of these women have varied across time periods.[3] Given a particular interest in the reform period, we can examine whether women in Chengdu who married after 1978 did things differently than women who married in earlier periods.

Here I intend to go beyond simply examining whether wedding behavior has changed over time in Chengdu. A number of more complex questions are of interest and may tell us something about shifts in family strategies. For example, how did social groups within Chengdu differ in their wedding behavior? Which types of individuals or families were most likely to have experienced arranged marriages, to have had elaborate weddings, or to have set up new households after marrying? Have the "social correlates" of different kinds of wedding behavior changed over time, and particularly in the post-1978 period? Is there any sign in our data, for instance, of a group of nouveaux riches families arising as a result of the reforms and distinguishing themselves by holding particularly elaborate weddings? Did families of Party members "hold the line" against the revival of elaborate weddings in the reform period, or did such families lead the way in this trend? These are ad hoc examples of the kinds of questions we can address with our Chengdu data. Since much evidence on how wedding behavior has changed over time has already been presented,[4] after reviewing that evidence briefly here, my main focus will be on the social sources of variation in wedding behavior in Chengdu and how those sources may have changed over time.

I should clarify at the outset that, although like my fellow authors I am interested in family strategies, the evidence I have to work with—the

3. The response rate for the survey was 87.7%. Chengdu is, of course, not "typical" of all of urban China, but it is not especially unusual in comparison with other major cities in China. (Chengdu is China's tenth largest city, with an estimated population of 2.6 million in 1985.) Inferring change over time from this kind of cross-sectional sample is, of course, not an easy matter. Many of the older women in our sample were not living in Chengdu at the time they first married, and many of the women who were getting married in that city in the 1930s and 1940s have either died or moved elsewhere. So the data presented here cannot, properly speaking, tell us how the wedding behavior of representative members of the Chengdu population varied across time periods. Instead, they should be interpreted as telling us how the wedding experiences of a representative sample of women living in Chengdu in 1987 differed depending upon the time at which they married.

4. See Martin King Whyte, "Changes in Mate Choice in Chengdu," in *Chinese Society on the Eve of Tiananmen*, ed. Deborah Davis and Ezra Vogel, 181–213 (Cambridge: Harvard University Press, 1990).

Chengdu survey data—does not contain any direct information about such strategies. We asked respondents questions about such things as who made the decision about whom to marry, how much was spent on the wedding, who paid for the celebration, and where the couple lived after the wedding. We did not, however, ask any questions about why things had been done in a certain way or about how the decisions were arrived at and with what family goals and concerns in mind. To address questions such as these properly would require a different research technique, involving intensive, in-depth interviews rather than a roughly one-hour-questionnaire survey. Even if we had used this alternative technique we would have faced diffi- culties, since the older respondents in our sample might have difficulty remembering and providing accurate reconstructions of family strategic thinking three or more decades earlier, and many of them (particularly those who experienced strictly arranged marriages) were not consulted at the time.

In the absence of direct information about family strategic thinking, I am forced to rely on inference here. My approach is to look for overall pat- terns in the data to see what those patterns might indicate about family strategies and changes in such strategies. I contend that if family strategies have been operating with any degree of success, we should see evidence of the operation of such strategies in our data on wedding behavior. If we do not find such interpretable patterns in our data, then we have evidence either that family strategies were not successful or that they did not exist in a coherent way in the first place. Inferring family strategies from such pat- terns in the data is not an easy or exact process.

CHANGES IN MATE CHOICE IN CHENGDU

How did wedding behavior change over time in Chengdu, and what do any trends tell us about changing families and family strategies in that city? In dealing with these questions, I focus on aspects of wedding behavior that tell something about changes in intergenerational relations.[5] This focus is important because it may help us deal with a central question in the study of family strategies: What is the proper unit of analysis? To put the ques- tion in a different way, when we want to study the formulation and negotia- tion of strategies for success in urban China, does it make most sense to look at individuals, at what I call new families, or perhaps at old families? Who, after all, is involved in these kinds of decisions? And might it not be that the locus of strategic thinking in regard to marriage has changed in

5. A more general examination of changes in a broad range of mate choice and wedding customs has already been published. See Whyte, "Changes in Mate Choice in Chengdu."

fundamental ways over time, from parents and family elders (the leaders of old families) to potential brides and grooms (those who will form the new families)? By examining what wedding behavior tells about shifts in relative power, social ties, and interdependency between generations, we may be able to draw inferences about basic changes in the nature and locus of family strategic thinking in contemporary China.

There are good reasons for assuming in advance that basic changes in the nature of intergenerational relations may have occurred in twentieth-century China. All that we know about the nature of marriage in late imperial China suggests that for most this was a relatively extreme form of arranged marriage in which the old family was the locus of power and the new family had little if any voice. Parents or other senior kin decided when it was time for children to marry and whom they should marry, and in many cases the young couple was not consulted and did not even meet until the day of the wedding. Sometimes a child betrothal or adoption of a future daughter-in-law as an infant was involved, making even clearer the total subordination of the younger generation to the wishes of their elders. Negotiations over brideprices and dowries and the financing of a wedding feast were also matters of family decision, rather than issues left for the young couple. Usually there was an expectation that the new family would be incorporated into the old through patrilocal residence, but even if not, the decision about where to live and how to earn a living were often matters determined more by the old family than the new. In some accounts from earlier times we learn of families making decisions to have one son study for the imperial examinations, another remain in the household and take over the family farm, and another go off to work in a market town or city, all in an effort to maximize chances for family success.[6] The power of the older generation and the role of that generation in making decisions about family strategy were reinforced and expressed in multiple ways in marriage behavior in late imperial China.

Changes that weakened the power of the old family in marriage matters were already under way before the Chinese Communist Party (CCP) came to national power in 1949. Both growing industrialization and commercialization and the spread of Western ideas about marriage and family life fostered trends toward greater independence of the young in the first half of

---

6. This scenario is somewhat idealized and would have applied mostly to families already well above the margin of subsistence. But in general a picture of the old family fairly explicitly dictating the lives of the young is a commonplace in descriptions of social life and social mobility in earlier times. See, for example, Ho Ping-ti, *The Ladder of Success in Imperial China* (New York: Science Editions, 1964); Yung-teh Chow, *Social Mobility in China* (New York: Atherton Press, 1966); Lin Yueh-hwa, *The Golden Wing* (London: Kegan Paul, 1947). The best-known fictional portrayal of the conflict over the power of the elders to control the fate of young family members is Pa Chin, *Family* (Garden City: Anchor Books, 1972 [originally 1933]).

the twentieth century.[7] After 1949 the CCP used its impressive power to campaign against arranged marriage and other manifestations of parental power. Both economic development and the socialist transformation of property relations carried out by the CCP should have weakened further the power and resources parents could wield in their efforts to dictate marriage matters.[8] Further economic development and the return of Western cultural influence during the reform period could be expected to accentuate these trends even more. How does the evidence from Chengdu fit these expectations?

The first aspect of marriage behavior to consider is the degree of freedom of mate choice—whether parents (or other family elders) or the young couple play the dominant role in deciding whom to marry. In this realm there have been clear changes, as the data presented in table 8.1 reveal. (This table and table 8.2 divide years of first marriage into periods that correspond roughly to important turning points in the history of contemporary China.) In general, there has been a shift from the old family to the new family in terms of who makes the selection of marital partners. (Other trends shown in the table have already been discussed in previous writings and will not be focused on here.) A more fine-grained analysis, making use of a summary scale and finer time divisions, reveals a somewhat more complex pattern. In figure 8.1 I display a three-year moving average of a summary Freedom of Mate Choice Scale across years of marriage.[9]

Figure 8.1 confirms that the change toward increasing freedom of mate choice was already under way prior to 1949 and that this trend continued during the 1950s. However, the figure also reveals that after about 1957 this shift more or less "stalled," with little net change toward greater freedom of mate choice during subsequent periods. Neither the storms of the Cultural Revolution nor the frenetic changes of the reform period had much effect on the freedom of young people in Chengdu to choose their own mates. To summarize briefly, I argue that the 1950s involved a massive structural change—the socialist transformation of the urban economy. That change

7. These trends are documented in Olga Lang, *Chinese Family and Society* (New Haven: Yale University Press, 1946). See also Marion Levy, *The Family Revolution in Modern China* (Cambridge: Harvard University Press, 1949).

8. The classic work on how various aspects of "modernization" produce changes that give young couples more autonomy is William J. Goode, *World Revolution and Family Patterns* (New York: Free Press, 1963).

9. The summary Freedom of Mate Choice Scale was constructed from the mean of the standardized scores of each respondent on six questions—those numbered 1, 2, 3, 6, 7, and 9 in table 8.1. A three-year moving average is constructed by taking the average of the scores for the years before and after a particular year. For example, the value for 1957 is an average of the values for 1956, 1957, and 1958. This procedure is followed to compensate for modest numbers of cases in each marriage year, and the result is a smoother and more readily interpretable graph.

TABLE 8.1. Changes in Aspects of Freedom of Mate Choice in Chengdu
(percentages)

	Year First Married				
	1933–48 (N = 71)	1949–57 (N = 107)	1958–65 (N = 82)	1966–76 (N = 116)	1977–8 (N = 21
Traditional arranged marriage	69	22	1	0	0
Type of marriage					
Arranged	68	27	0	1	2
Intermediate	15	33	45	40	41
Individual choice	17	40	55	59	57
Dominant role in mate choice					
Parents	56	30	7	8	5
Mixed	15	11	6	3	6
Respondent	28	59	87	89	89
Introduced to husband	91	76	54	59	60
Who provided the introduction?					
Own generation	38	43	75	75	74
Other	8	17	7	6	9
Parents' generation	53	40	18	19	17
Dated husband prior to marriage					
Often	12	17	24	40	48
Sometimes	6	18	27	13	21
Rarely	23	22	30	31	24
Never	59	44	18	16	7
No. of Romances					
None	73	29	9	5	5
One	24	63	74	66	67
More than one	3	8	18	29	28
Had other marital prospects	4	5	2	6	9
How much in love when married?[a]					
1. Completely	17	38	63	61	67
2.	26	29	22	26	19
3.	35	20	9	11	10
4.	9	4	4	1	3
5. Not at all	13	9	2	1	0

[a] Respondents were shown a five-point scale with only the end points labeled.

TABLE 8.2. Changes in Aspects of Wedding Behavior in Chengdu

	Year First Married				
	1933–48 (N = 71)	1949–57 (N = 107)	1958–65 (N = 82)	1966–76 (N = 116)	1977–87 (N = 210)
:dding ceremony held (%)	85	74	66	74	89
tendance at wedding (mean N)	60	55	66	66	102
:dding banquet held (%)	75	46	20	28	68
nquet attendance (mean N)	60	49	49	51	85
fts from husband to bride					
› giving)	34	18	21	22	31
ideprice (% giving)	18	9	5	6	9
›wry to bride (% giving)	56	36	26	32	71
tal spent on wedding (%)					
Under 500 yuan	82	89	94	80	15
500–999 yuan	10	8	6	13	32
1,000+ yuan	7	3	0	7	53
are of expenses paid by couple (%)					
0%	26	21	3	5	3
1–59%	11	10	6	10	30
60–99%	19	13	12	18	39
100%	43	56	80	68	28
stmarital residence (%)					
With bride's family	10	7	4	7	12
With groom's family	45	25	13	16	28
In own place	39	64	71	68	51
Other	6	4	12	9	9

reduced the power of parents dramatically, since they no longer controlled property or access to adult jobs, but urban young people gained increased autonomy only up to a point. The real winner was the bureaucratic system constructed by the CCP, which controlled education, employment, health care, housing, and all other important resources. Young people found that some of the freedom gained from parents was lost to the bureaucratic gatekeepers of the state (in schools, factories, etc.), individuals who were decidedly not indifferent to when and how young people married.[10]

10. This central role of the bureaucratic state is the decisive element left out of Goode's account of modernization and family change in capitalist countries. In the capitalist world, both governments and employers and other bureaucratic gatekeepers are largely indifferent to the private lives of the young, so that power lost by parents is gained by the young.

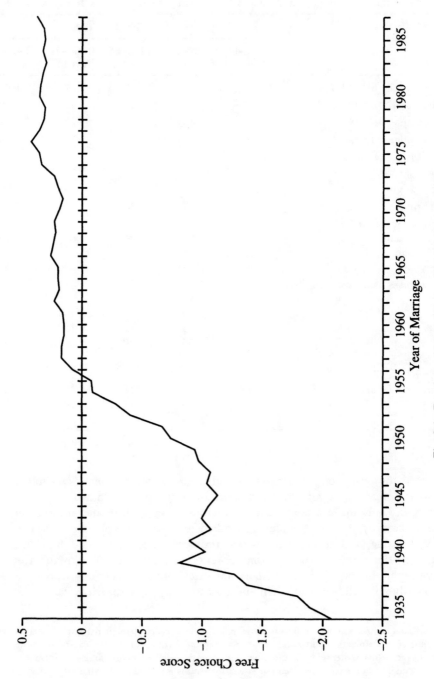

Fig. 8.1. Freedom of Mate Choice, Moving Average

A variety of measures of wedding celebrations and wedding finances are displayed in table 8.2. Also included in that table are responses to a question about where the couple lived after the wedding. There are dramatic changes across time visible in these figures, but the pattern is quite different from the one seen in table 8.1 and figure 8.1. Broadly speaking, what we see here is a curvilinear trend. Initially there are sharp shifts away from "traditional" patterns. By the late 1950s and 1960s fewer couples were having wedding ceremonies and banquets, fewer people were being invited to such events when they were held, marriage finance transactions (e.g., bride-prices, dowries) were less common, less money was being spent, more often the bride and groom were paying for any festivities themselves, and it was increasingly common for the new family to reside separately from either his or her parents.[11] In more recent times, however, all of these trends have been reversed. By the final period, the era of the reforms, wedding ceremonies, and banquets are once again increasingly common, more people are being invited to them, more is being spent on them, and it is less and less common for the young couple to finance their weddings themselves. By the same token, postmarital residence in a new household has become *less* common during the reform period, with moving in with the groom's or the bride's parents (most commonly still the former) once again on the rise (see also the figures presented in chapter 2 by Unger).[12] So in these realms we see not a stalling of a pattern of change, but an apparent reversal and return toward more "traditional" patterns.[13]

11. A variety of other aspects of change in wedding customs are not displayed in table 8.2. In general many couples who married between the 1950s and 1970s in urban China followed the models espoused by the CCP by holding a simple celebration with close friends and work-mates in the work unit, with tea and candy distributed to participants. In a few cases these "revolutionary" weddings included explicit political statements, such as a speech by the Party secretary encouraging devotion to the revolution, presentation of a set of Mao's writings to the couple, or having the couple bow to a bust or portrait of Mao Zedong. The role of the family is obviously strikingly deemphasized in such wedding ceremonies, which contrast very clearly with the traditional wedding, in which the family-run feast is the central event. The spartan nature of these "revolutionary weddings" helps explain why so much less was spent and why couples could finance things themselves. It might be noted that we asked a question about another officially espoused model, the "collective wedding," in which large numbers of couples are married at a single time in a public ceremony presided over by CCP officials. We found very few cases in our sample of such collective weddings in any time period.

12. Richard Barrett (personal communication) has found evidence from the 1985 In Depth Fertility Surveys that shows a similar trend of neolocal residence declining and patrilocal residence increasing during the 1980s in urban areas of several provinces (Beijing, Shandong, Liaoning, and Guangdong).

13. There are a number of "new" elements also visible in Chengdu wedding customs in the 1980s. For example, wedding banquets in restaurants are increasingly common, something that fits the Hong Kong more than the traditional Chinese model. Similarly, the wearing of a Western-style white wedding gown for a formal wedding picture is increasingly the norm, and

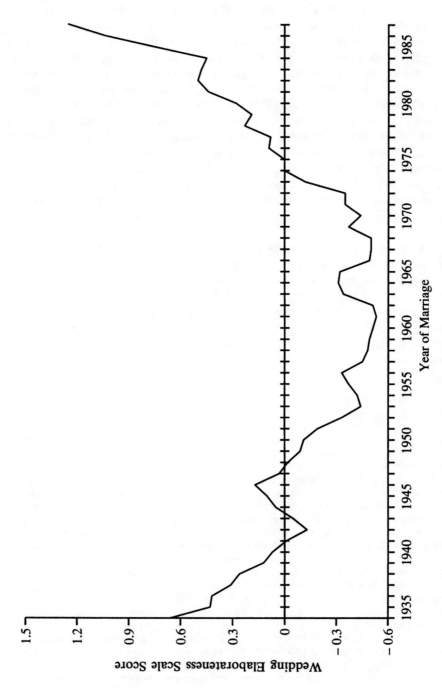

Fig. 8.2. Wedding Elaborateness, Moving Average

As earlier in regard to freedom of mate choice, we can examine whether a more fine-grained analysis will reveal further details about these trends in wedding elaborateness and expenditures. I constructed a mean scale of wedding elaborateness from a variety of the available measures, and in figure 8.2 I graph a moving average of scores on that scale against years of marriage.[14] Figure 8.2 reinforces the conclusions already reached about a curvilinear time trend, but adds a few extra details. According to this measure, the elaborateness or costliness of weddings in the reform period appears to be even greater than in the prerevolutionary period. Also, the decline in wedding expenditures is visible even before 1949, whereas the revival of wedding costs begins prior to Mao's death, rather than after 1978.

Put very simply, I think a variety of forces are at work in these reversals of wedding behavior. In part we see reflected here a return to something closer to normalcy after the Cultural Revolution, as lessened CCP monitoring of private life made it possible for families once again to follow cherished practices in celebrating weddings. Also at work, at least after 1978, is the new official encouragement of conspicuous consumption and the rapidly increasing incomes of urbanites, factors that made possible and respectable the sorts of lavish weddings that would have gotten people into trouble only a few years previously. (On this score the CCP continued to advocate spartan wedding celebrations while saying it was good to get rich and that envy provided a powerful incentive for economic improvement. Encouraging restaurants, photography shops, and other service facilities to cater to popular needs and make profits also helped to fuel the revived "wedding trade.")

Even though the post-1978 improvements in consumption standards applied to housing as well as to food, clothing, and other areas, the increases in urban housing space were not translated into improved chances for young couples to get a place of their own. My interpretation of this apparently contradictory finding, admittedly speculative, is that in the context of housing demands suppressed for so long, with many older people with stalwart work and political records waiting on housing lists for years, newly marrying couples had less chance than in previous periods of getting allocated housing on their own. By continuing to live with either her parents or his they might be able to move into new housing as it became

---

more and more couples are taking honeymoon trips. My claim is not that all aspects of wedding customs are reverting to traditional forms, but that those aspects of wedding celebrations that have implications for intergenerational relations are moving in that direction.

14. Included in the scale were seven items: those numbered 1, 2, 3, 4, 7, and 8 from table 8.2 and responses to a question about the monetary value of the dowry items (with zero used in cases with no wedding, banquet, or dowry). As with the Freedom of Mate Choice Scale earlier, this scale was formed by taking an average of standardized scores of each respondent on these seven items. This scale can be interpreted as measuring the elaborateness and costliness of the proceedings. Note that the postmarital residence measure is not part of this scale.

available during the 1980s.[15] (See the related discussion in the chapters by Davis, Unger, and Ikels.) In any case, in these realms we see a fairly consistent pattern that constitutes a reversal of the patterns that occurred in earlier years.

How are we to interpret the evidence presented so far? What do the data reviewed here tell us about shifting patterns in the relationship between generations in Chengdu families? What we do not see in this evidence is a pattern of "creeping individualism," of continuing growth in youth autonomy. Nor is the expectation of a linear trend toward more "modern" weddings borne out. Young people seem to have gained some power relative to their elders, at least when it comes to deciding whom to marry. However, their ability to live separately and rely on their own resources has actually diminished in recent years. We do not know, unfortunately, how in recent marriages it was decided how much to spend, how many to invite to the wedding, or where the couple would live afterward. But we can see that, even though the dominant role in choosing whom to marry is now in most cases played by "new families," in order to actually complete the process they have to rely on their "old families" in multiple ways. This continued and, indeed, revived intergenerational dependency may not mean that family elders are once again dictating matters to the young, but it would seem to require some sort of negotiation between generations over the nuts and bolts of how the wedding will be conducted and where the young couple will start out married life (a point also made by Davis in chapter 3). These results, taken as a whole, qualify my earlier discussion. This is not a situation in which powerless old families look on helplessly as the lives of their children are determined by an omnipotent and inflexible bureaucracy. Instead, continued family involvement and support appear to be vital to survival in the bureaucratic environment that is urban China. The trend toward increased youth autonomy from earlier in this century has been halted and in some respects even reversed.

SOCIAL BACKGROUND AND WEDDING BEHAVIOR

Now I turn to the questions of how subgroups within the Chengdu population differed in their wedding behavior and whether the sources of variation in such behavior changed across time periods. In the pages that follow I review a wide range of evidence bearing on these questions by examining the correlations between various background traits of our respondents (and

15. Figuring out how the housing supply affects patterns of postmarital residence is tricky. Young couples might end up with a place of their own for quite contradictory reasons—either because housing is so short that there is no space for them to move in with either set of parents or because housing in the city is so ample that young people can obtain their own place.

their old families) and their actual wedding experiences in various time periods.[16] From the large number of measures available from the Chengdu survey, I selected a limited range of important measures to examine, and consider only five basic aspects of wedding behavior: the degree of freedom of mate choice, the elaborateness of the wedding, whether or not there was a dowry presented by the bride's parents,[17] how much of the total wedding expenditures were borne by the young couple themselves, and whether the couple set up a new residence after the wedding. In terms of social background characteristics, I use a select subset of the available measures of three types: background characteristics of the individual bride and groom, background characteristics of their "old families," and "other" characteristics (i.e., traits that are not social status traits either of the bride and groom or of their families—for example, the year of the wedding, the age of the bride at the time, etc.).

Displayed separately here, the correlations between background characteristics and wedding behavior in three broad time periods—1933–57, 1958–77, and 1978–87, are collapsed further from the five categories used in previous tables. Each of these time periods has enough women in it (178, 198, and 210, respectively) to make analysis of correlations possible, but the main reason for these divisions is substantive. The first period involves the prerevolutionary era as well as the years after the CCP came to power but before the new socialist system was fully consolidated. The middle time period might be regarded as the years of full socialism or even "high Maoism"—they begin with the year in which Mao Zedong's visionary Great Leap Forward was launched and include the Cultural Revolution and its aftermath. The final time period is, of course, the era of the reforms initiated under the leadership of Deng Xiaoping.

What can we expect to learn by comparing correlations between social background traits and wedding behavior across these time periods? Of

---

16. The correlation is not the most appropriate statistic to use in examining many of these relationships, since most of our variables are ordinal or even nominal, rather than interval. However, most nominal variables can be rearranged to make them ordinal (for example, with occupations ranging from low status to high), and the use of interval statistics, such as the Pearson product-moment correlation, to summarize findings is claimed by most experts to be an acceptable shorthand that in most cases leads to similar conclusions as relying on cross-tabulations and ordinal statistics. (A large number of cross-tabulations were examined as a preliminary to preparing table 8.3, and that examination confirmed this impression.) Also, full tables on so many variables would be completely unwieldy.

17. The dowry is included as a separate measure even though this is one component part of the Wedding Elaborateness Scale. The reason for this "double counting" is that much previous literature suggests a particular importance for dowry exchanges in reflecting such things as continuing ties with the woman's natal kin and competition for high status. See the discussion in Rubie Watson and Patricia Ebrey, eds., *Marriage and Inequality in Chinese Society* (Berkeley: University of California Press, 1991).

course, we can consider a wide range of specific predictions about whether well-educated individuals, families with bad class backgrounds, or women who marry late (for example) had different types of weddings than others, and in all periods or only in one or two. However, my main interest in presenting the figures that follow is not to consider such specific predictions, but to look for overall patterns, and for any variation in those patterns across time periods.

To oversimplify somewhat: If we consider that our first broad time period captures marriages that occurred under basically presocialist conditions, then we can see what types of individuals and families had the most freedom of mate choice, the most elaborate weddings, and so forth, under those conditions. (We can also consider whether the distinctions found are similar to those uncovered in research on other nonsocialist societies.) If we designate the second period as the full socialist or high-Maoism period, then we might expect the predictors of variation in wedding behavior to have been somewhat different in those years (in comparison both with the pre-1957 period and with other societies). For example, the heightened emphasis on socialist values and vastly expanded bureaucratic control over people's lives under "high Maoism" might have produced a situation in which education and occupational status lost their predictive power in regard to weddings, but Party membership and class-origin labels gained predictive power.

If we find some clear differences between these first two time periods in the overall pattern of differentiation in wedding behavior, then we have a template against which to judge things in the final, reform period. Have the reforms sufficiently altered urban social structure in China and restored markets, material incentives, and meritocratic competition for personal advantage so that those social background traits that affected wedding behavior in the pre-1957 years reemerge as important after 1978? Or does the pattern of differentiation in wedding behavior in the reform period look much like that under high Maoism, suggesting that the dynamics of urban life have not changed as much under the reforms as many people suppose? Or is there some sort of completely new pattern of association between social background traits and weddings emerging in the reform era, unlike either the presocialist or high-Maoism eras? These are the sorts of ideas that motivated the analysis that follows.

Because the analysis of wedding behavior is spread over tables 8.3–8.7 (one table for each aspect of behavior considered), it may appear difficult to notice general patterns.[18] However, by looking across all five tables, the

---

18. Additional complexities concern how the various measures were constructed. Briefly, the Freedom of Mate Choice and Wedding Elaborateness Scales are interval measures whose construction was described earlier in the chapter; the dowry measure is a simple dichotomy

TABLE 8.3. Social Background and Freedom of Mate Choice Scale Scores
(Pearson correlation statistics)

	Period First Married		
	1933–57 (N = 178)	1958–76 (N = 198)	1977–87 (N = 210)
Couple's background			
Bride's educational level	.43**	−.04	.01
Groom's educational level	.31**	−.08	−.01
Bride's Party membership	.35**	−.03	.12
Groom's Party membership	.30**	−.08	−.05
Bride's occupational status	.25	−.05	.03
Groom's occupational status	.10	−.16*	.04
Bride's family characteristics			
Mother's educational level	.31**	−.11	−.01
Father's educational level	.35**	−.14	.11
Father's occupational status	.21**	−.02	.09
Parental urban origins	.18*	.04	−.06
Family's class origins	.16*	−.00	.09
Parental class label	−.22*	.10	.04
Other characteristics			
Year of marriage	.52**	.18*	−.05
Bride's age at marriage	.43**	.08	.04

*$p <= .05$
**$p <= .01$

main pattern I want to draw attention to should be clearly visible. Generally speaking, there are a number of fairly consistent background correlates of wedding behavior of those women who married during the years 1933–57 (see the first column in each table). In that period, it was common for brides and grooms who were well educated and who had well-educated par-

(see no. 7 in table 8.2), the measure of the couple's contribution is a 7-point measure from 0 to 100% (more detailed than is shown in table 8.2), and the postmarital residence measure is again a simple dichotomy of all other arrangements vs. neolocal (i.e., less detailed than the measure used in table 8.2). The various education measures are all 5-point ordinal measures ranging from illiterate to at least some college; the Party membership measure is actually 1 = masses, 2 = Communist Youth League, 3 = CCP; the occupation measures are 1 = industrial worker, 2 = service worker, miscellaneous, 3 = cadre or professional occupation; the parent urban origin measure is 1 = neither parent an urbanite, 2 = one parent an urbanite, 3 = both parents urbanites; the family class origin measure is 1 = landlord or capitalist, 2 = peasant, 3 = worker, 4 = poor urbanite, handicrafts, etc., 5 = cadre, employee, professional; and the parental class label measure is 1 = landlord, capitalist, rich peasant, 2 = petty bourgeois, 3 = peasant, 4 = worker, 5 = cadre or martyr.

TABLE 8.4.   Social Background and Wedding Elaborateness Scores
(Pearson correlation statistics)

	Period First Married		
	1933–57 (N = 178)	1958–76 (N = 198)	1977–87 (N = 210)
Couple's background			
Bride's educational level	−.14	−.09	−.08
Groom's educational level	.00	−.08	−.06
Bride's Party membership	−.23**	−.11	−.03
Groom's Party membership	−.21**	−.14	.03
Bride's occupational status	−.20	−.00	−.05
Groom's occupational status	−.02	−.08	−.01
Bride's family characteristics			
Mother's educational level	−.13	.01	−.01
Father's educational level	−.10	.02	−.13
Father's occupational status	−.07	.03	−.11
Parental urban origins	−.17*	−.04	.01
Family's class origins	−.03	.06	−.18*
Parental class label	.08	.04	.01
Other characteristics			
Year of marriage	−.32**	.25**	.25**
Bride's age at marriage	−.25**	−.09	−.20**
Freedom of mate choice scale score	−.39**	−.00	.00

*p <= .05
**p <= .01

ents, who belonged to the CCP or its youth auxiliary, who had high occupational status, and in which the bride had parents with urban roots and a father in a high-status occupation, to engage in more "modern" weddings—with greater freedom of choice, with less elaborate and expensive ceremonies, with the couple themselves paying a large share of the cost, with no dowry given by the bride's parents, and with the couple living in a separate household after the wedding.[19] Weddings in that period also tended to be

19. We do not have detailed information on the social backgrounds of the groom's parents to allow us to examine their characteristics separately. The strength of the associations noted in the text varies widely across tables and measures, and there are exceptions both to these patterns and some other measures that have an influence on one or another of the wedding measures. A few other background measures were examined (e.g., bride's father's Party membership) but were left out of the table because they did not have a clear effect on any of our wedding behavior measures.

TABLE 8.5.   Social Background and Presence of a Dowry
(Pearson correlation statistics)

	Period First Married		
	1933–57 (N = 178)	1958–76 (N = 198)	1977–87 (N = 210)
Couple's background			
Bride's educational level	−.20**	−.09	.06
Groom's educational level	−.09	−.10	.09
Bride's Party membership	−.25**	−.11	.05
Groom's Party membership	−.29**	−.08	.11
Bride's occupational status	−.24	.01	.07
Groom's occupational status	−.16*	−.03	.11
Bride's family characteristics			
Mother's educational level	−.18*	.10	.16*
Father's educational level	−.14	.05	.10
Father's occupational status	−.13	.06	.12
Parental urban origins	−.12	.00	−.10
Family's class origins	−.09	.05	.08
Parental class label	.12	.12	.01
Other characteristics			
Year of marriage	−.28**	.09	.07
Bride's age at marriage	−.16*	−.05	−.07
Freedom of mate choice scale score	−.28**	.03	.08
Neolocal postmarital residence	−.25**	−.03	−.10

*$p <= .05$
**$p <= .01$

more "modern" when the bride was older at the time she married and when the year of marriage was more recent. In addition, in those years there was a fairly consistent association across the various different wedding behaviors, such that couples who had more free choice in choosing their spouses tended to have simpler weddings, more payment by the couple, no dowry, and neolocal residence after the wedding (see the bottom rows in tables 8.4–8.7).

Although there are some weak points and inconsistencies in these patterns, in general they show that a set of altered wedding practices was emerging, and that people who had advantaged social statuses tended more often than others to hold such "modern" weddings. Furthermore, the patterns visible in this period are quite similar to those found in research

TABLE 8.6.   Social Background and Share Paid by Couple
(Pearson correlation statistics)

	Period First Married		
	1933–57 (N = 178)	1958–76 (N = 198)	1977–87 (N = 210)
Couple's background			
Bride's educational level	.28**	.12	−.07
Groom's educational level	.06	.07	−.11
Bride's Party membership	.18*	−.02	−.01
Groom's Party membership	.13	.05	.02
Bride's occupational status	.38*	.01	−.01
Groom's occupational status	.10	.12	.06
Bride's family characteristics			
Mother's educational level	.20*	.01	−.14*
Father's educational level	.32**	.05	−.08
Father's occupational status	.20	−.07	−.17*
Parental urban origins	.29**	−.11	.12
Family's class origins	.17*	−.17*	−.12
Parental class label	−.15	−.06	−.01
Other characteristics			
Year of marriage	.25**	−.15*	−.05
Bride's age at marriage	.34**	.11	.11
Freedom of mate choice scale score	.52**	.13	−.01
Wedding elaborateness scale score	−.43**	−.25**	−.14
Neolocal postmarital residence	.48**	.10	.00

$*p <= .05$
$**p <= .01$

on other societies that have modernized in a nonsocialist context.[20] The reasons for these associations between advantaged statuses and modern wedding behavior are much debated, and I will not try to resolve the existing debates here.[21]

20. Many aspects, such as freedom of mate choice, marriage without a dowry, and neolocal postmarital residence, are increasingly prevalent and are most often practiced by the best-educated and most modernized strata in capitalist societies. See the discussion in Goode, *World Revolution and Family Patterns.* However, simplified wedding celebrations are not part of a pattern Goode deals with, and the trend over time toward first simpler and then more elaborate weddings seems distinctive to the PRC.

21. One issue in the debates is at what point in the modernization process the situation turns from people who have high social status being the most elaborate and traditional in their

TABLE 8.7.   Social Background and Neolocal Postmarital Residence
(Pearson correlation statistics)

	Period First Married		
	1933–57 (N = 178)	1958–76 (N = 198)	1977–87 (N = 210)
Couple's background			
Bride's educational level	.25**	.12	.07
Groom's educational level	.15*	.25**	.01
Bride's Party membership	.18*	.18*	.06
Groom's Party membership	.23**	.01	.12
Bride's occupational status	.02	.12	−.03
Groom's occupational status	.17*	.08	−.01
Bride's family characteristics			
Mother's educational level	.14	.09	.08
Father's educational level	.20*	.16*	.03
Father's occupational status	.13	.07	−.09
Parental urban origins	.16*	.04	−.01
Family's class origins	.07	.05	.07
Parental class label	−.15*	−.09	.00
Other characteristics			
Year of marriage	.26**	−.04	−.06
Bride's age at marriage	.27**	.11	.05
Freedom of mate choice scale score	.38**	.12	.15*
Wedding elaborateness scale score	−.27**	−.08	−.02

*$p <= .05$
**$p <= .01$

When we turn to the second and third columns in tables 8.3–8.7, the picture looks different. Generally speaking, strong correlations are rare enough in those columns that they might almost have occurred through chance alone.[22] In other words, with the exception of some fairly clear

---

wedding behavior to being the most modern and simple. Another issue is whether culture or social structure is more important in producing the shifts toward modern weddings—in other words, whether the change comes mainly from differential exposure to Western ideas about modern marriages or from differential involvement in new, meritocratic opportunity structures.

22. The statistical significance measures used tell us this. P = .05 means a measure unlikely to occur by chance alone more than 1 time in 20. When we examine 28–34 separate correlations in the various subtables for these two columns, we would expect to find 1–2 correlations

trends related to the year of marriage, there appears to be no clear or consistent relationship between any of our social background characteristics and these aspects of wedding behavior in the years since 1958.[23] Furthermore, even the internal consistency of wedding behavior weakens or disappears in the post-1958 years. For example, it is logical to expect in any society that brides who are older when they wed will have more say in the matter; that couples who have more freedom of choice will have simpler weddings, will more often live neolocally, and will more often pay for much of the wedding cost themselves; and that couples who have elaborate weddings will be less likely to live neolocally. All of these patterns are clearly visible for those who married prior to 1957 (see the bottom portion of column 1 in tables 8.3–8.7), but not for those who married during the full socialist and reform periods. This decrease in internal consistency among various aspects of wedding behavior is especially puzzling.

In terms of our interest in the reform era, an additional implication of these findings is that the pattern of associations we find in the Deng era looks much like that in the Maoist period—in both periods most correlations with background traits are not significantly different from zero. There are few signs of any reemergence of the kinds of associations that existed prior to 1958. Because of this weakness, there is no point in looking within our Chengdu data to see whether Party members, cadres, new entrepreneurial elites, or others are behaving differently during the reform era. For those aspects of marriage behavior we are considering here, there is no clear evidence of such new trends in Chengdu. Social background traits do not seem to differentiate people in their wedding behavior in either the reform era or the preceding, Maoist period. The remainder of this chapter will be devoted to an effort to puzzle out the meaning of this curious set of findings.

TRANSFORMED SOCIAL STRUCTURE AND WEDDING BEHAVIOR

Why might the pattern of associations between individual and family status characteristics have disappeared in the full socialism and reform eras? My answer to this question becomes necessarily speculative, since there are no definitive ways to test various explanations with the Chengdu data. There are several possible explanations for the "disappearing correlations" in tables 8.3–8.7: (1) bad data, (2) declining variability, (3) random behavior,

---

surpassing statistical significance due to chance alone. In these tables we find from 1 to 5 of such correlations, little better than a chance result.

23. Credit for first noticing this curious disappearance of correlations in the later periods goes to my collaborator Xu Xiaohe, who discovered it while carrying out an analysis of changes in freedom of mate choice.

and (4) changes in underlying social structure and causation. I believe that the answer to our puzzle can be found in (4), but before explaining what changes are involved, I have to show why possibilities (1), (2), and (3) can be discounted.

An explanation premised on bad data involves the idea that our interviews were of such poor quality or our respondents were so confused or inaccurate in their responses that the resulting measures of background and behavior are loaded with random error, thus washing out any underlying correlations. Any study contains a certain amount of random error, and perhaps a study conducted under new and unusual conditions, such as our Chengdu survey, contains more than most. However, this explanation does not accord with the fact that relatively consistent correlations in the expected directions were found among the oldest women we interviewed, those who married prior to 1958. Other things being equal, the limited education and more severe memory problems of older women should produce more error in their answers than for younger women. Since there is no obvious reason why the degree of error should be worse for younger women, this first explanation can be discounted.

Another possibility involves the decline in variability in our data. Perhaps what we see here is evidence of an increasing homogenization of both behavior and backgrounds produced by the revolution. If everyone comes from pretty much the same background and behaves in pretty much the same way, then we would not expect to find very clear associations between background and behavior. This second explanation would be consistent with a pattern of correlations weakening over time, as is shown in tables 8.3–8.7. I examined this possibility by comparing across time periods the standard deviations of both the background traits and the wedding behaviors used in these tables (detailed results not shown here). Although in a few cases (e.g., father's occupational status, bride's educational level, Freedom of Mate Choice Scale), a decline in variability across marriage periods was visible, in most cases it was not.[24] In general there is enough variability in background traits and wedding behavior in the second and third marriage periods to expect some clear patterns of association to emerge. For this reason I conclude that the second explanation also can be discounted.

A third possible explanation for the patterns shown in tables 8.3–8.7 is random behavior. This idea involves the possibility that the reasons people have big weddings, defer to parental wishes in selecting a mate, or live independently after marriage are mostly determined by personal tastes and

24. In 14 out of the 19 measures used in tables 8.3–8.7 the standard deviations in the second or third marriage periods were as high as, or higher than, in the first period. In those cases there was no clear trend toward increased homogeneity for those who married after 1958.

idiosyncratic situations and constraints, so that no general associations between background traits and behavior will be visible. No doubt there is much that is personal and situational in the way weddings are observed in China, just as in any other society. But a large share of idiosyncrasy is not incompatible with social background traits exerting considerable influence. After all, social scientists deal with probabilistic explanations, and they typically expect to explain only a modest portion of the variability in individual behavior with their predictors. They are looking for common underlying patterns in their samples despite idiosyncrasies, and they do not aspire to explain the precise behavior of each particular individual within those samples. In any case, this explanation again runs afoul of the fact that we find quite acceptable associations in the expected direction among the pre-1957 marriages. There is no obvious reason why the degree of randomness of wedding behavior should have increased for those who married after 1958. This third explanation, like its predecessors, does not fit the patterns observed in the Chengdu data.

I have suggested that the most likely explanation of the weakening of the association between social background traits and wedding behavior, for couples who married after 1958, is that changes in urban social structure altered the sources of variation in individual behavior in basic ways. What sorts of changes do I have in mind? To oversimplify a great deal, I suggest that we see in the Chengdu data evidence of a major change in the nature of the urban social order in China from a status group/class/market system to a rank/network/bureaucracy system. This basic transformation had important implications for the role of families and family strategies in realms such as negotiating marriages.

To clarify this claim, it may be helpful to examine the assumptions that lie behind asking interviewees about their educational levels, occupations, Party membership, urban experience, and other related background traits. Asking such questions is the bread-and-butter approach used by most Western social scientists in their attempts to explain variation in individual attitudes and behavior, but this approach is based on research in capitalist or market societies. The reason these sorts of traits are asked about is that researchers assume that in these societies people who share certain background traits will have a variety of things in common that will affect how they behave and think. For example, well-educated women will differ from other women in a number of predictable ways, such as by having more access to desirable jobs and higher incomes, more knowledge about the world, and more "modern" ideas. In terms of the kinds of behavior we are interested in here, such women more often will make their own choices about whom to marry, they will have more modern-style weddings, and they will be more likely to set up a new household with their husbands when they marry. In general, groupings based on occupation, education, political membership, urban experience, or other similar traits become meaningful and important in such societies.[25]

The status groupings derived from such background traits may be the building blocks of larger and more complex solidarities in these societies, such as social strata, interest groups, and social classes. In general, the central idea here is that the markets and opportunity structures existing in capitalist societies produce competition for status and advantage that tends to make the kinds of social background traits we have been considering important influences on individual behavior. Our Chengdu data suggest that this sort of approach was useful for interpreting behavior of Chinese urbanites up into the 1950s, but not since then. Why the change?

I argue, as do others, that the socialist transformation of the mid-1950s produced a very different urban social order. A highly centralized state relied upon subordinate bureaucratic organizations to directly control the populace by administrative means. Labor markets and market distribution in other realms (e.g., housing, medical care, etc.) were effectively suppressed, and most individuals were locked into a high degree of dependency upon their work units (*danwei*) for access to the resources needed to survive.[26] This system was accompanied by severe scarcities in most realms and a weak legal system and convulsive political atmosphere, factors that made the decisions of bureaucratic gatekeepers appear highly arbitrary and unpredictable.

Individuals and families trying to survive in this system were ill-advised to simply accept the rules of the game and hope that bureaucratic favors would be bestowed on them for their individual efforts. Nor in most cases could they threaten to leave, compete for new opportunities, or organize collectively to gain better treatment. Instead, they had to try to survive and improve their lot by currying favor with superiors and by cultivating connections (*guanxi*) with gatekeepers, both within their enterprises and

25. The particular traits that are important may vary from society to society, and from locale to locale within any one society. For example, religion and rural vs. urban residence may be important differentiating factors in one society and quite unimportant in another. Many discussions of advanced capitalist societies assume that those traits related to what is called socioeconomic status—particularly education, occupational status, and income—will be particularly important influences on individual behavior and attitudes in such societies.

26. See the analysis in Martin King Whyte and William L. Parish, *Urban Life in Contemporary China* (Chicago: University of Chicago Press, 1984). Similar ideas have been further developed in Andrew Walder, *Communist Neo-Traditionalism* (Berkeley: University of California Press, 1986). Related arguments have been advanced for rural China as well. See, in particular, Edward Friedman, Paul Pickowicz, and Mark Selden, *Chinese Village, Socialist State* (New Haven: Yale University Press, 1991). Similar ideas have been used to interpret the social orders of the Soviet Union and Eastern Europe prior to 1989. See Kenneth Jowitt, "Soviet Neotraditionalism: The Political Corruption of a Leninist Regime," *Soviet Studies* 35, no. 3 (July): 275–97; Ivan Szelenyi, *Urban Inequalities under State Socialism* (New York: Oxford University Press, 1983).

outside—with doctors, housing office employees, store clerks, and many others. But individuals differed widely in their potential for developing supportive networks and their skills at doing so.

What are the sorts of factors that distinguish between success and failure when operating in this system? First, there is the type of work unit, for some units are much more able to provide resources to employees than others, and individuals of quite different personal background traits will share in the advantages or disadvantages of membership in a particular kind of unit.[27] A second important influence on success within this system is position and rank within the unit and whether these give control over or access to important resources and opportunities. A third important factor is the nature of one's social networks and the extent to which such networks can be used to meet individual and family needs. Wang Gongmin and Chen Zhiyuan may have quite similar educational backgrounds, occupations, and Party membership status, but if Wang is located in a favored work unit, has a position that gives him control over important resources, has cultivated a broad range of helpful connections, and has a strong and supportive family network to supplement those connections, while Chen lacks these things, their lives and their behavior will be quite different. Their social background traits will not have much influence on how they are treated, but their work units, positions, and connections will make all the difference in the world (see also the discussion in the Davis and Phillips chapters).

I suggest that as a result of the major changes in urban social structure that took place in the 1950s, the sorts of traits that affect individual and family behavior changed in fundamental ways. Traits that help form status groups in a market society became relatively unimportant, while new characteristics of individuals and their immediate environments gained salience. I also suggest that whether individuals had a fair amount of free choice in deciding whom to marry, held elaborate and expensive weddings, got new housing so they could live neolocally, and so forth, probably depended in predictable ways on the type of work units that employed both partners and key members of their "old families" and on the positions within those units and social networks of all the principals.[28] I also acknowledge that we did

27. Familiar examples are that individuals in military units and defense factories, the railway system, and large industrial plants tend to benefit from the special treatment those units receive, while those working in primary schools, small state stores, and neighborhood factories are not so well treated.

28. For example, in order to hold an elaborate wedding it is important to be able to mobilize enough funds and assistance for the event, to arrange for the banquet in a suitable place for a reasonable price, and to be able to avoid criticism for violating the official policy on frugal weddings. All of these things require connections and patronage. To obtain housing for neolocal residence one needs the right connections and the support of powerful individuals in work units and/or in housing management offices. Even the degree of freedom of mate choice will be

not ask the right kinds of questions in our Chengdu survey in order to test these ideas directly. To know whether my arguments are correct, we would need detailed questions about the nature of people's work units, their specific positions and degree of control over scarce resources within those units, and the nature of the kinship, friendship, and other social networks they are embedded in. Unfortunately, our Chengdu survey does not contain such questions.[29]

These ideas refer particularly to China's urban social structure during the full socialist era, roughly the years 1958–78.[30] What of the reform era? During the years since 1978 this system has been modified in important ways, with market reforms introduced in many realms. The Chinese and Western media in the 1980s were full of accounts of the resulting changes—for example, of new, family-run restaurants, of entrepreneurs setting up private companies, and of skilled personnel leaving state jobs to sell their services elsewhere.

To what extent have these reforms altered the social sources of popular behavior? From our data on wedding behavior in Chengdu, the answer is very little. This conclusion stems from the fact that the "disappearing correlations" observed in column 2 of tables 8.3–8.7 have not reappeared in the third columns of the tables, which deal with marriages in the reform era. Despite the modification of Maoist policies and the introduction of market reforms, there is little evidence that traits such as educational level, occupational status, and Party membership have regained importance in explaining wedding behavior.

My explanation for the limited impact of the reforms is that those most affected by them in urban areas, such as private entrepreneurs and the self-employed, remained a small portion of the total population (5 percent or

---

affected by the size and sex composition of the work unit, the degree of puritanism and control versus tolerance and protection exercised by supervisors, and the relative resources and networks of the couple vis-à-vis their parents. The high marriage ages in recent years mean that the great majority of both brides and grooms—85% or more—are already employed at the time they marry. This means that positions within the work units and personal networks of brides and grooms are more important than would be the case if marriages occurred at younger ages.

29. We did include questions about whether the work units of the bride, the groom, and the bride's father were state, collective, or private in ownership form. However, this question is too crude to allow us to get at many meaningful distinctions among types of work units.

30. During those years, the Chinese system was distinctive even when compared with the Soviet Union and Eastern Europe in the degree to which bureaucratic allocation was stressed and markets were suppressed. The most important distinction was that a labor market was virtually nonexistent in the Chinese case, while this was not so in the other cases. See the discussion in Martin King Whyte, "State and Society in the Mao Era," in *Perspectives on China*, ed. K. Lieberthal, J. Kallgren, R. MacFarquhar, and F. Wakeman (Armonk, N.Y.: M. E. Sharpe, 1992).

less) in most large cities such as Chengdu in the late 1980s, so that the mass media accounts mentioned above are decidedly atypical. Most urbanites remain highly dependent upon state enterprises for meeting their basic needs. Even if enterprises now have to orient themselves more to market forces, individual urbanites (as consumers, employees, patients, etc.) still face an environment filled with scarcities and organized predominantly by bureaucratic allocation. It is these more typical state factory workers, office clerks, and technicians who predominate in any general population sample, such as the one used in the present study.

A second influence that helps to suppress the influence of individual social background traits is the officially encouraged revival of conspicuous consumption. Displaying one's superior living standard, an act that was dangerous in the Mao era, is now looked upon with favor. China's urbanites have responded to this shift with alacrity, and in the process popular expectations about how you should dress, what consumer durables you should own, and how you should celebrate a wedding have been raised dramatically. As a result, it becomes increasingly difficult to meet those expectations without drawing on the aid and support of the extensive social networks cultivated in previous years. Since individuals with similar social backgrounds may have quite different social networks, and thus quite different potential for mobilizing such support, the influence of background traits on wedding behavior continues to be small. If these ideas are correct, personal status traits will become important influences again only if and when much more thoroughgoing economic and political reforms are instituted, reforms that reduce the role of networks of connections and make it possible to meet basic needs by relying on individual effort and meritocratic competition.

The evidence presented here for the shift from a status/class/market to a rank/network/bureaucracy system, and the maintenance of the latter well into the reform era, is admittedly very limited. The data analyzed in this chapter are consistent with such an interpretation, but they do not directly test it. But assuming for the moment that these arguments are correct, several obvious questions come to mind. Is Chengdu unusual in this regard, and would we see much more effect of the reforms in locales more centrally affected by them, such as in Shanghai or, even more so, in Canton? Is there a lag-time in popular adaptation to the reforms, such that if we go back and look at Chengdu marriages in the 1990s we will discover more signs of a revival of the influence of social background traits? Is the shift after the 1950s in the sources of individual behavior described here confined to wedding behavior, or would we see it as well in realms as diverse as political participation, leisure time pursuits, and fertility? Can we design questions informed by the rank/network/bureaucracy perspective that allow us to measure how individuals and families are situated in the urban pecking order and how that location influences their behavior and attitudes?[31] Only as future research deals with questions such as these will we be able to resolve fully the questions raised in the present analysis.

CONCLUSIONS

In the process of reviewing here changes in wedding behavior in Chengdu over the years, I have focused on the dramatic shift in the role played by individual and family background traits in explaining wedding behavior. I have speculated that this shift can be attributed to the major changes in the urban social order carried out during the 1950s, with that social order persisting into the 1980s despite reforms. The analysis has been somewhat unconventional, since I am interested not simply in describing changing Chinese wedding customs, but in using those customs as, in effect, a measuring gauge to judge the contours of the underlying social order. According to my measuring gauge, the transformations in the nature of that social order have been profound enough to undermine the utility of the approaches to explaining social behavior used by most Western scientists. But what does this analysis tell us about the nature and importance of family strategies in urban China today?

It might be supposed that when a highly centralized system of bureaucratic allocation takes over, as in China after 1957, the role of family networks and family strategies will decline into insignificance. Earlier conceptions of post-1949 China based on the totalitarianism paradigm sometimes used terms such as "atomization" to suggest that the revolution resulted in powerless individuals facing the omnipotent party-state without protection from supportive family and friendship networks. Much research now makes clear that at least for most people in urban China, the effect of the socialist system was more nearly the opposite of atomization. Precisely because the party-state was so powerful, but also because of the pervasiveness of shortages and the arbitrariness with which goods and services were distributed, individuals could not survive, let alone prosper, through individual effort and following the rules of the system. Getting by and getting ahead depended on finding ways to manage or to beat the system and, given the nature of that system, required the cultivation of as many useful social ties as possible. The result was a formally bureaucratic system, which at an informal level was riven with personalistic ties and private deals.[32]

31. New research under way, such as that conducted by Andrew Walder and collaborators in Tianjin, involves attempts to design questionnaires to tap connections and networks more directly than has been done before.

32. See the discussion in Zheng Yefu, "Connections," in *The Chinese: Adapting the Past, Facing the Future*, ed. Robert Dernberger, Kenneth DeWoskin, Steven Goldstein, Rhoads Murphey, and Martin Whyte (Ann Arbor: Center for Chinese Studies, 1991). Some analysts have

Useful social ties might have many origins—in status as co-workers, neighbors, friends, former classmates, relatives, and even as chance acquaintances. But kinship is a particularly useful basis for such ties. Kinship provides a ready-made network of ties that can be mobilized, rather than one that has to be created anew. Family connections tend to involve primordial loyalties that make them more reliable during times of political danger than most other kinds of social ties. Perhaps most important, relatives also tend to be highly dispersed geographically and situated in a broad range of work units and occupations. The heterogeneity involved in kinship relations provides a natural basis for mutually advantageous exchanges.[33] Socialist reforms in the 1950s may have undercut some of the structural grounds for relying on kin by attacking lineages and their corporate property and by eliminating family-run enterprises and the inheritance of capital. However, the new system sustained and perhaps even strengthened the reliance on a dispersed network of family relationships, as such networks became central to survival in confronting the bureaucratic system that was (and still is) Chinese socialism (see also the related discussion in chapters 2, 11, and 12).

Even as they heard their reformist leaders proclaiming a new era in which individuals would be able to succeed through meritocratic competition, bolstered by revived markets, strengthened legal codes, and rational administrative systems, young people contemplating getting married after 1978 found they could not do so without relying on a broad range of support and assistance from their families. We do not have any direct evidence in the Chengdu study on how family decisions about wedding celebrations and postmarital living arrangements are actually negotiated. We do have enough evidence, however, to state emphatically that family-based cooperation and negotiation between generations remain absolutely central in reform-era China.

---

suggested that the resulting system, with its strong emphasis on patron-client relations and personalistic favors, builds upon some of the worst features of the old imperial order. Chinese society after the 1950s, according to this argument, has more in common with feudalism than with either capitalism or socialism. See, for example, Tang Tsou, *The Cultural Revolution and Post-Mao Reforms* (Chicago: University of Chicago Press, 1986); Friedman, Pickowicz, and Selden, *Chinese Village, Socialist State.* Similar analyses have been advanced for the Soviet Union and Eastern Europe. For example, Zygmunt Bauman argues that the rank-based societies produced by state socialism embody a modern version of the sort of patrimonial order that Max Weber described as characteristic of feudalism. Bauman terms this modern variant "partymonialism." See his article, "Officialdom and Class: Bases of Inequality in Socialist Society," in *The Social Analysis of Class Structure,* ed. Frank Parkin (London: Tavistock, 1972).

33. Neighbors and workmates might be the source of more frequent interactions than relatives. However, as individuals in much the same boat, they do not provide as much opportunity for advantageous exchanges as do relatives located in distant markets or in work posts where the mixture of benefits and shortages is quite different. Diversity is a more fruitful basis for mutual advantage than similarity.

Plates

Market Town Wedding

Small-town bride about to enter her husband's home (Helen Siu)

Bridal car to carry her to banquet (Helen Siu)

Presentations before the family altar (Helen Siu)

A weeping bride is led away from her parents' home. (Stevan Harrell)

A proud mother-in-law ushers her new daughter-in-law into the bridal chamber. (Stevan Harrell)

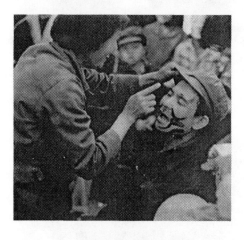

A relative of the bride paints the groom's parents' faces to ensure their good humor toward their daughter-in-law. (Stevan Harrell)

A new stem family poses for a formal portrait. (Stevan Harrell)

Family Portraits

Small-town fishing family (Helen Siu)

Multigenerational family in Shanghai (Graham E. Johnson)

Multigenerational family in rural Guangdong (Graham E. Johnson)

Entrepreneurs

Chengdu stallkeeper (Hill Gates)

Chengdu shopkeeper (Hill Gates)

The proud owner of a new house with modern furniture, Renhe, Panzhihua (Stevan Harrell)

Housing Styles

Shanghai apartment building,
constructed in the 1950s
(Deborah Davis)

Shanghai apartment building,
constructed in 1978 (Deborah
Davis)

Shanghai apartment building, constructed in 1988 (Deborah Davis)

Village house built with Canadian remittances, Duanfen, Taishan, Guangdong (Graham E. Johnson)

New house with traditional ritual couplets, Fucheng, Dongguan, Guangdong
(Graham E. Johnson)

Old-style mud-walled housing under construction in Yishala, Panzhihua, Sichuan (Stevan Harrell)

New-style mansion of twenty-nine rooms, home to a family of ten in Renhe, Panzhihua (Stevan Harrell)

PART THREE

Childbearing

NINE

The Peasantization of the One-Child Policy in Shaanxi

Susan Greenhalgh

POPULATION CONTROL:
THE STATE-SOCIETY CONFLICT AND ITS LOCAL MEDIATORS

A crucial component of China's development strategy is the control of population growth. Having seen rampant population growth eat up hard-earned economic gains in the past, the reformist leaders of the late 1970s were deadly serious about restraining reproduction. In January 1979 they announced the extraordinary policy of encouraging all couples to limit themselves to one child.[1] The concrete goals of the policy became clear in September 1980, when the Central Committee issued an "Open Letter" (*gongkai xin*) announcing a crash program to control population size within 1.2 billion by the year 2000 and demanding that all cadres and all Party and Youth League members take the lead in forming single-child families.[2]

For a regime that once prided itself on its deep understanding of the Chinese peasantry, the one-child policy was appallingly out of touch with rural reality. Virtually every policy goal—from restricting the number, thus also the sex, of children, to delaying family formation, to lengthening birth intervals—flew in the face of Chinese tradition and threatened to

The research on which this chapter is based was funded by a grant from the National Science Foundation, grant number BNS-8618121. I wish to thank Wang Zheng, Guo Huizhong, and Marilyn Beach for superlative assistance in coding and cleaning the data, and Li Nan for detailed comments on an earlier draft.

1. *Xinhua*, 26 January 1979, in *FBIS*, 31 January 1979, E9–10.
2. "Open letter from the Central Committee of the Communist Party of China to All Members of the Party and the Communist Youth League Concerning the Problem of Controlling the Country's Population Growth," in China Population Information Centre, *China: Population Policy and Family Planning Practice* (Beijing: CPIC, 1983), 1–4.

hobble one of the few reliable resources peasants had left after thirty years of socialism, the family.

Given the tremendous control the Chinese state wields over Chinese society in the domain of reproduction, a study of peasant fertility strategies alone will shed little light on the forces underlying family formation in rural China today. Chinese peasants follow essentially the same strategies employed by the oppressed everywhere—evasion, deception, manipulation, bribery, and all the rest.[3] An understanding of how reproduction has evolved in the era of the one-child policy must start instead with the state, its goals, and how they are pursued. In determining local fertility outcomes, however, the key actor may be neither state nor society, but those who occupy the interface between the two.

Between State and Society: The Local Cadres

Local cadres in China—that is to say, village-level officials—are charged with enforcing state policy among the rural populace. At the same time, they are firmly rooted in local society: they live in the village, they are linked to villagers by kin and friendship ties, and their livelihood is drawn from village resources. Over the past forty years, when state rules have challenged profoundly held local values or threatened peasant economic security, village cadres have often tried and sometimes succeeded in bending those rules to the advantage of their relatives and neighbors.[4]

During the collective era rural cadres appear to have mediated state-society conflicts by kowtowing to the state during periods of mobilization, but favoring society in quieter times.[5] It appears that most of the time local officials routinely distorted central policies to serve local interests. In cheating the state they were protected by structural features of the political system, in particular by the center's inability to monitor events in hundreds of thousands of villages, many poorly linked to communications networks, and by its chronically overloaded agenda, which allowed the microdeceptions at the grass roots to go unnoticed.[6]

The reform process has altered cadre relations with both state and society. In the post-1978 era resources have shifted down the administrative

3. Cf. James C. Scott, *Weapons of the Weak: Everyday Forms of Peasant Resistance* (New Haven: Yale University Press, 1985).

4. Jean C. Oi, *State and Peasant in Contemporary China: The Political Economy of Village Government* (Berkeley: University of California Press, 1989); John P. Burns, *Political Participation in Rural China* (Berkeley: University of California Press, 1988).

5. Jonathan Unger, "State and Peasant in Post-Revolution China," *Journal of Peasant Studies* 17, no. 1 (October 1989): 114–36.

6. David M. Lampton, "The Implementation Problem in Post-Mao China," in David M. Lampton, ed., *Policy Implementation in Post-Mao China* (Berkeley: University of California Press, 1987), 157–89.

hierarchy, enhancing the capacity of local cadres to twist Beijing's policies to local advantage.[7] Research in many sectors of economic policy has revealed that policy-making has been fragmented, with local power holders having a major impact on policy evolution.[8]

While gaining power relative to the state, local cadres have clearly lost influence over society. Reports from many localities suggest that in the immediate aftermath of the parceling out of collective land, peasants deemed their old leaders superfluous and refused to heed their word.[9] This pattern became solidified with the passage of time, as the elimination of many official duties led to a decline in cadre power and in the economic resources and social prestige that power had brought.[10] At the same time, new, more difficult duties were added to cadre workloads—enforcing the one-child policy is a prime example—dampening their enthusiasm for official work. During the 1980s cadres retained some important powers and gained some new ones, and these should be considered in an account of alterations in cadre status and power.[11] The overall picture current research paints, however, is one of decline in cadre power and a shift in cadre commitment from exemplary performance in official duties to self-enrichment in the private economy.

In the population arena, the one-child policy has provoked a locked-horns conflict between state and society over family size. By any except perhaps the cyberneticist's measure, the state devised an unworkable—one could even say a bad—policy that disregarded the basic needs of the rural population. If the post-1978 reforms did liberate local cadres from excessive state control, as recent research suggests, then village cadres had the opportunity to reshape the one-child policy, to peasantize it, as it were, to better fit the needs of their constituents. And if the reforms also lessened cadre control over the peasantry, then birth-planning workers may have had little choice but to modify the policy in response to peasant demands.

In the past few years an old debate over the strength of the Chinese

7. Barry Naughton, "The Decline of Central Control over Investment in Post-Mao China," in *Policy Implementation*, ed. Lampton, 51–80.

8. David M. Lampton, "Water: Challenge to a Fragmented Political System," in *Policy Implementation*, ed. Lampton, 157–89; Dorothy J. Solinger, "The 1980 Inflation and the Politics of Price Control in the People's Republic of China," in *Policy Implementation*, ed. Lampton, 81–118.

9. John P. Burns, "Local Cadre Accommodation to the 'Responsibility System' in Rural China," *Pacific Affairs* 58, no. 4 (Winter 1985–86): 607–25; Jonathan Unger, "The Decollectivization of the Chinese Countryside: A Survey of Twenty-eight Villages," *Pacific Affairs* 58, no. 4 (Winter 1985–86): 585–606.

10. Gordon White, "The Impact of Economic Reforms in the Chinese Countryside," *Modern China* 13, no. 4:411–40.

11. Oi, *State and Peasant.*

state has reemerged in new guise, that of state-society relations.[12] In her provocative book *The Reach of the State*, Vivienne Shue argues that previous observers got it wrong.[13] In her reading of the evidence, during the Maoist decades the state was hamstrung by the cellular structure of society, which allowed local cadres to weave protective webs over their village kingdoms. In the post-Mao era the extension of market reforms has torn off those protective webs, exposing the peasantry to the potentially fierce winds of state control. Jonathan Unger contends that it is Shue who has it wrong.[14] Drawing on primary interview data, he defends the orthodox position that state control was often formidable during Mao's lifetime. Far from showing the limits on state power, he says, the crumbs of resistance peasants and cadres managed to put up only revealed the state-imposed limits on their freedom. In his view, Dengism has at last brought some relief from state domination. With the weakening of many mechanisms of control, both the state's grip over local cadres and the cadres' power to exact compliance from the peasantry have loosened.

Objectives

This chapter examines the evolution of state-society relations in the area of population control. Which side is winning the struggle over family size, how, and why are questions aggregate statistics cannot answer. Using retrospective field data from village Shaanxi, I examine shifts in reproductive control in the reform era and the strategies local birth-planning cadres used to help engineer those shifts. Three questions are of primary concern.

First, how much control does the state wield over family formation in village China; and to what extent did the locus of reproductive control shift from state to society during the first decade of economic reform? The answers should advance the debate over the reach of the Chinese state during both late collective and reform eras.

Second, what components of the economic and political reform process have propelled the hypothesized shift in reproductive control? A number of observers have written about the apparent impact of the reforms on population policy enforcement, but little firsthand evidence has been

---

12. The interlinkages between state and society have become an important research focus among political sociologists, who believe that previous research on the state by political scientists, and on society by sociologists, neglected important connections and relationships between the two. See, for example, Joel S. Migdal, *Strong States and Weak Societies: State-Society Relations and State Capabilities in the Third World* (Princeton: Princeton University Press, 1988).

13. Vivienne Shue, *The Reach of the State: Sketches of the Chinese Body Politic* (Stanford: Stanford University Press, 1988).

14. Unger, "State and Peasant."

brought to bear on the issue. A better understanding of the mechanisms by which the reforms undermined policy enforcement would shed light on the larger process by which economic liberalization sparked demographic liberalization.

Third, what were the strategies of peasants in achieving their fertility goals, and of cadres in mediating the needs of state and society? An understanding of the trade-offs cadres worked out with peasant families, on the one hand, and state bureaucrats, on the other, would help us comprehend the delicate political balance that keeps the one-child policy on the books even as it appears to be largely inoperative on the ground.

The chapter begins by introducing the research locale and describing the process of economic reform that transformed the villages from collective brigades into collections of household agriculturalists. I then set out the reproductive demands of the state and the peasantry, taking "the state" to mean officials and organizations at provincial, municipal, and township (before 1984, commune) levels of the state bureaucracy. How peasant families coped with state reproductive demands, and how local cadres in turn coped with the conflicts between state and family demands are examined in the following two sections, which trace the evolution of de facto population policy in the villages over the period 1979–87. This chapter treats five major elements of the one-child policy: late marriage, late childbearing, second children, third and higher-order children, and child spacing. (Birth control is the subject of another study.) In the next section we step back from the implementation details to view the larger strategies local cadres used to smooth the bureaucrat-family interface. A conclusion summarizes the findings about the links between economic and demographic policy and spells out the larger implications for state-society relations in China.

This analysis is part of a larger project on the political economy of family and reproductive change in peasant China over the four decades 1947–87. The data used here were gathered as part of a field research project conducted in collaboration with Xi'an Jiaotong University's Population Research Institute. Carried out during the first six months of 1988, the project involved five stages of data collection: a reproductive survey of all ever-married women in the villages ($N = 1,011$), the gathering of family social and economic histories from a random subsample of families ($N = 150$), in-depth interviews with present and former cadres, collection of statistical data, and documentary research in local newspapers, journals, and other sources. Staff members of the Xi'an institute carried out the demographic surveys under my supervision; Chinese colleagues and I together conducted the family and cadre interviews and gathered the statistical data, living in the villages for a month and commuting from Xi'an the rest of the time; I was solely responsible for the documentary research. This chapter draws primarily on the reproductive histories and cadre interviews, but is informed by casual conversations and observations made throughout the research period.

ECONOMIC AND POLITICAL REFORM AND ITS EFFECTS ON POPULATION POLICY ENFORCEMENT

As no single locale can typify China, I begin by noting the distinctive features of the study province and villages so the reader may see how they fit into the larger picture.

The Provincial Context: Shaanxi in National Perspective

Throughout the post-1949 period fertility in Shaanxi has for the most part closely tracked the national average, making it an attractive site for research on reproduction.[15] As elsewhere, birth rates fell rapidly during the era of the later-longer-fewer (*wanxishao*) policy (1971–78), when strict controls on childbearing were first applied countrywide. From 5.5 births per woman in 1970, the provincial total fertility rate dropped to 2.7 in 1978.[16] During the period of the one-child policy, total fertility has vacillated, declining between 1979 and 1980, rising from 1980 to 1982, dropping again from 1982 to 1983, then moving upward yet again, reaching 3.0 in 1987.[17] After falling below the national average in the early years of the one-child era, provincial fertility rates climbed above the average in 1983–87. Although problems of underreporting argue for caution in interpreting the figures, available data suggest that since about 1983 Shaanxi has been among the laggards in enforcing the one-child policy.

The agricultural reforms introduced in the late 1970s and early 1980s have boosted provincial incomes, but not enough to pull Shaanxi out of the class of poor, least developed provinces.[18] Between 1980 and 1987, for example, the per capita income of agricultural households grew 2.3 times, rising from 142 to 329 yuan. However, Shaanxi peasants actually lost ground relative to the average Chinese peasant, whose income grew 2.4 times, from

15. Only during the Great Leap Forward did fertility levels in Shaanxi deviate significantly from the national average. Famine conditions in the province were less severe than elsewhere, producing a fertility trend that was smoother than that recorded countrywide.

16. Data from Ansley J. Coale and Shengli Chen, *Basic Data on Fertility in the Provinces of China, 1940–82* (Honolulu: Papers of the East-West Population Institute, no. 104, 1987), 168–69.

17. 1979–82 data from Coale and Chen, *Basic Data*. Later years from *China Population Newsletter* 6, no. 2 (April 1989): 7. Figures from the latter source are based on State Family Planning Commission surveys and are likely to be understated.

18. On Shaanxi's position as an economic underachiever, see Kenneth R. Walker, "Forty Years On: Provincial Contrasts in China's Rural Economic Development," *China Quarterly*, no. 119 (September 1989): 448–80.

191 to 463 yuan.[19] Acquisition of consumer durables also lagged. In 1986, for example, only six out of a hundred peasant households in the province owned televisions; countrywide, seventeen of every one hundred peasant families owned a TV set.[20]

Economic and Political Reforms in the Villages

Located in the Wei River Basin just west of the provincial capital of Xi'an, the three study villages are part of Weinan township (a pseudonym; 1987 population 26,000), which in turn is part of Xianyang city (1986 population 3.97 million).[21] The villages varied somewhat in size—their 1982 populations ranged from 1,436 to 707—but had similar social, economic, and political configurations. To avoid the problem of small sample size, in the analyses below the three villages are treated as one unit.

Vegetable growers for the nearby urban population, the villages were moderately well-off by Shaanxi standards, although only lower-middling by China-wide criteria. According to township records, 1987 per capita income was 402 yuan, roughly 122 percent of the provincial average of 330 (for the agricultural population), but only 87 percent of the national average of 463 yuan.[22]

The reforms introduced in the Shaanxi villages were similar in both content and timing to those promoted elsewhere.[23] In 1979 private plots were turned over to peasant households, and free markets were reopened, providing opportunities to earn cash for vegetables grown on those plots. Another source of cash income was short-term wage labor, which took the form of construction and transportation work in Xianyang and Xi'an. In 1979 such activities were organized by the production team. In 1980 "outside work" was fully privatized and, with urban centers close by, quickly became a common supplementary source of family income. While unskilled jobs outside the village were fairly abundant, opportunities for small-scale entrepreneurship were not. As late as 1987 the great majority of peasants continued to spend most of their time farming; "specialized households" were rare.

Decollectivization took place in phases. As early as 1979 the largest of the three villages experimented with contracting to small groups of four to

19. State Statistical Bureau (ed.), *Zhongguo Tongji Nianjian, 1988* (Statistical Yearbook of China, 1988) (Beijing: Zhongguo tongji chubanshe, 1988), 826.

20. Countrywide consumer durable data from State Statistical Bureau, *Tongji Nianjian*, 825. Shaanxi data from Shaanxi Provincial Bureau of Statistics, *Shaanxi Tongji Nianjian 1987* (Statistical Yearbook of Shaanxi 1987) (Xi'an: Shaanxi renmin chubanshe, 1987), 284.

21. *Shaanxi Tongji Nianjian.*

22. Provincial and national income figures from *Tongji Nianjian*, 826.

23. The following account of the reform process is based on interviews with present and former village and township accountants.

five households. The key package of reforms—the division of the collective land, the dismantling of the work-point system, and the introduction of household responsibility systems—took place in early 1982. Since that time peasants in the three villages have had virtually total control over the use of their plots and the marketing of their produce. The majority allocate the bulk of their land to the production of vegetables for the market, reserving small portions for grain for home consumption. Although parcels were reshuffled a few times during the first year or two after the initial division of land, from 1984 on the allocations have been relatively permanent. Small parcels are adjusted every three years, large parcels every fifteen.

The villages' periurban location combined with their vegetable-growing economy may have created a tougher climate for population policy enforcement than that faced by cadres in more rural grain-growing villages. In villages of both types, cadres retained control over the distribution of responsibility land, housing land (*zhuangjidi*), and key agricultural inputs such as chemical fertilizer. Cadres in the Shaanxi villages considered these, as well as their control over the electricity needed for irrigation, important sources of leverage over the peasants. In more remote grain-growing villages, however, cadres also gained power from their control over the distribution of other inputs, such as motor fuel, and access to draught animals, tractors, and marketing outlets.[24] None of these could bolster cadre power in the Shaanxi villages. Vegetable farming was done entirely by hand and with small tools, obviating the need for draught animals or tractors. And proximity to urban centers made the bicycle-driven cart the ideal means of transportation to market. These carts were so cheap that virtually every peasant household could own one. In addition, because their major crop was vegetables, after the distribution of collective land peasants in the Shaanxi villages were not required to sign production contracts with any level of government. In this context, enforcement methods such as "double contracts" linking production and reproduction quotas were clearly useless. Thus, while cadres in the study villages clearly had many levers with which to control peasant behavior, they probably had fewer such resources than local leaders in more remote grain-growing villages.

As part of the reform process collectives also relinquished control over their enterprises, both economic and medical. The cooperative health systems were abolished at the time of decollectivization, the brigade medical stations being contracted out to village doctors (*xiangcun yisheng*).

Designed to separate politics from economics and, more specifically, to roll back Party penetration of the economy, commune reform was carried out in April 1983. As elsewhere, at the commune level a township govern-

24. Jean C. Oi, "Peasant Households Between Plan and Market: Cadre Control over Agricultural Inputs," *Modern China* 12, no. 2 (April 1986): 230–51.

ment was officially established, while the commune was turned into an economic organization. At the formal level brigades became villagers' committees, and production teams were transformed into villagers' small groups. Informally, the elimination of many cadre duties brought an apparent decline in cadre power and, judging from how much time they spent in their fields, a loss of cadre commitment to official tasks.

Consequences for Population Policy Enforcement

In recent years a growing literature has dissected the effects of these reforms on population policy.[25] With few exceptions, that literature is based on secondary sources;[26] where it draws on firsthand research the fieldwork was conducted in the early 1980s, before some of the longer-term effects had become apparent.

The bulk of these studies deal with the consequences of the reforms for peasant fertility aspirations. The few discussions of effects on policy implementation tend to concentrate on disruptions of *economic* mechanisms, paying little heed to the fate of *administrative* tools. Furthermore, virtually all the literature on implementation problems focuses on difficulties in enforcing the rules on number of children; little has been written about the consequences of the economic reforms for enforcement of late marriage, late childbearing, and spacing rules.

Using the Shaanxi data, subsequent sections examine the effects of the reforms on both economic and administrative enforcement mechanisms, and on each of these policy elements (number of children, late marriage, late childbearing, spacing). Here we set the stage for that inquiry by setting out what is currently known about the impact of reform-era changes on economic enforcement methods.

Existing literature highlights three main mechanisms by which the post-1978 reforms are likely to have undermined population policy enforcement. First, it posits, the rise in peasant incomes impaired implementation by enabling couples to pay the fines for violating the policy rules without suffering great hardship.

---

25. See, for example, Wong Siu-lun, "Consequences of China's New Population Policy," *China Quarterly*, no. 98 (June 1984): 220–40; Martin King Whyte and S. Z. Gu, "Popular Response to China's Fertility Transition," *Population and Development Review* 13, no. 3 (September 1987): 471–93; Ashwani Saith, "China's New Population Policies: Rationale and Some Implications," *Development and Change* 15, no. 3 (1984): 321–58; Andrew Watson, "Agriculture Looks for 'Shoes That Fit': The Production Responsibility System and Its Implications," *World Development* 11, no. 8 (August 1983): 705–30; Delia Davin, "The Single-Child Family Policy in the Countryside," in *China's One-Child Family Policy*, ed. Elisabeth Croll, Delia Davin, and Penny Kane, 37–82 (New York: St. Martin's, 1985); Tyrene White, "Implementing the 'One-Child-per-Couple' Population Program in Rural China: National Goals and Local Politics," in *Policy Implementation*, ed. Lampton, 284–317.

26. A notable exception is White, "Implementing the Population Program."

Second, the abolition of team accounting disabled the system of economic incentives and disincentives by which the one-child policy was to be enforced. Under collective-income accounting, economic penalties were simply deducted from peasant income; when peasants gained control over their incomes, cadres lost the guarantee that they could collect the fines. Payment of incentives was also disrupted. During the collective era economic benefits were paid from the team welfare fund (*gongyi jin*). With decollectivization that fund largely disappeared, leaving few resources with which to award those complying with the policy.

Finally, commune reform exacerbated implementation difficulties by reducing the power and prestige of local cadres. Compounding the problem, local cadres were included in the distribution of land. Cultivating their plots was more rewarding than promoting birth planning—a task for which they received nominal compensation—depressing their commitment to their official work.

REPRODUCTION: STATE DEMANDS, PEASANT DEMANDS

When the one-child policy was announced in the late 1970s, state policymakers and Shaanxi villagers stood far apart on virtually every policy issue. We examine their positions on five key issues: the timing of marriage and of childbearing, second children, third and higher children, and child spacing.

State Demands

The large effect of the timing of demographic events on the rate of population growth was not lost on Chinese policymakers. Put simply, their aim was to slow the family's movement through its developmental cycle so as to depress the rate of generational turnover: by pushing first childbearing up to age twenty-four, they figured, they could reduce the number of generations in a century from roughly five to four. Building on the success of the later-longer-fewer policy of 1971–78, designers of the one-child policy set as their goals late marriage, late childbearing, few births, and quality births (*wanhun, wanyü, shaosheng, yousheng*). Shaanxi policy largely followed national policy on these basic reproductive demands; here we trace the evolution of provincial and municipal policy in the birth-planning regulations of the two administrative units.[27] The stress here is on the reproductive *rules*; how they were to be enforced is treated in subsequent sections.

Late marriage was a central element of provincial and municipal policy, appearing in virtually all sets of birth-planning regulations issued by the

27. A more extensive treatment of the evolution of formal policy in Shaanxi is Susan Greenhalgh, "The Evolution of the One-Child Policy in Shaanxi," *China Quarterly*, no. 122 (June 1990): 191–229. The following discussion is based on study of the original policy documents.

two units. Throughout the period of the one-child policy late marriage was set at age twenty-three and twenty-five for women and men, respectively.

Late childbearing became an important policy target only with the advent of the one-child policy. (Since the 1980 Marriage Law undermined the marriage ages in effect under *wanxishao* by establishing the legal minimum as twenty and twenty-two, those fashioning the one-child policy had to devise another way to delay childbirth.) In Shaanxi the one-child policy was not formally incorporated into official regulations until 1981. From that year on, virtually all provincial and municipal regulations advocated late childbearing, defining it as the delay of the first birth until the mother is over the age of twenty-four.

For the great majority of couples "few births" meant one birth. While the transitional policy of 1979–81 stipulated that "one is best, don't exceed two," from 1981 on the slogan was "advocate one birth, strictly limit second births, resolutely stop third births." From the beginning, however, provision was made for couples, especially village couples, who faced real hardships to have a second child. The number of such conditions increased over time. In the provincial regulations the number of special circumstances under which peasants were allowed a second child rose from five in 1981 to seven in 1982 to eleven in 1986. At the city level the number of conditions climbed from three in 1981 to six in 1982, to twelve, fourteen, or sixteen in 1985, depending on ecological zone. While most of the conditions were such that few couples were likely to fit them, in 1985 (city) and 1986 (province) all village residents whose first child was a girl became eligible to apply for permission to have a second child.

All those obtaining permission to have a second child were required to space four years between their first and second births. The spacing rule appeared in all the provincial and municipal regulations, changing from "over three years" in 1979 to "four years" in 1981–85, to "over four years" in 1986. Spacing between second and later children was, of course, irrelevant, as higher-order children were expressly forbidden.

These demands were not simply stated in the birth-planning regulations and then forgotten. On the contrary, top provincial officials kept the pressure on lower-level cadres by reminding them of these demands in frequent speeches and telephone conferences, as well as, no doubt, in internal circulars. Although such intrabureaucratic communications remain largely hidden from scholarly view, some indication of the nature of the demands made on local cadres can be gleaned from media reports of important speeches and conferences dealing with population policy. A review of such media items from 1981 to 1987 shows that during this period the provincial governor, deputy governor, first Party secretary, deputy Party secretary, and Standing Committee of the People's Congress made at least eight major, publicly reported speeches or announcements reminding local cadres and the population of the urgency of "vigorously" and "resolutely" enforcing the rules on late marriage, late childbearing, and number of children. (Spacing received less emphasis, presumably because the number of couples having second children was supposed to be limited.)[28] Thus, any laxity on the part of local cadres in enforcing these demands appears not to be attributable to indifference or inaction on the part of provincial authorities.[29]

Peasant Demands

It is hard to pin down who makes decisions on childbearing in Chinese peasant families. Discussions with many Shaanxi villagers suggest that in most cases it is a shared affair, with men and women, old and young, all attempting to influence the outcome. To understand peasant fertility demands, then, one needs to seek the views of both sexes and both generations.

Studies of ideal family size in China have generally shown that peasants queried during the 1980s have considered two the optimal number of children.[30] ("Family size" is convenient demographic shorthand for the number of children.) As important as the number of children, however, was their sex: two was best only if one was a girl, the other a boy.[31]

Residents of the Shaanxi villages apparently thought the same thing. Of the roughly 380 women who married between 1979 and 1987 and whose re-

28. This is a minimum count of such speeches and conferences, as it includes only those translated by the Foreign Broadcast Information Service (*FBIS*) and Joint Publications Research Service (*JPRS*). (These services most certainly missed relevant items in less widely distributed media such as the provincial birth-planning newspaper.) "Shaanxi Congress Standing Committee Session Held," Shaanxi Provincial Service, 1 May 1981 and 3 May 1981, in *FBIS*, 085 (4 May 1981), T2–T5; "Shaanxi: Ma Wenrui on Planned Parenthood Problem," Shaanxi Provincial Service, 25 February 1982, in *FBIS*, 039 (26 February 1982), T4–T5; "Shaanxi Planned Parenthood Work Report Issued," *Shaanxi Ribao*, 9 March 1982, 3, in *FBIS—Sociological, Education and Culture*, 80,836 (17 May 1982), 28–30; "Shaanxi Institutes Birth Control Regulations," Shaanxi Provincial Service, 30 July 1986, in *Daily Report—China*, 31 July 1986, T1; "Shaanxi Reports on Family Planning Work," Shaanxi Provincial Service, 13 October 1986, in *Daily Report—China*, 14 October 1986, T3; "Shaanxi Meeting Stresses Family Planning Propaganda," Shaanxi Provincial Service, 21 November 1986, in *JPRS*, 124 (18 December 1986), 84; "Shaanxi's Zhang Boxing Discusses Family Planning," Shaanxi Provincial Service, 10 July 1987, in *China—Daily Report*, 15 July 1987, T1–T2; "Shaanxi Family Planning Achievement," Shaanxi Provincial Service, 31 July 1987, in *JPRS*, August 1987, 83.

29. Numerous during 1981–83 and 1986–87, reminders of the reproductive rules dropped off somewhat during 1984–85, when the emphasis was on achieving numerical targets by improving education, contraception, and services. If local cadres were mere conduits for higher-level policy demands, we would expect a decline in enforcement efforts in 1984 and 1985, followed by an intensification of effort in 1986 and 1987. Instead we find a progressive relaxation of enforcement throughout the 1980s.

30. A very useful review of the literature is Whyte and Gu, "Popular Response."

31. Whyte and Gu, "Popular Response."

productive behavior will be examined below, 88 percent named a one-son-one-daughter family as the ideal. Four percent replied two sons and one daughter, 1 to 2 percent each answered one son, two sons, or one daughter, and another 3 percent were unable to make up their minds.

It was not only young women who thought small families were best. Men of all ages held the same view. Of 150 family heads asked their reaction to the old saying "more sons, more happiness" (*duozi duofu*), 91 percent rejected it outright. Four percent agreed, 3 percent thought it was right for some reasons and wrong for others, while a final 2 percent could not decide. While too many children had many drawbacks, too few children were also unacceptable. One child was clearly too few, for hazards of disease or accident could take it away, leaving a couple without issue. In short, two children were needed to guarantee one. And one of these had to be a boy. Thus, while one of each was deemed ideal, two children, including one son, were deemed essential.

There is no doubt that these responses were colored—to some unmeasurable degree—by features of the birth-planning program, in particular its antinatalist propaganda, which had been steady diet in the villages for over twenty years, and the fear of coercion its campaigns had instilled. However, the preferences for two-child, mixed-sex families may also have reflected genuinely held views, ones supported by the social and economic structures of village life. One's confidence in this possibility is increased when one hears the reasons villagers gave for wanting this offspring set. The fascinating subject of child "costs and benefits" could occupy a paper in itself; here I simply touch on the highlights to convince readers the peasants knew what they were talking about.

Students of peasant China are likely to ask two questions of the response that one son and one daughter are ideal. The first is why only one son, the second, why as many as one daughter? Taking the second first, peasants themselves were hard pressed when I asked them why they considered one daughter absolutely necessary. It seems they had never bothered to ask themselves this question. After repeated probing, the answer that emerged is that daughters provide crucial emotional support. The image that recurred was one of an elderly couple, unable to get around much any more, whose married daughter comes home to cook the meals, do the laundry, and generally keep them company. This was apparently a powerfully appealing idea, for a large number of informants, many of them men, produced it on their own.

As for why one son was sufficient, many informants noted the heavy economic burden entailed by raising many children. The costs not only of daily necessities but also of big-ticket items such as weddings and houses (expected at family division) have skyrocketed in the last decade, making the "cost of children" argument more compelling than it probably ever has been in rural China. The bottom line, however, was captured in the following expression: "One father can raise ten sons, but ten sons cannot support one father." In other words, when there is only one son, he has a clear obligation to support his elderly parents. When there are more than one they fight over who has to live with the parents, causing great humiliation and often even economic hardship for the older generation.

As for the timing of the phases of family formation, the older generation, whose opinions carried considerable weight, generally favored early marriage and childbearing. The reasons were both demographic and political. Demographically, the aim was to accelerate the family developmental cycle (precisely what the state sought to retard): the sooner one's son married, the sooner the grandchildren were born, the sooner grandparents could retire from heavy agricultural work to a more leisurely life of housework and child tending. The anxiety to hurry family formation was clearly also a product of the forceful and changeable fertility policy; in this political context peasants sought to marry and have their children as soon as possible, on the not-so-off chance the policy might become yet more restrictive.

THE EVOLUTION OF DE FACTO POPULATION POLICY I: LATE MARRIAGE AND LATE CHILDBEARING

Squeezed between a state promoting minuscule families and a society wanting modest families, what did local birth-planning cadres do? Treating village cadres as the creators of de facto policy—the adapters of de jure policy to local reality—the following sections trace the evolution of de facto policy on marriage and childbearing. The emphasis here is on *implementation* of the reproductive rules; as we shall see, economic and political reforms undermined enforcement mechanisms, narrowing the range of strategies available to birth-planning workers in the field.

Economic Incentives for Late Marriage

Late marriage was to be enforced through both economic and administrative mechanisms. Provincial and municipal regulations offered couples marrying late paid postnuptial vacations. During the collective era cadres could simply record the appropriate number of work-points for couples marrying late. With the abolition of unified team accounting, however, work-points were eliminated, leaving cadres without funds to pay vacation allowances.

In this incentive vacuum village cadres improvised. In the study villages couples marrying late were awarded a certificate giving them the privileges of having a child and of having it in a hospital free of charge. On close inspection, however, this new offer turned out to be an empty one.

First, as we shall see shortly, the de facto birth policy that evolved over the 1980s allowed virtually all couples, regardless of the age at which they married, to conceive their first child immediately after marriage. Thus, the privilege of having a child embodied in the certificate was no privilege at all. Second, the cost of a hospital delivery—about 50 yuan in 1987—was scarcely steep, and fell over time as a share of peasant income. In 1987, for example, a hospital delivery took a mere 3 percent of average household income.[32] Thus, a combination of changes stemming from the economic reforms—especially the elimination of work-points and rising peasant incomes—worked to empty the box of economic incentives available to birth-planning workers.

The Marriage Registration System

Late marriage was to be enforced through a strict registration system that required couples wishing to marry to obtain certification of marriage age from the village accountant. With that in hand, they were to proceed to the township police station to request a marriage certificate (*hunyin zheng*). As the reforms began to loosen administrative control, the commune tried to tighten it again with a new set of regulations. In January 1983 new regulations called for concentration of matrimonial study classes (in late marriage and late childbearing) and ceremonies during three annual holiday periods: International Labor Day (Wuyi, May 1), National Day (Guoqing, October 1), and Spring Festival (Yuandan, January or February). All those wishing to marry, the rules stated, must report one month earlier to the commune headquarters with their certificate. Only after passing an investigation and review and obtaining a marriage contract signed by their unit were they allowed to receive a marriage certificate. Strict penalties were on the books for those caught trying to escape the registration net by living together out of wedlock.

While the reforms contributed to the loss of control over marriage age by undermining the system of economic incentives, the timing of the shift in marriage age (documented below) suggests that another change played the decisive role. The 1980 Marriage Law set the legal minimum age at marriage at twenty and twenty-two for women and men, respectively. Since the new law was formulated and actively promoted by the political center, it clearly superseded provincial, municipal, and commune regulations that had called for higher ages at marriage. Peasants now had a centrally sanctioned excuse to lobby for earlier marriages, and cadres had no effective counter.

While local cadres lost their authority to strictly enforce the late-

32. The figure for average household income in 1987, 1,849 yuan, was calculated by multiplying the township per capita income of 402 yuan by the average number of persons per household in Xianyang city (4.6; figures from Shaanxi Provincial Bureau of Statistics, *Tongji Nianjian*, 64).

TABLE 9.1. Marriages in Three Shaanxi Villages, 1979–87

Year of Marriage[a]	% Registering Before Marriage (1)	% Registering 0–3 Mos. Before Marriage (2)	Average Age of Bride (3)	% Marrying Late (Age ≥ 23)[b] (4)	% Marrying Illegally (Age < 20)[c] (5)	No. (6)
1979	100.0	96.9	23.7	75.0	0	32
1980	100.0	81.6	23.0	68.4	0	38
1981	100.0	93.2	22.5	61.4	4.5	44
1982	97.7[d]	86.4	22.3	43.2	6.8	44
1983	100.0	82.1	21.8	39.3	8.9	56
1984	100.0	92.9	21.8	33.3	4.8	42
1985	100.0	91.7	21.7	16.7	0	36
1986	100.0	90.6	21.3	13.2	5.7	53
1987	100.0	91.7	20.9	13.9	8.3	36
All years	99.7	89.2	22.1	39.4	4.7	381

SOURCE: Calculated from reproductive histories.
NOTE: Table includes first marriages only. In same period seven second marriages occurred.
[a] Date of family wedding ceremony.
[b] Technically, "late marriage" requires that the bride be over 23 and the groom over 25. Here only the bride's age is considered.
[c] Legal marriage age for women set at 18 under 1950 Marriage Law and 20 under 1980 Marriage Law, effective 1 January 1981.
[d] One couple registered four months after marriage.

marriage regulations, they were clearly obligated to enforce the new legal marriage ages. Like most central directives, however, the 1980 Marriage Law was a general document that was strong on rules but weak on means of enforcement.[33] Lacking clear operational guidelines, local cadres took the system that had been devised to enforce late marriage and turned it into a tool to enforce legal marriage ages.

Table 9.1 shows how this transformation occurred. Between 1979 and 1987 the average female age at first marriage dropped from 23.7 years, just above the late-marriage age, to 20.9, just above the legal marriage age (col. 3). As cadres lost higher-level support for the late-marriage goal, the late-marriage rate for women plummeted from 75 to 14 percent (col. 4).

33. A convenient translation can be found in *Population and Development Review* 7, no. 2 (June 1981): 369–72.

Remarkably, throughout this period of flux in marriage age the marriage registration system remained intact. In every year virtually all couples registered their marriages with township officials before holding a family wedding ceremony (col. 1). Roughly 90 percent registered within three months of marrying (col. 2), suggesting close adherence to township rules on wedding procedures.

Inspection of the months in which weddings took place (data not shown) reveals that 85 percent of couples married around the time of the three holiday periods stipulated by the township. Seventy-eight percent took their vows during the Spring Festival (January and February), and another 4 percent each wedded during the Labor Day (May) and National Day (October) holidays. Clearly, the state had a lot to say about when weddings took place.

De Facto Policy on Late Marriage

The strategy local cadres evolved apparently entailed conceding marriage age to the peasants while appeasing officials higher up the state bureaucracy by rigorously enforcing the registration system and strictly carrying out the Marriage Law. Interviews with village birth-planning workers left the impression that upholding the Marriage Law was one of their proudest achievements. And uphold it they did. Between January 1981, when the law was put into effect, and December 1987, only 5 percent of women married before reaching the age of twenty (table 9.1, col. 5). The absence of a discernible trend in illegal marriage suggests that this handful of women marrying at eighteen and nineteen represent, not cases of lax enforcement of the law, but exemptions from the law fully authorized by local cadres. With explicit permission from local officials, families facing special difficulties were allowed to arrange early marriages for their sons. Most exemptions appear to have been granted for single-son families in which the mother was incapacitated; such families had a compelling need for a daughter-in-law to perform the cooking, cleaning, and other tasks reserved for women in rural China.

While late marriage remained on the books as a policy goal, then, it virtually disappeared from the de facto policy objectives local cadres sought to achieve. That village cadres had virtually abandoned late marriage as a goal emerged clearly from interviews with them in 1988. In one interview the birth-planning cadre of one village incorrectly identified the late-marriage ages for women and men as twenty-two and twenty-three; in another discussion she referred to the late-marriage ages as twenty and twenty-two, unwittingly substituting the legal marriage age for the late-marriage age. Clearly, the task in her mind was to keep couples from marrying before the legally stipulated minimum age.

Economic Incentives for Late Childbearing

Policymakers' second important timing goal, late childbearing, was inherently more difficult to enforce. (Registration systems do not easily control behavior within bedrooms.) As abortion of the first pregnancy was apparently not an acceptable means of control,[34] local cadres had only economic incentives with which to encourage the delay of first births. Provincial and municipal regulations of 1981 and 1982 offered generous paid maternity leaves for women postponing the birth of their first child beyond the age of twenty-four. In 1983, after the dismantling of the work-point system undermined the payment mechanism, commune leaders issued a new set of regulations offering women who both met the late-childbearing standard and accepted a one-child certificate (described below) cash awards of 20–30 yuan to be paid over the course of a two-month maternity leave.

In a newly privatized and rapidly growing economy, however, 20–30 yuan was a weak inducement to delay conception of a precious child. First, rapidly rising peasant incomes reduced the value of the award. Between 1983 and 1987, 25 yuan fell from 3 to 1 percent of average household income. Village cadres were also deprived of the means to pay the awards. The incentives were to be drawn from excess-child fines; as we shall see, however, collection of such fines dropped off over time, leaving those charged with encouraging late childbearing empty-handed.

De Facto Policy on Late Childbearing

With virtually no means to encourage delayed childbearing, local cadres had little choice but to simply abandon this policy goal. Data in table 9.2 suggest that this is precisely what they did. Between 1979 and 1985 the late-childbearing rate fell precipitously: from 84 percent in 1979, the proportion of women meeting the late criterion dropped to 18 percent in 1985 (col. 4). (Not enough women marrying in 1986 and 1987 had given birth by December 1987 to permit calculation of their intervals.) During that same period the average interval between marriage and first birth dropped from 17.5 months to 13.4 months (col. 2; the latter figure is biased downward slightly by the omission of a few women who had not given birth by December 1987). Of the seventy-eight women marrying in the last two years of observation, 1984 and 1985, fifty-one gave birth within a year of marriage, and ten had their first child nine months after matrimony (data not shown). The de facto rule on the timing of first births appears to have been: any time you want.

Interviews with village cadres confirm the story told by these statistics.

---

34. During the years 1979–87 only five first pregnancies ended in abortion. Neither the timing nor the answer to the survey question on the reason for the abortion suggests that those abortions were related to the birth-planning program.

TABLE 9.2.   First Births by Year of Marriage:
Three Shaanxi Villages, 1979–87

ar of arriage	% Having 1st Birth by End of 1987 (1)	Avg. Interval (Mos.) Between Marriage and 1st Birth[a] (2)	% Having Interval <9 Mos. (3)	% Meeting Late Childbearing Criterion (Age >24)[b] (4)	No. (5)
79	100.0	17.5	3.1	84.4	32
80	100.0	19.8	5.3	71.1	38
81	100.0	14.9	6.8	65.9	44
82	100.0	13.0	0	45.5	44
83	100.0	15.6	0	46.4	56
84	95.2	13.3[c]	0	37.5	42
85	94.4	13.4[c]	5.6	17.6	36
86	84.9	—	—	—	53
87	30.6	—	—	—	36
l years	90.3	—	2.8	52.1	381

URCE: Calculated from reproductive histories.
xcludes women having abortion or miscarriage between marriage and first birth.
roportion of all women having a first birth. Includes women having abortion or miscarriage between marriage and first birth.
igure biased downward slightly by omission of two women not having first birth by December 1987.

In response to a question about the status of late childbearing, village birth-
planning workers replied: "No regulations, no propaganda, no rewards."
The head of one village (*cunzhang*) said he had "heard of such things" as
late childbearing and late marriage, but "was not clear exactly what they
were."

THE EVOLUTION OF DE FACTO POPULATION POLICY II:
SECOND CHILDREN, THIRD AND HIGHER-ORDER CHILDREN, AND SPACING

Timing was a crucial component of the one-child policy, but the heart of
the policy lay in the number of children couples were encouraged to have.
While third and higher-order children were expressly prohibited, the rules
always included provisions for couples facing great hardship to have a
second, provided they spaced four years between the first and second. Indeed, as we have seen, the problem of second children was a difficult issue
for Chinese policymakers, one they eventually resolved by raising the number of conditions under which peasants were allowed a second offspring.
Ironically, efforts to improve enforcement by fitting the rules more closely

to peasant desires only made enforcement more difficult, for fluctuation in the official position created room for maneuver and manipulation at the local level, and peasants wasted no time rushing in.

How did local cadres control demands for second (and third) births and keep birth intervals of women fitting the special circumstances at four years? When the policy was first introduced three types of enforcement tools were available: administrative discipline, material rewards, and economic penalties. With the restructuring of the rural economy the force of each of these tools was blunted.

Administrative Discipline

The judicious use of administrative sanctions against selected birth-planning offenders was probably very effective in the late 1970s, when commune posts were deemed plum jobs. According to a set of commune-level documents, in 1979–82 twenty-eight high-status workers, including administrative cadres, teachers, women's team heads, and other officials, were relieved of their posts for violating the rules on number of children. Interviews with peasants revealed that workers in commune enterprises were also disciplined in this way.

The reforms, however, reduced the allure of commune work. As agricultural incomes rose, even workers with secure jobs in urban industry were tempted back to try their hand at "enlivening the rural economy." Teachers too left their posts for the promise of riches in the fields. As the relative income, and to a certain extent also the prestige, of commune jobs sank, the use of this form of administrative discipline against birth offenders dropped off. I uncovered no evidence of such firings after 1982.

Economic Incentives for One-Child Families

Economic measures also lost their punch. As elsewhere in China, in the Shaanxi villages couples promising to have only one child were awarded "one-child certificates" along with a host of material benefits. During the collective era benefits stipulated by the province included: priority in admission to kindergarten and school, in access to medical treatment and hospitalization, and in competitions for elevation to worker, soldier, and advanced-student status; priority in the allocation of housing land; monthly health stipends of three yuan; and adult grain rations and special consideration in the distribution of refined grain, sidelines, and other material goods; all to continue to age sixteen.

Village birth-planning cadres reported that during these years such incentives were both easy to award, as they came directly from team granaries and welfare funds, and appealing to parents, as the extra rations were paid immediately on the birth of the child. The dismantling of the collectives, however, eliminated the kitties from which the awards were to be paid. The result was a marked decline in single-child benefits, a process that can be traced in the provincial and municipal regulations.[35]

On the village level local cadres attempted to cope with the shift to household farming by offering single-child families double the normal allocation of responsibility land. This system, however, proved too inflexible. Much to the cadres' distress, it was extremely difficult to retrieve extra allocations from couples who went on to have a second child. In addition, land adjustments were infrequent, forcing couples to wait up to three years for their extra share. For these reasons the system was abandoned by two of the villages in 1984.

In 1987 the villages offered instead benefit packages of the following sort: four gifts twice a year (an award letter, candy, toys, and pen and notebook); monthly health stipends of five yuan; free attendance at the village kindergarten and local school; and free viewing of a movie or cultural program twice a year. To discourage further childbearing, parents who had accepted the one-child benefits but went on to have a second child were required not only to pay the excess-child fee, but also to return the accumulated value of the health stipends they had received.

The economic value of these benefits was clearly quite modest. The major incentive, the health stipend, amounted to only about 3 percent of average 1987 household income. The token size of the incentives, coupled with the fact that at most merely a handful of village couples actually intended to have only one child, probably explains why the birth-planning cadres described the single-child benefits as "unimportant to the peasants." What they meant, I see in retrospect, is that the benefits existed mainly on paper. Certainly, nothing in my six months' field experience led me to conclude that the one-child family was an important policy goal of cadres or reproductive aim of peasants.

Economic Penalties for Unauthorized Children and Short Spacing
The system of economic penalties was also disrupted by the abolition of team accounting. When income was paid in work-points, penalties could be directly deducted from a peasant's earnings. After peasants gained control of their income the task became one of persuading couples to hand over the fines, a difficult task given prevailing views about official policy.

In the villages studied excess-child and short-spacing fines were not formally collected until September 1979. In that year village cadres deducted amounts ranging from 500 to 1,200 work-points (the equivalent of 50 and 120 workdays) for having unauthorized third children (at that time second children were still permitted). Beginning in 1980 the fines were collected in cash. Following provincial guidelines announced in May 1981, from 1981–

35. Greenhalgh, "Evolution."

82 on (depending on the village) the fine for having unauthorized children or for spacing under four years was officially set at 420 yuan. This sum represented 10 percent of the "standard wage" (i.e., net agricultural income) in the township (estimated at 600 yuan) for seven years. For third births the fine was set at 840 yuan, or 10 percent of income for fourteen years. To ensure payment, the fines were supposed to be paid in one lump sum within a reasonable time after being levied.

Putting this system of fines into practice turned out to be very difficult indeed. On the one hand, since the fines were not adjusted for rising incomes, one might expect them to be increasingly easy to collect over time. The figures, though, seem to reflect the other hand. They suggest that peasant couples were unhappy about paying for the "privilege" of having children, regardless of the size of the payment, and did their best to avoid doing so. They avoided paying by bargaining with local cadres to get their fine reduced, by paying token sums, or by simply refusing to hand over any money. Both the portion of violators who were fined and the proportion of fines that were paid up declined with the decline of cadre power and influence over the peasantry.

These conclusions are based on the data in table 9.3, which examines trends in fines for unauthorized children and short spacing levied between 1979 and 1987. Shown in column 1, the proportion of couples having second and higher births (third and higher in 1979) who were fined for the offense rose from 44 percent in 1979, when the birth policy was just building up steam, to a high of 86 percent in 1980, then began to fall in 1981–83, reaching a low of 49 percent in 1984 before rising (for unknown reasons) to 60 percent in 1985.

In 1986 and 1987 the fine system broke down and was essentially abandoned. I discovered this fact, not from talking to the birth-planning cadres—who were not proud of the fact and tried to conceal it—but from studying the data they gave me. When I asked for longitudinal information on fines levied and collected, they provided detailed name lists running from 1979 to 1985. The request to fill in 1986 and 1987 was met with delay. The lists they finally produced gave only one fine, not indicating whether it represented the amount levied or the amount collected, and the numbers were all standard fines. Even in the years of good fine collection, standard fines were rarely collected. Later discussions with cadres not responsible for birth planning confirmed what the lists made me suspect, namely, that in 1986 birth-planning workers had begun to give up on collecting fines, and by 1987 the system had fallen into desuetude.

The destructive effect of decollectivization on cadres' ability to collect the fines is measured in columns 2–4. While the amount of fines *levied* quadrupled, rising from 4,565 yuan in 1981 (the first year all fines were paid in cash) to 18,420 yuan in 1985, the amount of money *taken in* only doubled,

TABLE 9.3.   Excess-Child and Short-Spacing Fines Levied and Collected:
Three Shaanxi Villages, 1979–87

ar	% of 2d and Higher Births Fined[a] (1)	Fines Levied[b] (Yuan) (2)	Fines Collected[b] (Yuan) (3)	% of Levied Fines Collected (4)	% of Fined Couples Obtaining Exemption (5)	No. of Couples Fined (6)
•79	43.8	1,625	1,405	86.5	25.0	8
•80	85.7	6,065	4,130	68.1	38.9	18
•81	70.6	4,565	3,341	73.2	28.8	24
•82	67.7	10,458	3,318	31.7	76.2	21
•83	67.5	14,280	3,360	23.5	85.2	27
•84	48.9	15,120	4,913	32.5	95.7	23
•85	60.3	18,420	6,861	37.2	82.9	35
•86c	—	—	—	—	—	—
•87c	0	0	0	—	—	0

•URCE: Individual-level data on fines provided by village wor⌐ ⌐'s heads and accountants.
⌐he figure for 1979 includes only third and higher births, as second births were permitted that year.
⌐ines paid in work-points in 1979–80, cash in 1981–85.
⌐ata for 1986 suspect; no fines levied in 1987. See text for explanation.

increasing from 3,341 to 6,861 yuan over the same period. The growing gap
between cadre effort and cadre success is documented in column 4, which
computes the level of fines collected as a proportion of fines levied. This
share dropped precipitously from 68 to 87 percent in the three years of
collective income accounting, 1979–81, to 24 to 37 percent in the years of
private income acquisition, 1982–85. Clearly, it was easy to deduct work-
points from team ledgers, but difficult to retrieve cash from peasant bureau
drawers.

Some of the political processes underlying this loss of cadre control are
revealed in column 5. These figures show the proportion of couples fined
who were exempted from paying part or all of the fee. The numbers suggest
that cadres were under intense pressure from peasants to lighten the load,
and that after decollectivization they increasingly gave in. From 25–39 percent during 1979–81, the proportion of couples granted exemptions rose to
76–96 percent in 1982–85. Clearly, the peasants were very successful in
cajoling, bargaining, bribing, or otherwise persuading the cadres to give in.

Analysis of the reasons exemptions were granted suggests that the situation changed from one in which cadres *bargained* with the peasants to com-
ply, trading exemption from the fine for contraceptive surgery, to one in
which cadres had to *bribe* the peasants to pay any money at all. In the
earlier years, especially 1980–83, the great majority of exemptions were

granted in exchange for proof of sterilization. By 1985 exemption-for-sterilization trades had disappeared entirely, being replaced by exchanges of exemption for insertion of an intrauterine device (IUD), a less draconian method of contraception much preferred by the peasantry. In these cases cadres at least got something in exchange for granting the exemption. Reflecting their growing loss of bargaining power, in other cases cadres were apparently forced to grant exemptions for no other reason than that the offending couples were willing to pay a portion of their fine. And these cases grew in number over time. From a figure of 13–31 percent of couples gaining exemptions in 1981–83, the proportion getting off easy simply for being a "fine-paying activist" or not refusing outright to honor the fine rose to 50 percent in 1984 and an astonishing 79 percent in 1985. By 1985 the peasants had clearly gained the upper hand in the matter of excess-child fines. This is no doubt why the cadres virtually suspended the fine system in 1986 and 1987.

De Facto Policy on Number of Children and Spacing

As routine enforcement mechanisms broke down under the weight of economic privatization, a de facto birth policy evolved that differed substantially from the one spelled out in the provincial and municipal regulations. Constrained from enforcing the policy preferred by the state, local cadres instead enforced a policy closer to that preferred by the people. Tables 9.4 and 9.5 reveal what that policy was and how it evolved over time.

For these Shaanxi villagers, we have seen, the optimal family included one son and one daughter. Given the odds of getting a girl and a boy on the first two tries, some families had to have three children to get one of each sex. The truly unfortunate had to have four.

Statistics on births by parity show that even during the years of greatest success in enforcement of state policy, peasants continued to have substantial numbers of second, third, and higher-order births (table 9.4). The proportion of first births is not a good index of the parity policy because it reflects the number of women marrying the year before (we saw earlier that couples were allowed to try for their first child immediately after marriage). A better measure is the proportion of third and higher births, which were expressly prohibited by state policy but ardently desired by the roughly 50 percent of couples whose first two children were of the same sex. Shown in column 4 of table 9.4, that share fell from 29.1 percent in 1979, the year the one-child policy was introduced, to a low of 7–8 percent in 1984–86, before climbing back to 13 percent in 1987. A more liberal informal policy on third and higher children, then, seems to have evolved only in 1986–87. (To prevent the birth of third and higher children in 1987, in most cases cadres would have had to take measures in 1986; for this reason the relaxation should be dated from the earlier year.)

TABLE 9.4.   Distribution of Births by Parity:
Three Shaanxi Villages, 1979–87
(percentage)

ar	First (1)	Second (2)	Third (3)	Third and Higher (4)	Fourth and Higher (5)	Total (6)	No. of Births (7)	No. of Marriages During Previous Year (8)
'79	32.7	38.2	25.5	29.1	3.6	100.0	55	11
'80	59.6	23.1	9.6	17.3	7.7	100.0	52	32
'81	52.1	32.4	12.7	15.5	2.8	100.0	71	38
'82	64.4	25.3	10.3	10.3	0	100.0	87	44
'83	51.2	37.8	9.8	11.0	1.2	100.0	82	44
'84	53.9	38.2	6.9	7.9	1.0	100.0	102	56
'85	40.8	51.0	6.1	8.1	2.0	99.9	98	42
'86	38.9	53.7	6.5	7.4	.9	100.0	108	36
'87	45.6	41.2	10.5	13.1	2.6	99.9	114	53
ll years	48.5	39.4	10.0	12.1	2.1	100.0	769	356

URCE: Calculated from reproductive histories.
TE: Includes all births, not just births to women marrying in 1979–87.

If substantial numbers of couples were having second children, were they waiting the stipulated number of years? Table 9.5 says no. Even in the years of closest adherence to formal policy the interval between first and second births never approached the four years dictated by state regulations. Women marrying in 1978, 1979, 1980, and 1981 waited about two and one-half years before having their second child (an event that occurred in 1981–85; data in col. 1). Women marrying later got away with even shorter intervals. The cohort married in 1982 waited just over two years, while that of 1984 saw just one year and eleven months elapse between their first and second births. By the mid- to late 1980s, it seems, there was no enforceable spacing policy in effect. As one village birth-planning cadre remarked, "Couples not waiting four years used to be fined; this practice was eliminated sometime before 1987, but I don't recall exactly when."

While data on parity and spacing tell part of the story of how local population policy evolved, the most important part is yet to come. The core conflict between state and society was over family size (in the state's formulation) or over size and composition (in society's). What we really want to know is how many couples got the two-child, one-of-each-sex families they wanted. The answer can be found in table 9.5. Here we find family

TABLE 9.5. Reproductive Outcomes by Year of Marriage: Three Shaanxi Villages, 1978–87

Year of Marriage	Avg. Interval Between 1st and 2d Birth (Mos.) (1)	Family Composition as of December 1987					Family Size as of December 1987 (No. of Children)					No. of Women Marrying
		At least 1 S and 1 D (2)	2 or 3 S (3)	2 or 3 D (4)	1 S or 1 D (5)	No Children (6)	4 (7)	3 (8)	2 (9)	1 (10)	0 (11)	
1978	31.3	54.5%	18.2	18.2%	9.1%	0%	0%	0%	90.9%	9.0%	0%	11
1979	32.5	59.4	21.9	15.6	3.1	0	0	21.9	75.0	3.1	0	32
1980	30.7	52.6	31.6	10.5	5.3	0	2.6	5.3	86.8	5.3	0	38
1981	28.8	65.9	22.7	6.8	4.5	0	0	13.6	81.8	4.5	0	44
1982	26.0	52.3	22.7	18.2	6.8	0	2.3	9.1	81.8	6.8	0	44
1983	25.6	46.4	14.3	10.7	28.6	0	0	1.8	69.6	28.6	0	56
1984	22.7	47.6	7.1	14.3	26.2	4.8	0	2.4	66.7	26.2	4.8	42
1985	—	13.9	2.8	11.1	63.9	8.3	0	0	27.8	63.9	8.3	36
1986	—	1.9	0	0	81.1	17.0	0	0	1.9	81.1	17.0	53
1987	—	0	0	0	30.6	69.4	0	0	0	30.6	69.4	36
All years	—	38.0%	13.5%	9.7%	28.8%	9.9%	.5%	5.4%	55.4%	28.8%	9.9%	392

SOURCE: Calculated from reproductive histories.

NOTE: Percentages under family composition and family size represent the percentage of women marrying in a given year. S = son, D = daughter.

composition as of December 1987 by marriage cohort. The "as of December 1987" is crucial, for with the exception of couples with one spouse sterilized, all couples had the potential for further childbearing should they decide to go to the trouble (or should the official policy change, an unlikely prospect).

On the basis of informed speculation about reproductive intent,[36] the ten marriage cohorts can be divided into three groups: those married from 1978 to 1982, most of whom had probably completed the process of family formation by the end of 1987; the cohorts of 1983–84, a majority of whom had finished childbearing; and couples married in 1985–87, most of whom had definitely not ceased reproductive activities. The group of greatest interest is the first, few of whom will go on to have more children. Of these, 57 percent (statistic not shown) achieved the ideal of at least one son and one daughter. Another 24 percent had two or three sons, considered an acceptable substitute for one of each kind. A further 13 percent had two or three daughters,[37] considered an unfortunate outcome indeed, while 5 percent had only one child, an unacceptable state of affairs.

Eighteen percent (with one child, or only girls) may seem like a high level of reproductive dissatisfaction, but data on contraception suggest that the majority of women in these circumstances were planning to become pregnant again. For while 85 percent of all couples married in 1978–82 were contracepting at the end of 1987, a substantially lower 55 percent of couples with one child or daughters only were using birth control (data not shown). And the great majority of these were using the easily removable IUD. Only four couples were sterilized; in two of these cases a son had died *after* the operation was performed, indicating an intention to have a son and one or more other children. Should all these couples who were not sterilized go on to have another child, and should 50 percent of those be boys, then overall 90 percent of those married in 1978–82 will end up with families of a sort considered ideal or close to it.

If peasant families did fairly well in achieving their compositional goals, how well did the state do in attaining its family-size targets? Columns 7–11 of table 9.5 suggest that state policymakers did even better, at least on this measure of policy performance. Overall, only 0.5 percent of couples marrying in this decade had four children, and a slightly higher but still respectably low 5.4 percent had three children. State policymakers were always ambivalent about second children, and it looks as though peasants exploited this ambivalence by pressing for a policy of (at least) two children for all. Fully 82 percent of the couples married in 1978–82 had two

36. Informed by data on contraceptive practice.
37. The gap in the proportion of couples with 2 or 3 sons (24%) and 2 or 3 daughters (13%) is probably due to the tendency for those with daughters to try again for a son. The "missing daughters" issue will be carefully examined in a future paper.

children, and another 12 percent had three or four. Local cadres' strategy, apparently, was to oblige state and society at once. The de facto policy they evolved allowed virtually all peasant families to have two children, and all but a small minority of biologically unlucky couples to end up with a son and a daughter, or two sons. At the same time it largely succeeded in achieving the state's goal of eliminating third and higher births.

CADRE STRATEGIES:
MEDIATING THE STATE-SOCIETY INTERFACE

In evolving de facto population policy for their villages, local birth-planning cadres worked out a compromise that placated both state and society, even if it pleased neither. What quid pro quos enabled them to do so?

Satisfying Peasant Families

Having dealt with a long stream of insufferable state policies over the years, Chinese peasant families probably did not take long to decide that the one-child policy was of this type. Neglecting basic survival requirements, it had no legitimacy in the eyes of village society. The view in the Shaanxi villages was that the minimally legitimate population policy was one that allowed couples two children, one of which was a son. Widely held by ordinary peasants (as is indicated by responses to survey questions), this view was also sanctioned by local Party officials, one of whom quietly allowed a relative to have a third child after the first two turned out to be girls.

As birth-planning cadres were basically of society rather than of the state, it is not surprising that they biased the policy to favor their kind. Over nine years they gradually peasantized the policy, permitting most couples to end up with two children, including one son; and allowing families to accelerate their movement through the developmental cycle by approving female marriage at age twenty rather than twenty-three, consenting to the conception of the first child immediately after marriage, and forgoing spacing requirements.

Yet these concessions were not granted cost-free. Even with their hands increasingly tied by the erosion of enforcement tools, cadres did their best to make life difficult for peasants infringing on the remaining rules. For example, couples were administratively prevented from marrying before the legal minimum age, premarital pregnancies were effectively prohibited, and, at least in the early years, couples desiring exemptions from excess-child fines were required to undergo contraceptive surgery. Over time a modus vivendi evolved in which a combination of growing local consensus on legitimate policy, application of some economic and administrative measures, and probably also fear of further sterilization campaigns worked to maintain enforcement of de facto policy at reasonable levels.

Appeasing State Bureaucrats

If local cadres effectively abandoned so many policy goals—indeed, they dropped virtually all the one-child goals except the prohibition on higher-order children—how did they appease policymakers in the state bureaucracy? Certainly, one trick they used—one of the oldest in the books—was to try to fool their superiors by sending up doctored records of policy implementation and performance. And when officials higher up the state bureaucracy called for sterilization campaigns, village cadres cooperated with township officials in co-opting couples with ample numbers of children into undergoing the dreaded sterilization operations.

Yet these rather token efforts could hardly have sufficed to close the hole between official goals and unofficial performance. Given the size of that hole, how is it that state bureaucrats did not "crack down" on the local cadres and insist on better performance?[38] The answer, of course, is that the state bureaucrats' hands were tied. After all, it was the state itself that bore responsibility for undermining the mechanisms by which the one-child policy was to be enforced. It was policymakers in Beijing who had introduced the rural economic reforms, ironically, the very same year they had introduced the single-child policy. The top leadership too was accountable for the 1980 Marriage Law, which undermined the legitimacy of the late-marriage rule. Finally, state wavering and policy fluctuation on the issue of second children opened a "big hole" into which peasants in great numbers jumped. (The aim of the central-level policy that first significantly relaxed rules on second children was to "open a small hole to close a big hole.")[39] Itself ultimately to blame for undermining the one-child policy, the state could not complain too loudly when local cadres failed fully to enforce it.

Floating administrative levels above village society, state bureaucrats were also totally dependent on local cadres for policy implementation. The local cadres were their only link to the peasantry; without their cooperation, problematic as it was, the policy could not have been carried out at all. And a close look at policy enforcement in the villages suggests that local cadres were giving more than a pro forma performance. If not the one-child policy, birth-planning workers were at least enforcing some population policy, and one that accorded with state goals. In the villages studied, local cadres achieved a record of solid accomplishment in some important areas: they

38. Provincial policymakers did try to improve enforcement by instituting a "cadre responsibility system," under which cadres who failed to achieve birth-planning targets had their salaries docked. This system, however, reached only down to the township level. Even there, it was not very efficacious, among other reasons because the salary reduction was extremely small.

39. This policy was spelled out in Central Document no. 7, issued in April 1984. See Susan Greenhalgh, "Shifts in China's Population Policy: Views from the Central, Provincial, and Local Levels," *Population and Development Review* 12, no. 3 (September 1986): 491–515.

upheld the Marriage Law with admirable thoroughness; they prevented third and fourth births, except where the first two or three were girls; and they continued to remind the people, through wall slogans, tours of propaganda vehicles, and other educational means, that population control was good for nation and individual alike. Recognizing that local cadres were doing a good job in a difficult situation—at least they were not actively subverting state goals—and that finding replacements to perform this thankless task would not be easy, state bureaucrats probably concluded that they were getting the best they could expect.

CONCLUSION

What light do the Shaanxi data shed on the larger issues of economic-demographic policy links and state-society relations? The answers are the subject of this conclusion.

Links Between Economic Reform and Population Policy

Existing literature posits a number of pathways through which the reforms disrupted the system of economic incentives by which the one-child policy was to be enforced. The field data from Shaanxi allow us to go beyond these general hypotheses to document precisely how and when those enforcement mechanisms came apart, and with what effect on each of the policy's demographic targets. In the study villages the incentive system was disabled by the opening of free markets in 1979–80, only to be crippled by the dissolution of the collectives in 1982–83. Loss of economic tools, coupled with changes in the legal environment, devastated enforcement not only of rules for the number of children but also of the timing rules. Every one of the timing goals—late marriage, late childbearing, and spacing— was dropped from the de facto policy enforced in the villages, with calculable effects on population growth rates.

The field data also shed new light on the reforms' effects on administrative enforcement mechanisms. One form of administrative discipline— the firing of commune cadres—was rendered obsolete by the reforms, as the appeal of commune posts faded before that of agricultural entrepreneurship. However, the marriage registration system remained a powerful tool for shaping the age at marriage and time of wedding. Cadre control over the household registration system served a similar function; its effects, however, were most apparent in the control of contraception. Thus, while the economic mechanisms were enfeebled, cadres retained certain administrative controls that facilitated policy implementation.

Finally, the Shaanxi village data also provide a window on the political process that pushed cadres' backs up against the wall. Newly empowered by the reforms, peasants bribed, cajoled, and otherwise manipulated birth-planning workers to grant so many exemptions that the system of fines had eventually to be abandoned.

The view from the villages thus suggests that in ways certainly unanticipated by China's leaders, economic and political reform weakened the enforcement of population policy, undermining the achievement of state demographic goals, which were, in turn, crucial to the attainment of state economic goals. The size of the demographic impact depends on the extent to which the dynamics of policy implementation in the Shaanxi villages were general to village China as a whole.

Reproduction has been a particularly fruitful arena in which to observe this process, as state goals are so clear-cut, policy enforcement mechanisms so copious, and outcomes so eminently measurable. However, the process by which the freeing of economic controls loosens sociodemographic controls is a general one, which should extend to all areas of social life that fell under the umbrella of state control in the collective era. The unraveling of systems of rural old-age support, health care, and migration control, for example, could be greatly clarified by tracing out the links between economic and political policies, on the one hand, and social outcomes, on the other.

Reproductive Control: From State to Society?

Trends in reproductive control in Shaanxi appear to support the orthodox view that the reach of the state was very long at the end of the Maoist period. Data from the late 1970s suggest that under the collective regime the state wielded truly awesome control over peasant reproduction, pushing female age at marriage above twenty-three, getting the great majority of women to adhere to late-childbearing rules, and strictly limiting the number of third and higher-order children. This was a remarkable display of state power, given what can be inferred about peasant reproductive preferences at the time.

As in other policy sectors, during the 1980s a good deal of this power was lost. By 1987 the average age of brides had fallen by three years, while the share of women meeting the state's late ages at marriage and childbearing had sunk to abysmally low levels. Despite the one-child-with-exceptions policy officially in effect, nearly all women who had completed their childbearing had two or more children.

While reproductive control clearly shifted in the direction of society, too much freedom should not be read into these data. State controls had become indirect, but not inoperative. For example, marriage age had fallen— but not below the legally stipulated age. Although couples had gained freedom from the late-marriage rule, they remained subject to the marriage registration system. Society had gained important freedoms, yet the state had maintained its grip over crucial aspects of family formation.

One of the state's major sources of reproductive control was its capacity to launch birth-planning campaigns. Preliminary analysis of the Shaanxi data suggests that campaigns were conducted in a more lenient fashion as the 1980s wore on. Nevertheless, one can speculate that the memories of highly coercive campaigns in the past, as well as still-present fears of being targeted for sterilization in future campaigns, must have been powerful deterrents to those tempted to challenge state policy.

At the grass-roots level the shift from state to state-cum-peasant reproductive control was engineered by the local cadres. Although they had gained power relative to the state, they had lost power relative to society. As a result, they were increasingly absorbed into society, overwhelmed by it, and constrained to accept its rules. Microdeceptions grew into macrodeceptions, and state policy was slowly but surely altered to fit societal demands.

In a complex process of mutual influence and learning, the peasantization of informal policy at the grass roots was communicated up the political hierarchy, with visible effects on formal policy. At the provincial and municipal levels, rules on the timing and number of children remained in place, but conditions for having second children were broadened, and implementation methods were modified to better accord with reform-era conditions.[40] Nor were national-level policymakers blind to the limits on their power in the villages. At the political center too, basic reproductive rules remained unchanged, while conditions for having second children were expanded and the population target for the end of the century was raised.[41] Thus, state and society moved closer together, and state policy itself was altered to reflect fundamental societal needs.

40. Greenhalgh, "Evolution."

41. The number of conditions for second children was increased in 1984 and 1988; the year 2000 target was raised in 1985. See Zeng Yi, "Is the Chinese Family Planning Program 'Tightening Up'?", *Population and Development Review* 15, no. 2 (June 1989): 333–37, and Greenhalgh, "Shifts."

TEN

Cultural Support for Birth Limitation among Urban Capital-owning Women

Hill Gates

> *The sky is bright and the earth is bright.*
> *We have a baby that cries at night.*
> *If the passerby will read this right,*
> *He'll sleep all night till broad daylight.*

POPULAR SICHUAN CHARM OF THE 1920S, PASTED ON WALLS, AND
EFFICACIOUS WHEN READ OR WHEN THE SUN SHINES. (DAVID C. GRAHAM,
RELIGION IN SZECHWAN PROVINCE, CHINA)

"You like this baby a lot. How about I give him to you? I already have these two boys, and they're too active. We don't need any more. I'm too busy to take care of this one. I don't want any money for him—I'll just give him to you."

It is awkward to refuse the gift of a healthy, pretty, month-old infant whom one has too enthusiastically admired. I have had to do this several times in my career as an anthropologist in Taiwan; usually the proferred child is a girl. Now, with three sons under five, this young mother clearly had too much of what is always assumed to be a Chinese woman's ultimate Good Thing—sons. Her oldest, at five, was already capable of taking numbered tickets in return for bags of clean laundry, enabling his mother to make daily dashes for the take-out food the family mostly ate. Soon he would be able to make change and fold clothes, giving her real help. But now, the commotion of four automatic washing and drying machines, of the television in the family's only other room, of the pachinko games in the shop next door, and of the boys' baby martial arts on the tatami bed was driving her near the brink.

"My husband helps with the boys after work, but he can't do laundry properly. The customers get mad, so I don't ever leave him in charge. This is a good business, but the noise really makes me tired, and now there's another child to listen to! I wish I'd stopped after the first one!"

The "family strategy" that most affects contemporary Chinese families is the decision to rear fewer children than Chinese families have historically wanted. This strategy is especially favored by women who own substantial capital in a household business. Analyses of peasant and petty-commodity-producer households have generally treated households (or coresident families) as molecular units that single-mindedly pursue a joint family fertility strategy, with all members in agreement about what is best for the group. Feminist critics of this conflict-free image have alerted us to the differing goals sometimes pursued by female versus male, or young versus old members of the household.[1] In the negotiations that result from their different interests and structural positions, there are both winners and losers. Winners control the group strategy, sometimes against considerable opposition. These might be called "directed family strategies," dependent on a special (and perhaps fragile) imbalance of power. I will argue that certain Chinese and Taiwanese women can obtain that power under economic conditions that obtained in the 1980s, and that they are likely to use it to lower their own fertility.

It is well known that in many societies, complex combinations of lowered infant mortality, higher participation in the female labor force, urbanization, and increased time spent in school, combined with good contraception, result in women's bearing fewer children—often only one or two. My focus here is on a much narrower point: that even in a culture often singled out as extremely pronatalist, women *as childbearers* are often eager to take advantage of new opportunities for limiting births, and they find considerable support for this in some versions of Chinese culture reproduced by women.

The women who I believe are most likely to find such cultural support for birth limitation are women in what I call the petty-capitalist class, most especially petty-capitalist women who are the principal owners of the capital that founded their small businesses. The communities with many petty-capitalist households studied by Harrell and by Johnson (this volume) may owe some of their demographic distinctiveness to the special opportunities that private ownership of means of production offers to Chinese women.

Since birth limitation has been a frequent, if not consistent, state policy in the People's Republic for at least two decades, especially in cities and among state workers, fertility has declined dramatically. This was especially true under the one-child policy of the early 1980s. In Chengdu in 1981, total fertility fell to 1.88.[2] (In Taibei in the same year it was 2.20.)[3] But fer-

---

1. E.g., Winnie Lem, "Gender and Social Reproduction in Petty Commodity Production," in *Marxist Approaches in Economic Anthropology*, ed. Alice Littlefield and Hill Gates, 103–18 (Lanham, Md.: University Press of America, 1991).

2. Liu Gongkang, ed., *Zhongguo Renkou, Sichuan Fence* (Zhongguo caizheng jingji chubanshe, 1988), 95. Note that this and the following figure for Taibei are total fertility, not total marital fertility rates (the statistic used in the remainder of the chapter), the latter being unavailable for Chengdu.

3. Directorate-General of Budgets, Accounting, and Statistics. *Statistical Yearbook of the Republic of China*, 1986. Supplementary table 12.

tility continues to vary considerably in different segments of the population. It is of both theoretical and practical importance to determine what factors operate to make the universal, abstract, national strategy into the specific, concrete, family strategy.

In this chapter I explore the mind-set that women of culturally optimal childbearing age bring to their childbearing choices. Put most simply: young Chinese women, when they do not fear want in later life, and where they have the social power to choose alternative uses for their time and energy, often willingly and voluntarily limit their children to one or two. This attitude is a response both to the practicalities of daily life and to a complex cultural pattern that structures kinship ideology in ways that are sometimes supportive of birth limitation.

While industrialization and urbanism generally condition voluntary reductions in the number of children women bear, urban Chinese women and their Taiwanese sisters have downsized their families with unusual alacrity, given the strongly pronatalist ideology and practice of the very recent past. Their speed in responding to the changed conditions that make a one- or two-child family the rational choice is not often braked by nostalgia for the good old days of six, eight, or fourteen children, by ambivalence about the utility of abortion, or even by the pressures for more grandchildren that some parents-in-law continue to apply. Women spoke to me as if they had internalized virtually nothing of the philoprogenitiveness on which much of Chinese culture is widely assumed to be based. This is perhaps the most important point of this study because it helps to contradict the widely held notions that there is a single normative Chinese kinship model, and that men and women are equally responsive to its imperatives.[4]

My data derive in part from field experience since 1968 with urban women in Taiwan, but especially from systematic interviews in 1988 there and in Sichuan—seventy-five in Taibei, and one hundred in Chengdu. They, and most of their families, are part of a petty-capitalist class—which I describe more fully below—because in nearly all cases the largest part of the household income comes from family business. Many of the women run the business as its principal manager and supplier of capital, while others have invested less than half, or even none, of the capital with which they work. These subsets of women in petty-capitalist families differ substantially in fertility, as will be shown. The data indicate—though with samples of this size, they cannot prove—that within the wider petty-capitalist context, women who have capital invested in their household enterprises negotiate down the number of children they bear for their husbands' families.

Determining whether women have capital invested in the household business, and how much that capital might be, is not simple. Government

---

4. See, for example, the sections on Chinese kinship and gender in Jack Goody's *The Oriental, the Ancient and the Primitive* (Cambridge: Cambridge University Press, 1990).

figures separating women (or worse yet, households) into categories such as "self-employed," "unpaid family worker," and the like, can be very misleading. Women frequently assign "ownership" of their businesses to their husbands when talking to strangers; capital for such firms may come from a woman's wedding presents or premarital savings; an unemployed "housewife" may profit from rental properties or run a substantial, though officially invisible, money-lending operation. A woman's economic clout in her own household is carefully screened from public view. Careful interviewing of known subjects in a social context with which the analyst is familiar produces reasonably reliable data on such matters, but at the cost of small sample sizes.

The principal argument of this chapter applies well to the family strategies directed by the Chengdu women, but the argument itself is best made and most clearly illustrated by the use of data from both Chengdu and Taibei. With extremely able assistance in each place,[5] I queried small-business women of a wide range of ages about their business practice, their fertility histories, and their thoughts about childbearing and work. I asked them about their sources of capital, including the gifts (often of money) made at engagements and weddings. These descriptions of marriage exchanges often revealed perceptions of their childbearing obligations. While my colleagues and I attempted to obtain complete information on these four areas from each woman, we left our questions open-ended, with ample scope for thoughtful response.

Many of the Taibei women I had known previously; I had seen what they did, as well as what they said. Here I draw also on a set of thirty-five women's life-history interviews conducted in and around Taibei in 1986. In Chengdu, in addition to the core sample of one hundred subjects found through a Women's Federation's introduction to the Chengdu Small Business Association, I interviewed an additional dozen women outside these channels. Some of the Chengdu women I have now visited repeatedly. In both Taiwan and China, my associates and I encountered women who refused to be interviewed, or who gave grudging and uninformative responses under gentle pressure. But in both places we were sometimes received with genuine enthusiasm. The question we were asking: "How do you run a

5. Chen Xiaowei and Lu Hana helped in Taibei; Hua Xinghui, Jiang Yinghong, and Li Jufang of the Sichuan Provincial Women's Federation assisted in Chengdu. Each of these contributed very substantially to clearer formulation of problems and more effective fieldwork. I am grateful for their work and their companionship. I gratefully acknowledge too the necessary support given by the Rockefeller Foundation's program in Women's Status and Fertility; the many kindly "extras" supplied by Women's Federation workers at many levels; the collegial atmosphere of the Institute of Ethnology, Academia Sinica, Taiwan, where I had the status of a Visiting Scholar; and the generous flexibility of my colleagues at Central Michigan University, who carried my teaching load while I worked on this project.

business and a family at the same time?" was, of course, the central question of their lives. When they had time enough to do so, they were usually eager to talk about it. One of the things they clearly said, over and over, was that childrearing was a burden to be limited as much as possible.

Chinese women do not choose to limit this burden only because childcare and childbearing are sometimes uncomfortable, painful, and exhausting, and at worst fatal. They do so as well because they have access to a secondary model of kinship relations that is submerged within a more visible kinship ideology. This model, especially clear among petty capitalists, rationalizes childbearing as a measurable contribution made to meet a specific obligation, and also rationalizes its limitation. The view men typically take is often quite different, but the two kinship models I will present here are specific, not to gender, but to mode of production.

PETTY CAPITALISM AND KINSHIP

Where commodity production is common, social arrangements and ideological responses form that reflect and enable it. In Chinese societies at least, people who are deeply engaged in petty-capitalist production (petty-commodity production by firms organized by kin ties) experience and re-create kinship differently from those who are not simultaneously capital owners and labor providers in an active market. The ideologically more salient model of "traditional Chinese kinship," or "the Confucian family," differs in a number of ways from petty-capitalist versions of kinship. The idealized model, which I will refer to as "the tributary kinship model," is derived from the operation of a tax-and-tribute sphere of production and circulation that in late imperial times assumed most of the population living an uncommoditized, agrarian life. This assumption was wrong for most Chinese even in late imperial times; it is certainly wrong for people living in contemporary Taiwan and urban China. But tributary kinship continues to be reproduced in partial form through a variety of practices.[6] The very considerable continuities in Chinese kinship observable throughout China's experiment with socialism and Taiwan's engagement with capitalism have been generated by these practices. Commoditization, where and when it has been strong, encourages people to act out a much wider range of

6. Tributary kin relations are still maintained in China through such legal requirements as that obliging adult children and grandchildren (since the Marriage Law of 1980) to support their parents economically; through the inheritability of state-sector jobs; during the period of People's Communes, through the frequent congruence of production teams and brigades with lineage segments; and by a number of other mechanisms. In Taiwan, the Guomindang government has consistently made its version of neo-Confucianism central to education, and has done nothing practical to discourage strict patrilineality in inheritance. This complex issue is discussed further in my manuscript "China's Motor: The Petty Capitalist Mode of Production."

kinship behaviors, many of them considered heterodox outside the communities that develop them.[7]

Petty-capitalist kinship behavior remains partially constrained within the limits of the tributary model. The latter has greater prestige and more legal protection and is continuously re-created by households in some other classes. Like tributary kinship, petty-capitalist kinship is thus organized around patri-corporations made up of a line of male agnates working and transmitting a body of productive property. It stresses hierarchy, patrilineality, and partible equal inheritance of means of production. Kinship behavior that departs from these principles has been punished historically by colluding officials and patriarchs whose interests lie with the continued congruence of patriliny and control of major means of production.[8]

People immersed in highly commoditized environments, however, constantly manipulate tributary constraints. The selling of goods, of labor, and occasionally of people influences decisions about marriage, divorce, adoption, and child rearing; the constant calculation of costs in the marketplace accustoms people to, obliges, and ultimately legitimates the calculation of costs within the household. Popular morality comes to commend the accumulation or maintenance of productive "capital" even at the expense of household members not essential to the preservation of the agnatic line.

Where petty capitalism is strong, households are shaped by contracts and market transactions, not only by "blood and bone." Those seeking heirs buy sons when agnatic nephews are not available, and sometimes when they are. Men, at times, transform kin ties into the cement of great landowning and trading corporations, or, lacking the appropriate kinsmen, construct lineages by agreeing to be coparceners in a joint estate.[9] Daughters, and women generally, are especially likely to be commoditized, marriages take many forms, and brideprices may come to wholly outweigh dowries. Women may long to bear many sons who will later support them, or may prefer only one or two children so that they may better support themselves. The connection of individual family members with the wider political economy can differ greatly. A woman may be a wage-earning silk-reeler or factory worker; a homebound mother, housekeeper, and unpaid hand in a family shop; or the owner-manager of a frame-knitting factory or a restaurant. Each job will position her differently in her household, espe-

7. A good prerevolution example of heterodox but locally normative kinship behavior is what Janice M. Stockard calls delayed transfer marriage in her 1989 book, *Daughters of the Canton Delta* (Stanford: Stanford University Press).

8. Judith Stacey (*Patriarchy and Socialist Revolution in China*, Stanford University Press, 1983) and Margery Wolf (*Revolution Postponed: Women in Contemporary China*, Stanford University Press, 1985) have argued this case convincingly for the post-1949 period.

9. See Jack Goody, *The Oriental, the Ancient and the Primitive*, 52–92, for a recent and hard-headed summary of the literature on Chinese lineages.

cially if members of that household have already accustomed themselves to market models of capital and labor.

The petty-capitalist model of kinship is characterized, then, by its subordination to the patrilineal principles of tributary kinship; by looser criteria for adoption; at some times and places by the development of large and economically powerful lineages; by the contractualization of relationships; by wide variation in treatment of women and forms of marriage; and by market-driven demographic tendencies. To survive and flourish in such a social environment, women obey its rules when they must, but are sharply attuned to what is negotiable in the bundle of kinship rights and duties incumbent on a daughter, a daughter-in-law, a wife, a mother.

Particularly important for this study was the assumption I shared with many of my subjects that ownership of means of production creates power within the sphere of kinship in a commercialized environment. Women who owned most of the capital that founded their businesses had very considerable decision-making power vis-à-vis relatives who might also be shareholders. Such women actively sought to limit their childbearing and childcare tasks, and used the cultural patterns discussed below to rationalize and legitimize birth limitation to their husbands, their parents-in-law, and themselves.

Implicit in women's statements about childbearing are two expectations. The first is that if a woman marries, she agrees at least to try to have children, preferably a boy. The bearing of children in return for a permanent home is the core of tributary Chinese kinship for women; a relationship of long-term generalized reciprocity is assumed to exist among family members. A woman's principal contribution to the family is the children she bears.

The second expectation relates to the role of kin seniors in childcare; it assumes that family members have rights based not on kin position, but on direct contribution to the household. It assumes as well that, to some degree at least, money and children are interchangeable contributions. Many women feel that their duty to bear children is a contingent one. Women working to earn income cannot bear and care for many children alone. If Mother-in-law wants lots of grandchildren, she must help care for them. If she will not, the working daughter-in-law's duty is fulfilled after one child or one son. A daughter-in-law can expect a direct, immediate return—the mother-in-law's work in childcare—for what the younger woman gives to her husband's agnatic line through her earnings. Short-term exchanges evaluated in terms of the known costs of childcare characterize kin relations.

These two expectations are contradictory. They speak to the operation in Chinese life of two concurrent models of kinship expressing different economic logics. These models are based on and congruent with the two historically significant modes of production that have governed relations of production and distribution in Chinese life for many centuries. In Taiwan, and in China for the class of women I interviewed, the petty-capitalist mode was much emphasized in the 1980s. Implicit bargains within the family were struck not only on the basis of kinship status—daughters-in-law sometimes obey mothers-in-law *because of their positions in a kin hierarchy*—but also on the basis of precisely quantifiable contributions, *because mothers-in-law will contribute childcare.*

Power over material resources was always a principal source of patriarchal and parental authority in China, along with the law and custom that enforced filiality. The greatest prerevolution enemy of that authority has been expansive commoditization, which sometimes enabled women and the young to slip the leash by supporting themselves and families of their own choice. Two informants, a Shandongnese in her sixties and a Taiwan Hakka in her forties, told me recently of literally buying themselves free of their father's power by paying their own brideprices to him. Wages from a Qingdao textile mill and earnings from tailoring bought these women a chosen life rather than a dictated one.

We should remember that the Chinese economy has encompassed both a long secular trend toward commoditization since the Song, and many temporary or regional bursts of commoditization that bloomed and faded over that time. Taiwan's unusual developmental history and the 1949 revolution in China brought women more income-earning possibilities than ever before because of their regular and systematic inclusion in the agricultural work force and their more limited participation in large-scale enterprise and, when policy permitted, in petty capitalism.

Fujianese petty capitalists pioneered the commodity production of rice, sugar, tea, forest products, fertilizers, and timber in Taiwan in the eighteenth and nineteenth centuries. In the early 1990s, small-scale family firms are still immensely important in its highly productive and only partially capitalist economy. In China, the official post-1949 position on petty capitalism (seen inaccurately as capitalist by Stalinist theoreticians) has oscillated wildly from the limited acceptance of the early fifties and early sixties to the near-extirpation of the late fifties and sixties to the Dengist free-for-all that began in 1979 in Chengdu and lasted until July 1989—the month after Tiananmen.[10] Experience and memory have maintained the assumptions and expectations of the market as elements in kinship practice in Taibei and Chengdu. Nearly ten years of observing or participating in private production had taught or reaccustomed the women I interviewed in 1988 to an increasingly classical market. Such women bargain hard, in kinship as in sacks of Sichuan pepper or bolts of polyester suiting.

10. For a post-Tiananmen follow-up on the women petty capitalists of this sample, see my "Eating for Revenge: Consumption and Corruption in Chengdu," *Dialectical Anthropology* 16, nos. 3–4 (1991): 233–50.

Charlotte Ikels's chapter for this volume explores intergenerational contracts in reform-period China; Susan Greenhalgh has argued for the utility of positing an implicit family contract that explains differential parental expectations of their daughters' and sons' contributions to their natal families in contemporary Taiwan.[11] According to Greenhalgh, parents characteristically require that daughters turn over more of their premarital earnings than sons because (a) children should repay parents for the expense of rearing them, and (b) daughters have only the years until they marry to repay this debt. Sons will remain with parents for life and can thus be given more leeway in repayment. The distinction points up the precise calculations made possible and then smuggled into kin relations by immersion and participation in a thoroughly commoditized economy. Her position complements a view of implicit intrafamilial contracts derived from petty capitalism.

Informants from both Taibei and Chengdu often described their childbearing plans, or their experiences with children, in what can only be described as highly economizing ways. A young Taibei fish-stall keeper rejected further childbearing on the grounds that one loses at least two months of work time after a birth, which is a lot of income to forgo. A Chengdu mother wanted a boy because "it's easy to find work for them. Only one-quarter of girls find suitable work." Some reasoning was convoluted: a Taibei flower-arranging teacher was pressed by her mother-in-law to have a third child (after two sons) to give to her husband's childless brother. Because the brother was rich, and they themselves had become poor, she refused "because I didn't want to be accused of doing it so our family could make a claim on his property."

The women I interviewed in 1988 were directly exposed to a secondary model for kinship because of their occupations. They illustrate petty-capitalist influence well, metaphors and explanations deriving from its logic flowing trippingly from their tongues. They plan their childbearing with care (now that contraceptive methods are available). They abort frequently and pragmatically. They often calculate precisely the costs of bearing and rearing children, seeing them as trade-offs against other purchasable satisfactions or uses of time. Their discussions of their marital obligations to bear children are grounded on the idea that other things—the income from a flourishing business, for example—can substitute for a large number of children in the eyes of their husbands' families. And women attribute their ability to resist pressures for more children to money that is absolutely their own.

11. Susan Greenhalgh, "Sexual Stratification . . . in East Asia," *Population and Development Review* 11, no. 2 (1985): 265–314.

HOW MANY CHILDREN ARE ENOUGH?

Do petty-capitalist women who own their own means of production differ from women of other classes in their actual fertility? At present, this question cannot be answered definitively. Demographic information is almost never categorized on the basis of ownership (or secure control) of means of production, whether by household, individual, or gender. Many rural as well as urban households in China and Taiwan are petty-capitalist, engaging in the production of commodities with household labor. But many are not, especially in mountainous regions distant from markets for their potential products. Peasant households, which produce principally for taxes and subsistence and in only tiny quantities for local exchange, engage with the wider economy differently from petty capitalists, whose production for exchange sustains the household. Determining which rural and urban households make up the petty-capitalist class thus requires data on production for exchange and on ownership or control of means of production—data are obtainable only through direct fieldwork.

The fertility of women in petty-capitalist households depends too on whether they are majority owners in an enterprise, or merely unpaid family labor. In most rural petty-capitalist households in China, women cannot contract independently for land with local authorities; rural petty-capitalist women in Taiwan almost never inherit land. The principal means of agricultural production are thus rarely in women's hands. Their negotiations with family members over the number of children they will ideally bear are conducted without the power given by ownership of capital. A class analysis of petty-capitalist fertility based solely on commodity-producing households (urban and rural) would be seriously incomplete without specifying capital ownership and thus the very varied degree of power held by women in petty-capitalist households. Such data are expensive to collect and virtually nonexistent. For Taiwan, however, we can piece together some information that supports the contention that petty-capital-owning women have low fertility.

In Taibei, I divide my field sample of women along two dimensions: age, and degree of ownership. Because the total number of women is small, only two possibilities in each dimension are considered. The age cohorts are women born in 1950 and before, and those born after 1950. This is a natural break. Younger women who reached childbearing years in late 1960s Taibei had ready access both to effective methods of birth limitation and to a flourishing market for their own skills. Older women, born prior to 1950, had few means of birth control and faced a labor market that generally excluded married women.

Cross-cutting the two age cohorts are two capital-ownership sets. I divide the sampled women into majority owners, who contributed half or more of the founding capital for their family businesses, and minority owners, who contributed less than half. I calculate total marital fertility rates for four subsamples: younger majority owners, younger minority owners, older majority owners, and older minority owners.

In Taibei, twenty-four younger majority owners have noticeably lower total marital fertility rates (4.300) than twenty-one younger minority owners (5.066). Twenty-one older majority owners also have lower total marital fertility rates (6.497) than four older minority owners (8.311).

This last figure, predictably, is the highest, perhaps even too high because of small sample size. It conforms, however, to my expectations for older minority-owner women in petty-capitalist households. In the economic environment of their childbearing years, their husbands and kin seniors wanted large numbers of children who could be flexibly employed in the family enterprise, or as outside wage labor. They themselves, with only a small share in the business, were both motivated and obliged to bear many children. Women of the same-age cohort with majority capital ownership had fewer children.

The drop in fertility among younger women in both ownership sets results from changing expectations on the part of society and entire households (due to changed economic environment, lowered infant mortality, higher participation in the women's labor force, increased years of schooling, etc.). But the differences between "majority owners" and "minority owners" in both age groups suggest a genuine power differential between women thus situated.

Total marital fertility for the Taibei ward of Guting (in which most of these seventy women lived) as a whole for 1986 was 6.160. Guting is heavily populated with petty-capitalist households, only a minority of which are run on women's capital. Such heavily petty-capitalist wards as Guting compare predictably with Nangang ward, where concentrations of wage-workers lowers the total marital fertility rate to (1986) 4.300.[12]

Because private commodity production has been sharply restricted for most of the postrevolution period in China, parallel comparison among Chengdu petty-capitalist households can only be limited. Nine older majority-owning women from the Chengdu sample had a total marital fertility rate of 4.202, compared with the rate of 5.807 for sixteen minority owners. These women had their children before the birth-limitation program began and, for many of them, while private production was a legitimate part of the urban economy. Even the younger women, some of whom

12. Taiwan, Republic of China, *Taiwan-Fukien Demographic Fact Book* (Taipei: DGBAS, 1986), table 15.

have not completed their childbearing, but who live under Chengdu's still-strict one-child policy, differ when we take ownership of means of production as a variable: forty-four majority owners had a total marital fertility rate of 2.258, while the five minority owners had a rate of 4.583. To attach social-class meaning to the published fertility data on Chengdu—or China—as a whole would require far more fieldwork than I have done there. The total marital fertility rate for Sichuan in 1985, however, was 3.224.[13]

As in Taiwan, I infer that petty-capitalist households tend to have more children than average *unless* the childbearer is a majority-capital-owner—in which case, they tend to have fewer than average. The sample—large in respect to the detailed fieldwork necessary to assemble it—is small by demographers' standards. Statistical tests would supply only spurious measures of significance and are thus inappropriate. That differences in marital fertility among the subsets of the sample conform so closely to the model is persuasive, however, if not definitive, that the logic of petty capitalism is employed by childbearing women.

Behind fertility figures lies a complex of behavior and belief through which political-economic pressures are translated into action. Understanding that complex requires careful attention to what women do in changing circumstances. Women's desire for children to meet affective needs and to care for them in old age is a central assumption in studies of Chinese kinship. Margery Wolf makes it the keystone of her analysis of women and the family: emotional and economic countercurrents in patrilineal households are generated by women seeking security through the birth of sons and through their emotional attachment to the mother.[14] Chinese patriarchy, past and present, offers only the most marginal economic and social support to women except in their role as mothers. Until recently, sons were the essential hedge not only against neglect and loneliness, but against immiseration and premature death. While conditions for women have altered significantly for Chinese women in both Taiwan and China in this century, many women still fear sonlessness.

But fear that one will starve without a son is not evidence for a love of either children or childbearing. Young women seem often to approach their need to become mothers much as many people approach the need to earn a living: start early, work hard, get it over with, and hope the investment of effort will suffice for its purpose. Of villagers in Zengbu, Guangzhou, Sulamith Potter says: "Objectively, care is needed both in childhood *and* in old age, but. . . in China, the moral emphasis is on the importance of caring

13. Computed from Wang Jichuan, "Determinants of Fertility Increase in Sichuan," *Population and Development Review* 14, no. 3, table 6.
14. Margery Wolf, *Women and the Family in Rural Taiwan* (Stanford: Stanford University Press, 1972).

for the old. Child care is a means to an end, a form of long-range self-interest."[15]

A desire to bear enough children to provide support in later life for propertyless farm wives tells us nothing at all about what young women might do if they had a choice of careers. One of the many things that makes contemporary small-business women in Taibei and Chengdu so very interesting is that they do, in fact, have a choice.

What we know of Chinese attitudes toward motherhood comes largely from people who cannot, or no longer must, bear and care for children: from men and from older women. "Duo zi, duo fu" (the more children, the more prosperous) is elliptical in a classic Chinese way: it is agentless. "The more *I* bear children, the more *the family* prospers" may often be the real meaning of the proverb. I have never heard a woman, in China or in Taiwan, present this bit of folk wisdom to me as a speech out of her own mouth. "Parents say" (or "parents-in-law," or "everyone"; or "in traditional society they say") "duo zi, duo fu." Women themselves say, "I didn't calculate [infertile days], I just had what came," or "I just gave birth until I was all birthed out," or "I had no right to object, and no means to prevent it," or, most simply, "I didn't dare resist." A vision of the past in which only "others" emphasize the advantages of many births is as common in Taibei as in Chengdu, where women have been exposed to much more, and more authoritative, birth-limitation propaganda.

A woman who has ruined her health and used up the energy of her youth and middle years in childbearing and childcare is likely to die prematurely—as Chinese women statistically did. Life expectancies for Chinese women were lower than those for men;[16] it is probable that deaths in childbirth were in part responsible for this. Women being interviewed often spoke of relatives or friends who died in childbirth. The reality was recreated in horripilating stories such as the one told by an elderly Chengdu wine brewer:

> Lots of women died in childbirth. Or the placenta didn't come out, so they would die. The husband's family would bury such women quickly [such women leave very dangerous ghosts]. In one case, blood leaked out of the coffin so an official saw it and thought it was a murder. He had the coffin opened, and the woman was alive, trying to scratch her way out! Having heard such stories, we women were all afraid of childbirth.

Those for whom maternity did not become a fatal condition often took years to recover their energies from as much as two decades of serial births.

15. Sulamith Heins Potter, "Birth Planning in Rural China: A Cultural Account." Working Paper no. 103, Women in International Development, Michigan State University, 1985.

16. State Statistical Bureau, PRC, 1985. Table/Average Life Expectancy at Birth in Selected Areas, 211.

For them, the promised "prosperity," if it materialized at all, came at the expense of their bodies. Women are not unaware of this; compulsion was and is often brought to bear on them to sacrifice leisure, health, and life itself for their principal family duty.

From my first fieldwork in Taiwan in 1968, I have been struck with the open unhappiness of young mothers in the Taibei working-class neighborhoods I frequent. They are outspoken in their distaste for the boring, tiring, dirty job of caring for a baby or toddler, and thought me a bit bizarre for the attention I paid to their infants. A Chengdu dye-worker who bore seven children before contraception was available added a much-needed laugh to a painful interview with her description of locking her young children up when she went to work, and returning every day to a house full of puddles.

Let me suggest, before anyone else does, that American mothers also often find childcare tedious and fatiguing. American culture, however, discourages such admissions—maternity is so sentimentalized that an outburst of irritation with the mother's daily grind is sufficient to create the uneasy, counter-to-expectation "joke" of many cartoons and situation comedies. American culture instead encourages the expression of positive sentiments toward the very young, and the open enjoyment of the immediate rewards of motherhood—the pleasures of nursing, of cuddling, of infant smiles and baby's first words.

Chinese culture offers much less encouragement to manifestations of maternal pleasure. In popular iconography, healthy boy babies are frequently depicted, but mothers nursing or tending children are rarely shown. Birth-assisting goddesses (such as Taiwan's Zhu Sheng Niangniang) are almost never represented with a child. Chinese mothers enjoy their babies, especially the first child (or first boy), in the same restrained and private way they are culturally permitted to express other feelings. They speak more than middle-class Americans do, however, about the unpleasant parts of their relationships with infants, just as they are far more direct in making negative comments about older children. By the time Old Three, Four, and Five come along, mothers have little time or energy for tender moments.

For several months I once slept on the same tatami platform with a Taiwan couple (divided from them by a thin plywood wall) who had just had their fourth daughter. When tiny Zhuzhu awakened her weary mother, she was gently fed, but also roundly and regularly (if tritely) cursed as a "loving-to-be-beaten wanting-to-die slave." Women burdened with the hand-washing of clothing, daily marketing, and numerous other chores of pre-1980s Taibei and present-day Chengdu are simply being honest when they consistently describe childcare as "excessively hard/bitter/demanding" (*tai ku*), or, simply, "exhausting" (*xingku*).

Though women are often direct in unguarded moments, they are usually unwilling to articulate negative attitudes toward mothering in response to direct questioning. Many veil their responses in deferential discourse guided by powerful state and family ideologies. The persistent Guomindang emphasis on a Confucian role for women as wives and mothers, and on the sanctity of families pivoting around self-sacrificing, home-loving women frames and constrains Taibei women's descriptions of their feelings. So do the power and opinions of their husbands and parents-in-law. China's one-child policy and its inconsistently enforced but widely known position that women have both a right and a duty to gain greater independence through work "out in society" send the opposite message to the women of Chengdu. Comparison of the two sets of women enables us to shovel away at least some of the hegemonic overburden, revealing the behavioral content of their choices.

In 1988, I asked women to tell me about their childbearing choices and about who had attempted to influence them. Parents-in-law and husbands naturally predominate. Predictably, the Taibei sample contains not a single example of a man who wanted fewer children than his wife. Many agreed with their wives on the number they wanted; a few wanted more than the woman herself wished to bear.

In both cities, women claimed that parents-in-law were the most frequent source of pressure to bear more children. If we include mothers as well, kin seniors account for 52 percent of that pressure in Taibei and 7 percent in Chengdu, in contrast to 10 percent brought by husbands in Taibei and none in Chengdu. Women agree better with their husbands than with kin seniors on this matter; women are also motivated to blame kin seniors rather than husbands.

Sixty-eight percent of Taibei women said they were under no pressure from others, as did 92 percent of Chengdu women. Fifty-seven percent of Taibei and 66 percent of Chengdu women's answers indicated satisfaction with number and sex of the children they had borne. The degree of satisfaction Chengdu women feel is clearly overstated among younger women who are mandatory one-child mothers. In more informal discussions, they very commonly prefer two children, one of each sex. The lower rate of satisfaction by Taibei women may result from the greater pressure they feel from family members *or* from simple accidents of birth. Their responses suggest considerable similarity between the two groups, and a general preference within them for approximately two children.

It can be argued that data from Chengdu, where a carefully supervised one-child policy was implemented during the 1980s, is of little worth in determining what women would choose to do. I cannot absolutely refute such a contention. When we put the Chengdu sample beside that from Taibei, however, we find strong similarities. And when the women speak—whether in the neutral or slightly pronatalist atmosphere of Taibei, or the one-baby-maximum world of Chengdu—they say the same things.

A twenty-six-year-old owner of a Chengdu film-processing shop and a growing retail clothing business wanted to delay having her child into a clearly distant, perhaps unreachable future, when she would have built an empire solid enough for even her incompetent husband to manage. "Then I will retire and have a baby." A thirty-two-year-old Taibei hairdresser did not want to have children immediately, perhaps not at all. "But my mother-in-law cried and cried, so I gave in and had my son. My parents-in-law and husband want me to have another. I won't until my business is more stable. A woman has to have her own business or she will be looked down on; she should be economically independent so her husband's family will respect her." Two shopkeepers, one in each city, both had such difficult first births that they have decided one was enough. A Chengdu restauranteur in her late thirties stopped with one daughter in 1974, long before policy required it. "I believed in birth control very strongly. So, as soon as I had passed the month, I took my husband to the hospital for a vasectomy, one of the first in the city." An equally strong-minded Taibei fish seller opposed family pressures to have more than two children by insisting on condoms, saying, "I can decide whether I want to have another child or not. A mother has to earn money. She has no time to take care of too many children." A seller of sweet snacks much enjoyed in Chengdu, who bore two boys to a dissolute man in the hungry sixties, told me, "I didn't want a lot of kids, and wasn't pressured into it. Children are a burden. These days, two people caring for a baby are tired, all the more me alone with two to care for. When the babies cried, I sometimes just threw the quilt over them to stifle the sounds of their crying." A woman with a small Taibei shoe store was unable to resist her parents-in-law's demand for three children (though she aborted a fourth). Since she had to have them, "I wanted to bear the three children as quickly as possible so I could take care of the store. My first and second children were brought up by my mother," and they now help her with Number Three. Over and over, from women in both cities: "Two is best, a boy and a girl; then you have insurance if one of them dies"; or: "One or two is enough. In today's society, parents don't need children to support them in old age. I can earn enough myself." "People always want boys, but girls are better to their parents," "are more obedient," "but have to be protected more."

Parents in both cities referred obliquely to changing social mores in their frequently expressed concern for successfully developing filiality in their children. A young Chengdu couple running an outrageously successful restaurant were perfectly satisfied with their one boy, although they could easily have had a second, back in the mid-seventies. "I was too busy [working in a factory days and making clothes to sell at night] to have a second, and we really didn't want the expense of another," said the wife. Her husband agreed: "Today's children are too bad. It's meaningless to have a lot. They might go bad, and end up in jail." Many women stressed the importance of obedience, and thus the special advantages of small families and of having daughters. But daughters are not always obedient: a sixty-five-year-old clothing wholesaler complained that "my second daughter has been useless to me, so one would have been enough. I'm not feudal."

Occasionally, I heard a more "traditional" voice. Both a Taibei and a Chengdu woman said they wished to have lots of children because they *like* children, and so do their husbands. Said a Chengdu knitwear producer whose daughters were grown by the time it became possible to start businesses: "I had four, which is a lot by today's standards. Still, if I could have managed one more, we'd have another helper and not need to hire one." But this is retrospect, which just as often looks in a different direction, as in this comment by a former dyeworks co-owner: "I was sorry after Liberation that we had had so many [five], because then our business was collectivized" (so they couldn't use the labor). And women in both cities often stated that one was the absolute minimum: "You can't not have *any*! Then why marry at all?"

Like other women who earn cash incomes, petty-capitalist women wish to have, and indeed do have, relatively few children compared with their mothers and grandmothers. They are sometimes also seen as having earned the right to do so. "In former times," said a woman whose family business before Liberation was a Chinese medicine store, "women worked only at home, and so should have more children. Now, they also work outside, so they can have fewer." Speaking of her sister-in-law's numerous progeny, a Chengdu woman said, "She kept having them because she lived in the country and work-points weren't worth much, so her husband made her have them all. If she had worked for money, she could have refused on grounds of her work." The forty-eight-year-old wife of a Taibei car-repair-shop owner, whose fecund mother-in-law (thirteen *live* births) had shown little sympathy for her ten births and one abortion, saw clearly the value of one's own income. "Women who work after marriage absolutely won't have so many. It's not necessary and it's too hard on you. But women couldn't go out to work in my time, and so we didn't have the opportunity to have fewer." Three or four, she thinks, would have been plenty. Taibei women often make the same point more succinctly: "Shei you qian, shei jiu shi lao da" (Whoever has the money is number one).

COPING WITH CHILDCARE

A strong cultural imperative gives mothers the primary responsibility for their children's care and rearing. Under the Qing, women could be punished by the state for neglecting to train children (especially daughters) properly;[17] custom certainly holds them responsible, at least for children under five or six years. Women continue to accept this without question. A Chengdu clothing wholesaler with a boy and a girl was pressured by her husband to have a third child to give to the husband's elder brother. She refused, pointing out that "caring for and bearing children is mine to do, so you keep out of it."

Despite the heavy and essential emphasis on women as mothers, Chinese culture also encourages and enables women to escape the burden of child-care. They do this in several time-honored ways: adopting out or otherwise disposing of babies, especially girls, when their care would especially tax a woman who already has young children; putting children into school/daycare arrangements as early as possible; turning children over to house-hold members, including other very young children; leaving children with relatives in other households, often at a considerable distance.

It is well known that infanticide and the selling of children, particularly girls, were common in China in the past,[18] and recur occasionally in the present.[19] Even in Taiwan some poor families sell boys.[20] That children have often been sold, and sometimes killed, is part of people's daily under-standings. Whether such events are viewed with horror or merely ruefully, everyone knows that, not long ago, babies could be disposed of with little likelihood that punishment would ensue for their families. Happily, these events now are rare; the more commonplace practices described below are far more significant in maintaining the unsentimental approach to child rearing I am asserting.

ADOPTION

Out-adoption as a solution to the problem of too many children faded very quickly in Taiwan with the advent of reliable contraception and abortion in

17. For a particularly horrible example, see Gary Hamilton, "Patriarchalism in Imperial China and Western Europe: A Revision of Weber's Sociology of Dominance," *Theory and Society* 13, no. 3 (1988): 393–425.

18. Infanticide, direct or indirect, and the selling of kinfolk were, of course, well known in many other societies. Their commonplace occurrence in China in recent times leaves a deeper mark on present-day society than parallel but obsolete practices do on Euro-American culture.

19. See Mary Erbaugh, "Chinese Women Face Increased Discrimination," *Off Our Backs* 20, no. 3 (Mar. 1990): 9, 33, for a recent and well-informed summary of this problem in China. Simon Long (*Guardian*, February 2, 1990) reported the freeing in 1989 of more than 7,000 women and children in Sichuan as part of a national campaign against kidnapping, slave-trading, and bride-selling. Poor regions in Sichuan are especially notorious for this.

20. In addition to the child offered to me by the laundry-keeper, I occasionally hear of such sales in the course of fieldwork. Twin boys had just been sold by a Taibei couple on welfare whom I interviewed in 1985, for example.

the 1960s. While we lack comparable data for China as a whole, I encountered only a few cases of adoption in or out in the Chengdu sample among women who came to childbearing years after the mid 1960s, when contraception and abortion became available to those who wanted them. It is instructive, therefore, to consult the conclusions from Taiwan household-register data drawn by Arthur P. Wolf and Huang Chieh-shan about pre-contraception adoption.

As a part of a marriage form in which infant girls were fostered by their future parents-in-law, adoption was extremely frequent in northern Taiwan from at least eighty years prior to 1930, when such "minor marriages" radically diminished. For some time, approximately 70 percent of girls were adopted out shortly after birth.[21] Seeking to account for the timing in a woman's childbearing career of decisions to adopt girl children, Wolf and Huang found that the work load of care for previously born children was important in determining whether a newly born girl would be kept as a daughter or adopted out as some other family's foster daughter-in-law.[22]

Such very high rates of adoption were unevenly distributed in China, being found mostly in southeastern regions,[23] and were far from universal. But adoption of girls was widely practiced and probably very frequent throughout China. Demand for girls as daughters, daughters-in-law, servants, and apprentice prostitutes ensured that families that did not choose to abandon superfluous children, or dared not do so, could dispose of them easily in, or under the guise of, adoption.[24] While much diminished, such practices are known, discussed, and part of the experience of many living women.

CARE BY SIBLINGS

With the growth of universal education in Taibei and Chengdu, older children are much less available to care for younger ones at home than they once were. As every urban mother knows, the early years of schooling are both obligatory and the time in which a child's future career is adumbrated. Despite the horrendous educational competition, a city child who can easily learn the special skills required for success in Chinese schools truly stands on a golden escalator. For a while at least, Mother will make few demands on her time, including eschewing help with baby. With aston-

21. Arthur P. Wolf and Huang Chieh-shan, *Marriage and Adoption in China, 1845–1945* (Stanford: Stanford University Press, 1980), 230.

22. Wolf and Huang, *Marriage and Adoption*, 290.

23. Wolf and Huang, *Marriage and Adoption*, 1–11, especially 6.

24. See Maria H. A. Jaschok, *Concubines and Bondservants: The Social History of a Chinese Custom* (London: Zed Books, 1988).

ishing rapidity, families in which older children care for very young siblings have vanished.

DAYCARE AS EDUCATION

Childcare even for today's smaller families remains a pressing problem. Daycare that emphasizes the establishment's educational functions is extremely popular in Taibei and increasingly so in Chengdu. Many women meet their own needs for manageable small businesses simultaneously with other women's need and wish for daycare by setting up privately run preschools and kindergartens. A great many women in my sample in both cities put their children in care as early as the "teachers" would take them, usually as soon as they were toilet trained.

Mothers who own and run small businesses, many home-based, often *could* keep young children with them at work at least part of the time, and many can afford to hire in-home care. The labeling of daycare for very little children as "schools," however, gives mothers a strong rationale for putting their children in outside care. Early socialization to school may indeed make it easier for children to do well in the state elementary schools, as the women say it does. Having their children safely in custody during the workday also makes it much easier for women to work and to enjoy brief periods of leisure. A Chengdu woman employed before Liberation in her family's cloth store thought one of the best reasons to find paid work was that "if you have income, you can put your children in kindergarten."

Schooling for their daughters meant very different things for the wife and husband with whom I shared the sleeping arrangements described above. Xiao Ping, seven and in first grade, was an important role model for her sister, Xiao Cui, five years old and rapidly growing stir-crazy. With four little girls to care for, and not a penny in her pocket, their mother, Lim A-Bi, had not been off the block—hardly out of the apartment—since her marriage at sixteen to a fortyish Hunan bus driver. Xiao Cui was climbing the walls, or at least the furniture.

Lim A-Bi sent for reinforcements. The eldest girl's former daycare "teacher" came to take Cui-cui for a free day's schooling. The child came home enchanted, and spent the next three days writing the half-dozen characters she had been taught, over and over, in her very own little notebook. Her parents spent the next three days arguing about whether to pay for more. The cranky bus driver (wearing an armored orthopedic corset while driving ten-hour days in Taibei traffic, he could hardly be other than cranky) was adamant. "A kid can learn to line up and march in a few days: that's all they really learn in daycare, anyway. I'm not paying money for Xiao Cui to play when she can stay here and play at home for free." A week later, Xiao Cui was black and blue from forehead to chin from fall-ing off the television onto her neat little nose. Till the bruises faded, her mother would frequently poke her—hard—on the nose, saying, "Hurts, doesn't it?"

HIRED CARE AT HOME

Women petty capitalists often say that a principal reason for starting a home business is that it enables them to combine work with childcare. Meeting the demands of both young children and a new business is clearly a strain, however; petty-capitalist women also say they are too busy to over-see their younger children while working, even if the work is done at home.

The Taibei women in my sample, like all but the richest of present-day Taiwan families, can no longer afford live-in amahs. Mothers in Chengdu who earn (at an estimate) over 150 yuan a month find it worthwhile to take in a country teenager for room, board, pocket money, and the implicit promise of bright lights and city boyfriends. But few women outside of a few intellectuals and petty capitalists have such incomes. *Laobanniang*— "boss ladies"—in both cities often fob their child off on an apprentice or paid worker for part of the workday. Most seem reluctant to hire in a full-time nursemaid, preferring to save the cost of keeping her, to make other use of the necessary sleeping space, and to avoid untoward complications with their husbands.

LONG-TERM CARE OUTSIDE THE HOME

Chinese mothers often leave children for long periods in the care of relatives or hired care-givers outside their own homes. Young Chinese intellec-tuals studying abroad, including women, endure (often with much pain) separation from even a very young child, left behind in China with its grandmother. Those who choose such separation justify it in terms of the extraordinary benefits—in which the child will eventually share—of their training, and argue that the child will not suffer, because it remains in a familiar setting with a relative. "After all, we're all one family, aren't we?" Women are thus supported in undertaking independent activities by an attitude that suggests that *their* care for the child is not essential. It is a task that others could do for her.

Female intellectuals abroad follow a pattern common to many women in Taibei and Chengdu. Working women frequently send their children to live during the workweek or for longer periods with relatives or trusted, paid nursemaids. In Chengdu, the eight-year-old son might sleep on the sofa on weekends, when home from his grandmother's, or the fourteen-year-old daughter, with her younger sister, when she returned each month from staying with an aunt who lived near her school. A woman who ground medicines in the family shop and cooked for a large household of relatives and employees in the 1940s put the last three of her four children into paid care until each was two and a half. Because she was working, her husband paid part of the cost; the rest she paid herself.

Unsurprisingly, women prefer to put their children in the care of relatives, especially their own mothers or mothers-in-law. Each choice has its advantages. Women generally trust their mothers more not to alienate the child's affections, and to follow child-rearing standards with which they are familiar. Also, a woman may give her mother money "for the child's food" or even as payment for childcare. They thus finesse the problem that husbands, generally, do not want wives to give their own mothers money, while women usually want to or feel they should. A mother-in-law is less likely to receive payments for the work itself: after all, she is caring for *her* lineal descendant. Sometimes even "money for food" is eliminated, apparently on these grounds. It is thus materially more advantageous, as well as emotionally more comfortable, for older women to take in their daughters' children than their sons'. Much the same can be said for a woman's sisters. Having a child room and board with a woman's relative connects her with what may be her most important relationships, again rationalizing the allocation of childcare duties away from the woman herself.

Taibei women have depended on nonresidential relatives for long-term childcare at least since the 1930s. Guo A-Gui, a sixtyish kitchen worker, told me that she and her sister turned each of their children over to their mother in those years. This enabled Guo not only to work during the day, but also to spend the evenings out at opera performances.[25] Chengdu women of the same age group sometimes did the same.

In the absence of complete information, I estimate that one-fourth of the Chengdu and one-fifth of the Taibei women had left children in living arrangements with their mothers, mothers-in-law, or more rarely, another relative. "If there is no old person to care for the children, it is hard for women to work," said a sixty-two-year-old Chengdu factory owner. Often this childcare arrangement is interrupted only by the relative's death and may be almost total when the woman has no husband. A forty-two-year-old Chengdu restauranteur widowed after three children has had them all raised by her husband's elder sister in the countryside. "I visit them occasionally on Sundays, and I pay Sister-in-law three hundred to four hundred yuan a month."

25. Hill Gates, *Chinese Working-Class Lives: Getting By In Taiwan* (Ithaca: Cornell University Press, 1987), 87–88.

MOTHERS-IN-LAW

Of the alternatives available, most women agree that the best solution to their childcare problem is, of course, their own mothers. The second best solution, the mother-in-law as baby-sitter, is more complex than it appears. The economic relations between women and their mothers-in-law offer critical insights into the slippage in Chinese families between two visions of kinship obligation.

Chinese daughters-in-law have often been described as servants of their mothers-in-law: washing, cooking, bringing tea, bearing and caring for the grandchildren, whom mother-in-law can dandle or not as she sees fit. For most families, I doubt that grandmothers were ever so entirely free of obligation, although I have known lazy and exploitative mothers-in-law.[26] Especially in regard to childcare, older Chinese women in many settings have complained mightily that the leisure they expected from acquiring a daughter-in-law has vanished, because the daughters-in-law have all gone out to work. Some mothers-in-law may well have had an exaggerated view of their future privileges during the years when they were the daughters-in-law. I have interviewed elderly as well as young women whose mothers-in-law did most of the childcare while they themselves worked in the fields or for wages. Taibei women make this especially clear.

A twenty-four-year-old who runs a fish stall with her husband, and has had two children, expects no pressure from her mother-in-law to have more "because Mother-in-law is so tired of taking care of children." A woman, thirty-six, whose small family factory makes noodles, has stopped after a girl and a boy because "I'm too busy, and Mother-in-law won't take care of them for me," though she observes that her mother-in-law could force her to have a third if she had no son. A twenty-seven-year-old motorcycle mechanic had three children, then refused to have any more, despite her husband's wishes. "My parents-in-law couldn't take care of them for me."

---

26. It would be wrong to omit from this record the acts of kindness young women often receive from older ones, even in the structurally difficult in-law relationship. In Chengdu, the mother-in-law of a thirty-seven-year-old spiced-goose maker wanted her to wait until she was thirty before having a child, because she herself had suffered so from early and repeated childbearing. The mother-in-law took her to three hospitals to arrange an abortion, but without a certificate from a work unit, she was unable to do so. A young shopkeeper began her business because her mother told her that having no occupation but housekeeping and caring for one child was bad for her. An auto mechanic with three children born before contraception became widely available would have stopped at two; at that time, one needed a work unit's permission for sterilization. After her own daughter-in-law bore a girl, the woman made sure she got a careful tubal ligation. And, in the saddest of the Chengdu cases, a rising state-factory forewoman was advised by her mother to cure the painful and lingering aftereffects of a bad voluntary abortion by having a second, and illegal, child. The pregnancy cured her ills, but lost her her job.

Perhaps most interesting, a forty-year-old restaurant keeper justified having only two children in the face of the generally higher expectations of the 1960s by saying, "My parents-in-law had no influence over how many babies I had because [when we married] they didn't give us anything."

CONCLUSIONS

One need not be a reactionary, I think, to see the persistence of many patterns from the Chinese past in contemporary China and Taiwan. Social novelties, however desired and desirable, are likely to be widely adopted only if they find support from existing practice and popular sentiment as well as from state intervention and official ideology. The rapid drop in birthrates in China, even allowing for all their failures, and the even more counter-intuitive drop in Taiwan, which began *before* the government birth control program, has been facilitated by young women's wish to be free of prolonged childbearing and childcare. Under certain conditions, that wish is supported by petty-capitalist kinship expectations, which encourage women to negotiate and bargain over the children they bear. While they often consider China's one-child rule excessive, urban petty-capitalist women bearing children outside of or before that policy often voluntarily limit births to three, two, or even one child. As a woman from much-commoditized rural Zhejiang said in 1980, reflecting on the newly implemented one-child policy, "Why would we have borne so many children if there had been a way of avoiding it?"[27]

27. Arthur Wolf, fieldnotes, 1980 (Zhejiang, Hong Shan, 23). My thanks to Professor Wolf for this quote.

PART FOUR

Hardship and Dependencies

ELEVEN

Strategies Used by Chinese Families Coping with Schizophrenia

Michael R. Phillips

The acute or chronic inability of individuals to fulfil their expected functional roles because of age, illness, or injury is a universal phenomenon. A primary function of the family cross-culturally is to provide for the short-term and long-term care of disabled family members while minimizing the effect of the disability on the overall success of the family. The strategy a family adopts to achieve this goal is influenced by a number of factors: the severity of the disability; the family's beliefs about the cause, appropriate management, and likely outcome of the disability; the stage in the life cycle that the individual is disabled (i.e., at birth, as a young adult, in mid-life, or in old age); the cultural ideology about desirable family outcomes and about expected intrafamilial rights and obligations; the availability of extrafamilial social support services; and the socioeconomic resources of the family. Strategies used to cope with disability are highly dynamic; changes in any of these factors—such as a decrease or increase in severity of the disability or a change in the family's beliefs about the disability—result in modifications in the family strategy. Thus analysis of the strategies families adopt to cope with the disability of a family member provides a unique perspective on the constraints that cultural ideology and socioeconomic conditions place on family choices.

Schizophrenia is one of several illnesses that are frequently associated with serious and chronic social dysfunction, so it is a suitable index condi-

The author thanks the leaders and the collaborators from Shashi Psychiatric Hospital, the Department of Psychiatry of Hunan Medical University, Huilong Guan Hospital (Beijing), Jilin Neuropsychiatric Hospital, and Nanjing Neuropsychiatric Hospital for their assistance in collection of the data discussed in this chapter. This research was funded in part by a grant from the Rockefeller Foundation for collaborative research between the Shashi Psychiatric Hospital and the Department of Social Medicine and Health Policy of Harvard University.

tion for assessment of the strategies that families use to cope with disability. It is a universally prevalent disorder of unknown etiology,[1] which usually starts during early adulthood. It typically has a fluctuating course characterized by relatively short episodes of florid symptoms—hallucinations, delusions, bizarre behavior, and disorganized thinking—followed by much-longer quiescent periods during which sufferers manifest varying degrees of residual symptoms: affective flattening, poverty of thought, and lack of motivation. The most commonly used treatments (antipsychotic drugs) can usually decrease the severity and frequency of relapses of florid symptoms, but they have limited effectiveness in treating the more chronic residual symptoms. Schizophrenia affects young adults in whom the hopes of future family success reside, so it is a severe blow to the morale of family members. In societies such as China where there are few social support services for the mentally ill and where mental illness is highly stigmatized, families are the primary care-givers for schizophrenic patients; they adopt a wide variety of structural and functional strategies with greater or lesser success. This chapter discusses the effect that schizophrenia has on family strategies in China and looks at the influence recent socioeconomic changes have had on these strategies.

The difficult choices facing families with a schizophrenic member are poignant examples of the dilemma that faces all families in post-Mao China. The rapid ideological and socioeconomic changes are transforming the opportunity structure and, I contend, the ideal paradigms of family behavior; so families must now try to select strategies that satisfy the dictates of both the hierarchical, family-centered Confucian paradigms and those of the egalitarian, individual-centered paradigms seen in Western cultures. Most families are only partially aware of the dilemma; their methods of family decision making and the strategies they adopt to achieve family success are unstable amalgams of elements from these two contradictory worldviews. But for families of the chronically disabled the choices are starker and the decisions are more conscious. In an era when the authority of urban parents over adult children is rapidly diminishing and "free choice" marriages are becoming the norm, parents of schizophrenic adults closely supervise the lives of their disabled children and arrange their marriages. In an era when economic well-being is an increasingly important indicator of social status, and when the reduction in state-sponsored social welfare is

---

1. There are, of course, a wide range of theories about the cause of schizophrenia. The most radical position is that schizophrenia and all other mental illnesses do not exist: T. S. Szasz, *The Myth of Mental Illness* (New York: Harper and Row, 1961). The position taken in this chapter is that biological factors are the primary cause of schizophrenia in most instances of the disorder, but that sociocultural factors strongly modulate the age of onset, severity of symptoms, frequency of relapse, and degree of social dysfunction. Treatment should, therefore, combine biological (medication) and psychosocial interventions.

increasing the economic burden of chronic illness, these families usually follow the ethical dictates of Confucianism and continue to provide for schizophrenic family members despite the detrimental effect this has on the economic and social status of the family. Thus Chinese families respond to the catastrophe of having a chronically disabled member by adopting more traditional patterns of family behavior even though they realize that their behavior is out of step with the trends of the times. They are acutely aware of the contradictions that all families in post-Mao China must resolve, contradictions that will intensify as the reform process proceeds.

METHOD

This chapter includes data collected from three separate studies that 1 conducted during my stay in China from 1985 through 1990. The first study (hereafter, Changsha study) was a collaborative project between the Department of Psychiatry at the University of Washington in Seattle and the Department of Psychiatry of the Hunan Medical University in Changsha, which ran from December 1985 until June 1987.[2] Patients who were officially resident in Changsha (population: 1.3 million) and who met the American Psychiatric Association criteria for schizophrenia were recruited from the outpatient psychiatric clinic at Hunan Medical University.[3] The patient and one or more family members were seen on a monthly basis at the clinic for six to eighteen months.

The second study (hereafter, multicenter study)[4] enrolled a random

2. M. R. Phillips, Q. J. Shen, Y. P. Zheng, et al., "Zai Zhongguo dui 'Jiating Qinmidu he Shiyingxing Liangbiao (FACES II)' he 'Jiating Huanjing Liangbiao (FES)' de chubu pingjia" (Preliminary evaluation of the Family Adaptability and Cohesion Scale [FACES II] and the Family Environment Scale [FES]), *Zhongguo xinli weisheng zazhi* (*Chinese Mental Health Journal*) forthcoming.

3. The first study (in Changsha) used the diagnostic criteria for schizophrenia from American Psychiatric Association, *DSM-III: Diagnostic and Statistical Manual of Mental Disorders* (3d ed.) (Washington, D.C.: American Psychiatric Association, 1980), 181–93. The second and third studies (the multicenter study and the study in Shashi) used the criteria from American Psychiatric Association *Diagnostic and Statistical Manual of Mental Disorders* (3d ed. rev.): *DSM-III-R* (Washington, D.C.: American Psychiatric Association, 1987), 187–98. The official Chinese diagnostic criteria for schizophrenia were in a state of flux at the time I conducted these studies, so I decided that using the American criteria would be more appropriate. The Chinese criteria are quite similar to American criteria except that in the Chinese criteria the minimum duration of symptoms needed is three months, whereas the duration required by the American criteria is six months. Thus the American criteria are somewhat more stringent; had I used the Chinese criteria, the sample would have included more patients who had one brief psychotic episode that subsequently resolved completely.

4. M. R. Phillips, W. Xiong and Z. A. Zhao, *Jingshenbing yinxing yangxing zhengzhuang liangbiao shiyong youguan wenti* (Issues involved in the use of scales for the assessment of negative and positive symptoms in psychiatric patients) (Wuhan: Hubei Science and Technology Publishing House, 1990).

selection of schizophrenic patients admitted to four large psychiatric hospitals (in Beijing; Nanjing; Siping, Jilin; and Shashi, Hubei) from July 15, 1988, to November 30, 1988. On the day of admission the patient and a family member were administered a one-hour structured interview that collected extensive social and demographic information about the patient and about the household in which the patient lived.

The third study (hereafter, Shashi study) is an ongoing collaborative study between the Shashi Psychiatric Hospital and the Department of Social Medicine of Harvard University, which started in May 1988. At the time of admission to hospital, schizophrenic patients who are urban residents of Shashi or Jingzhou (approximate populations: 270,000 and 100,000, respectively) are enrolled in the study. Extensive clinical, demographic, and social data are obtained, and the one and one-half hour Camberwell Family Interview is administered to family members.[5] Families are then randomly assigned to treatment and control groups. After discharge from hospital, patients assigned to the treatment group attend the outpatient clinic with one or more family members on a monthly basis. Control subjects receive no special intervention. This chapter utilizes data on thirty-three treatment-group families and thirty-two control-group families that were followed for six to twenty-four months.

The three studies collected data on 428 Chinese families with a schizophrenic member. The characteristics of the patients are presented in table 11.1. (In table 11.1 and in subsequent tables the total number of cases reported may be smaller than the sample size because some cases have missing data.) Collectively, these studies provide extensive quantitative and qualitative data about the strategies used by Chinese families who have a schizophrenic family member. All of the families in these studies, however, come from clinical sources, and so families that do not bring their ill family member to see a psychiatrist are not represented. This sample, then, overrepresents patients with more severe symptoms and patients that have state-sponsored health insurance.

The other major methodological issue is that the data for the Changsha study and for the treatment-group families in the Shashi study were

---

5. J. Leff and C. Vaughn, *Expressed Emotion in Families: Its Significance for Mental Illness* (London: Guilford Press, 1985). The Camberwell Family Interview is an extensive semistructured interview that uses family members' descriptions of their interactions with the patient over the course of the illness to determine the degree of "expressed emotion" family members have toward the patient. Several replicated studies in Britain and the United States have shown that patients from families with high expressed emotion (as assessed by the scale) are significantly more likely to relapse than patients from families with low expressed emotion. Since families are such an important part of the care-delivery system for schizophrenic patients in China, I expect that after suitable revisions of the instrument it will be possible to replicate these findings in China.

TABLE 11.1. Characteristics of 428 Chinese Patients with Schizophrenia

	All Patients (N = 428)	Changsha Outpatients[a] (N = 64)	Shashi Inpatients[a] (N = 65)	Multicenter Study Inpatients (N = 299)
Sex				
Male	255 (59.6%)	34 (53.1%)	41 (63.1%)	180 (60.2%)
Female	173 (40.4%)	30 (46.9%)	24 (36.9%)	119 (39.8%)
Age				
Mean ± SD	32.3 ± 11.3	28.1 ± 10.2	33.0 ± 11.5	33.1 ± 11.3
Range	(16–70)	(17–60)	(16–70)	(16–70)
Age at onset				
Mean ± SD	24.1 ± 8.0	21.8 ± 6.6	24.0 ± 8.5	24.5 ± 8.1
Range	(11–64)	(14–43)	(11–53)	(12–64)
Duration of illness (yrs.)				
Mean ± SD	8.0 ± 6.9	6.6 ± 6.1	8.0 ± 6.3	8.4 ± 7.2
Range	(0.5–37)	(1–37)	(1–25)	(0.5–34)
No. of admissions				
Mean ± SD	3.4 ± 4.0	1.5 ± 1.5	5.9 ± 7.5	3.3 ± 3.0
Range	(0–50)	(0–8)	(1–50)	(1–25)
Years of education				
Mean ± SD	9.1 ± 3.1	9.7 ± 3.0	9.0 ± 2.9	9.0 ± 3.2
Range	(0–20)	(0–17)	(0–20)	(0–17)
Medical insurance status				
Unit pays	321 (75.0%)	38 (59.4%)	57 (87.7%)	226 (75.6%)
Family pays	107 (25.0%)	26 (40.6%)	8 (12.3%)	73 (24.4%)

NOTE: See text for definition of the three subsamples. SD = standard deviation.

[a] Comparison of outpatients (Changsha study; $N = 64$) and inpatients (Shashi study and multicenter study; $N = 364$) found several significant differences. The outpatients are younger (t-test = 3.3, df = 426, two-tailed $p = 0.001$); have an earlier age of onset (t = 2.5, df = 421, $p = 0.012$); have a shorter duration of illness (t = 2.2, df = 421, $p = 0.032$); have fewer hospitalizations (t = 4.2, df = 424, $p < 0.001$); and are less likely to have medical insurance coverage ($\chi^2 = 8.8$, df = 1, $p = 0.003$).

obtained in the context of a long-term clinical relationship.[6] All subjects were fully informed of the nature of the research study, but they had to overcome both their discomfort in talking with a Chinese-speaking Cauca-

6. The complex epistemological issues of the clinician-ethnographer are discussed at length in E. B. Brody, "The Clinician as Ethnographer: A Psychoanalytic Perspective on the Epistemology of Fieldwork," *Culture Medicine and Psychiatry* 5 (1981): 273–301.

sian physician and their unfamiliarity with talking about family issues in a clinical setting. In most cases I did not find these problems major obstacles. In contrast to previous reports about the emotional reserve of Chinese subjects,[7] I found that most family members would openly express their anguish and frustration when given an opportunity to do so. The family strategies discussed in this chapter are those adopted by families prior to my clinical intervention.

SCHIZOPHRENIC DISABILITY AND ITS EFFECT ON HOUSEHOLD FUNCTIONING

Case 1. Mrs. Ma is a twenty-seven-year-old woman whose problems started five years ago when her angry interactions with other employees and episodes of "talking crazy" led to dismissal from her job as a cashier and, eventually, to psychiatric hospitalization. One year after the onset of these problems, her parents, who were eager to find her a spouse, located an army sergeant who wished to leave the army and move to the city. There was a two-month "courtship" during which Mrs. Ma's father composed love letters, which she copied and sent to the man. They then met briefly five times and were married. She became pregnant two years later. As the pregnancy progressed she started wandering in the streets, shouting her husband's name and stopping cars to see if he was driving; she had an abortion and was readmitted to the psychiatric hospital. One year later she again became pregnant; during the pregnancy she became progressively more irritable and had to be rehospitalized after an episode in which, according to her mother, "she smashed a TV and other household goods, stabbed her husband in the arm, and struck her father on the head with an iron bar so severely that he needed ten sutures to close the wound." After her discharge from hospital, her husband went to court to apply for a divorce. Her parents tried to prevent the divorce, but her husband won the case on the grounds that he had been tricked into the marriage.

One and one-half years after her third hospitalization Mrs. Ma remains on medication and has not had any further outbursts of violence, but she is unwilling to participate in social activities or to consider resuming employment. She continues to sleep alone in her conjugal apartment but spends her days in the nearby apartment of her parents. Her father still has poor sleep and a poor appetite because of his concern about his daughter. Her mother complains about Mrs. Ma's laziness and unwillingness to help with the housework and about the financial burden of caring for her. Mrs. Ma's

---

7. T. Y. Lin, "Mental Disorders and Psychiatry in Chinese Culture: Characteristic Features and Major Issues," in *Chinese Culture and Mental Health*, ed. W. S. Tseng and D. Y. H. Wu, 369–93 (London: Academic Press, 1985).

illness has profoundly changed her parents' household: "Every evening we are tense and cannot relax until she has taken her medicine and returned to her apartment to sleep—we are afraid that she may explode again and kill us. We had hoped for a peaceful retirement but now that's not possible."

The most authoritative figures available report the point prevalence of schizophrenia as 6.06 per 1,000 in urban China and 3.42 per 1,000 in rural China.[8] Given a population of 1.1 billion and an urban:rural population split of 25:75, there are 4.5 million persons with schizophrenia in China at any given time. Less than 3 percent of these patients are hospitalized in the nation's 803 psychiatric institutions,[9] approximately 3.4 percent live on their own, and I estimate that no more than 3 percent reside in prisons, nursing homes, or on the streets. The remainder, over 90 percent, live with their families. By contrast, only 40 percent of the 1.2 million schizophrenic patients in the United States live with their families.[10] Thus in China, as in other countries with underdeveloped services for the mentally ill, families are the primary care-givers for schizophrenic patients.

Providing care for schizophrenic family members when they have acute symptoms is only one of the burdens of illness for the family. As the illness progresses, the chronic inability of affected family members to perform expected functional roles has an even greater effect on the household. Every aspect of patients' social functioning is severely affected. Many are unable to sustain gainful employment or to get married. For those who do marry and have children, their ability to adequately perform marital and parent-

---

8. Coordinating Epidemiological Group for Twelve Regions, "Duo lei jingshenbing, yaowu yilai, ji renge zhangai de diaocha ziliao fenxi" (Analysis of survey results of all types of psychiatric illnesses, drug and alcohol dependence, and personality disorders), *Zhongguo shenjing jingshen ke zazhi* (Chinese Journal of Neurology and Psychiatry) 19, no. 2 (1986): 70–72. This is by far the largest and most rigorous epidemiologic study of psychiatric disorders yet done in China. Nevertheless, the unexpectedly large difference in urban and rural prevalences casts doubt on the thoroughness of case-finding in the countryside.

9. State Statistical Bureau, *Zhongguo Tongji Nianjian 1989* (1989 Statistical Yearbook of China) (Beijing: Chinese Statistical Publishing House, 1989), 889. Psychological Medicine Research Center of West China Medical University, *Quanguo Jingshen Weisheng Yiliao, Jiaoyu, Keyan Jigou: Minglu* (National registry of psychiatric treatment, educational, and research institutions) (Sichuan Psychology Association, 1990). In total, there are about 127,000 psychiatric beds in Chinese institutions. The Ministry of Public Health operates 414 acute-care psychiatric hospitals with 81,000 beds. The Ministry of Civil Affairs operates 190 chronic-care psychiatric hospitals with about 35,000 beds. The Ministry of Public Security operates 23 forensic psychiatric hospitals with about 6,000 beds. And there are an estimated 5,000 beds in psychiatric research centers, in psychiatric wards in general or military hospitals, and in hospitals operated by other ministries or collectives. Approximately 80 percent of the psychiatric beds in the country are occupied by schizophrenic patients.

10. E. F. Torrey, *Surviving Schizophrenia: A Training Manual* (rev. ed.) (New York: Harper and Row, 1988), 8.

ing functions is severely reduced. Affected family members are often socially isolated, have difficulty in performing routine household chores, and, in extreme cases, are unable to care for their own personal hygiene.

The ability of schizophrenic patients to obtain and sustain employment is significantly impaired. Overall, 18.8 percent of the patients in this sample have never been engaged in productive labor, 40.0 percent are unable to sustain their previous employment, and 41.2 percent are currently employed. Currently employed patients include cadres (9 percent), technical-professional workers (9 percent), industrial workers (73 percent), urban agricultural workers (3 percent), and businessmen or service-trades workers (3 percent). The rate of employment is significantly less than expected: Pasternak found that 87 percent of male urban residents between sixteen and fifty-nine years of age are gainfully employed, and 80 percent of female urban residents sixteen to fifty-four are gainfully employed[11]—the corresponding rates in this sample are 40.7 percent and 36.7 percent, respectively. There are no significant differences in the employment status between male and female patients. Of the 341 currently or previously employed patients, 301 (88.3 percent) are in state-sector jobs that provide medical insurance.

The employment rate of Chinese schizophrenic patients is, however, probably higher than that of schizophrenic patients in the West. Accurate data on employment of schizophrenic patients in the West are not available, but the most optimistic experts believe that under ideal conditions 20 percent of American schizophrenic patients could hold full-time jobs and a further 20 percent could maintain part-time jobs; the actual rates are certainly much lower than these ideal rates.[12]

Table 11.2 shows that the marital competency of these subjects is also seriously impaired. Of the 423 patients, 49.6 percent have never married. This rate is much higher than expected: according to the national rates of marriage by age the expected never-married rate in these subjects is 28 percent.[13] Of the 188 currently married patients in this sample, 78.2 percent live in neolocal households, 17.0 percent live with the patient's parents (11.7 percent patrilocal and 5.3 percent uxorilocal), and 4.8 percent live in the household of the patient's sibling. In circumstances where the patient

11. B. Pasternak, *Marriage and Fertility in Tianjin, China: Fifty Years of Transition* (Honolulu: East-West Population Institute, 1986), 15.

12. Torrey, *Surviving Schizophrenia*, 252–53.

13. State Statistical Bureau, *Statistical Yearbook of China 1986* (Hong Kong: Economic Information and Agency, 1986), 80. The expected rate of never-married persons in the sample is calculated by multiplying the number of persons at each age by the proportion of the general population at that age who have never married, summing these products, and then dividing by the sample size (423) to obtain an overall expected rate for the sample. The expected rate of divorce for once-married persons is calculated in a similar fashion. Unfortunately, the census data do not separately report age-specific marital status for males and females, so it was only possible to adjust the expected rates for age and not for sex.

TABLE 11.2.   Marital Status of 423 Chinese Schizophrenic Patients

Marital Status	All Patients (N = 423)		Male Patients (N = 252)		Female Patients (N = 171)	
	N	%	N	%	N	%
Never married	210	49.6	143	56.7	67	39.2
Currently married	188	44.4	95	37.7	93	54.4
Divorced	17	4.0	12	14.8	5	2.9
Separated or widowed	8	1.9	2	0.8	6	3.5

NOTE: There are significant differences in the marital status of male and female patients. Male patients are less likely to get married, and if they do get married they are more likely to get divorced ($\chi^2 = 17.5$, df = 3, $p < 0.001$).

fell ill before marriage, couples that do not establish their own household inevitably live with the patient's family regardless of the sex of the patient.

The rate of divorce among once-married schizophrenic patients—8.0 percent (15/213)—is almost tenfold the expected rate of 0.81 percent. Male patients are significantly less likely to get married than female patients (43.3 percent versus 60.8 percent), and if they do get married they are significantly more likely to get divorced (11.0 percent versus 4.8 percent). Of the twelve male and five female divorced patients in this sample, four men live on their own, eight men and four women live with their parents, and one woman lives with a married sibling.

What effect does a family member with such disabilities have on the functioning of a household? Table 11.3 shows the opinions of family members from 293 urban Chinese households with a schizophrenic member (data from the multicenter study). It demonstrates that the schizophrenic illness of a family member has a profound effect on the economic, social, and emotional well-being of the household. Economically, the illness limits the productive labor of the ill family member, interferes with the work of other family members who must care for the ill person, and often results in considerable treatment costs. In urban households (where most patients have state-sponsored health insurance) the major economic effect is on the earning potential of the household: the per capita yearly income of urban households with a schizophrenic member is significantly lower than the national average (860 yuan versus 1,192 yuan).[14]

The functional disability of a schizophrenic family member often requires structural and functional modifications in the household. The household

14. State Statistical Bureau, *1989 Statistical Yearbook of China*, 729.

TABLE 11.3. Effect of Schizophrenic Illness on the Functioning of 293 Chinese Households

Function/Type of Household[a]	Effect on Household Function (%)				Mean Score[b]	Two-tailed p-value[c]
	None	Mild	Moderate	Severe		
Economic conditions of household						
Male patients' households	9.2	26.4	28.7	35.6	1.91	>0.05
Female patients' households	13.4	21.8	30.3	34.5	1.86	
Work function of healthy family members						
Male patients' households	13.8	21.3	32.2	32.8	1.84	>0.05
Female patients' households	11.8	15.4	32.8	40.3	2.02	
Emotional stability of healthy family members						
Male patients' households	4.6	6.9	29.3	59.2	2.43	0.055
Female patients' households	1.7	7.6	20.2	70.6	2.60	
Relationships between healthy family members						
Male patients' households	24.1	25.9	37.9	12.1	1.38	<0.007
Female patients' households	47.9	9.2	33.6	9.2	1.04	
Social activities of healthy family members						
Male patients' households	17.3	29.5	40.5	12.7	1.49	>0.05
Female patients' households	20.2	21.0	43.7	15.1	1.54	
Overall effect						
Male patients' households	3.5	12.7	35.3	48.6	2.29	>0.05
Female patients' households	0.8	12.6	31.1	55.5	2.41	

NOTE: These are the subjective opinions of household members about the effect of the patient's illness in the year before the patient's admission to hospital, obtained at the time of admission.

[a] The sample comprised 174 male patients' households and 119 female patients' households.

[b] The mean score is computed by converting the four grades to a four-point scale: none = 0, mild = 1, moderate = 2, and severe = 3. Thus the maximum mean score is 3.

[c] This is the p-value for the normal variate for the difference in mean rank scores (using the Mann-Whitney Test) between male and female patients' households.

types of 420 Chinese families with a schizophrenic member are presented
in table 11.4, and the status of the affected family member in these households is presented in table 11.5. Both the census data and Pasternak's
work[15] suggest that this sample has a lower than expected rate of single-
person households (4.3 percent) and a higher than expected rate of "other"
types of households (4.0 percent). In the West, socially isolated schizophrenic patients often use welfare payments to live on their own in single-person
households,[16] but in China single patients rarely receive housing from their
workplaces, so they are required to live with relatives. Families with a
schizophrenic member may be more likely than other families to resort to
relatively unconventional household arrangements: in seven households unmarried adult patients are living with their elderly grandparents, and in
twenty-four households adult patients live in their siblings' homes. Compared with female patients, male patients were more likely to live alone,
more likely to live in their parental household, and, if they live in their own
conjugal household, more likely to be the head of their own household.

FAMILY STRATEGIES USED TO COPE WITH SCHIZOPHRENIA

Case 2. Mr. Cai is a twenty-three-year-old man who first developed problems five years ago when he became fearful that others were out to harm
him, cursed the national leaders, and wandered away from home for days
at a time. His mother thought that "it was something to do with spirits,"
and so she took him to a shamanistic healer. When this intervention was in-
effective, his father, who thought Mr. Cai had a "psychological problem,"
had him admitted to the psychiatric hospital. Mr. Cai's unusual beliefs and
behavior resolved quickly with antipsychotic medication, but he refused to
take medication after discharge; he has been hospitalized with the same
pattern of symptoms six times in the last five years. In the intervals between hospitalizations he is socially isolated and unable to function well
enough to obtain regular employment.

Mr. Cai's mother is a fifty-five-year-old woman who recently retired
from a responsible position "because I need to take care of him [Mr. Cai]
at home." She desperately seeks out shamans and others who claim that
they can cure her son; her husband has criticized her for this on several
occasions. She is an important member of their local residents committee
and has used this position to obtain 50 percent coverage of her son's drug
costs from her former employers and to guarantee an urban residence permit to a young woman from the countryside who has agreed to marry her

15. State Statistical Bureau, *Statistical Yearbook of China 1986*, 83; Pasternak, *Marriage and
Fertility in Tianjin, China*, 36.
16. Torrey, *Surviving Schizophrenia*, 8.

TABLE 11.4. Household Types in 420 Chinese Families with a
Schizophrenic Member

Type of Household	All Patients (N = 420)		Male Patients (N = 249)		Female Patients (N = 171)	
	N	%	N	%	N	%
Single person	18	4.3	17	6.8	1	0.6
Nuclear	295	70.2	166	66.7	129	75.4
Stem	82	19.5	50	20.1	32	18.7
Joint	8	1.9	4	1.6	4	2.3
Other	17	4.0	12	4.8	5	2.9

NOTE: The household types of male and female patients are significantly different ($\chi^2 = 11.6$, df = 4, $p = 0.021$).

TABLE 11.5. Household Status of 420 Chinese Patients with Schizophrenia

Relationship of Patient to Head of Household	All Patients (N = 420)		Male Patients (N = 249)		Female Patients (N = 171)	
	N	%	N	%	N	%
Patient is head of household	85	20.2	76	30.5	9	5.3
Patient is spouse of Household head	88	21.0	15	6.0	73	42.7
Patient is unmarried of household head	169	40.2	108	43.4	61	35.7
Patient is married child of household head	47	11.2	31	12.4	16	9.4
Patient is sibling of household head	24	5.7	13	5.2	11	6.4
Patient is grandchild of household head	7	1.7	6	2.4	1	0.6

NOTE: The head of household is the person listed in the household registry as such. There are highly significant differences between male and female patients' relationships to the household head ($\chi^2 = 101.7$, df = 5, $p < 0.001$).

son. Five years after the onset of the illness she remains distraught: (sobbing) "This is the biggest trouble of my life. I have no hope. Whatever we can do, we will do for him. I can't die now because I need to take care of him."

Mr. Cai's father is a fifty-eight-year-old worker who is even more severely affected by his son's illness: "When he gets ill my heart breaks. I sleep poorly because of his illness. Whenever he is not at home, I can't eat and I lose weight. Sometimes I get so upset about him I cry." After Mr. Cai's first hospitalization his father quit his job as a state worker and opened a bicycle-repair shop where he works twelve hours a day seven days a week to make enough money to pay for his son's multiple hospitalizations: "All the money I make is organized for his use." When Mr. Cai is reasonably well, his father arranges part-time work for him at the bicycle-repair shop. To guarantee Mr. Cai's long-term security, his father has decided to rent out two flats in their privately owned home and to give this income to his son rather than selling the flats and dividing the proceeds equally among his three children; his wife and two older children are strongly opposed to this plan.

Confronted with the disability of a family member, families first try to resolve the problem by accessing a care-delivery network that includes extended family, friends, folk healers, and professional health-care providers. If the care-delivery system is unable to "cure" the disability, and the individual is permanently unable to perform expected social roles, the family must then develop strategies that provide for the long-term security of its ill family member while protecting the interests of the family as a whole. The strategies developed to achieve these goals are the product of a dynamic interaction of patient, family, and social factors. What follows is a partial list of these factors and how they influence the strategies Chinese families utilize in the management of schizophrenia.

Family, Folk, and Professional Explanatory Models of Disability
In the early stages of a disability family strategies aim to cure the disability, return ill family members to their normal functional roles as soon as possible, and resume interrupted long-term plans for family advancement. The steps the family follows to achieve these goals are strongly determined by the meanings it attaches to the dysfunctional behavior of its disabled family member. The idiosyncratic and polysemous meanings attributed to the behavior by individual family members are condensed into the family's "explanatory model,"[17] which provides a tentative explanation of the behavior

17. A. Kleinman, *Patients and Healers in the Context of Culture* (Berkeley: University of California Press, 1980), 83–118.

and a potential course of action. The family initially attempts to deal with the problem within the family, but if the disability is serious, it may seek the advice and assistance of an expanding circle of informants and care providers.

In China the family, not the affected individual, plays the dominant role in the selection of treatment choices; if family members have varying views, it is usually the view of the household head that prevails. The hierarchy of resort to care providers is determined by the family's explanatory model and by the relative availability of different types of providers in the community. Exposure to the wider cultural conceptions of the causes, appropriate treatment, and likely outcome for the disability—the folk and professional explanatory models—influences the family's explanatory model and leads to alternative family strategies for the management of the disabled person. Chinese families are very pragmatic in their utilization of healthcare providers: they often try a variety of modalities (either sequentially or concurrently) to find the method that generates the most desirable outcome.

Chinese folk models ascribe mental illnesses to imbalances in the supernatural, physiological, or psychosocial environment of the ill person.[18] In rural areas supernatural explanations such as spirit possession, wrath of ancestors, and imbalances of cosmological forces are seen as important causes of mental disturbances: 70 percent of the families with a mentally ill member in the countryside consult native shamans at some point during the illness.[19] In both rural and urban areas many families have assimilated traditional medical concepts that consider mental aberrations the result of either an excess or a deficiency of physiological functions (e.g., eating, bowel movements, sexual activity) that disrupts the *yin-yang* balance; families that subscribe to such organic causes try dietary measures, take vitamins, or seek treatment by herbalists or physicians of traditional Chinese medicine.

Psychological factors (e.g., excessive introversion, laziness, a "strong" personality) and psychosocial stressors (e.g., pressure of studies, failure in love affairs, conflicts at work, family tensions, being sent down to the countryside) are common explanatory models used by urban families. Families with such beliefs first try to reduce the stressors by manipulating the social environment of the affected person. My clinical cases include families in which (1) parents exhort their children to be less "lazy"; (2) a parent took

18. K. M. Lin, "Traditional Chinese Medical Beliefs and Their Relevance for Mental Illness and Psychiatry," in *Normal and Abnormal Behavior in Chinese Culture*, ed. A. Kleinman and T. Y. Lin, 95–111 (Dordrecht, Holland: Reidel, 1981).

19. S. X. Li and M. R. Phillips, "Witch Doctors and Mental Illness in Mainland China: A Preliminary Report," *American Journal of Psychiatry* 147 (1990): 221–24.

an ill child on a two-month sight-seeing trip around the country to relieve the stress of school; (3) parents arranged alternative employment for a child who felt workmates were plotting against him; (4) parents arranged a rapid marriage to resolve the symptoms that occurred "because of a failed love affair"; and (5) parents had the patient live with a distant relative to reduce exposure to intrafamilial stresses in the natal household.

If these cosmological, physiological, and psychosocial interventions fail, the family may suspect that the problem is a "mental illness"; but the intense stigmatization of mental illnesses in China inhibits most families from seeking professional psychiatric care. If, however, the ill person manifests socially disruptive behavior, the family is obligated by neighbors, school administrators, work leaders, or the police to seek immediate treatment.[20]

The professional psychiatric explanatory model of mental illnesses currently in vogue in China is an amalgam of American biological psychiatry (which attributes most mental aberrations to alterations in the structure or function of the brain) and of the more holistic approach of traditional Chinese medicine (which ascribes mental illness to physiological or psychosocial disharmonies). Recommended treatments for serious mental disorders are almost invariably somatic, such as antipsychotic drugs, electroconvulsive shock therapy, herbs, acupuncture. I find that families usually accept Western drugs but are unlikely to accept the professional Western explanatory model of brain dysfunction unless it is couched in the more familiar terms of physiological imbalances.

At first families tend to see every remission of symptoms as the hoped-for cure, but when it becomes evident that a particular treatment is only palliative and not curative, they may become angry with the care providers and seek out alternative forms of treatment. They are often willing to make almost any sacrifice or to try the most unlikely methods if there is hope of a cure. Cases from my clinical practice include several such families: families that have exhausted their savings to pay the exorbitant fees of itinerant healers who claim they can cure the disorder; intellectuals or high-level cadres who, despite considering shamanistic practices superstitious charlatanism, seek out native shamans for their ill family members when more conventional methods fail; families who accept the extravagant claims of *qi gong* "masters" (who have recently had a dramatic increase in popularity) until their recommendations to stop medication and to practice physical

20. In some situations it is not the family but other social authorities who decide about the treatment of a mentally ill person. Students living away from home may, in emergency cases, be sent directly to a psychiatric hospital; mentally ill persons who have committed serious crimes may be remanded to a forensic psychiatric hospital without the consent of family members; and persons living on the streets who are obviously mentally ill and who have no known family may be treated in a chronic-care psychiatric hospital.

disciplines lead to the patient's relapse; and one family with two children that emigrated to a distant province in the unshakable belief that the changed environment would cure their son.

Social Services for the Disabled and Social Attitudes About Disability

Family choices for the treatment and long-term care of their disabled members are constrained by the availability of treatment and social service options in the community and by the social rules that define access to the available facilities. Underdeveloped countries such as China have limited health and social services, particularly in the countryside, and so families must often try to maintain the disabled person within the household. This pattern of family-based care for the disabled is reinforced by the social ethic that families "care for their own,"[21] and by the legal requirements of family members stipulated in the Marriage Law (Ikels, chapter 12, this volume).

The institutional attitudes of workplaces and other social agencies and the personal attitudes of employers and other influential social actors can either restrict or expand the options available to families. In societies such as China where there are no professional social workers who can act as intermediaries for the disabled, family members must negotiate for the patient in order to obtain desired changes in the patient's social environment. They negotiate with the patient's workplace about medical coverage, disability payments, return to employment after hospitalization, and changes in the patient's responsibilities at work. Parents of ill students negotiate with school administrators about temporary leaves of absence, reenrollment after treatment, changes in the patient's course of study, and premature graduation. Family members must also negotiate with their own employers to get temporary leaves of absence or early retirement so they can care for the patient at home. To achieve a favorable outcome in these negotiations, family members of disabled persons must become adept at the "strategies of supplication" described by Davis (chapter 3, this volume).

Another determinant of the family's strategy is the stigmatization of the disability in the society. The willingness of families to use the available health care and social service options and to negotiate on the patient's behalf depends on the degree of stigma attached to the disability. The family must decide if the potential benefits of enlisting aid from the health-care delivery system and negotiating with the official representatives of social institutions are worth more than the loss of family status that occurs when they admit to having a disabled member. In China, as in many other countries, mental illnesses are more heavily stigmatized than other disabilities

21. J. Hsu, "The Chinese Family: Relations, Problems, and Theory," in *Chinese Culture and Mental Health*, ed. W. S. Tseng and D. Y. H. Wu, 95–112 (London: Academic Press, 1985).

because they are often viewed as the results of the social or moral errors of the family.[22] Popular press reports about the numbers of murders and other crimes committed by the mentally ill magnify the public's fear of mental illness and perpetuate this social stigmatization.[23] Persons with mental illnesses can be refused a marriage certificate, and the siblings of a mentally ill person will have difficulty finding a spouse because of fears that they are genetically tainted. In many academic centers and industries those who have received treatment for mental illness must undergo a formal (and occasionally demeaning) evaluation process before they can be accepted back at school or on the job. It is little wonder that Chinese families with mentally ill patients want to keep it secret.

Case 3. Mr. Zhou is a twenty-seven-year-old single cadre with eleven years of schooling who first fell ill seven years ago. His parents report that at that time "he felt others were following him and that his teacher wanted to harm him," so they decided to have him hospitalized. He never returned to school; after ten months of resting at home he took up employment as an administrative cadre in a factory. Over the next five years he had three more episodes and a second hospitalization. His problems included extreme anxiety, fear about going out on the street because "strangers may harm me," discomfort in listening to music "because it gives me bad thoughts," repetitive thoughts about meaningless numbers, strange eating habits ("I won't eat eggs because they are bad for the intelligence"), and extremely uncomfortable interactions with females because of "my excessive preoccupations with finding a wife." He frequently had to ask leave from work to "rest at home."

The parents, particularly Mr. Zhou's mother, have been extremely anxious that no one find out about their son's illness, both for his sake and for the sake of the family's stature in the community. They paid the high cost of his hospitalizations themselves rather than have the money reimbursed by the health insurance scheme at his workplace (filing a claim would require disclosing his illness). Despite my recommendations, they are reluctant to reduce his medication for fear that he will have a relapse that will expose his illness to others. Mr. Zhou's twenty-two-year-old sister, who has lived in the same household over the last seven years, does not, as yet, know that he has a mental illness, "because she would be upset if we told her." Over the last two years I have seen Mr. Zhou and his parents more than twenty times; I have never been told their real names, the names of their workplaces, or the location of their residence.

22. T. Y. Lin and M. C. Lin, "Love, Denial and Rejection: Responses of Chinese Families to Mental Illness," in *Normal and Abnormal Behavior in Chinese Culture,* ed. A. Kleinman and T. Y. Lin, 387–401.

23. See, e.g., "Schizophrenic Criminals Face Police Action," *China Daily,* 23 June 1988, 3.

Characteristics of the Patient

The long-term security needs of disabled persons vary depending on the severity of the disorder and on the marital and employment status of the person at the time of onset of the disability. The family strategy for management of the disability must, therefore, be tailored to the specific circumstances and characteristics of the patient.

Sex. Acceptable functional roles vary by sex, thus the options available to families are different for male and female disabled persons. In China the role of housewife or housekeeper is an acceptable social position for females, so there is less pressure on females with mental illnesses to obtain regular employment than on males. The generally better social outcome for female schizophrenic patients (a higher proportion are married and independent of their natal families) is partially due to the wider range of acceptable functional roles available to females.

Marital status. In China, the parents of persons who are unmarried dependents at the time of onset of a disability assume almost total control over the disabled person's life and may prolong this expanded parental role much longer than is customary. Once parents accept the chronicity of the disability, one of the most urgent agendas is to find a spouse who will care for the ill person after the parents' death. Schizophrenic patients usually lack the social skills and social networks needed to find a spouse for themselves, so in virtually all instances parents make the selection for their child and undertake the marital negotiations. The extended parental authority and arranged marriages seen in these families goes against the current of social change in China, which is leading to decreased parental authority and to more "free choice" marriages.[24]

Typically, urban families attract women from the countryside or men from the army by offers of urban residence registration and employment in enterprises where the patient's parents have some influence. This practice of finding mates of lower status is a departure from the traditional ideal marriage between "matching doorways"—*dangmen hudui*[25]—and from the current pattern of high status homogamy in Chinese marriages described by Whyte (chapter 8, this volume). The engagement period is short, with few face-to-face meetings, and the married couple is encouraged to have a child immediately, as this will cement the marriage. It is usually understood that the patient's family will continue to assume partial responsibility for the care and maintenance of the patient after marriage. The higher

24. Martin Whyte and William Parish, *Urban Life in Contemporary China* (Chicago: University of Chicago Press, 1984), 117–24.

25. Pasternak, *Marriage and Fertility in Tianjin, China*, 26–27.

proportion of patrilocal versus uxorilocal residence among married schizo-phrenic patients (11.7 percent versus 5.3 percent) supports Lin and Lin's contention that Chinese families marry off their mentally ill daughters to get rid of the responsibility but marry their mentally ill sons to produce male grandchildren.[26] My clinical work with these families, however, indicates that the need to terminate responsibility to dependents by making them jural adults through marriage is the overriding motivation of parents for both male and female schizophrenic patients.

Case 4. Mr. Tuan is a thirty-eight-year-old man whose first hospitalization occurred fifteen years ago when he believed that people were following him and that strange voices were talking to him; he has been rehospitalized seven times over the subsequent years. Three years after the onset of his problems, he made inappropriate advances to his younger brother's fiancée; his parents decided that this proved his problems "were due to unreleased sexual energy," and so they arranged for him to marry a woman from the countryside (whom they did not inform about his psychiatric hospitalizations). His parents obtained an urban residence permit for the woman, organized a job for her as a maintenance worker in a technical college, and arranged for the couple to get housing at the college. After eleven years of marriage, Mr. Tuan's wife continues to be dominated by and beholden to her father-in-law. Neither she nor Mr. Tuan had the courage to voice any disagreement when his father decided to move their ten-year-old son to Mr. Tuan's sister's household.

In some cases patients refuse to marry, either because they have unrealistic expectations for a spouse or because they have no interest in any form of social interaction; the parents then try to convince the patient's sibling(s) to assume responsibility for the patient when they (the parents) die. When there are no siblings or when the siblings refuse (they are not, by law, re-quired to assume this responsibility), the parents may try to convince more distant relatives to assume responsibility for the patient or apply for place-ment of the patient in one of the few welfare institutions for the chronically mentally ill.

If the patient is married and has established his or her own household at the time of onset of the illness, the spouse is usually the primary decision-maker in the care of the ill person. This is a more difficult responsibility than in the parental case because the spouse must assume a new and often unwelcomed role. In China, patients' spouses actively seek the assistance of their natal family and of their in-laws in making decisions about the man-agement of the patient, but over time these extended family members tend

26. Lin and Lin, "Love, Denial and Rejection."

to be less and less willing to assist the beleaguered spouse. After division of the natal household (*fen jia*) the responsibilities of kinship become contingent on reciprocal benefit;[27] since there are considerable social disadvantages and no benefits in being associated with a mentally ill person, many family members distance themselves from the patient and his or her spouse.

Families of disabled persons are particularly eager to avoid the divorce of the ill person because divorce usually means that the responsibility for the patient will revert to the natal family. Spouses recruited by the patient's parents may divorce the patient because the reality proves much worse than what was portrayed to them before the marriage or because they have already achieved their goal of urban residence and employment. In cases where the patient falls ill after marriage, divorce is more likely if the marriage has been a short and unhappy one; if the marriage had been satisfactory prior to the onset of illness, the spouse is much more willing to make the continuing sacrifices necessary to sustain the marriage.

Employment status. In China the employment status at the time of onset of a disability is crucial because individuals who are employed in state-sector jobs have guaranteed health insurance coverage and disability payments, usually for life. Without such security, the economic pressures on the family caused by the disability are considerable, and the family's strategy must first aim to provide economic security for the patient. If the disability is so severe that employment, even partial employment, will never be possible, the family assigns the ill person to a nonproductive role in the household and provides for him or her with the productive labor of other household members. For most disabilities, however, ill persons retain some degree of employability despite their disability. In urban areas persons with limited abilities have great difficulty entering and remaining in the wage-oriented labor market; family members must often expend considerable resources to help the disabled person overcome barriers to employment.

In the past parents in state-sector jobs were able to retire early and give their jobs to their disabled children (the *dingti* option), but this privilege was rescinded in 1983. Parents who have relatively high status in their workplaces are still able to arrange for the employment of their disabled child at their unit; this arrangement has the advantage that the parents are in a good position to negotiate any needed changes in the patient's work environment. If unable to place the patient at their own unit, parents may trick other units into accepting their child without informing the unit about

27. M. Cohen, *House United, House Divided: The Chinese Family in Taiwan* (New York: Columbia University Press, 1976), 57–85.

the illness, or they may pay high fees to send their disabled child to a private training college to get a technical diploma that can be used to obtain a job. When the patient is unable to perform a regular job, families try to organize part-time or temporary work. Occasionally, families open small shops with the express purpose of providing employment for their disabled family members.

If the patient is working at the time of onset of the mental illness or obtains a job subsequent to the onset of illness, the family's strategy focuses on helping the patient sustain the job and on ensuring that the patient receives health and disability benefits. Once the work unit is aware of the patient's mental illness, family members negotiate with workplace leaders about hospitalization and about returning to work after hospital discharge. If the patient has difficulties completing expected tasks, family members try to have the patient assigned duties that are more compatible with his or her abilities.

The extent the disability interferes with performance of functional roles. The family strategy must assign the functional roles that the patient is unable to perform (e.g., wage earner, housekeeper, childcare provider, supporter for elderly adults) to other family members. In households where there are many duties and few persons who can assume these duties (e.g., a stem family with one frail elderly grandparent and preschool-age children), the disability of one person will put a heavy burden on the others. Sometimes the disability of a key family member results in temporary or permanent structural changes in the family. In nuclear families with small children, for example, the psychiatric hospitalization of one parent often results in the transfer of the patient's children to a grandparent's home or the recruitment of a grandparent or other retired family member into the nuclear household.

The long-term dependence of the patient necessitates the creation of a new family role: the "patient care-giver." If the patient is relatively independent, the major responsibilities of this role will be to help the patient make important decisions and to assist the patient to achieve desired goals by serving as an interlocutor between the patient and relevant social actors. If the patient needs extensive direct supervision of his or her daily activities, the time and effort needed to perform this care-giver role may dictate changes in the functional roles of family members or recruitment of new family members. In 20 percent of the families in this study, for example, family members (usually the patient's mother) retired prematurely from work to assume the care-giver role. Occasionally more distant relatives are temporarily or permanently recruited to the household to supervise the daily life of the patient. If the family cannot find the personnel to perform this function, it may seek long-term hospitalization for the patient.

Protection of the Interests of Other Family Members

In selecting strategies for the management of chronic disability within the family, Chinese families must compromise two competing cultural values: self-sacrifice to provide for dependents; and judicious investment of family resources in the careers of family members who are most likely to increase the social status of the family. Chinese families often go to extremes of self-sacrifice to assist their disabled members to achieve and sustain the socially desirable goals of education, employment, and marriage; but when it becomes evident that the effort is wasted, the family is faced with a dilemma. Should they reduce their support for the disabled person and use the family resources in ways that are more likely to produce beneficial effects for the family as a whole, or should they sacrifice the goals of the family to the needs of the disabled person? In the urban families I have treated, parents usually conclude (after much soul-searching) that they must do whatever is possible for the disabled child and leave the capable children to fend for themselves. If family members have different views on the issue, arguments about the distribution of family resources may lead to serious and long-standing family conflict.

Families must also protect healthy family members from the direct and indirect harm caused by the disabled person. A few schizophrenic patients are violent toward their family members; if the episodes of violence are severe or frequent, the family may decide to transfer the patient to another household or, if possible, to get the patient hospitalized in a long-term facility. A patient's children, another major source of concern for family members, are often cared for by grandparents because the family does not believe that the patient is an adequate parent. Families also adopt strategies that minimize the effect of the stigma of mental illness on the family: they may restrict the social activity of the patient to decrease the likelihood that he or she will shame the family, and they may move the patient's siblings to live with distant relatives to increase the siblings' chances of finding suitable spouses.

THE EFFECT OF RECENT SOCIOECONOMIC CHANGES

The socioeconomic changes in China since 1978 have had a major effect on every aspect of life. Strategies used by families to manage disability have had to adapt to this new socioeconomic environment. Overall, the decreased availability of free health care, the increased competitiveness of employment, and the trend toward increased personal autonomy have made it more difficult for families to adjust successfully to the disability of a family member. But the large urban areas have seen some developments that, if extended to the rest of the country, will lighten the burden for the families of the disabled.

Availability of Health Care

The significantly reduced numbers of urban residents entering state-sector jobs has resulted in a decrease in the proportion of the urban population that receive free health care.[28] Moreover, my own data show that many state firms are decreasing their expenditures for health care by tightening eligibility criteria for health benefits or by increasing the proportion of copayment by the user. With the economic retrenchment of the last two years some smaller firms have been unable to pay for the health care of their employees, who must now cover these expenses themselves. At the same time the pressure for health institutions to become efficient and profitable has resulted in a rapid increase in the costs of treatment[29]—over the last two years the average cost of a two- to three-month psychiatric hospitalization has increased from 500 yuan to 1,000 yuan. The overall effect of these changes is to make health care less available and less equitable. Since disabled persons are high utilizers of health services who are unlikely to have state-sponsored health insurance, they are severely affected by these changes.[30]

The decreased accessibility to health care is changing families' strategies for the management of disabled family members. Families in which the patient nominally has full medical benefits must be more active in dealing with the patients' workplace to overcome the bureaucratic barriers that enterprises are erecting to limit their health care expenditures. An increasing proportion of families with uninsured, disabled family members are simply unable to afford medical care, so they try to maintain the patient in the home or seek out other, less expensive, interventions. In the case of uninsured schizophrenic patients, most families pay for the first hospitalization in the hope that this will lead to a full remission; but when they realize that hospital treatment is palliative not curative, they are less likely to have the patient hospitalized a second time or, if the patient is rehospitalized, may demand the earliest possible discharge. Some psychiatric hospitals have recently opened "observation wards" where family members provide all the nursing care for the patient during a brief seven- to ten-day admission; this

28. My own data show that 25 percent of urban residents who get admitted to a psychiatric hospital have no medical insurance. The central government is aware of the magnitude of the problem, but there are, at present, no visible changes at the grass-roots level: "All Chinese to Enjoy Health Care by the Year 2000," *China Daily*, 8 September, 1990, 1.

29. G. E. Hendersen, E. A. Murphy, S. T. Sockwell, J. L. Zhou, Q. R. Shen, and Z. M. Li, "High-technology Medicine in China: The Case of Chronic Renal Failure and Hemodialysis," *New England Journal of Medicine* 318, no. 15 (1988): 1000–1004.

30. The government is aware of these problems and has allocated 30 million yuan per year (for the five-year period starting in 1989) to provide treatment for various disabilities: "Major Programme to Aid the Disabled," *China Daily*, 1 December 1988, 3. This degree of support will have little effect on the problem.

is a less-expensive option, which economically limited families with severely disturbed patients may be obliged to select.

Employment

Economic retrenchment and unemployment have resulted in an increasingly competitive job market that tends to exclude those with marginal employability—the disabled. It is now much more difficult for urban families to obtain a secure state-sector job for their disabled family member. Lacking the connections to arrange such a position, many families must either settle for jobs in collective or private enterprises that provide limited (if any) social security benefits or give up entirely on trying to find employment for their disabled family member.[31]

For disabled persons who have obtained employment or who were employed at the time of onset of their disability, the new responsibility system has increased the pressure to perform up to expected standards. Several of my patients who have regained their work skills following a psychiatric hospitalization are unable to return to work because their fellow workers do not want to accept someone whose inferior performance might affect the productivity bonuses of all. Many firms now require persons who take leave for psychiatric treatment to undergo a complicated evaluation process before returning to work. Economic pressures have caused some enterprises to decrease the time ill workers are paid 100 percent of their salary (usually six months) and to reduce the amount of disability payments (usually 60 to 80 percent of the previous salary) paid to workers who become officially "disabled." Thus the right to continued employment and social welfare benefits is no longer guaranteed; to safeguard these rights, families with a disabled member must now be much more active in their negotiations with the leaders of the patient's workplace.

One positive change has been the development of welfare enterprises and factories that employ varying numbers of disabled persons. These enterprises are either fully under the supervision of the Ministry of Civil Affairs (which administers most of the state welfare programs) or are state or collective enterprises that are given tax incentives if 30 to 50 percent of their workers are disabled persons. As of March 1988 there were 24,000 such enterprises that hired 395,000 disabled persons;[32] but demands for increased economic efficiency have threatened many of these sheltered workshops with closure.[33] Unfortunately, very few of these enterprises are willing to hire persons with mental disorders.

31. A draft law on the protection of the handicapped that is currently under consideration by the State Council should, eventually, make it easier for families to obtain employment for their disabled members: "Law for Handicapped Ready for Discussion," *China Daily*, 4 September 1990, 3.

32. "Rural Handicapped Need Special Help," *China Daily*, 17 March 1988, 3.

33. "Deng Pufang Appeals for Help," *China Daily*, 22 March, 1989, 3.

Changes in Social Values

The increased cost of health care and the decreased ability of the disabled to obtain employment with social security benefits is increasing the economic burden of disability for the family. At the same time, the reforms have enhanced the importance of economic factors in the determination of social status in Chinese society, and so families with disabled members now find it more difficult to improve or even maintain their social status. Several of the families I treat have not bought such items as televisions, refrigerators, or washing machines, because of the expenses incurred for treatment of their ill family member or because they feel that they must save for the economic security of the patient.

Exposure to the West is slowly enhancing the value placed on independence and personal autonomy and diminishing the value placed on responsibilities within the extended family;[34] as these new values become more firmly established, adult disabled persons will be less willing to be chronically dependent on their family, and family members will feel less morally obligated to provide lifelong support for the disabled individual. In my own clinical work there are several cases in which patients have been divorced by dissatisfied spouses or chronically hospitalized by families; it is my impression that such cases, though still uncommon, are on the increase. Lin and Lin report that rejection of seriously mentally ill family members is a common final outcome in Chinese families living in Westernized societies.[35] The socioeconomic changes currently in progress in mainland China may produce a similar outcome; if this occurs, there will be increasing pressure on the state to build more chronic-care facilities for the mentally ill.

Destigmatization

One change that may decrease the rate of rejection of disabled members from households is the official recognition and destigmatization of disabilities. The election of Deng Xiaoping's paralyzed eldest son, Deng Pufang, as chairman of the Disabled Persons' Federation of China and his frequent efforts to publicize the plight of the disabled and to change government policy on their behalf have helped to demystify disabilities, to focus public attention and resources, and, most important, to lighten the burden of guilt and shame that the families with disabled members bear.

Progress in decreasing the stigmatization of mental illnesses has been slower than with other disabilities, but there has been some progress. The most visible sign that psychiatry has finally moved out from the shadows was that the opening banquet of the 1988 meeting between the American

34. A. Y. King and M. H. Bond, "The Confucian Paradigm of Man: A Sociological Perspective," in *Chinese Culture and Mental Health*, ed. W. S. Tseng and D. Y. H. Wu, 29–45 (London: Academic Press, 1985).
35. Lin and Lin, "Love, Denial and Rejection."

Psychiatric Association and the Chinese Psychiatric Association was held in the Great Hall of the People. The recent development of counseling centers, crisis intervention centers, child behavior clinics, telephone hot lines, parenting training classes, and so forth in the large urban areas indicates an increased awareness of the importance of psychological factors.[36] A spin-off effect of this psychologization of the urban intellectuals is that mental illnesses are demystified; they are seen as extreme manifestations of the psychosocial stressors that are experienced by all. It is unclear how quickly and how extensively this new "popular" view of mental illness will infiltrate the public consciousness, but as it does it will relieve some of the guilt and shame experienced by the families of the mentally ill, who will then be more willing, presumably, to utilize available services. In my own clinical work with urban families, an increasing proportion of families identify social stressors as the primary etiology of schizophrenia; this may be an early indicator of the "psychologization" of mental illnesses in China.

Demographic Transition

One other factor that is affecting the strategies of families with disabled members is the decrease in family size. With smaller families more functional roles must be assigned to each individual, and so the loss of one family member through disability has a greater effect on the family. Single-child families in which an unmarried child develops a serious disability are particularly hard-pressed: there is no one who can assure the security of the parents in their old age, and there is no sibling who can assume responsibility for the disabled child when the parents die. If the parents are unable to find a spouse for their disabled child, they may seek the assistance of their extended families in providing for their own and their child's future, but in most cases the child will become a ward of the state when they die. The numbers of such cases will inevitably increase as the family size decreases.

DISCUSSION

This chapter discusses the results of a series of studies that collected extensive quantitative and qualitative data on 428 urban families of schizophre-

---

36. A long list of articles in the *China Daily* from 1985 onwards chronicle the burgeoning of psychological training and counseling in China: "Parents Study Art of Child-rearing," 21 October 1985, 1; "Volunteer Helpers Flock to Counselling Course," 11 February 1987, 3; "Family Advice," 2 October 1987, 3; "China's Suicide Prevention Center," 25 February 1988, 3; "Campus Kids Get a Weight off Their Minds," 22 September 1988, 1; "China's Mediation System Unique," 10 October 1989, 4; "Intimate Elder Sisters Allay Teenagers' Worries," 25 October 1989, 3; "Tianjin Has Now Got a Hot Line to a Shrink," 25 December 1989, 1; "Some Behavior Problems Solved at Children's Clinic," 14 February 1990, 5.

nic patients in China; 331 of the families were interviewed for one hour at the time the patient was admitted to hospital, and 97 families were seen monthly in an outpatient clinic over a period of six months to two years. The data were collected from clinical sources and so they cannot be considered representative of families with schizophrenic members who do not utilize psychiatric services. Nor can the results for these urban families be considered representative of rural Chinese families.[37] Given these qualifications, the data justify several conclusions about families with schizophrenic members in China:

1. The schizophrenic illness of a family member has a severe effect on the functioning of a household.
2. Families with schizophrenic members must undertake a difficult revision in the family's strategy for success. Some or all of the functional roles of the patient devolve to other family members, and the family must assume the additional function of caring for the patient. If the personnel and resources of the household are insufficient to meet these unexpected demands, families resort to structural changes.
3. In China, family members closely supervise the lives of relatives with schizophrenia: they determine the pattern of health-care seeking; they undertake necessary negotiations with schools and workplaces; they find a spouse for the patient (if the patient is not married at the time of onset of the illness); and, when necessary, they assume responsibility for the care of the patient's children.
4. The socioeconomic resources of the family are a major determinant of the strategies adopted to manage disabled family members. Families with limited resources are less able to obtain treatment for the patient, less able to recruit a spouse to their family to care for the patient, and less able to obtain employment for the patient.
5. The recent socioeconomic changes in China are, in sum, making it increasingly difficult for families to cope with the schizophrenic illness

37. The multicenter study also collected data on 164 rural families, but space limitations prevented me from presenting them here. The findings were broadly similar for urban and rural families except that (1) a much higher proportion of rural families do not have health insurance; and (2) rural schizophrenic patients have better outcomes than urban schizophrenic patients because the social and intellectual demands of agricultural labor are lower than those of industrial labor and because the heads of autonomous rural households have the flexibility to define roles that maximally utilize a disabled person's productive ability. These findings suggest that the lower chronicity of schizophrenia found in underdeveloped countries by the International Pilot Study of Schizophrenia may also be found within a single country where there are underdeveloped and developed subpopulations: World Health Organization, *Schizophrenia: An International Follow-up Study* (New York: Wiley, 1979). A detailed comparison of the differences between hospitalized rural and urban schizophrenic patients is presented in W. Xiong and M. R. Phillips, "Chengxiang zhu yuan jingshenfenliezheng bingren de bijiao" (Comparison of urban and rural hospitalized schizophrenic patients), submitted manuscript.

of a family member. If current trends continue, there may be more schizophrenic patients who are ejected from households.

The Role of Traditionalism and Modernism in Chinese Family Strategies
One of the most consistent findings in these families is that if a patient gets married after the onset of illness, the introductions and marriage arrangements are almost always orchestrated by the patient's parents. This is in dramatic contrast to the findings of the five-cities study (Unger, chapter 2, this volume), which found that 0.94 percent of marriages are arranged and 15.79 percent of marriages are initiated by introductions from relatives. Parents of schizophrenic patients in Western societies do not commonly arrange marriages for their ill children (this is my clinical impression; I am unaware of any statistics on this issue). Why, then, do Chinese parents of schizophrenic patients act in this way? I suggest that the traditional Chinese practice of arranged marriages, though rapidly being replaced by "free choice" marriages, is still a paradigm in Chinese culture that, given the situation of a child who lacks the social skills needed to find his or her own spouse, can be utilized as a blueprint for action by Chinese parents. The paradigm is, however, transformed in the new social context: in most circumstances the parents of adult schizophrenic children negotiate directly with the prospective spouse rather than with the prospective spouse's relatives.

Contemporary Chinese culture provides a wide palette of different paradigms for social behavior that could be placed on a traditionalism-modernism continuum: one pole includes the most traditional Confucian models of social behavior, which emphasize the social interdependence of individuals and the subjugation of the self to promote social harmony, and the other pole includes the most modern "Western" models, which emphasize independence, assertiveness, and individualism. K. S. Yang has developed this traditionalism-modernism concept in a series of studies in Taiwan covering a span of over twenty years.[38] His results suggest separate traditionalism-modernism continua for different types of social behavior (e.g., child rearing, marital relationships, professional relationships); and he hypothesizes that the behavior of Chinese individuals and families is strongly influenced by where their particular beliefs place them on these continua. This is a useful heuristic model that enhances understanding of Chinese social behavior, but it does not give sufficient weight to the role of particularistic factors in determining the strategies of social actors.

At any point in time a specific Chinese community—such as urban PRC, rural PRC, Hong Kong, Taiwan, Overseas Chinese communities—

38. K. S. Yang, "Chinese Personality and Its Change," in *The Psychology of the Chinese People*, ed. M. H. Bond, 106–70 (Hong Kong: Oxford University Press, 1986), 106–70.

has modal paradigms for different types of social behavior (i.e., the behaviors that are most frequently observed), and the members of the community have a range of ideal paradigms of behavior that they consciously or unconsciously try to emulate. When selecting a strategy for action in a specific situation, however, a variety of particularistic factors incline social actors to act in ways that diverge from the ideal and modal paradigms; the disability of an adult child, for example, induces parents to adopt more traditional paradigms of parent-child relationships. In different circumstances these same actors may make different choices: for example, the parents of the schizophrenic patients in this study did *not* arrange the marriages of their nonschizophrenic children. Thus analysis of family strategies must simultaneously consider at least four dimensions: (1) the range of paradigms of family behavior available in the culture; (2) the modal paradigms of family behavior in the community; (3) the internalized ideal paradigms of family behavior held by the social actors involved; and (4) the status of particularistic factors that are known to affect the family behavior under consideration.

Ethical Considerations Inform the Strategies of Chinese Families

In case after case I found that parents chose to expend all their resources on the treatment and long-term care of their schizophrenic child. Even when it became clear that the child would be chronically disabled, they continued to sacrifice the economic and social status of the family to assist their ill child. Why were these families consciously diverging from the strategies predicted by economic determinism? One father gave a representative response: (plaintively) "We've spent everything we saved for our retirement and for the marriages of our other children on her. But what else could we do? She's our daughter."

The ethical importance of the mutual rights and obligations in family relationships (particularly the parent-child relationship) is a central tenet of Confucian doctrine, which has been reinforced by the stipulations of China's Marriage Law. For parents with schizophrenic children the moral imperative to provide for their dependent adult child is more compelling than the social imperative to improve (or sustain) the economic and social status of the family. This ethical responsibility continues until the child marries and establishes an independent household; if the child is unable to achieve these goals, parents feel obliged to "take care of him until we [they] die." Spouses of mentally ill patients, especially those who married the patient before the onset of illness, also experience a moral obligation to care for the disabled individual; but they rarely go to the extremes of self-sacrifice seen in parents of the disabled. Siblings of mentally ill persons, though occasionally willing to help in the management of the patient, do not usually feel a strong moral obligation to provide for the patient.

When confronted with the option of either supporting a disabled relative or advancing the economic status of the family, family members must weigh the effect of their decision on the two different aspects of "face" described by Redding and Wang:

> Lian is moral worth and contains the idea of being a "decent" human being. It is ascribed rather than achieved and loss of it is serious. Mianzi carries with it the idea of reputation based on one's own efforts. It is more achieved than ascribed and, although useful in life, it is not essential. Its absence is not a cause for condemnation.[39] (P. 286)

If the family's actions contravene the ethical expectations of society, the damage to lian will far outweigh any possible gain in mianzi; and so strong ethical imperatives often result in choices that are not in the best economic interests of the family. A society's ethical standards, however, change over time. It is probable that the slow but definite erosion of the Confucian family system by Western individualistic values, industrialization, and urbanization will result in a weakening of the moral imperative to care for disabled family members.

39. G. Redding and G. Y. Y. Wong, "The Psychology of Chinese Organizational Behavior," in The Psychology of the Chinese People, ed. M. H. Bond, 267–95.

TWELVE

Settling Accounts:
The Intergenerational Contract in an
Age of Reform

Charlotte Ikels

One of the major problems facing people in any society is how to act while still vigorous and capable so as to ensure support and care in old age. While the means used to achieve these goals are many and diverse, in essence they generally involve both economic and social strategies. In particular, older people, by providing economic and other supports to the young (and middle-aged), hope thereby to be laying the foundation for their own support in later life. Social scientists have analyzed this intergenerational dynamic extensively in terms of exchange theory or reciprocity;[1] in this chapter the concept of an "intergenerational contract" is used to highlight the binding nature of such exchanges.

THE INTERGENERATIONAL CONTRACT

Both the Chinese constitution and the Chinese government have made abundantly clear that care of the aged in China is primarily a family responsibility, an unavoidable part of a contract between the generations. In

1. See, for example, Steven M. Albert, "Caregiving as a Cultural System: Conceptions of Filial Obligation and Parental Dependency in Urban America," *American Anthropologist* 92, no. 2 (1990): 319–31; Toni C. Antonucci, Rebecca Fuhrer, and James S. Jackson, "Social Support and Reciprocity: A Cross-Ethnic and Cross-National Perspective," *Journal of Social and Personal Relationships* 7 (1990): 519–30; J. Dowd, "Aging as Exchange: A Preface to Theory," *Journal of Gerontology* 30 (1975): 584–95; Nancy J. Finley, M. Diane Roberts, and Benjamin F. Banahan III, "Motivators and Inhibitors of Attitudes of Filial Obligations Toward Aging Parents," *Gerontologist* 28, no. 1 (1988): 73–78; Paula Hancock, David J. Mangen, and Kay Young McChesney, "The Exchange Dimension of Solidarity: Measuring Intergenerational Exchange and Functional Solidarity," in *Measurement of Intergenerational Relations*, ed. David J. Mangen, Vern L. Bengtson, and Pierre H. Landry, Jr., 156–86 (Newbury Park, Calif.: Sage Publications, 1988); Charlotte Ikels, "Delayed Reciprocity and the Support Networks of the

this respect neither the Communist Revolution nor the post-1978 reforms represents any significant break from what traditional Chinese have always regarded as the surest route to a secure old age, namely, that "rearing a son for old age is like storing grain for a famine" (*yang er fang lao, ji gu fang ji*). For centuries filial piety was extolled as the highest virtue, and caring for elderly parents was regarded as a key form of its expression.

The traditional Chinese family system ideally rewarded filial sons by providing them access to the resources of the senior generation. In rural areas the primary resource was land; in urban areas it might have been the family business. In the absence of adequate material resources the senior generation might have provided in their place social resources in the form of personal contacts useful for negotiating for temporary employment or for an apprenticeship. Calculations of financial and social gains were, of course, not the only factors expected to motivate filial care. As elsewhere, a sense of obligation for all that parents had already done for one, as well as ties of affection, was expected to make the care of parents seem "natural," an inescapable aspect of the parent-child bond.

Even parents without resources or without the affection of their children were not entirely powerless. In a small village or a tightly knit community any child known to be unfilial risked public censure and jeopardized his other social relationships. Thus, harmony in the family (or at least the appearance of harmony) was an indicator of how well family members conformed to social ideals and served to enhance the relative standing of all its members. Ikels found that a concern for "face" or family reputation continues to be an important consideration in the resolution of intergenerational conflict even in urban areas.[2] (See also Phillips, chapter 11, in this volume.) Traditionally, supernatural sanctions also played a role in encouraging correct familial behavior. Neglected ancestors made their displeasure with their treatment known by causing illness or misfortune in the families of their descendants.[3] Similarly, powerless individuals with griev-

---

Childless Elderly," *Journal of Comparative Family Studies* 19 (1988): 99–112; Alice James, William L. James, and Howard L. Smith, "Reciprocity as a Coping Strategy of the Elderly: A Rural Irish Perspective," *Gerontologist* 24, no. 5 (1984): 483–89; and Jeffrey P. Rosenfeld, "Disinheritance and Will Contests," in *Family Systems and Inheritance Patterns*, ed. Judith N. Cates and Marvin B. Sussman, a special issue of *Marriage and Family Review* 5, no. 3 (1982): 75–86.

2. See Charlotte Ikels, "The Resolution of Intergenerational Conflict: Perspectives of Elders and Their Family Members," *Modern China* 16, no. 4 (1990): 379–406. This article reports the responses of 200 urban elders and their family members to five vignettes describing problematic family situations. The elders and a younger family member were asked separately to propose "workable" solutions to the dilemmas depicted. In many cases informants proposed solutions with an eye to "what the neighbors would think" about a particular course of action or the family's inability to resolve the problem.

3. Emily Ahern, *The Cult of the Dead in a Chinese Village* (Stanford: Stanford University Press, 1973).

ances in this life were known to commit suicide so that as supernaturals they could seek revenge on their persecutors.[4] Although the significance of the supernatural realm was officially denigrated for three decades of Communist rule, the resurgence of temple festivals in the last decade suggests that for many Chinese the supernatural remains a power to be reckoned with. Perhaps most important of all in inspiring filial behavior was the child's knowledge of the power of the example he set for his own children. In the absence of any alternative to family care in old age, a man who neglected his parents risked experiencing similar treatment in his own old age.

Historically, the inheritance of property and the care of parents were primarily the concerns of sons. As Greenhalgh points out in the case of Taiwan, the intergenerational contract for daughters was (and continues to be) both more short-term and more overtly economic.[5] Daughters are required to make contributions to their natal families only so long as they remain unmarried. Parents with limited resources view every expenditure on daughters, who will marry into other families, as losses, but they view those on sons, who will remain members of their natal families throughout their lives, as investments. Greenhalgh argues that given sexual inequality in wages and occupations (a situation that admittedly is at least partially a consequence of parental decisions to restrict the educational opportunities of girls), parental strategies of underinvestment in daughters compared with sons is rational. A study in urban Hong Kong also found that despite the frequency with which Chinese parents state that daughters are emotionally closer than sons (to say nothing of daughters-in-law) and despite the fact that in urban areas a move into a married daughter's home is socially less disruptive to the parents than in the countryside, the great majority of elderly parents were living with sons and not with daughters, and for the same reasons cited by Greenhalgh: the economic potential of sons is generally greater than that of daughters.[6]

Deborah Davis has investigated the issue of parental preferences for living arrangements in urban families in Wuhan and Shanghai and notes an interesting trend.[7] In the decade prior to the introduction of the Deng reforms parents seemed almost equally concerned with daughters' as with sons' prospects. Thus married daughters (including those with brothers) were frequently found living with their husbands in their own natal households. Similarly, parents were nearly as likely to exercise the *dingti* option of

4. Charlotte Ikels, *Aging and Adaptation: Chinese in Hong Kong and the United States* (Hamden, Conn.: Archon Books, 1983).

5. Susan Greenhalgh, "Sexual Stratification: The Other Side of 'Growth with Equity' in East Asia," *Population and Development Review* 11, no. 2 (1985): 265–314.

6. Ikels, *Aging and Adaptation*.

7. Deborah Davis, *Long Lives: Chinese Elderly and the Communist Revolution*, rev. ed. (Stanford: Stanford University Press, 1990). See also Deborah Davis, chapter 3 in this volume.

retirement in favor of a child on a daughter's behalf as on a son's. Davis argues that these deviations from traditional practices were less a reflection of an increased preference for daughters than of the involvement of the state in hampering parental strategizing for old age. For example, during the decade of the Cultural Revolution parents had little control over the fates of their children—sons and daughters were sent to the countryside or assigned urban jobs on the basis of current policies regardless of parental plans. Similarly, when the *dingti* option was liberalized in the late 1970s, parents, knowing that the policy was not likely to be permanent, brought back as quickly as possible whichever child was still living in the countryside. By the late 1980s, however, Davis noticed that married daughters were no longer such frequent members of their natal households and concluded that in China, as in Taiwan and Hong Kong, greater economic opportunities for males meant that greater investment in sons was again a rational parental strategy.

POST-MAO REFORMS AND THE ELDERLY

The significance of the post-Mao reforms for the elderly and their family members has been to raise the stakes involved in the intergenerational contract; that is, both parties have more to gain or lose now than they had prior to the reforms. For example, changes in housing policy have converted privately owned housing from an inconsequential asset to one of great value,[8] while wage reform, mandatory retirement, and increasingly restrictive health-care coverage have lowered the relative economic position of the elderly and made them more dependent on the young and middle-aged.

Housing Reform

In the late 1970s the quantity and quality of housing stock in China's older cities were appalling, and by 1980 the national and local governments, as well as individual work units, made the improvement of housing a priority. Urban housing reforms include restoring the property rights of private owners, increasing the amount of housing stock, and encouraging private, rather than work-unit, ownership of new housing. In Guangzhou (Canton), the site of the research on which this study is based, about one-third of the

8. In 1985 the Chinese government felt compelled to promulgate the first inheritance law since the founding of the PRC precisely because of the increasing frequency of disputes involving property distributions. The inheritance law guarantees the right of a decedent to bequeath property as he or she sees fit and in the absence of a will spells out clearly who has rights in a decedent's property. For the text of the law and its interpretation, see Liu Shuzhen, *Jicheng fa bai ti wenda* (One hundred questions and answers about the inheritance law) (Beijing: Beijing shifan chubanshe, 1986).

housing is privately owned, much of it in the names of Overseas Chinese. During the Cultural Revolution, however, these owners or their agents lost the right to occupy or sell their property, to set rents, and to choose their tenants. To restore the confidence of Overseas Chinese and thereby to induce them to invest in the homeland, these policies were overturned, and owners were allowed to reoccupy or sell their housing, set rents, and even evict tenants.[9] All of these measures served to heighten the interest of the younger generation in the senior generation's property.

In October 1989 another wave of housing reforms was officially introduced in Guangzhou. One of the aims of these reforms is to facilitate the withdrawal of work units from the responsibility of providing and maintaining housing for their workers. Implementation has been gradual, but by the spring of 1991 many occupants of old work-unit-provided housing were facing the decision whether to buy their apartments at greatly subsidized prices or to accept substantial rent increases. The privatization of this housing means that even more families will control assets worth fighting about.

Initially, the construction of new housing was largely by work units but was increasingly by "companies" for sale to work units and individual buyers. Because of the high costs of land acquisition and resettlement in the oldest three districts of the city, most of the new housing has been going up in areas that had until recently been primarily agricultural. From the point of view of the elderly, with their limited mobility, such locations can be very unattractive, for they are often too far from medical facilities and not convenient to shops or markets. Thus, some elderly are forced to ponder the question whether it is more desirable to follow one's son to new housing or to remain behind in their familiar and accessible neighborhoods.

Workplace Reforms

The elderly have been particularly affected by changes in the wage system and in the enforcement of retirement. The introduction of bonuses to encourage greater worker productivity has increased the gap between a worker's pre- and postretirement incomes, since retirement income is based on a fixed percentage of the basic wage and does not include the bonus. Despite high rates of pension receipt by urban dwellers, as Unger points out in chapter 2 in this volume, many elderly, especially women, receive quite modest monthly amounts. Despite concerns about reduced incomes, many elderly were essentially forced to retire in the early 1980s. The implementation of mandatory retirement was intended both to provide employment

9. The actual implementation of these reversals proved to be a decade-long process because tenants could not be evicted unless they had somewhere else to go, and rents of long-term tenants could be raised only incrementally. New tenants (often those without urban household registration) could be charged whatever the market would bear.

opportunities for newly returned "sent-down" youths and current school-leavers and to remove elders who might be inclined to resist the liberalizing policies that Deng was pushing. While middle- and lower-level workers in state enterprises with ample retirement benefits are often happy to retire as soon as eligible, top-level personnel are frequently reluctant to give up the perquisites and powers associated with their positions.[10] Retirees from impoverished units, who cannot tolerate any reduction in their already minimal incomes, frequently supplement their pensions with earnings from the reform-legitimated private sector as shoe repairers, barbers, or petty entrepreneurs.

Health care costs have become an issue for many elderly and their fami-lies, less because of reforms in the health care system itself than because of cost-consciousness on the part of work units, which are responsible for pro-viding coverage to workers. In an effort to reduce costs, work units have been pushing for more cost-sharing by the individual. Thus, some enter-prises have set ceilings on the amount they will pay per outpatient visit for medication or have excluded certain high-cost diagnostic tests or treat-ments. Long-term care requiring the hiring of private attendants is rarely covered at all. The minority of elderly without any coverage is, of course, in an even more difficult situation.

In a sense, all of the reforms described above can be viewed as reduc-tions or withdrawals of state subsidies from urban dwellers and their re-placement by greater financial responsibility on the part of the individual family. In this context younger family members are likely to be more alert to the costs of fulfilling the terms of the intergenerational contract and more sensitive to perceived inequities in parental distributions of property. This chapter explores the functioning of the intergenerational contract during the late 1980s and early 1990s by examining family organization in two hundred urban households. The focus is on aid flows between the genera-tions, with particular emphasis on the ways families manage the long-term health problems so frequently associated with old age. I first examine the characteristic living arrangements of the elderly and the factors that con-tribute to them. I then consider the nature of the needs of the elderly, in terms of housing, income, health care, and assistance in daily living, and the impact of living arrangements on the meeting of these needs. Last, I speculate on how increases in the value and availability of housing and changes in employment opportunities are likely to affect the operation of the intergenerational contract.

10. For example, one of my high cadre informants died in late 1989 at the age of ninety. He had never officially left work even though he showed clear signs of cognitive impairment as early as 1987.

THE STUDY POPULATION AND SETTING

The data on which this chapter is based were gathered in two phases: the first covered a seven-month period beginning in June 1987, the second a five-month period beginning in February 1991. One hundred households in each of two neighborhoods of Guangzhou, the capital of Guangdong province, make up the sample. To assure a range of educational and occupational backgrounds, two urban districts known to differ in these respects were chosen as the initial sampling frame. Yuexiu district was selected as an area representative of commercial, service, and industrial workers, while Dongshan district was selected as an area representative of technical, administrative, and professional workers. In actuality there is, of course, considerable overlap in the occupational categories of the residents of the two districts.

Each of the street committees (*jiedao*) within the two city districts was assigned a number, and three street committees within each district were randomly selected and proposed to the respective City District Offices as possible sites for the research. Each of the City District Offices, together with representatives from the Guangdong Academy of Social Sciences (the researcher's host institution), then selected one street committee from among the three as the target neighborhood within its jurisdiction. Three residents committees within each of the chosen street committees were then randomly selected by the researcher, and a total listing of all households containing at least one member seventy years of age or older was obtained from the local police station. Since a final sample of one hundred households from each of the two districts was desired, a proportional quota of households was randomly selected from each residents committee.

In the course of interviewing, it became clear that residents of the two neighborhoods differed not only in occupation but also in place of origin. Compared with Yuexiu, Dongshan had more older residents who came from outside the immediate environs of Guangzhou and its surrounding countryside. Specifically, Dongshan was home to more families of Overseas Chinese from the Taishan county area of Guangdong, as well as to more Mandarin-speaking "northerners" from outside the province. Most of these older people had been living in Guangzhou since at least the mid-1950s and were thoroughly familiar with the local context.

Informants lived in a wide range of housing types: old, privately owned two- and three-story buildings, free-standing single-family buildings best described as cottages, and most frequently, old (or new) work-unit-owned multistory apartment buildings. Regardless of building type, nearly all accommodations were run-down and overcrowded, the combined result of years of scanty investment in housing stock and the gradual growth of the urban population.[11] The resulting housing shortage has led to high rates of doubling up by families regardless of preferences for intergenerational living.[12]

Households selected for inclusion in the study were visited a day in advance by a person from the local residents committee, who presented them with a letter explaining the nature of the research and encouraged them to participate. Although the household registration lists contained many inaccuracies, the overall response rate (percentage of those invited to participate who agreed to do so) was 99 percent. In the case of elders too impaired to be interviewed, another person in the household was asked to provide the necessary information.

The high response rate can be attributed to several factors. First, the topic of caring for the aged has been given high priority and much publicity in China since the mid-1980s when population projections revealed that the number of elderly was increasing rapidly. According to Tian,[13] in 1982 China had 49.7 million people aged sixty-five or over; by the year 2000 this figure is expected to reach 86.5 million. Thus, participating in the study could be viewed as a patriotic duty. Second, the households in the study could all be expected to be particularly interested in the topic, since they already contained an elderly member. Third, in terms of logistics the elderly are easier to contact than younger informants. They are less likely to be employed, to have competing demands on their time, and to be mobile. Fourth, the two neighborhood samples were geographically compact. Prospective informants had already seen us about the neighborhood, could discuss the experience with others already interviewed, and could verify that the interview was likely to be tolerable—so tolerable, in fact, that all the (surviving) households interviewed in 1987 agreed to be reinterviewed in 1991.

All interviews took place in the informants' homes, usually with at least one other family member present. In addition, the interviewer was usually accompanied by a representative of the Guangdong Academy of Social Sciences as well as a member of the local residents committee or of the street committee. Under these circumstances only the most basic data could be easily collected, although many families went into considerable detail about their own experiences attempting to cope with the health problems of elderly family members. In the course of the one- to two-hour interview in

11. Much of the new affluence in Guangzhou has been used to improve the material quality of life. During the 1987 interviews families were busy amassing household appliances, but by 1991 they were turning directly to home improvements, that is, laying tiles over bare concrete floors and installing lighting fixtures.

12. Davis (chapter 3) and Jonathan Unger (chapter 2) in this volume.

13. Tian Xueyuan, "China's Elderly Surveyed," *Beijing Review*, November 14–20, 1988, 26–28.

1987, data on the following topics were gathered: residential history, marital history, work history, current income sources, health and functional status, household composition and organization, location of and contact with close kin, leisure activities, and perceptions of intergenerational conflicts. At the close of the interview or on a separate occasion a younger family member was also interviewed on the last topic. In the second phase of data collection the interviewing format and content were similar to the first except that the topics of death and death ritual were added and there was no separate interview with a younger family member.

Because this is a study of an urban population, its findings cannot be generalized to the entire Chinese population. Urban elders, who make up about 20 percent of the elderly population, are a privileged group in terms of resources. Compared with the rural aged, they are more highly educated, more likely to be receiving pensions, more likely to have subsidized medical care, and more likely to have access to a wide range of medical facilities. In short, from the point of view of their families, urban elderly probably remain net producers to their households longer than the rural elderly.

The extension of the findings of this study to other urban populations within China should also be qualified, because Guangzhou itself has some unusual characteristics, the most important of which are its long tradition of overseas contacts and its proximity to Hong Kong. Many residents of Guangzhou have relatives living abroad who, over the course of the years, have sent remittances back to be used for the purchase of private housing or for the support of the elderly. Thus, a substantial minority of the elderly with no visible means of support in fact receives some financial assistance directly or indirectly from these overseas sources. Of perhaps greater significance for the well-being of the elderly is the presence of Hong Kong some ninety miles away. A substantial proportion of the elderly have at least one child living and working in Hong Kong. On the one hand, the lure of the Hong Kong economy means that some elderly have had their local support networks compromised by the emigration (both illegal and legal) of their children. On the other hand, the Hong Kong economy puts extra cash into the hands of the emigrants, which, in turn, frequently finds its way back to their elderly parents. Furthermore, some elderly are themselves former residents of Hong Kong and as such may move freely back and forth across the border.

Another feature to be considered is the current high standard of living now possible in the Pearl River delta.[14] Much of coastal Guangdong province serves as a magnet for migrants from poorer areas of the province as well as for residents of less prosperous provinces. Thus, for example,

14. Ezra F. Vogel, *One Step Ahead in China: Guangdong under Reform* (Cambridger: Harvard University Press, 1989).

Guangzhou currently attracts young women from neighboring Hunan and Guangxi, who will work for less money than the local residents. These young women are eagerly sought after as *baomu* for the impaired elderly. At the same time, now that the standard of living in the countryside is so much higher, a significant proportion of the elderly are themselves leaving Guangzhou to live in their native villages.[15] Do these out-movers differ in some special way from the elderly who choose to remain in the city? One hypothesis is that people return to the countryside to assure themselves a burial rather than a cremation—their almost certain fate if they die in the city. Are these people in fact nearing death? If so, presumably they are already in ill health, and their relocation removes them from the urban health care system as well as from their families. Is the burden of providing care to the urban elderly being shifted onto the rural population? At this point I have insufficient data to answer this question, but it is certainly worth pursuing.

LIVING ARRANGEMENTS

The two most important conditions governing the provision of family care to the elderly are the existence and proximity of appropriate family members. For these reasons almost any study attempting to assess the likely impact of an aging population on a nation's resources will include statistics on marital status or living arrangements or both.[16] In the United States, given American preferences for neolocal residence, the first-choice care-giver of an elder is normally that elder's spouse. While adult children may offer supplementary care, the bulk of care-giving is provided by a spouse, since she (or he) is likely to be the only person other than the elder present in the household. In the absence of a spouse, an adult child assumes responsibility.

In some societies a particular child is clearly designated in advance as the likely care-giver. In prewar Japan, for example, this was normally part of the role of the firstborn son, who would succeed to headship of the house-

15. I was unable to contact 156 of the original 359 elderly drawn from the household registration lists because they were no longer living at their official residence. Residents committee personnel generally had a pretty good idea of the missing elders' whereabouts, and they reported that 31 percent of these elders (or 13 percent of the total sample) had returned to live long-term or permanently in the countryside. Most of the other missing elderly were living elsewhere in Guangzhou.

16. See, for example: Gary Andrews, Adrian J. Esterman, Annette J. Braunack-Mayer, and Cam M. Rungie, *Aging in the Western Pacific* (Manila: World Health Organization, 1986); Chen Ai Ju and Gavin Jones, *Aging in ASEAN: Its Socio-Economic Consequences* (Singapore: Institute of Southeast Asian Studies, 1989); and E. Heikkinen, W. E. Waters, and Z. J. Brzezinski, *The Elderly in Eleven Countries: A Sociomedical Survey* (Copenhagen: World Health Organization, 1983).

hold while his younger brothers set up branch households nearby or migrated. In the United States, there are no culturally prescribed rules for assigning care-giving responsibilities other than the vague sentiment that daughters are more likely to be care-givers than sons. In China, Confucian norms prescribed that adult sons remain members of their parents' household and contribute their labor and wages to the household as a whole so long as the parents remained alive. In actuality the idea of "dividing" the family budget was likely to be raised as soon as the sons began marrying. As Cohen and Harrell point out in the case of Taiwan, timing of division is based primarily on economic considerations, specifically on whether the constituent subunits (*fang*) believe they are better off apart rather than together.[17] One of the key issues to be negotiated during the process of division is the nature of the sons' responsibilities for care of their elderly parents.

While brothers may select from a wide range of alternative patterns of care, the guiding principle is that all other things being equal, sons should share equally in the care. If they do not share equally, they usually do not benefit equally in the division of household resources—for example, the son who takes on a disproportionate share of responsibility will acquire more property (land, housing, or other resources) than his brothers. Alternatively, if division precedes the need for care, sons who feel they have been dealt with unfairly by their parents (or their own brothers) might refuse to help out.[18]

A study of the elderly conducted in urban Hong Kong in the mid-1970s found that a majority of the elderly were "living with adult children."[19] This simple phrase, however, masks three distinctive living arrangements: (1) Parents living with unmarried children, twenty-one cases; (2) parents living with a married child as well as unmarried children or additional married children, thirteen cases; and (3) parents living with one married child,

17. Myron Cohen, "Developmental Process in the Chinese Domestic Group," in *Family and Kinship in Chinese Society*, ed. Maurice Freedman, 21–36 (Stanford: Stanford University Press, 1970); Myron Cohen, *House United House Divided: The Chinese Family in Taiwan* (New York: Columbia University Press, 1976); Stevan Harrell, *Ploughshare Village: Culture and Context in Taiwan* (Seattle: University of Washington Press, 1982).

18. Because of frequent complaints of elder abuse and elder neglect, by the late 1980s some provinces were passing laws to protect the rights of the elderly including their right to care from their adult children. Guangdong province instituted its own such law in February 1991. Article 6 of the law spells out adult children's obligations to provide for their parents, and Article 7 guarantees the rights of the elderly to remarriage and to freedom from interference by their children. The text of the law appears in *Lao Ren Bao*, no. 3, 1991. Children's concerns about the disposition of parental property and the possible claims of stepchildren to such property are thought to be major reasons for their interference in remarriage plans. The juxtaposition of these two articles suggests the significance of the link between care provision and property provision.

19. Ikels, *Aging and Adaptation*.

thirty-seven cases. These three ways of living with adult children are essentially sequential in nature and have different implications for the balance of power between the generations. In the first two instances the housing is that of the senior generation, and the children are still living in the households in which they were raised. In the third instance, of the thirty-seven families, fourteen had lived together continuously and twenty-three had not. *All* cases of discontinuous residence ended with the moving of the elderly into the household of the married child, and all of these moves came about primarily as the result of the needs (e.g., poverty, ill health, loss of previous residence, loneliness) of the senior generation (though in three cases the in-moving elder was also seen as a source of household help). Clearly, in this last living arrangement, the balance of power favors the younger generation.

There are three major reasons for the high rates of coresidence of the elderly and their unmarried children in Hong Kong. First, this particular cohort of elders was not raised with the small-family ideal but produced offspring into its forties. Second, leaving one's natal family to establish one's own household was frowned upon for any reason other than matrimony or to pursue higher education. Third, housing costs in Hong Kong were high, and most young people were unlikely to have the incomes necessary to live on their own. Thus, many couples in their sixties still had children in their homes, though as these married out or found satisfactory housing, they would eventually leave their parents behind.

The situation for widowed parents, especially for those who had been widowed for many years, was somewhat different. While some of their children could marry out, secure in the knowledge that others were still living with the widowed parent, an only child or the last child left at home seems to have found it very difficult to move out of the nest, viewing such a move as a form of abandonment. If the widowed parent was also in poor health, emotionally frail, or incapable of self-support, residential separation of the generations was nearly impossible. Given high rates of early widowhood and associated discouragement of remarriage, many elderly women in this cohort have always lived with their children. Generally, only intact couples were likely to experience some period of single-generation living in old age.

In Guangzhou the same demographic principles, childbearing into the forties and high rates of widowhood, apply. Similarly, the moving out of a child for reasons other than matrimony or higher education is frowned upon, and given the housing shortage that prevailed until very recently, young people have found it very difficult to establish their own households, less for financial reasons than for rules governing priority of access. Thus, as in Hong Kong, the great majority of elderly Cantonese (68 percent in this study) reside with adult children, and even more than in Hong Kong, this coresidence occurs in the household of the senior generation. Table

TABLE 12.1.   Living Arrangement by Sex
(percentages)

Living Arrangement	Males (N = 77)	Females (N = 123)	Total (N = 200)
Living with spouse (subtotal)	76	15	39.0
Only	14	3	7.5
And unmarried child(ren)	12	1	5.0
Married child(ren) and unmarried child(ren)	17	3	8.5
And married child(ren)	21	7	12.5
And married child(ren) but eat/budget separately	5	0	2.0
And other	7	1	3.0
Living without spouse (subtotal)	24	83	61.0
With unmarried child(ren)	3	3	3.0
With married child(ren) and unmarried child(ren)	5	7	6.5
With married child(ren)	6	42	28.5
With married child(ren) but eat/budget separately	1	2	2.0
With other	0	22	13.5
Alone	9	7	8.0
Total	100	98	100.0

NOTE: Total less than 100 is due to rounding.

12.1 summarizes the living arrangements of the two hundred elders in the study.

As table 12.1 clearly indicates, there are major sex differences in living arrangements, with males five times more likely than females (76 over 15 percent) to still be living with a spouse (with or without others). There are three main reasons for this disparity. First, women tend to marry men who are several years older than they, and, thus, women are more likely than men to experience the death of their spouse. Second, age-specific mortality rates are higher for men than for women. Third, traditionally it was culturally acceptable for widowed men to remarry, but not for widowed women. Legally there are no restrictions on the remarriage of the elderly of either sex, and, in fact, official policy is attempting with limited success to popularize remarriage in old age.[20]

20. Charlotte Ikels, "New Options for the Urban Elderly," in *Chinese Society on the Eve of Tiananmen*, ed. Deborah Davis and Ezra F. Vogel, 215–42 (Cambridge: Harvard University Press, 1990).

In terms of a balance of power, the great majority of living arrangements involving an elderly married couple (in contrast to an elderly widowed person) enhance the position of the senior generation because (1) they are associated with residence in housing allocated to the senior generation; (2) decades of continued residence mean that the neighbors are generally familiar with the family's history and circumstances; (3) the man nearly always has his own pension, as do nearly half the women; and (4) the senior female nearly always controls the common budget.

It is important to note, however, that the *common* budget is likely to represent less than half of the incomes and expenditures of the younger family members. Coresident married children retain most of their wages for their own use—for example, to pay for clothing, transport, educational fees for their own children, recreation, gifts, meals outside the home, and new appliances such as televisions and washing machines, that are generally made available to other family members for the duration of the coresidence. The money that adult children turn over to their mother or mother-in-law is generally regarded as their contribution to the food that the senior female purchases and prepares for the household as a whole, and according to most of the informants, the younger generation itself determines what constitutes an appropriate sum. Some children who live elsewhere nevertheless take their evening meal with their parents or board one or more of their school-age children with their parents, and they too contribute the cost of their meals. Interestingly, some of the unmarried sons in this study were exempted from making any contributions to the family budget on the grounds that they were saving up for their marriage expenses. As Davis points out, failure to assist a son in meeting his marriage expenses is viewed by both old and young as a violation of the terms of the intergenerational contract and might be seen as releasing the son from his obligation to look after his parents.[21]

What does household division mean in the context of these urban families? If the families remain under the same roof, division means little more than that the younger generation ceases to contribute to the common food budget and begins to prepare and take its meals separately. Division is most likely to occur when there are other married children in the household or when the senior female dies and a member of the younger generation takes over her responsibilities. Depending on the circumstances, the senior generation either chooses to cook and eat on its own or joins one of the junior households (or, less frequently, one parent joins one and the other another). When a member of the junior generation controls the common budget, the elder usually does not contribute to it. To some extent the lack of a contribution is an artifact of the composition of the household; that is, a

21. Davis, chapter 3 in this volume.

younger person is likely to control the budget only when the senior female is extremely disabled. In such cases the senior women are predominantly in their eighties or nineties and not receiving pensions.

Whether households divide or not, one interesting aspect of the financial arrangements between the generations is that direct cash transfers (apart from contributions for meals) are neither regular nor frequent. Parents without pensions have almost no discretionary funds, inasmuch as coresident children seldom provide any kind of allowance. It is as if the unwritten contract states that each generation must allow the other to share accommodations if there are no alternatives, that the senior generation is entitled to free board and care (including the costs of medical care), and that the junior generation is responsible for its own expenses. Although urban men are only infrequently in this situation, the absence of discretionary funds seems to disturb them more than women because of their sense of entitlement; that is, they expect in their old age to be able to go to the teahouse, smoke cigarettes, and have an occasional drink. Without cash of their own they are effectively cut off from normal peer activities.

Elders who do receive cash for their own use from children are usually not living with them. These are parents who have one or more children living in Hong Kong or overseas. Hong Kong children come back several times a year, bring modern household appliances, take their parents to eat in fancy hotels, and give them gifts of money. Overseas children send remittances several times a year, enabling their parents to live independently, to hire outside helpers, or to spend as they see fit if they are already living with other children. Yang observed a similar phenomenon in rural areas of Zhejiang where parents lamented that rural sons supplied them with grain (and services) but not with cash, whereas sons who worked in towns sent back cash.[22]

The nearest urban equivalent to inheriting land from one's parents is inheriting one's job. As Davis points out, many former sent-down youth benefited greatly from the expansion of this policy (*dingti*) in the late 1970s and early 1980s when the Chinese government encouraged older workers to retire in favor of the young.[23] Unlike land, however, a job is not divisible, and a parent could pass it on to only one of his or her children. Furthermore, the *dingti* option was likely to be acted on independently of the issue of household division.

22. Yang Haiou, "The Future Family Support System for the Rural Elderly: The Consequences of the One-Child Policy and the Latent Impacts of the Current Economic Reform." Paper presented at the 41st Annual Meeting of the Association for Asian Studies, Washington, D.C., 1989.

23. Deborah Davis, "Unequal Chances, Unequal Outcomes: Pension Reform and Urban Inequality," *China Quarterly*, no. 114:223–42, 1988. Also Deborah Davis, "Urban Job Mobility," in *Chinese Society on the Eve of Tiananmen*, ed. Deborah Davis and Ezra F. Vogel, 85–108.

Nevertheless, it is tempting to speculate that parents might choose to link the passing on of a job to filial obligations, that is, to retire in favor of a son who would subsequently be perceived as more obligated than his brothers to look after them. Elsewhere Ikels found that an important "historical" variable affecting care-giver selection was the shared belief that a particular child "owed" the parents more than his or her siblings did;[24] in the Chinese context job inheritance might be viewed as incurring a greater debt to repay. At this point it is difficult to discern such a pattern in the Guangzhou data. Of the forty cases (in thirty-five households) in which parents retired so that their children could inherit their position, nineteen beneficiaries were sons and twenty-one were daughters. (My data almost certainly understate the frequency with which the *dingti* option was exercised, for I only gradually became aware of its possible importance and did not systematically ask about it while interviewing.) Given that Cantonese elderly still rely primarily on their sons for support (table 12.2), passing a job on to a daughter does not seem to reflect strategic thinking. However, as Davis indicates, during most of the 1970s parents' strategies were subject to state policies hampering predictability.[25] Parents themselves indicated that their reason for retiring in favor of a particular child was to bring him or her back from the countryside (it is not clear whether any of their other children were still in the countryside at the time).

As can be seen from table 12.2, preference is definitely given to coresidence with sons. Parents having both sons and daughters were living with sons eight times as often as with daughters (56.4 percent to 6.8 percent). But the mere fact of having sons did not automatically mean living with them. Of 156 elders having at least one son, 8 lived with daughters only, 9 lived with spouses only, 9 lived alone, and 20 lived with others (grandchildren, other relatives, former employers, etc.).

Rather than detail the circumstances that led to each and every alternative living arrangement, I want to make a cautionary statement about the limitations of viewing living arrangements as predictors of family care. While they certainly do tell us something about the proximity of relevant categories of kin, they tell us little about family dynamics and nothing about the availability of kin who do not share the household. In times of need most Chinese elderly, whether they live with children or not, do have resources on which they may draw for support. In the following section I introduce several illustrative cases that demonstrate how families mobilize (or fail to mobilize) to meet their elders' needs.

24. Charlotte Ikels, "The Process of Caretaker Selection," *Research on Aging* 5, no. 4 (1983): 491–509.

25. Davis, chapter 3 in this volume.

TABLE 12.2.   Living Arrangement by Sex of Surviving Child(ren)
(percentages)

	Has Sons Only (N = 39)	Has Both (N = 117)	Has Daughters Only (N = 28)	Has None (N = 16)	Total (N = 200)
⸝ving Arrangement					
With son	56.4	56.4	0	0	44
With both	0	18.8	0	0	11
With daughter	0	6.8	64.3	0	13
With spouse only	10.3	4.3	10.7	18.75	7.5
With other	25.6	8.5	17.9	50.0	16.5
Alone	7.7	5.1	7.1	31.25	8
⸝tal	100.0	99.9	100.0	100.0	100.0

⸝TE: Total less than 100 is due to rounding.

THE NEEDS OF THE ELDERLY

The minimal needs of the elderly include housing, income, health care, and managing the activities of daily living. As is indicated above, housing in the strict sense of having a roof over one's head is not a problem for the elderly. Most were assigned housing many years ago and have simply continued to live in it. It may be overcrowded, run-down, and lacking in amenities, but it is cheap, and every older person has shelter of some sort. The predominance of pensions means that nearly all men and nearly half of the women in the study have independent sources of income. Those who do not have pensions still do not, so long as they remain healthy, constitute much of a financial drain on their families, since their requirements are few. As we saw above, the family really only has to cover the costs of their meals. Elders for their part, especially elderly women, provide many services for the young and are generally viewed as earning their keep.

Nevertheless, we observed a number of cases in which financial issues were clearly a source of tension between the generations. For example, one seventy-three-year-old widow living with her older married son and his family (in housing assigned by his unit) receives no financial assistance from them, although they do eat together. According to residents committee personnel, the family has had a bad relationship for the duration of the seven years it has lived in the neighborhood. During the interview the son many times corrected his mother rudely while she sat stoically on the edge of the bed. Her daughter-in-law declined to greet us or to say anything throughout the interview, though she remained a hostile presence, determinedly clipping her toenails and pacing back and forth to the balcony. On being asked to comment on a story about a case of suspected elder abuse, the old woman related her own bad relationship with her daughter-in-law, stating that the young woman never so much as says hello or good-bye when passing her while she is on security duty at the entrance of the building. Her six-hour tour of duty provides her with thirty yuan a month, her only source of income. Apparently, several years ago the residents committee invited her to do this work in an effort to alleviate the tension in the family by providing her with an independent source of funds.

Another older woman's independent source of income and her reluctance to share it with her children has caused at least one child to express disgruntlement about the situation. Four years ago, after having been retired for three years, Mrs. Tai, now seventy-five years old, started her own cooked-food business because she was dependent on her children and did not feel she had enough money. Since she was still able to work, she hired a young woman to prepare food in her home, which she herself sells at a stall. None of her eight children is involved in the business, nor do any of them even live in her house—a cottage-type structure which she had built over ten years ago with funds supplied by a son in the air force—though two live very close by. One evening we stopped by the nearby daughter's house to ask her opinions about stories depicting intergenerational conflict. One of the stories dealt with an old man who was unwilling to turn over to his son the management of the cash box in his small business. In the presence of her mother, the daughter commented: "He doesn't trust the son. Coax him [to turn over control of the cash box]. Help him until he collapses or dies— *then* he'll give it over to the son. Like my mother—we'll still get the money [when she dies]. She won't even let anyone live over there."

An elder is most likely to need care when he or she becomes ill or so impaired that he or she can no longer manage the daily routine and requires that someone else take up the slack and provide special personal services to the elder—for example, supervision, help with dressing, accompaniment on outings. In terms of financing, medical coverage in the urban areas is quite generous (particularly in comparison with rural areas where the family generally is responsible for all medical costs), though the extent of coverage is dependent on the nature of one's work unit. Among the study population 55 percent had between 90 and 100 percent of normal medical costs covered by their unit; 23 percent had between 50 and 89 percent covered, and only 13 percent had no medical coverage. The remaining 9 percent either received a fixed monthly sum (usually quite small) to cover medical care costs, whether they were ill or not, or were covered on a sliding scale with a fixed monthly maximum.

More important than health per se is the issue of functionality—for example, the degree to which a health problem or a combination of health problems hamper an individual's ability to manage daily life. Liang and Gu

TABLE 12.3.   Types of Assistance Needed
(percentages, $N = 200$)

Range	None	Supervision	Household Tasks	House-bound	Personal Care	Bedfast	No.
–74	89	0	4	6	1	0	84
–79	80	1[a]	8	8	1	1	66
–84	50	0	14	21	11	4	28
and over	27	0	23	41	9	0	22
erall	74	0.5	9	12.5	4	1	

his individual had psychiatric problems.

reviewed seven regional studies carried out in China and concluded that between 11 and 15 percent of Chinese aged sixty and over suffer some degree
of physical disability, with 10 percent being moderately disabled and 3 to 5
percent being severely disabled or bedridden.[26] Of the two hundred elders
in this study 30 percent experienced moderate or major disabilities in walking, 19 percent in seeing, and 16 percent in hearing. Fourteen percent
showed evidence of substantially impaired cognitive functioning, but this
figure almost certainly understates the proportion of the sample with moderate to major mental impairments inasmuch as twelve elders could not be
rated with confidence because of their deafness or language difficulties.
These rates are higher than those found by Liang and Gu, primarily because the population studied is older—with a minimum age of seventy
rather than sixty.

The impairments listed have diverse consequences for the affected individuals. Deafness, for example, obviously hampers conversation, but it does
not affect one's ability to go out, run a household, or look after oneself.
Similarly, mobility problems need not have great significance if neither the
affected individual nor his family members consider it necessary or desirable for the older person to go out. Table 12.3 presents the impact of these
various disabilities in terms of the kind of assistance the affected elder
requires.

As Liang and Gu point out, institutional long-term care is almost exclusively reserved for the childless elderly, whereas those elderly with families
must rely almost entirely upon them for support in daily living.[27] In many

26. Jersey Liang and Gu Shengzu, "Long-term Care for the Elderly in China," in *Caring for
an Aging World: International Models for Long-term Care, Financing, and Delivery*, ed. Teresa Schwab,
265–87 (New York: McGraw-Hill, 1989).
27. Liang and Gu, "Long-term Care."

cases several individuals work together to provide care to an affected family member, but more often a single person emerges as the primary care-giver. Among the households in this study 63 percent of the care provided to disabled elderly family members is provided primarily by a single individual with minor contributions from others. In only 37 percent of the cases was care so equally shared that it was not possible to identify a primary care-giver.

To illustrate the nature of the demands placed on the family and to provide some sense of the complexity of the care-giving situations encountered in Guangzhou, four cases are described below.

Case 1. Mr. and Mrs. Jeung were both originally Cantonese, but most of their working life was spent in Tianjin at a music college. When Mr. Jeung retired in 1965, the couple and the younger of their two sons (they have no daughters) returned to Guangzhou where they rented half an apartment in a two-story house owned by an old friend. At the time of the first interview their older son was living in Beijing; their younger son had since married and lived with his wife and daughter very nearby. The Jeungs' combined pensions amounted to about 230 yuan a month. In addition, seventy-nine-year-old Mrs. Jeung earned an occasional 5 yuan for teaching piano classes at kindergartens or churches. As former employees of a state unit, their normal medical costs (excluding hospital meals) were completely covered.

Despite their seeming affluence, however, the Jeungs' monthly medical expenses were more than double their monthly income. Three months prior to the first interview eighty-one-year-old Mr. Jeung suffered a stroke that left him bedridden and in need of twenty-four-hour care in the local district hospital. Mrs. Jeung herself could not provide this care easily because she has arthritis in her knees and shoulders as well as bone spurs. Consequently, she hired a sixty-seven-year-old woman for more than 17 yuan a day to stay at the hospital twenty-four hours a day looking after Mr. Jeung. Fifteen yuan were paid directly to the woman while over two were paid to the hospital to cover the cost of her meals. Mrs. Jeung said several times that the only way they could manage this sum was through the help of friends.

Before his illness Mr. Jeung had done most of the food shopping and sometimes helped with the cooking. Following his hospitalization their son brought his mother breakfast every morning. After breakfast nearly every day Mrs. Jeung boiled a traditional restorative tonic for her husband and brought it to the hospital. The day preceding the interview her daughter-in-law had taken the tonic to the hospital during her lunch hour because Mrs. Jeung had gone to a hospital specializing in the treatment of high blood pressure to get expert advice on her husband's prognosis. She returned from that visit feeling glum. The costs of staying at the special facility exceeded what Mr. Jeung's medical plan would cover. Furthermore, she had observed that one of the patients who had already been there for several years had yet to regain the ability to speak, and she doubted the value of moving her husband there. Because her son and daughter-in-law were both employed, they could not easily participate in caring for Mr. Jeung.

Case 2. The following case provides a clear illustration of how the various parties to the intergenerational contract can interpret the terms differently. In 1986 eighty-five-year-old Mr. Fok and his eighty-three-year-old wife formally divided their property among their three sons and their senior grandson (oldest son of their oldest son); their three daughters waived their rights to any shares. Prior to division the senior Foks owned four dwellings: a village house (given to their oldest son), two small dwellings in Dongshan they had been allocated when their original urban dwelling was taken over by the government (one of these was given to their middle son, the other to the senior grandson), and a three-story house in Dongshan in which they and other family members lived. This house had been built with money provided by the Foks' youngest daughter, a driving instructor in Hong Kong. At division the youngest son was given the third floor and half the first floor, the senior grandson was given the second floor, while the old couple retained half the first floor for their own use.

The division process had not been amicable; in fact, the residents committee had to come in and mediate when two of the brothers actually came to blows. As a condition of division the oldest son (through his oldest son) agreed to provide for old Mrs. Fok, while the youngest son agreed to provide for Mr. Fok. Since neither of the parents had pensions or medical coverage (they had come to Guangzhou in the 1950s when they themselves were already about fifty and thus too old to obtain employment in the state sector), they were totally dependent on their sons for support. Operationally, this support meant primarily meal provision, but eventually in Mrs. Fok's case it meant meeting substantial medical bills. In the winter of 1990–91 Mrs. Fok had surgery for gallstones and spent two months in the district hospital. The costs of her care came to between 5,000 and 6,000 yuan, which the oldest son paid. He felt, however, that this was an exceptionally heavy burden for one son to carry and requested that his two brothers help him with these expenses. At first both brothers argued that this was not their responsibility, but the middle brother eventually yielded to his older brother and sisters' argument that he had received a share of the parental property and surely owed something. The youngest brother, however, refused to pay anything, insisting that he was responsible only for old Mr. Fok.

In an effort to resolve the impasse the youngest daughter returned from Hong Kong. She supported the youngest son in his claim that the middle son should contribute but that he should not. She herself contributed 1,000 yuan toward her mother's medical bills *and* redefined the future property division (recall that she was the original source of funds for the building of the three-story residence). Under the terms of the original division the old couple had retained the rear half of the first floor of their dwelling; at their deaths it was expected to go to the youngest son, who already used the front half for his home appliance repair business. Under the redefinition the rear half is now to go to the senior grandson because he and his father paid for the bulk of Mrs. Fok's medical care. In actuality the case is not yet closed as both the parents are outraged that their youngest son will not accept any responsibility for his mother's expenses and have instituted a legal suit to require him to pay.

Case 3. In contrast to the Fok family, the eight siblings in the Gunn family provide an example of harmonious functioning and shared responsibility in dealing with their mother's housing and health problems. Between the first and second interviews, an interval of less than four years, Mrs. Gunn, a widow in her early eighties, moved six times and lived with five of her eight children. At the time of the first visit Mrs. Gunn had been living with her younger son's family in a building owned by an Overseas Chinese. In 1988 her daughter-in-law, with whom she got along very well, died of stomach cancer. In April of the following year Mrs. Gunn went on a three-month visit to her older son in Hong Kong. When she returned, her younger son and his new wife soon had a child. Mrs. Gunn did not get along with the new daughter-in-law as well as she had with the first and was particularly concerned that her granddaughter (by the first daughter-in-law) was being treated unfairly by her stepmother.

During the 1990 Spring Festival most of Mrs. Gunn's children assembled in Guangzhou; they felt that under the circumstances she was under too much stress in her younger son's household and pressed her to move in with any of them. Although she did not actually want to move, Mrs. Gunn had little choice, for the Overseas Chinese landlord had reclaimed the house in which she lived and was waiting for them to leave. Her younger son was being assigned housing with considerably less space in another part of Dongshan. Consequently, she moved in with her oldest daughter, a widow living in the same old neighborhood. Then, almost immediately, from April to October of 1990, Mrs. Gunn went to Beijing where her third and fourth daughters lived and stayed with one of them.

When she returned to her oldest daughter's house in Guangzhou, both her oldest daughter and her second daughter felt that she had deteriorated physically. They worried that she had circulatory problems, so in the spring of 1991 they sent her to the hospital for a general work-up. While in the hospital, Mrs. Gunn suddenly had a very severe attack of herpes zoster, which initially threatened her eyesight and required a great deal of care. Although a *baomu* was hired to look after her, at least two or three children or children-in-law (including those living in Hunan province and in Hong Kong) were usually present also. One day her oldest daughter, who has a heart condition, collapsed at the hospital while trying to look after her. Therefore, to relieve the strain on her oldest daughter, Mrs. Gunn, upon her release from the hospital, went to live with her second daughter in another district of Guangzhou. (This arrangement cannot be long-term, because the second daughter's entire family is about to emigrate to Canada.)

As a retired kindergarten teacher Mrs. Gunn has 100 percent medical coverage and also receives a pension of 180 yuan. Nevertheless, her hospitalization and subsequent care at home cost the family about 4,000 yuan. Part of this sum went for the *baomu*, part of it for an intravenous medication available only from Hong Kong, and part of it for gifts to doctors who came from specialty clinics to treat Mrs. Gunn at home. Fortunately, these financial obligations were met relatively easily because Mrs. Gunn's children had held a meeting in early 1991 to formalize their contributions to her welfare. Prior to the meeting the various children had contributed as they saw fit, but as a result of the meeting, care and financial obligations were divided up more systematically. The three children in Guangzhou (the two oldest daughters and the younger son) are expected to provide housing and the bulk of daily care. The older son, living in Hong Kong, and the youngest daughter, living in Australia, each contribute HK $500 (a total of approximately US $125) a month to Mrs. Gunn's upkeep. The two daughters in Beijing and the one in Hunan are expected to be available for emergency assistance, such as looking after her in the hospital or providing housing. Interestingly, no property transfers have been involved in these care decisions, for Mrs. Gunn has no property beyond whatever she has been able to save out of her pension.

Case 4. Ninety-year-old Mrs. Fong is originally from Taishan county. Like many women of that area, she lived with her parents-in-law while her husband worked overseas (in Cuba), where he died in 1954. Because of her husband's absence, Mrs. Fong bore only one child, a daughter, but she had the foresight to purchase a son, who eventually left the village for work. During the 1950s her son's unit was transferred to Shaoguan, a remote part of Guangdong province. In 1956 Mrs. Fong joined her married daughter (who had also married a man working abroad) in Guangzhou and subsequently followed her to Hong Kong, where she stayed until 1984. By that time her daughter was already in her late sixties and in failing health. At the same time Mrs. Fong's son retired and returned to Guangzhou to live.

He moved into his sister's privately owned house (in which his own wife
and children had been living all along) and was joined by his elderly
mother.

Mrs. Fong has arteriosclerosis, but she does not require any special
medical services. This is fortunate, for she has no health coverage at all.
Her son retired from a relatively impoverished state enterprise that provides him with a flat payment of eight yuan a month to be used for medical
expenses. However, Mrs. Fong does require extensive assistance simply to
get through the day. She has a knee problem that dates from her Hong
Kong days and cannot get around without a cane; she never leaves the
house. More important, she is severely impaired mentally. She has nearly
no memory, seldom talks (though when she does, she is extremely repetitive), has a bad temper, and cannot really look after herself. Her sixty-one-
year-old retired daughter-in-law related how Mrs. Fong does not even know
enough to change her clothes. She will wear the same thing for days and resist all efforts to persuade them to allow them to wash her clothing. They
have had to forcibly undress her.

THE FUTURE OF FAMILY CARE-GIVING

From the above four cases we can see that proximity of kin is a crucial variable affecting the provision of care to the elderly. During most of the Maoist
era and even into the 1980s, the Chinese government has promoted policies
that, by constraining opportunities for geographic mobility, have simultaneously promoted the availability of family care-givers.[28] These policies
include deferring the construction of new housing, restricting migration,
and discouraging job changing. Furthermore, the one policy that did separate young people from their parents, that of sending urban youth to the
countryside, was modified early on so that at least one child could remain
in the city. The subsequent broadening of the *dingti* option enabled hundreds of thousands, if not millions, of those who were "sent down" to return
to the city and to their parents' own work units. Not only were potential
care-givers in place, but the policy of allowing women to retire at age fifty
and fifty-five with full benefits meant that they could provide care to a disabled elder without compromising the financial standing of their families or
jeopardizing their own futures.

How are the economic policies that have been developing over the past
decade likely to affect the availability of family care-givers and their willingness to provide care? The single most important question now facing Chinese

---

28. Charlotte Ikels, "Family Caregivers and the Elderly in China," in *Aging and Caregiving:
Theory, Research and Policy*, ed. David E. Biegel and Arthur Blum, 270–94 (Newbury Park,
Calif.: Sage, 1990).

elders, whether to continue sharing dwelling space with the younger generation or to live separately, is a direct consequence of the enormous boom in housing construction that has been under way for nearly a decade. Increased opportunities for job mobility also contribute to the dispersal of children and to the need to make decisions about housing, though, as Davis points out, in the urban areas job mobility is more apparent than real.[29] As a result of the increasing availability of housing, more and more young couples are able to acquire apartments of their own and no longer need to spend years of their married life in their natal households with their parents. This increased availability of housing means that many older people whose spouses are still alive at the time their youngest child marries are likely to spend some years living only as a couple. One result of this living arrangement will be more situations such as the Jeungs encountered—when one elder becomes ill or disabled, almost all of the care will fall on the coresident spouse. This is especially likely now that much of the new housing is being built on the outskirts of the city far from the natal households of the new occupants. When one of the elderly partners dies, the survivor will have to decide whether to remain in his or her own territory until no longer able to do so or, leaving old friends and neighbors behind, to join a married child in unfamiliar territory. The younger generation for its part will be forced to ponder its own filial obligations in more detail. Instead of assuming that, by default, the last son to marry will simply remain with a widowed parent, brothers (and to a lesser extent sisters) will have to spend more time negotiating parent-care responsibilities, as the Foks and the Gunns have done.

Under the new circumstances proximity will continue to be important, but historical and situational factors will come to play a more important role in determining the distribution of these responsibilities, and the assumptions now implicit in the intergenerational contract may have to be clearly spelled out. Historical factors could include calculations of which child is more obligated by virtue of having received special parental investments by, for example, being the beneficiary of the *dingti* option or of child-care services. Situational factors, such as who can provide care with the least disruption to their own family when parental needs become apparent, will also necessitate both intragenerational and intergenerational strategy sessions to determine who can best provide the necessary care. Thus, in the absence of any competing family obligations, a retired child or child-in-law is a likely candidate for the role of care-giver.

The provision of care by an elderly spouse, a residentially distant child, or a still working child presents more logistical difficulties than does care provided by someone young and coresident or living just down the street. If

29. Davis, "Urban Job Mobility."

the Chinese government continues to expect families to provide the bulk of elder care, it will be necessary to develop support services for these families. Homemaker services, respite care services, and mutual aid organizations are all neighborhood-based programs that would allow the elder to remain in his or her own residence and at the same time would lessen the burden taken on by the family. Alternatively, workplace-based programs, such as daycare centers or care-giver leave policies, could alleviate the stress of providing parent care. Some forms of congregate living, such as retirement apartments for the relatively well elderly or nursing homes for those whose children are unable to provide direct care, could be expanded. Currently, most welfare homes for the elderly restrict admission to the childless and needy elderly, but increasingly such homes are beginning to admit elders whose children cannot look after them but are able to pay for care.[30]

CONCLUSIONS

As is indicated in the introduction to this chapter, the traditional intergenerational contract was generally understood to require sons to support their parents in old age. Material and psychological incentives along with the threat of social and supernatural sanctions usually made living up to the contract more attractive to the younger generation than reneging on it. In the reform era the strength of these forces has been weakened as the young take advantage of the new opportunities to live and work in communities other than the ones in which they were raised. Nowhere is this more apparent than in the rural area, where the shift from the collective to the individual household as the unit of production has undermined the power of the village (formerly team or brigade) head to penalize neglectful adult children by witholding their wages.

Great official concern has been expressed recently about both the willingness of adult children to support their parents and how best to take preventive action to avoid abuse. According to a report in the *Legal Daily*, such abuse and neglect in Zhejiang caused the deaths of at least 187 elderly Chinese between 1988 and 1990.[31] These "abnormal" deaths, of which many were suicides, were the result of being denied medical treatment, being coerced into turning over property, and being bullied and tortured. Local authorities were accused of not paying much attention to these cases and of failing to prosecute the persons responsible.

Sun reports that some localities are now requiring written contracts of support between elderly parents and their children.[32] Such contracts are

30. Liang and Gu, "Long-term Care."

31. *Legal Daily*, 1990. Cited in Lena H. Sun, "China Seeks Ways to Protect Elderly," *Washington Post*, October 23, 1990.

32. Sun, "China Seeks Ways."

not, of course, a new idea, but requiring them of newlyweds and involving officials rather than relatives to witness them are new. The vice-chairman of the Qindu county (Shaanxi province) committee on aging clarified the need for contracts by pointing out that "it is very common for children, especially sons who are the traditional care-providers, to quarrel among themselves about who will take care of the parents." This issue of conflict among siblings, whose individual resources may now vary substantially compared with the prereform period, is the same phenomenon Cohen discusses in Taiwan.[33] The sons are so concerned about the exploitation of their conjugal families by one another that determining how to meet the needs of the senior generation becomes one more source of contention.

In the urban areas, as we have seen, elders are less vulnerable to the quarrels among their sons because they normally have their own pensions and subsidized medical care. Nevertheless, it is clear that "serving" the elderly—that is, assisting them in the tasks of daily living—may become a source of contention among their children. Parents now appreciate more than ever the need to think strategically and to nurture a sense of filial obligation in their children. Thus parents sometimes exempt unmarried sons from contributing to the household budget, provide childcare for adult children living elsewhere, and make themselves agreeable coresidents by staying out of young people's affairs. In these ways they hope to lessen the impact on themselves of the new opportunities young people have to seek distant jobs and to move into separate housing.

33. Cohen, *House United.*

CONTRIBUTORS

Deborah Davis is professor and chair of the Department of Sociology at Yale University. She is the author of *Long Lives: Chinese Elderly and the Communist Revolution* and coeditor with Ezra Vogel of *Chinese Society on the Eve of Tiananmen.* She is working on a book on occupational mobility in urban China entitled *Getting Ahead, Falling Behind,* and on an edited volume on Chinese city life in the early 1990s.

Hill Gates, after receiving a B.A. from Harvard/Radcliffe, an M.A. from the University of Hawaii, and a Ph.D. from the University of Michigan, taught anthropology for twenty years at Central Michigan University. She is now a senior research associate in the Institute for International Studies at Stanford University. She has written *Chinese Working-Class Lives: Getting By in Taiwan,* recently coedited (with Alice Littlefield) essays entitled *Marxist Approaches in Economic Anthropology,* and done extensive field research in Sichuan, Fujian, and Taiwan, especially on class and gender.

Susan Greenhalgh is an anthropologist and senior associate in the Research Division of the Population Council. She has conducted field research in Taiwan and Shaanxi and has published widely on issues of gender, family, reproductive politics, and political economy. She is completing a book on family entrepreneurship among the offshore Chinese.

Stevan Harrell is professor of anthropology and director of the University Honors Program at the University of Washington in Seattle. He has conducted field research in northern Taiwan and southern Sichuan. His most recent edited volumes are *Violence in China* (with Jonathan Lipman) and *Culture Change in Postwar Taiwan* (with Huang Chün-chieh). He has finished a long book manuscript on the history of the human family, and he plans a shorter one on ethnicity and development in southern Sichuan.

Charlotte Ikels is associate professor of anthropology at Case Western Reserve University in Cleveland. Prior to coming to Case Western in 1985 she was a research associate at Harvard University. She has conducted research on Chinese elderly and family care-giving in Hong Kong, the United States, and Guangdong. Her publications include a book, *Aging and Adaptation: Chinese in Hong Kong and the United States*, as well as numerous articles and book chapters. She is coeditor of a special issue of the *Journal of Cross-Cultural Gerontology* on aging in China.

Graham E. Johnson is a member of the Department of Anthropology and Sociology at the University of British Columbia in Vancouver. He has conducted field research in Hong Kong, the Pearl River delta, and various Chinese communities in Canada. He has recently completed a monograph on the rural transformation of the Pearl River delta in the 1980s entitled *Peasants of the Pearl*.

Michael R. Phillips is a psychiatrist associated with the Shashi Psychiatric Hospital, Shashi, Hubei, China. He is also affiliated with the University of Washington and with Harvard University. He is the author of several articles on cross-cultural psychiatry as well as a recent book (in Chinese) on techniques of psychiatric assessment.

Mark Selden is chair of the Department of Sociology at the State University of New York, Binghamton. His recent books include *Chinese Village, Socialist State* (with Edward Friedman and Paul Pickowitz), *The Political Economy of Chinese Socialism*, and *Reinventing Vietnamese Socialism: Doi Moi in Comparative Perspective*.

Helen F. Siu is professor of anthropology at Yale University. She has conducted field research in the Pearl River delta since the 1970s. She is the author of *Agents and Victims in South China: Accomplices in Rural Revolution* and has compiled two anthologies of modern Chinese literature, *Mao's Harvest: Voices from China's New Generation* (coedited with Zelda Stern) and *Furrows: Peasants, Intellectuals, and the State: Stories and Histories of Modern China*.

Jonathan Unger, a sociologist, is head of the Australian National University's Contemporary China Centre. He has published eight books, including *Education under Mao: Class and Competition in Canton Schools* and, as coauthor, *Chen Village under Mao and Deng*. His most recent book, as editor, is *"Using the Past to Serve the Present": Historiography and Politics in Contemporary China*.

Martin King Whyte is professor of sociology and associate of the Center for Chinese Studies at the University of Michigan. He is the author of numerous studies of contemporary social life in China. His most recent book is a study of changes in premarital and marital relations in the United States, *Dating, Mating, and Marriage*.

BIBLIOGRAPHY

Ahern, Emily M. 1973. *The Cult of the Dead in a Chinese Village*. Stanford: Stanford University Press.

Albert, Steven M. 1990. "Caregiving as a Cultural System: Conceptions of Filial Obligation and Parental Dependency in Urban America." *American Anthropologist* 92, no. 2:319–31.

American Psychiatric Association. 1980. *DSM-III: Diagnostic and Statistical Manual of Mental Disorders*. 3d ed. Washington, D.C.: American Psychiatric Association.

———. 1987. *Diagnostic and Statistical Manual of Mental Disorders: DSM-III-R*. 3d ed., rev. Washington, D.C.: American Psychiatric Association.

Andrews, Gary R., Adrian J. Esterman, Annette J. Braunack-Mayer, and Cam M. Rungie. 1986. *Aging in the Western Pacific*. Manila: World Health Organization.

Antonucci, Toni, Rebecca Fuhrer, and James S. Jackson. 1990. "Social Support and Reciprocity: A Cross-Ethnic and Cross-National Perspective." *Journal of Social and Personal Relationships* 7:519–30.

Ash, Robert F. 1988. "The Evolution of Agricultural Policy." *China Quarterly*, no. 116 (December): 529–55.

Aston, T. H., and C. H. E. Philpin. 1985. *The Brenner Debate: Agrarian Class Structure and Economic Development in Pre-Industrial Europe*. Cambridge: Cambridge University Press.

Banister, Judith. 1984. "Population Policy and Trends in China 1978–1983." *China Quarterly*, no. 100 (December): 717–41.

———. 1987. *China's Changing Population*. Stanford: Stanford University Press.

Bauman, Zygmunt. 1972. "Officialdom and Class: Bases of Inequality in Socialist Society." In *The Social Analysis of Class Structure*, edited by Frank Parkin. London: Tavistock.

Becker, Gary. 1981. *A Treatise on the Family*. Cambridge: Harvard University Press.

Beneria, Lourdes, and Gita Sen. "Class and Gender Inequalities and Women's Role in Economic Development: Theoretical and Practical Implications." *Feminist Studies* 8, no. 1:157–74.

Bernstein, Thomas P. 1989. Review of *The Reach of the State: Sketches of the Chinese Body Politic*, by Vivienne Shue. *Journal of Asian Studies* 48:373–75.

Bian Yanjie. 1990. "Equal Education and Unequal Outcome." Paper presented at Yale University conference on Gender and Inequality, January 19.

Blau, Peter, Terry Blum, and Joseph Schwartz. 1982. "Heterogeneity and Intermarriage." *American Sociological Review* 47:45–62.

Blau, Peter, and Joseph Schwartz. 1984. *Crosscutting Social Circles*. New York: Academic Press.

Boserup, Ester. 1970. *Women's Role in Economic Development*. London: Allen and Unwin.

Brody, E. B. 1981. "The Clinician as Ethnographer: A Psychoanalytic Perspective on the Epistemology of Fieldwork." *Culture Medicine and Psychiatry* 5:273–301.

Buck, John Lossing. 1986 [1937]. *Land Utilization in China*. Nanking: University of Nanking, 1937. Reprint. Taipei: Southern Materials Center.

Burns, John P. 1985–86. "Local Cadre Accommodation to the 'Responsibility System' in Rural China." *Pacific Affairs* 58, no. 4 (Winter): 607–25.

———. 1988. *Political Participation in Rural China*. Berkeley: University of California Press.

Cai He. 1987. "Chengshi jiating jiegoude bianhua ji qushi" (Alterations and trends in the structure of the urban family). *Shehuixue* (Sociology). People's University Reprint Series C4, no. 6. First published in *Juece yu xinxi* (Policy and News) (Wuhan), no. 9, 1987.

Caldwell, John. 1976. "Toward a Restatement of Demographic Transition." *Population and Development Review* 2, nos. 3 and 4 (September and December): 321–66.

Carter, Anthony T. 1984. "Household Histories." In *Households*, edited by Robert McC. Netting, Richard R. Wilk, and Eric J. Arnould, 44–83. Berkeley and Los Angeles: University of California Press.

Chan, Anita, Richard Madsen, and Jonathan Unger. 1984. *Chen Village: The Recent History of a Peasant Community in Mao's China*. Berkeley: University of California Press.

Changes and Development in China (1949–1989). 1989. Beijing: Beijing Review Press.

Chaolian xiangzhi (Township Gazetteer of Chaolian). 1946.

Chayanov, A. V. 1986. *The Theory of Peasant Farm Organization*. Madison: University of Wisconsin Press.

Chen Ai Ju and Gavin Jones. 1989. *Aging in ASEAN: Its Socio-Economic Consequences*. Singapore: Institute of Southeast Asian Studies.

Chen Chung-min. 1985. "Dowry and Inheritance." In *The Chinese Family and Its Ritual Behavior*, edited by Hsieh Jih-chang and Chuang Ying-chang, 117–27. Monograph Series B, no. 15. Taipei: Institute of Ethnology, Academia Sinica.

Chen Gusong and Zhao Dehua. 1987. "Zhongguo jiating ningju li pouxi" (Analysis of the cohesive power of the Chinese family). In *Zhongguo hunyin jiating yanjiu* (Research on Chinese marriages and families). Beijing: Shehui kexue wenxian chubanshe.

Chen Qinghua. "Pingdi Yizu de jiating bianqian" (Changes in the Yi family of Pingdi). Unpublished paper.

Chen Wanzhen. 1987. "Wo guo hunyin zhuangkuang de tongji fenxi" (A statistical analysis of the state of affairs of marriage in China). *Renkouxue kan* (Journal of Demography), no. 1.

Chesneaux, Jean. 1973. *Peasant Revolts in China, 1840–1949.* Stanford: Stanford University Press, 1973.

Chiao, Chi-Ming. 1933. "Rural Population and Vital Statistics for Selected Areas in China 1929–1931." Cornell University M.S. in agriculture.

China Population Information Centre. 1983. "Open Letter from the Central Committee of the Communist Party of China to All Members of the Party and the Communist Youth League Concerning the Problem of Controlling the Country's Population Growth." In *China: Population Policy and Family Planning Practice,* 1–4. Beijing: CPIC.

Chow Yung-teh. 1966. *Social Mobility in China.* New York: Atherton Press.

Chu, G. C. 1985. "The Emergence of the New Chinese Culture." In *Chinese Culture and Mental Health,* edited by W. S. Tseng and D. Y. H. Wu, 15–27. London: Academic Press.

Coale, Ansley J. 1985. "Fertility in Rural China: A Reconfirmation of the Barclay Reassessment." In *Family and Population in East Asian History,* edited by Susan B. Hanley and Arthur P. Wolf. Stanford: Stanford University Press.

Coale, Ansley J., and Shengli Chen. 1987. *Basic Data on Fertility in the Provinces of China, 1940–82.* Papers of the East-West Population Institute, no. 104. Honolulu: East-West Population Institute.

Cocks, Joan. 1989. *The Opposition Imagination: Feminism, Critique, and Political Theory.* London and New York: Routledge.

Cohen, Myron L. 1968. "A Case Study of Chinese Family Economy and Development." *Journal of Asian and African Studies.*

———. 1970. "Developmental Process in the Chinese Domestic Group." In *Family and Kinship in Chinese Society,* edited by Maurice Freedman, 21–36. Stanford: Stanford University Press.

———. 1976. *House United, House Divided: The Chinese Family in Taiwan.* New York, Columbia University Press.

———. 1990. "Lineage Organization in North China." *Journal of Asian Studies* 49:509–34.

Colburn, Forest D., ed. 1989. *Everyday Forms of Peasant Resistance.* Armonk, N.Y.: M.E. Sharpe.

Connor, Walker. 1979. *Socialism, Politics, and Equality.* New York: Columbia University Press.

Coordinating Epidemiological Group for Twelve Regions. 1986. "Duo lei jingshenbing, yaowu yilai, ji renge zhangai de diaocha ziliao fenxi" (Analysis of survey results of all types of psychiatric illnesses, drug and alcohol dependence, and personality disorders). *Zhongguo Shenjing Jingshen Ke Zazhi* (Chinese Journal of Neurology and Psychiatry) 19, no. 2:70–72.

Croll, Elisabeth. 1981. *The Politics of Marriage in Contemporary China.* Cambridge: Cambridge University Press.

———. 1987. "New Peasant Family Forms in Rural China." *Journal of Peasant Studies* 14, no. 4:469–97.

Davin, Delia. 1985. "The Single-Child Family Policy in the Countryside." In *China's*

One-Child Family Policy, edited by Elisabeth Croll, Delia Davin, and Penny Kane, 37–82. London: Macmillan.

Davis, Deborah. 1988. "Patrons and Clients in Chinese Industry." *Modern China* 14, no. 4:487–97.

———. 1988. "Unequal Chances, Unequal Outcomes: Pension Reform and Urban Inequality." *China Quarterly*, no. 114:223–42.

———. 1989. "Chinese Social Welfare Policies and Outcomes." *China Quarterly*, no. 119 (September): 577–97.

———. 1989. "My Mother's House." In *Unofficial China: Popular Culture and Thought in the People's Republic*, edited by Perry Link, Richard Madsen, and Paul Pickowicz, 88–100. Boulder, Colo.: Westview press.

———. 1990. "Urban Job Mobility." In *Chinese Society on the Eve of Tiananmen: The Impact of Reform*, edited by Deborah Davis and Ezra F. Vogel, 85–108. Cambridge: Harvard University Press.

Davis-Friedmann, Deborah. 1983. *Long Lives: Chinese Elderly and the Chinese Revolution.* Cambridge: Harvard University Press.

———. 1985. "Chinese Retirement: Policy and Practice." *Current Perspectives on Aging and the Life Cycle* 1:295–313.

———. 1985. "Intergenerational Inequality and the Chinese Revolution." *Modern China* 11, no. 2 (April): 177–201.

———. 1991. *Long Lives: Chinese Elderly and the Communist Revolution.* 2d ed., rev. and exp. Stanford: Stanford University Press.

Delman, Jorgen, Clemens C. Ostergaard, and Flemming Christiansen, eds. 1990. *Remaking Peasant China: Problems of Rural Development and Institutions at the Start of the 1990s.* Aarhus, Denmark: Aarhus University Press.

Diamond, Norma. 1975. "Collectivization, Kinship, and the Status of Women in Rural China." In *Toward an Anthropology of Women*, edited by Rayna Reiter, 372–95. New York: Monthly Review Press.

Dowd, J. 1975. "Aging as Exchange: A Preface to Theory." *Journal of Gerontology* 30:584–95.

Duara, Prasenjit. 1988. *Culture, Power and Village Communities in North China: 1900–1949.* Stanford: Stanford University Press.

Ebrey, Patricia. 1986. "Early Stages in the Development of Descent Group." In *Kinship Organization in Late Imperial China, 1000–1940*, edited by Patricia Ebrey and James Watson, 16–61. Berkeley: University of California Press.

Edelman, Robert. 1987. *Proletarian Peasants: The Revolution of 1905 in Russia's Southwest.* Ithaca: Cornell University Press.

Erbaugh, Mary. 1990. "Chinese Women Face Increased Discrimination." *Off Our Backs* 20, no. 3 (March 1990): 9, 33.

Feeney, Griffith, et al. 1989. "Recent Fertility Dynamics in China: Results from the One Percent Population Survey." *Population and Development Review* 15, no. 2 (June): 297–322.

Femia, Joseph V. 1981. *Gramsci's Political Thought: Hegemony, Consciousness, and the Revolutionary Process.* Oxford: Clarendon Press.

Finley, Nancy J., M. Diane Roberts, and Benjamin F. Banahan III. 1988. "Motivators and Inhibitors of Attitudes of Filial Obligation Toward Aging Parents." *Gerontologist* 28, no. 1:73–78.

Fitzgerald, Stephen. 1972. *China and the Overseas Chinese*. Cambridge: Cambridge University Press.

Fox, Greer L. 1975. "Love Match and Arranged Marriage in a Modernizing Nation: Mate Selection in Ankara, Turkey." *Journal of Marriage and the Family* 37:180–93.

Freedman, Maurice. 1958. *Lineage Organization in Southeastern China*. London: Athlone Press.

———. 1966. *Chinese Lineage and Society: Fukien and Kwangtung*. London: Athlone Press.

———. 1970. "Ritual Aspects of Chinese Kinship and Marriage." In *Family and Kinship in Chinese Society*, edited by Maurice Freedman, 163–87. Stanford: Stanford University Press.

Friedman, Edward, Paul Pickowicz, and Mark Selden. 1991. *Chinese Village, Socialist State*. New Haven: Yale University Press.

Gamble, Sidney. 1968 [1954]. *Ting Hsien: A North China Rural Community*. New York: Institute of Pacific Relations. Reprint. Stanford: Stanford University Press.

———. 1963. *North China Villages: Social, Political and Economic Activities Before 1933*. Berkeley: University of California Press.

Gates, Hill. 1987. *Chinese Working-Class Lives: Getting By in Taiwan*. Ithaca: Cornell University Press.

———. 1989. "The Commoditization of Chinese Women." *Signs* 14, no. 4:799–832.

———. n.d. "Fertility and Women's Capital in Two Chinese Societies." MS.

———. 1991. "Eating for Revenge: Consumption and Corruption in Chengdu." *Dialectical Anthropology* 16, nos. 3–4:233–50.

———. n.d. *China's Motor: The Petty Capitalist Mode of Production*. MS.

Geertz, Clifford. 1963. *Agricultural Involution: The Process of Ecological Change in Indonesia*. Berkeley: University of California Press.

Goldstein, Melvyn C., Ku Yachun, and Charlotte Ikels. 1990. "Household Composition in Two Rural Villages in the People's Republic of China." *Journal of Cross-Cultural Gerontology* 5, no. 2:119–30.

Goode, William J. 1963. *World Revolution and Family Patterns*. New York: Free Press.

———. 1982. *The Family*. Englewood Cliffs, N.J.: Prentice-Hall, 1982.

Goody, Jack. 1976. *Production and Reproduction*. Cambridge: Cambridge University Press.

———. 1990. *The Oriental, the Ancient and the Primitive: Systems of Marriage and the Family in the Pre-industrial Societies of Eurasia*. Cambridge: Cambridge University Press.

Goody, Jack, and Stanley J. Tambiah. 1973. *Bridewealth and Dowry*. Cambridge: Cambridge University Press.

Graham, David C. 1928. *Religion in Szechwan Province, China*. Washington, D.C.: Smithsonian Institution.

———. 1961. *Folk Religion in Southwest China*. Washington, D.C.: Smithsonian Institution.

Gramsci, Antonio. 1988. *Gramsci's Prison Letters: A Selection Translated and Introduced by Hamish Henderson*. London: Zwan Publications.

Greenhalgh, Susan. 1985. "Sexual Stratification: The Other Side of 'Growth with Equity' in East Asia." *Population and Development Review* 11, no. 2:265–314.

———. 1986. "Shifts in China's Population Policy: Views from the Central, Provincial, and Local Levels." *Population and Development Review* 12, no. 3 (September): 491–515.

———. 1990. "The Evolution of the One-Child Policy in Shaanxi." *China Quarterly*, no. 122 (June): 191–229.

Griffin, K., ed. 1984. *Institutional Reform and Economic Development in the Chinese Countryside.* London: Macmillan.

Gu Jirui. 1985. *Jiating xiaofei jingjixue* (The economics of family consumption). Beijing: Zhongguo caizheng jingji chubanshe.

Gu Quanzhong, Chen Yangming, and Qian Fang. 1987. "Status and Needs of the Elderly in Urban Shanghai: Analysis of Some Preliminary Statistics." In *Journal of Cross-Cultural Gerontology* 2.

Hajnal, John. 1982. "Two Kinds of Pre-industrial Household Formation Systems." *Population and Development Review* 8, no. 3 (September): 449–94.

Hamilton, Gary. 1988. "Patriarchalism in Imperial China and Western Europe: A Revision of Weber's Sociology of Dominance." *Theory and Society* 13, no. 3:393–425.

Hancock, Paula, David J. Mangen, and Kay Young McChesney. 1988. "The Exchange Dimension of Solidarity: Measuring Intergenerational Solidarity." In *Measurement of Intergenerational Relations*, edited by David J. Mangen, Vern L. Bengston, and Pierre H. Landry, Jr. Newbury Park, Calif.: Sage.

Hanley, Susan B., and Arthur P. Wolf, eds. 1985. *Family and Population in East Asian History.* Stanford: Stanford University Press.

Hardee-Cleaveland, Karen, and Judith Banister. 1988. "Fertility Policy and Implementation in China 1983–1986." *Population and Development Review* 14, no. 2 (June): 245–86.

Hareven, Tamara K. 1987. "Reflection on Family Research in the People's Republic of China." *Social Research* 54, no. 4 (Winter): 663–89.

Harrell, Stevan. 1982. *Ploughshare Village: Culture and Context in Taiwan.* Seattle: University of Washington Press.

———. 1985. "Why Do the Chinese Work So Hard?" *Modern China* 11, no. 2:203–26.

———. 1990. "Ethnicity, Local Interests, and the State: Yi Villages in Southwest China." *Comparative Studies in Society and History* (July).

———. Forthcoming. "Marriage, Mortality, and the Developmental Cycle in Three Zhejiang Lineages." In *Chinese Historical Microdemography*, edited by Stevan Harrell. Berkeley: University of California Press.

Harrell, Stevan, and Sara Dickey. 1985. "Dowry Systems in Complex Societies." *Ethnology* 24, no. 2:105–20.

Hashim, Wan. 1988. *Peasants Under Peripheral Capitalism.* Bangi: Penerbit Universiti Kebangsaan Malaysia.

Heikkinen, E., W. E. Waters, and Z. J. Brzezinski. 1983. *The Elderly in Eleven Countries: A Sociomedical Survey.* Copenhagen: World Health Organization.

Henderson, Gail E. 1990. "Increased Inequality in Health Care." In *Chinese Society on the Eve of Tiananmen: The Impact of Reform*, edited by Deborah Davis and Ezra F. Vogel, 263–82. Cambridge: Harvard University Press.

Henderson, Gail, and Myron S. Cohen. 1984. *The Chinese Hospital: A Socialist Work Unit.* New Haven: Yale University Press.

Hendersen, Gail E., E. A. Murphy, S. T. Sockwell, J. L. Zhou, Q. R. Shen, and Z. M. Li. 1988. "High-technology Medicine in China: The Case of Chronic Renal Failure and Hemodialysis." *New England Journal of Medicine* 318, no. 15:1000–1004.

Hinton, William. 1990. *The Great Reversal: The Privatization of China, 1978–1989.* New York: Monthly Review Press.

Ho, D. Y. F. 1986. "Chinese Patterns of Socialization." In *The Psychology of the Chinese People*, edited by M. H. Bond, 1–37. Hong Kong: Oxford University Press.

Ho Ping-ti. 1964. *The Ladder of Success in Imperial China.* New York: Science Editions.

Honig, Emily, and Gail Hershatter. 1988. *Personal Voices.* Stanford: Stanford University Press.

Howe, Christopher. 1971. *Employment and Economic Growth in Urban China 1949–1957.* Cambridge: Cambridge University Press.

Hsiao, Kung-ch'uan. 1960. *Rural China: Imperial Control in the Nineteenth Century.* Seattle: University of Washington Press.

Hsu, J. 1985. "The Chinese Family: Relations, Problems, and Theory." In *Chinese Culture and Mental Health*, edited by W. S. Tseng and D. Y. H. Wu, 95–112. London: Academic Press.

Hu Renxi. 1987. "Shiqu gaoling laoren zhuzhu qingkuang chouyang diaocha" (Sample survey of the housing situation of the very old in the urban districts). In *Gaoling laoren wenti yanjiu*, edited by the Research Group of Shanghai Municipal Committee on Problems of the Elderly, 71–80. Shanghai: Shanghai shi laonianxue xuehui mishuzhu.

Hu Ruquan. 1986. "Cong Tianjin, Wuhan deng chengshide diaocha kan woguo chengshi laonianren jiating shenghuo" (The family life of elderly urban Chinese, as witnessed through surveys of Tianjin, Wuhan, and other cities). *Shehuixue yanjiu* (Sociological Research), no. 4.

———. 1986. "Shitan 'Wangluo jiating'" (A discussion of 'Networked families'). *Zhongguo funu bao* (China Woman's Paper) (March 7): 3.

Huang, Philip C. C. 1985. *The Peasant Economy and Social Change in North China.* Stanford: Stanford University Press.

———. 1990. *The Peasant Family and Rural Development in the Yangzi Delta, 1350–1988.* Stanford: Stanford University Press.

Huang Shu-min. 1987. "The Strategy of Prosperity in a Chinese Village." *Journal of Developing Societies* 3, no. 2:119–36.

———. 1988. "Transforming China's Collective Health Care System: A Village Study." *Social Science and Medicine* 27, no. 9:879–88.

———. 1989. *The Spiral Road: Change in a Chinese Village Through the Eyes of a Communist Party Leader.* Boulder, Colo.: Westview.

———. 1990. "Folk Reproductive Medicine in North China: The Cultural Constructs of Pregnancy, Childbirth, and Post-Natal Care." Paper presented at the Third International Congress on Traditional Asian Medicine, Bombay, India, January 4–7, 1990.

Ikels, Charlotte. 1983. *Aging and Adaptation: Chinese in Hong Kong and the United States.* Hamden, Conn.: Archon Books.

———. 1983. "The Process of Caretaker Selection." *Research on Aging* 5, no. 4:491–509.

———. 1988. "Delayed Reciprocity and the Support Networks of the Childless Elderly." *Journal of Comparative Family Studies* 19:99–112.

———. 1990. "Family Caregivers and the Elderly in China." In *Aging and Caregiving: Theory, Research and Policy*, edited by David E. Biegel and Arthur Blum, 270–84. Newbury Park, Calif.: Sage.

———. 1990. "New Options for the Urban Elderly." In *Chinese Society on the Eve of Tiananmen: The Impact of Reform*, edited by Deborah Davis and Ezra F. Vogel, 215–42. Cambridge: Harvard University Press.

———. 1990. "The Resolution of Intergenerational Conflict: Perceptions of Elders and Their Family Members." *Modern China* 16, no. 4:379–406.

———. 1991. "Aging and Disability in China: Cultural Issues in Measurement and Interpretation." *Social Science and Medicine* 32, no. 6 (March): 649–65.

James, Alice, William L. James, and Howard L. Smith. 1984. "Reciprocity as a Coping Strategy of the Elderly: A Rural Irish Perspective." *Gerontologist* 24:483–89.

James, William E., Seiji Naya, and Gerald M. Meier. 1987. *Asian Development: Economic Success and Policy Lessons*. San Franciso: International Center for Economic Growth.

Jaschok, Maria H. A. 1988. *Concubines and Bondservants: The Social History of a Chinese Custom*. London: Zed Books.

Johnson, Elizabeth, and Graham Johnson. 1976. *Walking on Two Legs: Rural Development in South China*. Ottawa: International Development Research Centre.

Johnson, Graham E. 1982. "The Production Responsibility System in Chinese Agriculture: Some Examples from Guangdong." *Pacific Affairs* 55, no. 3 (Fall): 430–52.

———. 1986. "1997 and After: Will Hong Kong Survive? A Personal View." *Pacific Affairs* 59, no. 2 (Summer): 237–54.

———. 1989. "Rural Transformation in South China? Views from the Locality." *Revue Européene des Sciences Sociales* 27, no. 84:191–226.

———. 1992. "The Political Economy of Chinese Urbanization: Guangdong and the Pearl River Delta." In *Urbanizing China*, edited by Gregory Guldin. Westport, Conn.: Greenwood Press.

Johnson, Kay Ann. 1983. *Women, the Family and Peasant Revolution in China*. Chicago: University of Chicago Press.

Jowitt, Kenneth. 1983. "Soviet Neotraditionalism: The Political Corruption of a Leninist Regime" *Soviet Studies* 35, no. 3:275–97.

Judd, Ellen. 1989. "Niangjia: Chinese Women and Their Natal Families." *Journal of Asian Studies* 48:525–44.

Kaufman, Joan. 1989. "Family Planning Policy and Practice in China." *Population and Development Review* 15, no. 4 (December): 707–30.

Kelley, Jonathan, and Herbert Klein. 1977. "Revolution and the Rebirth of Inequality: A Theory of Stratification in Postrevolutionary Society." *American Journal of Sociology* 83:78–99.

Keyes, Charles F. 1983. "Peasant Strategies in Asian Societies: Moral and Rational

Economic Approaches—A Symposium: Introduction." *Journal of Asian Studies* 42, no. 4 (August): 754.

King, A. Y., and M. H. Bond. 1985. "The Confucian Paradigm of Man: A Sociological Perspective." In *Chinese Culture and Mental Health*, edited by W. S. Tseng and D. Y. H. Wu, 29–45. London: Academic Press.

Kleinman, Arthur. 1980. *Patients and Healers in the Context of Culture*. Berkeley: University of California Press.

Kojima, Reiitsu. 1987. *Urbanization and Urban Problems in China*. Tokyo: Institute of Developing Economics.

Kraus, Richard. 1989. *Pianos and Politics in China*. New York: Oxford University Press.

Kubler-Ross, Elisabeth. 1969. *On Death and Dying*. London: Macmillan.

Lampton, David M. 1987. "The Implementation Problem in Post-Mao China." In *Policy Implementation in Post-Mao China*, edited by David M. Lampton, 3–24. Berkeley: University of California Press.

———. 1987. "Water: Challenge to a Fragmented Political System." In *Policy Implementation in Post-Mao China*, edited by David M. Lampton, 157–89. Berkeley: University of California Press.

Lang, Olga. 1946. *Chinese Family and Society*. New Haven: Yale University Press.

Lao Ren Bao (Elderly News). 1991. Issue 3.

Lardy, Nicholas. 1983. *Agriculture in China's Modern Economic Development*. London: Cambridge University Press.

———. 1984. "Consumption and Living Standards in China, 1978–83." *China Quarterly*, no. 100 (December): 849–65.

Lavely, William. 1990. "Industrialization and Household Complexity in Rural Taiwan." *Social Forces* 69, no. 1 (September): 235–51.

———. 1990. "Marriage and Mobility under Rural Collectivism." In *Marriage and Inequality in Chinese Society*, edited by Rubie Watson and Patricia Ebrey. Berkeley: University of California Press.

Lavely, William, and Ronald Freeman. 1990. "The Origins of the Chinese Fertility Decline." *Demography* 27, no. 3 (August): 357–67.

Lee, Yok-shiu F. 1988. "The Urban Housing Problems in China." *China Quarterly*, no. 115 (September): 387–407.

Leff, J., and C. Vaughn. 1985. *Expressed Emotion in Families: Its Significance for Mental Illness*. London: Guilford Press.

Lem, Winnie. 1991. "Gender and Social Reproduction in Petty Commodity Production." In *Marxist Approaches in Economic Anthropology*, edited by Alice Littlefield and Hill Gates. Lanham, Md.: University Press of America.

Levy, Marion. 1949. *The Family Revolution in Modern China*. Cambridge: Harvard University Press.

Li Dongshan. 1985. "Lun ju zhi" (On systems of accommodation). *Shehui diaocha yu yanjiu* (Social Investigations and Research), no. 5.

Li Minghua et al. 1983. "Wuchang qu qinggong lian'ai hunyin xianzhuang diaocha" (Investigation into the current circumstances of falling in love and marriage among young workers in a Wuchang [Wuhan] district). *Shehui* (Society), no. 6 (1983).

Li, S. X., and M. R. Phillips. 1990. "Witch Doctors and Mental Illness in Mainland China: A Preliminary Report." *American Journal of Psychiatry* 147:221–24.

Li Shaoming. 1989. "Panzhihua shi gongyequ de jianshe dui zhoubian nongcun de yingxiang" (The effect of the construction of the industrial district in Panzhihua city on surrounding villages). Paper presented at the Conference on Urban Anthropology, Beijing, December.

Li Xiaorong. 1988. "Panzhihua shi Yishala Yi cun shehui jingji diaocha" (An investigation of the society and economy of Yishala Yi village in Panzhihua city). *Minzuxue luncong*.

Liang, Jersey, and Gu Shengzu. 1989. "Long-term Care for the Elderly in China." In *Caring for an Aging World: International Models for Long-term Care, Financing, and Delivery*, edited by Teresa Schwab, 265–87. New York: McGraw-Hill.

Lin, K. M. 1981. "Traditional Chinese Medical Beliefs and Their Relevance for Mental Illness and Psychiatry." In *Normal and Abnormal Behavior in Chinese Culture*, edited by A. Kleinman and T. Y. Lin, 95–111. Dordrecht, Holland: Reidel.

Lin, K. M., and Arthur M. Kleinman. 1988. "Psychopathology and Clinical Course of Schizophrenia: A Cross-Cultural Perspective." *Schizophrenia Bulletin* 14:555–67.

Lin, T. Y. 1985. "Mental Disorders and Psychiatry in Chinese Culture: Characteristic Features and Major Issues." In *Chinese Culture and Mental Health*, edited by W. S. Tseng and D. Y. H. Wu, 369–93. London: Academic Press.

Lin, T. Y., and M. C. Lin. 1981. "Love, Denial and Rejection: Responses of Chinese Families to Mental Illness." In *Normal and Abnormal Behavior in Chinese Culture*, edited by A. Kleinman and T. Y. Lin, 387–401. Dordrecht, Holland: Reidel.

Lin Yueh-hwa (Lin Yaohua). 1947. *The Golden Wing*. London: Kegan Paul.

Ling Bi. 1986. "Shanghai shide laoren jiating" (Families of the elderly in urban Shanghai). *Shehuixue yanjiu* (Sociological Research), no. 4.

Little, Daniel. 1989. *Understanding Peasant China: Case Studies in the Philosophy of Social Science*. New Haven: Yale University Press.

Liu Bingfu. 1986. "Wo guo jiating zai 'hexinhua' ma?" (Are Chinese families 'nuclearizing'?). *Shehuixue* (Sociology), no. 3. First published in *Xuexi yu shijian* (Study and Practice), no. 5, 1986.

Liu Gongkang, ed. 1988. *Zhongguo Renkou, Sichuan Fence* (Chinese population, analysis of Sichuan). Zhongguo caizheng jingji chubanshe.

Liu Shuzhen. 1986. *Jicheng fa bai ti wenda* (One hundred questions and answers about the inheritance law). Beijing: Beijing shifan chubanshe.

Liu Ts'ui-jung. Forthcoming. "Demographic Constraint and Family Structure in Chinese Lineages." In *Chinese Historical Micro-Demography*, edited by Stevan Harrell. Berkeley: University of California Press.

Liu Ying. 1984. "Wo guo chengshi jiating jiegoude guimo he leixing" (The size and types of family structure in China's cities). *Shehui* (Society), no. 5.

———. 1986. "Tianjin Huningrong wu chengshi jiating diaocha chuxi" (Initial analysis of Tianjin's Huningrong neighborhood in the five-cities family survey). *Shehuixue yanjiu* (Sociological Research), no. 4.

Liu Ying and Bi Suzhen, eds. 1987. *Zhongguo hunyin jiating yanjiu* (Research on Chinese marriages and families). Beijing: Shehui kexue wenxian chubanshe.

Liu Yirong. 1981. "Yinggai zhongshi yanjiu yishihu de sheji wenti" (We must research the problem of one-room apartments). *Jianzhu xuebao*, no. 5:61–63.

Liu Y. L. 1988. "Dui woguo shixing jiankang baojian ruogan wenti de shentao" (Discussions of issues involved in the implementation of health insurance in our country). *Zhongguo weisheng jingji* (Chinese Health Economics) 2, no. 60:22–24.

Liu Zhiwei. 1990. "Lineage on the Sands: The Case of Shawan." Paper presented in the panel "Lineage Power and Community Change in Republican South China," at the annual meetings of the Association for Asian Studies, Chicago.

Long, Simon. 1990. "7,000 Slaves Freed." *Guardian*, February 2.

Lu Shiming and Hu Anqi. 1989. "Shanghai zhufang zhidu gaige de gouxiang" (An analysis of Shanghai housing reform). *Shanghai gaige*, no. 2:34–35.

Lu Xing. 1989. "Shanghai zhumin dui shangpinfang de xianchuan he qianjing de kanfa" (Shanghai residents' attitudes toward the present and future of commercial housing). *Shehui xue*, no. 3:33–35.

Luther, Norman Y., Griffith Feeny, and Weiman Zhang. 1990. "One Child Family or Baby Boom? Evidence from China's 1987 One-per-hundred Survey." *Population Studies* 44:341–57.

McDonald, Peter. 1987. "Adjustments of Rural Family Systems to Economic and Social Change: A Review of Goode's Theory of Convergence." Paper presented at the Seminar on Changing Family Structures and Life Courses in LDC's, Honolulu, Hawaii, January.

McGee, T. G. 1989. "Urbanasasi or Kotadesasi? Evolving Patterns of Urbanization in Asia." In *Urbanization in Asia*, edited by L. Ma, A. Noble, and A. Dutt, 93–108. Honolulu: University of Hawaii Press.

McGough, James P. 1984. "The Domestic Mode of Production and Peasant Social Organization: The Chinese Case." In Chayanov, *Peasants and Economic Anthropology*, edited by E. Paul Durrenberger, 183–201. Orlando, Fla.: Academic Press.

Maclachlan, Morgan D. 1987. "From Intensification to Proletarianization." In *Household Economies and Their Transformation*, edited by M. D. Maclachlan. Lanham, Md.: University Press of America.

Maclachlan, M. D., ed. 1987. *Household Economies and Their Transformation*. Lanham, Md.: University Press of America.

Marcuse, Herbert. 1968. *Negations: Essays in Critical Theory*. Boston: Beacon Press.

Middelhoek, Jan. 1989–90. "Urban Housing Reform in the PRC." *China Information* 4, no. 3 (Winter): 56–72.

Migdal, Joel S. 1988. *Strong States and Weak Societies: State-Society Relations and State Capabilities in the Third World*. Princeton: Princeton University Press.

Mosher, Steven. 1982. "Birth Control: A View from a Chinese Village." *Asian Survey* 22, no. 4 (April).

Murray, Dian. 1987. *Pirates of the South China Coast, 1790–1810*. Stanford: Stanford University Press.

Myrdal, Jan. 1965. *Report From a Chinese Village*. New York: Pantheon.

Naughton, Barry. 1987. "The Decline of Central Control over Investment in Post-Mao China." In *Policy Implementation in Post-Mao China*, edited by David M. Lampton, 51–80. Berkeley: University of California Press.

Nee, Victor. 1989. "A Theory of Market Transition." *American Sociological Review* 54 (October): 663–81.

Nee, Victor, and Su Sijin. 1990. "Institutional Change and Economic Growth in

China: The View from the Villages." *Journal of Asian Studies* 49, no. 1 (February): 3–25.

Netting, Robert McCee, Richard R. Wilk, and Eric Arnould, eds. 1984. *Households*. Berkeley and Los Angeles: University of California Press.

Notestein, Frank W., and Ch'iao Ch'i-ming. 1937. "Population." In *Land Utilization in China*, by John Lossing Buck, 367. Nanking: University of Nanking.

Oi, Jean C. 1986. "Peasant Households between Plan and Market: Cadre Control over Agricultural Inputs." *Modern China* 12, no. 2 (April): 230–51.

———. 1989. *State and Peasant in Contemporary China: The Political Economy of Village Government*. Berkeley: University of California Press.

Pa Chin. 1972 [1933]. *Family*. Garden City: Anchor Books.

Pan Yunkang. 1985. "Shilun Zhongguo hexin jiating he xifang hexin jiatingde yi tong" (An attempt to discuss the differences and similarities between Chinese and Western nuclear families). *Shehuixue* (Sociology), no. 3 (1985). First published in *Tianjin shehui kexue* (Tianjin Social Science), no. 2.

Pan Yunkang, ed. 1987. *Zhongguo chengshi hunyin yu jiating* (Chinese urban marriages and families). Jinan: Shandong renmin chubanshe.

Pan Yunkang and Lin Nan. 1987. "Zhongguo chengshi xiandai jiating moshi" (A model of contemporary Chinese urban families). *Shehuixue yanjiu* (Sociological Research), no. 3.

Parish, William. 1984. "Destratification in China." In *Class and Social Stratification in Post-Revolution China*, edited by James L. Watson, 84–121. London: Cambridge University Press.

———. 1985. *Chinese Rural Development: The Great Transformation*. Armonk, N.Y.: M.E. Sharpe.

Parish, William L., and Martin King Whyte. 1978. *Village and Family in Contemporary China*. Chicago: University of Chicago Press.

Pasternak, Burton. 1983. *Guests in The Dragon: The Social Demography of a Chinese District*. New York: Columbia University Press.

———. 1983. "On the Causes and Consequences of Uxorilocal Marriage in China." In *Family and Population in East Asian History*, edited by Susan B. Hanley and Arthur P. Wolf, 309–36. Stanford: Stanford University Press.

———. 1986. *Marriage and Fertility in Tianjin, China: Fifty Years of Transition*. Papers of the East-West Population Center, no. 99. Honolulu: East-West Population Institute.

Peng Xizhe. 1989. "Major Determinants of China's Fertility Transition." *China Quarterly*, no. 117 (March): 1–37.

Perry, Elizabeth J., and Christine Wong, eds. 1985. *The Political Economy of Reform in Post-Mao China*. Cambridge: Harvard University Press.

Phillips, M. R., Q. J. Shen, Y. P. Zheng, et al. Forthcoming. "Zai Zhongguo dui 'jiating qinmidu he shiyingxing lianbiao (FACES II)' he 'jiating huanjing liangbiao (FES)' de chubu pingjia" (Preliminary evaluation of the Family Adaptability and Cohesion Scale [FACES II] and the Family Environment Scale [FES]). *Zhongguo xinli weisheng zazhi* (Chinese Mental Health Journal).

Phillips, M. R., W. Xiong, and Z. A. Zhao. 1990. *Jingshenbing yinxing yangxing zhengzhuang liangbiao shiyong youquan wenti* (Issues involved in the use of scales for the assessment of negative and positive symptoms in psychiatric patients). Wuhan: Hubei Science and Technology Publishing House.

Plakans, Andrejs. 1984. "Serf Emancipation and the Changing Structure of Rural Domestic Groups in the Russian Baltic Provinces: Linden Estate, 1797–1858." In *Households*, edited by Robert McCee Netting, Richard R. Wilk, and Eric J. Arnould, 245–78. Berkeley and Los Angeles: University of California Press.

Popkin, Samuel I. 1979. *The Rational Peasant: The Political Economy of Rural Society in Vietnam*. Berkeley: University of California Press.

Potter, Sulamith Heins. 1983. "The Position of Peasants in Modern China's Social Order." *Modern China* 9, no. 4:465–99.

———. 1985. "Birth Planning in Rural China: A Cultural Account." Working Paper no. 103, Women in International Development, Michigan State University.

Potter, Sulamith H., and Jack M. Potter. 1990. *China's Peasants: The Anthropology of a Revolution*. Cambridge: Cambridge University Press.

Powers, E. A. 1971. "Thirty Years of Research on Ideal Mate Characteristics: What Do We Know?" *International Journal of Sociology of the Family* 1:1–9.

Putterman, Louis. 1989. "Entering the Post-Collective Economy in North China." *Modern China* 15, no. 3 (July): 275–320.

Qian Jianghong et al. 1987. "Wo guo da zhong chengshi qingnian jiehun xiaofei yanjiu" (Research into the marriage expenditures of young people in China's large and medium-size cities). *Zhongguo shehui kexue* (Chinese Social Science), no. 3.

———. 1988. "Marriage Related Consumption." *Social Sciences in China*, no. 1: 208–28.

Qiu Liping. 1987. "Wo guo chengshi jiating jiegou biandong jiqi fazhan moxing yanjiu" (Research into changes and developmental models relating to China's urban family structures). *Renkou yanjiu* (Demographic Research), no. 5.

Redding, G., and G. Y. Y. Wong. 1986. "The Psychology of Chinese Organizational Behavior." In *The Psychology of the Chinese People*, edited by M. H. Bond, 267–95. Hong Kong: Oxford University Press.

Robinson, J. C. 1985. "Of Women and Washing Machines: Employment, Housework and the Reproduction of Motherhood in Socialist China." *China Quarterly*, no. 101 (March): 32–57.

Rosen, Stanley. 1992. "Women, Education and Modernization." In *Education and Modernization: The Chinese Experience*, edited by Ruth Hayhoe. Elmsford, N.Y.: Pergamon Press.

Rosenfeld, Jeffrey P. 1982. "Disinheritance and Will Contests." In *Marriage and Family Review*, edited by Judith N. Cates and Marvin B. Sussman, special issue, 5, no. 3:75–86.

Ruddle, Kenneth, and Zhong Gongfu. 1988. *Integrated Agriculture-Aquaculture in South China: The Dyke-Pond System of the Zhujiang Delta*. Cambridge: Cambridge University Press.

Saith, Ashwani. 1984. "China's New Population Policies: Rationale and Some Implications." *Development and Change* 15, no. 3:321–58.

Sartorius, N., et al. 1986. "Early Manifestations and First-contact Incidence of Schizophrenia in Different Cultures." *Psychological Medicine* 16:909–26.

Schoppa, Keith. 1989. *Xiang Lake: Nine Centuries of Chinese Life*. New Haven: Yale University Press.

Scott, James C. 1976. *The Moral Economy of the Peasant: Rebellion and Subsistence in Southeast Asia*. New Haven: Yale University Press.

———. 1985. *Weapons of the Weak: Everyday Forms of Peasant Resistance*. New Haven: Yale University Press.

Selden, Mark. 1988. "Income Inequality and the State in Rural China." In *The Political Economy of Chinese Socialism*, by Mark Selden, 129–52. Armonk, N.Y.: M.E. Sharpe.

———. 1992. *The Political Economy of Chinese Development*. Armonk, N.Y.: M.E. Sharpe.

Shanin, T. 1972. *The Awkward Class: Political Sociology of a Peasantry in a Developing Society: Russia 1910–1925*. Oxford: Oxford University Press.

Shen Kuixu. 1981. "Zhengque quli zhujai sheji yu fen pei di guanxi" (Resolve the relationship between housing supply and allocation). *Jianzhu xuebao*, no. 12:59–64.

Shen, Y. C. 1985. "The Mental Health Home Care Program: Beijing's Rural Haidan District." In *Chinese Culture and Mental Health*, edited by W. S. Tseng and D. Y. H. Wu. London: Academic Press.

Shepherd, John R. n.d. "Marriage Mode and Marriage Market." Unpublished paper.

Shirk, Susan. 1982. *Competitive Comrades*. Berkeley: University of California Press.

Shue, Vivienne. 1980. *Peasant China in Transition: The Dynamics of Development Toward Socialism, 1949–1956*. Berkeley and Los Angeles: University of California Press.

———. 1988. *The Reach of the State: Sketches of the Chinese Body Politic*. Stanford: Stanford University Press.

Sicular, Terry. 1985. "Rural Marketing and Exchange." In *The Political Economy of Reform in Post-Mao China*, edited by Elizabeth J. Perry and Christine Wong, 83–110. Cambridge: Harvard University Press.

Simkus, Albert. 1984. "Structural Transformation and Social Mobility: Hungary 1938–1973." *American Sociological Review* 49:291–307.

Siu, Helen. 1989. *Agents and Victims in South China: Accomplices in Rural Revolution*. New Haven: Yale University Press.

———. 1989. "Recycling Rituals: Politics and Popular Culture in Contemporary Rural China." In *Unofficial China: Essays in Popular Culture and Thought*, edited by Richard Madsen, Perry Link, and Paul Pickowicz. Boulder, Colo.: Westview.

———. 1989. "Socialist Peddlers and Princes in a Chinese Market Town." *American Ethnologist* 16, no. 2 (May): 195–212.

———. 1990. "The Politics of Migration in a Market Town." In *China on the Eve of Tiananmen: The Impact of Reform*, edited by Deborah Davis and Ezra F. Vogel, 61–82. Cambridge: Harvard University Press.

———. 1990. "Recycling Tradition: Culture, History and Political Economy in the Chrysanthemum Festivals of South China." *Comparative Studies in Society and History* 32, no. 4 (October): 765–94.

———. 1990. "Subverting Lineage Power: Local Bosses in the 1940's." Paper presented in the panel "Lineage Power and Community Change in Republican

South China," at the annual meetings of the Association for Asian Studies, Chicago, April 1990.

——. 1990. "Where Were the Women? Rethinking Marriage Resistance and Regional Culture in South China." *Late Imperial China* (December): 32–62.

Skinner, G. William. 1964–65. "Marketing and Social Structure in Rural China" (in three parts). *Journal of Asian Studies* 24, nos. 1–3:3–44; 195–228; 363–99.

——. 1985. "Rural Marketing in China: Repression and Revival." *China Quarterly*, no. 103 (September): 393–413.

Smelser, Neil J. 1963. "Mechanisms of Change and Adjustments to Change." In *Industrialization and Society*, edited by Bert F. Hoselitz and Wilbert E. Moore, 32–54. Paris: UNESCO and Mouton.

Smythe, Lewis S. C. 1935. "The Composition of the Chinese Family." *Chin-ling Hsueh-pao* 5, no. 1.

Solinger, Dorothy J. 1987. "The 1980 Inflation and the Politics of Price Control in the People's Republic of China." In *Policy Implementation in Post-Mao China*, edited by David M. Lampton, 81–118. Berkeley: University of California Press.

——. 1989. "Capitalist Measures with Chinese Characteristics." *Problems of Communism* 38 (January–February): 19–33.

Stacey, Judith. 1983. *Patriarchy and Socialist Revolution in China*. Berkeley and Los Angeles: University of California Press.

State Statistical Bureau of PRC. 1985. *A Survey of Income and Household Conditions in China*. Beijing: New World Press.

——. 1989. *A Survey of Income and Expenditure of Urban Households in China, 1986.* Beijing and Honolulu: China Statistical Information and Consultancy Service Centre and the East-West Population Institute.

Stockard, Janice M. 1989. *Daughters of the Canton Delta: Marriage Patterns and Economic Strategies in South China, 1860–1930.* Stanford: Stanford University Press.

Su Xing. 1987. *Wo guo chengshi zhuzhai wenti* (Our country's urban housing problem). Beijing: Zhongguo shehui kexue chubanshe.

Sun, Lena H. 1990. "China Seeks Way to Protect Elderly." *Washington Post*, October 23.

Szasz, T. S. 1961. *The Myth of Mental Illness*. New York: Harper and Row.

Szelenyi, Ivan. 1983. *Urban Inequalities Under State Socialism*. New York: Oxford University Press.

Taeuber, Irene B. 1970. "The Families of Chinese Farmers." In *Family and Kinship in Chinese Society*, edited by Maurice Freedman, 63–85. Stanford: Stanford University Press.

Taylor, Jeffery R. 1988. "Rural Employment Trends and the Legacy of Surplus Labour, 1978–1986." *China Quarterly*, no. 116 (December): 736–66.

Taylor, Robert. 1973. *Education and University Enrolment Policies in China, 1949–1971.* Canberra: Australian National University.

Thaxton, Ralph. 1983. *China Turned Rightside Up: Revolutionary Legitimacy in the Peasant World.* New Haven and London: Yale University Press.

Thireau, Isabelle, and Mak Kong. 1989. "Travail en famille dans un village du Hebei." *Etudes chinoises* 8, no. 1 (Spring): 7–40.

Thorns, David. 1989. "The New International Division of Labor and Urban

Change: A New Zealand Case Study." In *Pacific Rim Cities in the World Economy*, edited by M. P. Smith, 68–101. New Brunswick: Transaction Books.

Thornton, Arland, and Thomas E. Fricke. 1987. "Social Change and the Family: Comparative Perspectives from the West, China, and South Asia." *Sociological Forum* 2, no. 4:746–79.

Tian Xueyuan. 1988. "China's Elderly Surveyed." *Beijing Review* (November 14–20): 26–28.

Tien, H. Yuan, and Che-fu Lee. 1988. "The Chinese Family and Induced Population Transition." *Social Science Quarterly* 69, no. 3 (September): 605–28.

Tilly, Charles. 1975. "Reflections on the History of European State-Making." In *The Formation of National States in Western Europe*, edited by Charles Tilly, 3–83. Princeton: Princeton University Press.

Tilly, Louise, and Joan W. Scott. 1978. *Women, Work and Family*. New York: Holt, Rinehart and Winston.

Topley, Marjorie. 1975. "Marriage Resistance in Rural Kwangtung." In *Women in Chinese Society*, edited by Margery Wolf and Roxanne Witke, 67–88. Stanford: Stanford University Press.

Torrey, E. F. 1988. *Surviving Schizophrenia: A Training Manual*. Rev. ed. New York: Harper and Row.

Tsou, Tang. 1986. *The Cultural Revolution and Post-Mao Reforms*. Chicago: University of Chicago Press.

Tu, Edward, Jersey Liang, and Shaomin Li. 1989. "Mortality Decline and Chinese Family Structure." *Journal of Gerontology* 44, no. 4 (July): 157–68.

Udry, J. Richard. 1965. "The Influence of the Ideal Mate Image on Mate Perception and Mate Selection." *Journal of Marriage and the Family* 27:477–82.

———. 1971. *The Social Context of Marriage*. 2d ed. Philadelphia: Lippincott.

Unger, Jonathan. 1979. "China's Troubled Down-to-the-Countryside Campaign." *Contemporary China* 3, no. 2:79–92.

———. 1982. *Education Under Mao: Class and Competition in Canton Schools, 1960–1980*. New York: Columbia University Press.

———. 1985–86. "The Decollectivization of the Chinese Countryside: A Survey of Twenty-eight Villages." *Pacific Affairs* 58, no. 4 (Winter): 585–606.

———. 1989. "State and Peasant in Post-Revolution China." *Journal of Peasant Studies* 17, no. 1 (October): 114–36.

Vogel, Ezra F. 1989. "Guangdong's Dynamic Inner Delta." *China Business Review* (September–October): 56–62.

———. 1989. *One Step Ahead in China: Guangdong under Reform*. Cambridge: Harvard University Press.

Wachter, K. W., E. A. Hammel, and Peter Laslett. 1978. *Statistical Studies of Historical Social Structure*. New York: Academic Press.

Walder, Andrew G. 1979. "Industrial Organization and Socialist Development in China." *Modern China* 5:233–92.

———. 1986. *Communist Neo-Traditionalism: Work and Authority in Chinese Industry*. Berkeley: University of California Press.

———. 1990. "Collective Benefits and Social Stratification in Urban China." Paper presented at the 42nd Annual Meeting of the Association for Asian Studies, Chicago, April 5–8.

Walker, Kenneth R. 1989. "Forty Years On: Provincial Contrasts in China's Rural Economic Development." *China Quarterly*, no. 119 (September): 448–80.

Wang Jichuan. 1988. "Determinants of Fertility Increase in Sichuan." *Population and Development Review* 14, no. 3, table 6.

Wang Sung-hsing. 1968. "Pooling and Sharing in a Chinese Fishing Community: Kuei-shan Tao." Ph.D. diss., University of Tokyo.

Wasserstrom, Jeffrey. 1984. "Resistance to the One-Child Family." *Modern China* 10:345–74.

Watson, Andrew. 1983. "Agriculture Looks for 'Shoes That Fit': The Production Responsibility System and Its Implications." *World Development* 11, no. 8 (August): 705–30.

Watson, James L. 1982. "Chinese Kinship Reconsidered: Anthropological Perspectives on Historical Research." *China Quarterly*, no. 92:589–622.

Watson, Rubie, and Patricia Buckley Ebrey, eds. 1991. *Marriage and Inequality in Chinese Society*. Berkeley: University of California Press.

Weinstein, Maxine, T. H. Sun, M. C. Chang, and R. Freedman. 1990. "Household Consumption, Extended Kinship, and Reproduction in Taiwan, 1965–1985." *Population Studies* 44, no. 2 (July): 217–39.

White, Gordon. 1987. "The Impact of Economic Reforms in the Chinese Countryside." *Modern China* 13, no. 4:411–40.

White, Lynn T. 1978. *Careers in Shanghai*. Berkeley: University of California Press.

White, Tyrene. 1987. "Implementing the 'One-Child-per-Couple' Population Program in Rural China: National Goals and Local Politics." In *Policy Implementation in Post-Mao China*, edited by David M. Lampton, 284–317. Berkeley: University of California Press.

Whyte, Martin King. 1985. "The Politics of Life Chances in the People's Republic of China." In *Power and Policy in the PRC*, edited by Yu-ming Shaw, 244–65. Boulder, Colo.: Westview.

———. 1990. "Changes in Mate Choice in Chengdu." In *Chinese Society on the Eve of Tiananmen: The Impact of Reform*, edited by Deborah Davis and Ezra F. Vogel, 181–214. Cambridge: Harvard University Press.

———. 1990. *Dating, Mating, and Marriage*. New York: Aldine.

———. 1992. "State and Society in the Mao Era." In Kenneth Lieberthal, Joyce Kallgren, Roderick MacFarquhar, and Frederick Wakeman, eds., *Perspectives on China*. Armonk, N.Y.: M. E. Sharpe.

Whyte, Martin King, and S. Z. Gu. 1987. "Popular Response to China's Fertility Transition." *Population and Development Review* 13, no. 3 (September).

Whyte, Martin King, and William L. Parish. 1984. *Urban Life in Contemporary China*. Chicago: University of Chicago Press.

Whyte, Martin King, and Burton Pasternak. 1980. "Sociology and Anthropology." In *Humanistic and Social Science Research in China*, edited by Anne F. Thurston and Jason H. Parker. New York: Social Science Research Council.

Whyte, Martin K., Ezra F. Vogel, and William Parish. 1977. "Social Structure of World Religions: Mainland China." In *Annual Review of Sociology*, no. 3:179–207.

Wilke, Richard R. 1984. "Households in Process: Agricultural Change and Domestic Transformation Among the Kekchi Maya of Belize." In *Households*, edited by

Robert McC. Netting, Richard R. Wilke, and Eric J. Arnould, 227–44. Berkeley and Los Angeles: University of California Press.

Wolf, Arthur P. "Introduction." 1974. In *Religion and Ritual in Chinese Society*, edited by Arthur P. Wolf, 1–18. Stanford: Stanford University Press.

———. 1985. "Chinese Family Size: A Myth Revitalized." In *The Chinese Family and Its Ritual Behavior*, edited by Hsieh Jih-chang and Chuang Ying-chang, 30–49. Monograph Series B, no. 15. Taipei: Institute of Ethnology, Academia Sinica.

———. 1985. "Fertility in Prerevolutionary China." In *Family and Population in East Asian History*, edited by Susan B. Hanley and Arthur P. Wolf. Stanford: Stanford University Press.

Wolf, Arthur P., and Huang Chieh-shan. 1980. *Marriage and Adoption in China, 1845–1945*. Stanford: Stanford University Press.

Wolf, Eric. 1965. *Peasants*. Englewood Cliffs, N.J.: Prentice-Hall.

———. 1969. *Peasant Wars of the Twentieth Century*. New York: Harper and Row.

———. 1986. "The Vicissitudes of the Closed Corporate Peasant Community." *American Ethnologist* 13:325–29.

Wolf, Margery. 1972. *Women and the Family in Rural Taiwan*. Stanford: Stanford University Press.

———. 1985. *Revolution Postponed: Women in Contemporary China*. Stanford: Stanford University Press.

Wong Siu-lun. 1984. "Consequences of China's New Population Policy." *China Quarterly*, no. 98 (June): 220–40.

Woon Yuen-fong. 1984. *Social Organization in South China, 1911–1949: The Case of the Kuan Lineage of K'ai-ping County*. Ann Arbor: Center for Chinese Studies.

———. 1989. "Social Change and Continuity in South China: Overseas Chinese and the Guan Lineage of Kaiping County, 1949–1987." *China Quarterly*, no. 118 (June): 324–44.

———. 1990. "International Links and Socio-economic Development of Modern China: An Emigrant Community in Guangdong." *Modern China* 16, no. 2:139–72.

———. 1991. "From Mao to Deng: Life Satisfaction Among Rural Women in an Emigrant Community in South China." *Australian Journal of Chinese Affairs*, 25.

World Health Organization. 1979. *Schizophrenia: An International Follow-up Study*. New York: Wiley.

Worsley, Peter. 1984. *The Three Worlds: Culture and World Development*. London: Weidenfeld and Nicholson.

Wu chengshi jiating yanjiu xiangmu zu. 1985. (Research Project Group on the Families of Five Cities). *Zhongguo chengshi jiating* (Chinese urban families). Jinan: Shandong renmin chubanshe.

Wu Xingci and Li Zhen. 1988. "Gun San Haak in the 1980's: A Study of Chinese Who Return to Taishan County for Marriage." *Amerasia* 14, no. 2.

Xiong, W., and M. R. Phillips. n.d. "Chengxiang zhu yuan jingshenfenliezheng bingren de bijiao" (Comparison of urban and rural hospitalized schizophrenic patients). Submitted manuscript.

Xu Jingze. 1985. "Wo guo jiating jiegoude tedian jiqi fazhan qushi chutan" (Initial investigation into the characteristics and developmental trends in the structure of Chinese families). *Shehuixue* (Sociology). People's University Reprint Series C4, no. 2 (1985). First published in *Wenshizhe* (Literature, History and Philosophy), Jinan City, no. 1.

Yang, C. K. 1959. *The Chinese Family in the Communist Revolution*. Cambridge: MIT Press.

Yang Dali. 1990. "Patterns of China's Regional Development Strategy." *China Quarterly*, no. 122 (June).

Yang Haiou. 1989. "The Future Family Support System for the Rural Elderly: The Consequences of the One-Child Policy and the Latent Impacts of the Current Rural Economic Reform." Paper presented at the 41st Annual Meeting of the Association for Asian Studies, Washington, D.C.

Yang, K. S. 1986. "Chinese Personality and Its Change." In *The Psychology of the Chinese People*, edited by M. H. Bond, 106–70. Hong Kong: Oxford University Press.

Ye Nanke and Tang Zhongxun. 1990. "Laonianren shenghuo zhiliang chutan" (A preliminary investigation into elderly people's quality of life). *Shehuixue* (Sociology), no. 1. First published in *Renkou Yanjiu* (Population Research), no. 6, 1989.

Yu Luojin. 1986. *A Chinese Winter's Tale*. Hong Kong: Renditions.

Yuan Fang. 1987. "Zhongguo Laonianren zai jiating, shehui zhongde diwei he zuoyong" (The status and functions of the Chinese elderly in the family and society). *Shehuixue*, no. 4. First published in *Beijing daxue xuebao, zhe she ban* (Beijing University studies, philosophy and social science edition) 3, no. 1, 1987.

Yuan Jihui. 1986. *Chengshi laonian shenghuo yanjiu* (Research on the urban elderly). Vol. 2. Suzhou: Shanghai daxue wenxueyuan.

———. 1989. *Dangdai laonian shehuixue* (Contemporary gerontology). Shanghai: Fudan daxue chubanshe.

Yuan Jihui, Chou Liping, and Dong Jiahua. 1987. "Shanghai shiqu gaoling laoren shenghuo zhuangkuang diaocha baogao" (An investigative report into the living conditions of the truly aged of a Shanghai urban district). *Shehuixue yanjiu* (Sociological Research), no. 3.

Zeng Yi. 1989. "Is the Chinese Family Planning Program 'Tightening Up'?" *Population and Development Review* 15, no. 2 (June): 333–37.

Zeng Yi and James Vaupal. 1989. "The Impact of Urbanization and Delayed Childbearing on Population Growth and Aging in China." *Population and Development Review* 15, no. 4 (December): 707–30.

Zhang Qingwu. 1989. "Guanyu chengshi liudong renkou wenti di sikao" (Reflections on the problem of the urban floating population). *Zhongguo renkou kexue*, no. 3:50–55.

Zhang Yulin. 1986. "The Shift of Surplus Agricultural Labor." In *Small Towns in China*, edited by Fei Xiao-tong, 170–210. Beijing: New World Press.

Zheng Guizhen. 1988. "Shanghai shi jiating jiegou yu yang lao shiye" (Shanghai's urban family structure and facilities for the care of the elderly). *Zhongguo renkou kexue* (Chinese Demography), no. 5.

Zheng Yefu. 1991. "Connections." In *The Chinese: Adapting the Past, Facing the Future*, edited by Robert Dernberger, et al. Ann Arbor: Center for Chinese Studies.

Zhonggong Zhongyang Bangongting. 1989. *Dongguan shi'nian: 1979–1988* (Dongguan ten years: 1979–1988). Shanghai: Shanghai renmin chubanshe.

Zhongguo chengshi jiating (Chinese urban families). 1985. Jinan: Shandong renmin chubanshe.

Zhou Ying. 1988. "Wo guo xiandaihua guocheng nongcun jiating" (Rural families in the transition to modernization). *Renkou yanjiu*, no. 2:17–21.

Zhou Ying, ed. 1988. *Chengshi zhuzhai gaige cankao ziliao* (Reference materials on the urban residential housing reform). Beijing: Xinhuashe "Jingji cankao" bienjibu.

Zhuang Jia. 1988. *Ren yu ren* (The Human Relationship). Canton: Guangdong renmin chubanshe (Guangdong People's Publisher).

Zou Naixian. 1987–88. "Qingnian fangzhi nügong shenghuo fangshi xuqiu bianhuade diaocha" (Survey of changes in young female textile workers' demands on life). *Chinese Sociology and Anthropology* 20, no. 2 (Winter) (in English). First published in Chinese in *Qingnian yanjiu* (Youth Studies), no. 10, 1985.

Zweig, David. 1989. "Struggling Over Land in China: Peasant Resistance After Collectivization, 1966–1986." In *Everyday Forms of Peasant Resistance*, edited by Forrest D. Colburn. Armonk, N.Y.: M.E. Sharpe.

YEARBOOKS

Beijing Shehui Jingji Tongji Nianjian 1987–1989 (Social and Economic Statistical Yearbook of Beijing). Beijing: Zhongguo tongji chubanshe.

Directorate-General of Budgets, Accounting, and Statistics. *Statistical Yearbook of the Republic of China. 1986.*

Guangdong Tongji Nianjian 1985–1989 (Statistical Yearbook of Guangdong). Beijing: Zhongguo tongji chubanshe.

Guangxi Tongji Nianjian 1989 (Statistical Yearbook of Guangxi). Beijing: Zhongguo tongji chubanshe.

Guangzhou Nianjian 1989 (Guangzhou Yearbook). Guangzhou Nianjian Bianzuan Weiyuanhui. Guangzhou: Wenhua chubanshe.

Guangzhou Tongji Nianjian 1988–1989 (Statistical Yearbook of Guangzhou). Zhongguo tongji chubanshe.

Hubei Tongji Nianjian 1988 (Statistical Yearbook of Hubei Province). Wuhan: Hubei sheng difang zhibian weiyuanhui.

Shaanxi Tongji Nianjian 1987 (Statistical Yearbook of Shaanxi). Shaanxi Provincial Bureau of Statistics. Xi'an: Shaanxi renmin chubanshe.

Shanghai Tongji Nianjian 1988–89 (Shanghai Statistical Yearbook). Shanghai: Zhongguo tongji chubanshe.

Statistical Yearbook of China 1986. State Statistical Bureau. Hong Kong: Economic Information and Agency.

A Survey of Income and Expenditure of Urban Households in China, 1986. Beijing and Honolulu: China Statistical Information and Consultancy Service Centre and the East-West Population Institute, 1989.

A Survey of Income and Household Conditions in China. State Statistical Bureau of PRC. Beijing: New World Press, 1985.

Taiwan-Fukien Demographic Fact Book. Taipei, Taiwan, Republic of China, 1986.

Tianjin Tongji Niangjian 1985, 1988. Beijing: Zhongguo tongji chubanshe.

Wuhan Nianjian 1986 (Wuhan yearbook). Wuhan: Wuhan nianjian bienzuan weiyunhui bienji chuban.

Zhongguo Chengshi Tongji Nianjian 1987 (China's Urban Statistical Yearbook). Beijing: Zhongguo tongji xinxi zixun fuwu zhongxin and zhongguo jianshe chubanshe.

Zhongguo Laodong Gongzi Tongji Nianjian 1989 (Yearbook of Labor and Wage Statistics). Beijing: Laodong renshi chubanshe.

Zhongguo Nongcun Tongji Nianjian 1988 (Chinese Rural Statistical Yearbook). Beijing: Zhongguo tongji chubanshe.

Zhongguo Shehui Tongji Ziliao 1987 (Chinese Social Statistics for 1987). Beijing: Zhongguo tongji chubanshe.

Zhongguo Tongji Nianjian, 1987–1989 (Statistical Yearbook of China). State Statistical Bureau, ed. Beijing: Zhongguo tongji chubanshe.

Zhongguo Tongji Zhaiyao 1987 (Summary of Chinese Statistics). Beijing: Zhongguo tongji chubanshe.

INDEX